AN AFTER ACTION REPORT

GULF WAR DEBRIEFING BOOK

Andrew Leyden

Edited by Camille Akin

HELLGATE PRESS
GRANTS PASS, OREGON

GULF WAR DEBRIEFING BOOK

An After Action Report

Published by Hellgate Press®

HELLGATE PRESS
an imprint of PSI Research
300 North Valley Drive
Grants Pass, Oregon 97526 USA

(541) 479-9464 *telephone*
(541) 476-1479 *fax*
psi2@magick.net *email*

Hellgate Press is a Registered Trademark of Publishing Services, Inc., an Oregon corporation doing business as PSI Research.

Edited by Camille Akin
Cover and interior design by Steven Burns

Library of Congress Cataloging-In-Publication Data
Leyden, Andrew, 1966–
Gulf War debriefing book : an after action report / by Andrew Leyden.
p. cm.
Includes bibliographical references (p.).
ISBN 1-55571-396-3
1. Persian Gulf War, 1991. 2. Operation Desert Shield, 1990-1991. I. Title.
DS79.72.L5 1997
956.7044'2--dc21
97-5411
CIP

Printed and bound in the United States of America
First edition 10 9 8 7 6 5 4 3 2 1 0

Printed on recycled paper when available

"To those who know firsthand
that this was not a bloodless war."

Contents

Preface

When President George Bush spoke before the country on 16 January 1991, he was watched on television by more Americans than had ever watched television before. For those who did not see him, they still remember that very first moment that they heard the war had begun. Whether it was on their living room couch, in an automobile, or in a restaurant, that single moment that someone said "the war has started" will echo in their memories for a long time to come.

With the cessation of hostilities, many people began to forget the barrage of images that they had been shown during January and February 1991. They may remember a few things here and there, a picture of a POW or a liberated Kuwaiti, but the details of the war soon became a blur. This loss would be a shame.

"Another Gulf War book by another wannabe armchair general." This has become a common refrain as people walk past the bookstores filled with works on "the inside story" and "the hidden truth" behind Operation Desert Storm. Written usually by men with "retired" after their names, these books provide some insight into our nation's operations in the Persian Gulf, but also contain some misinformation and certainly have a few paragraphs based on opinion rather than fact.

However, despite the sound-bite, short-attention span of the majority of society, there remains a "silent minority" interested in the simple truth — just the facts. While it is difficult to prove what did and did not happen in any situation, I have endeavored to compile as many facts on Operation Desert Storm as I could fit into this book. Just as the Gulf War was compared to Vietnam, we will see future wars compared with the Desert Storm standard. Policymakers will draw upon similarities and compare differences in a surprisingly large number of events throughout the world that, on the face, have nothing to do with the Persian Gulf. However, when future U.S. security policy is made, it should be noted that much of the rationale for these decisions will come from our operations in Kuwait.

Much of this book is based upon reports from the Pentagon and the military community in Washington. From these detailed reviews of weapons and tactics, the defense community learned what went right and what went wrong, and what can be done in the future to make things better. Policymakers, and to a larger extent, politicians, oftentimes reach a conclusion, and then going looking for the facts to back them up. Hopefully, by laying out as many facts as I can about Operation Desert Storm, a solid base for decision-making will exist before future conclusions are reached.

Andrew Leyden
March 1997

About the Author

Andrew Leyden is a former defense advisor to two U.S. representatives in the Congress. During that time, he offered briefings, advice, and research into various weapons programs and force structure of the U.S. military. He has traveled the country on inspection tours and helped solve military problems ranging from inadequate troop housing to cost overruns in major weapons systems. In addition, he served as an international observer in Nigeria during a change of government ceremony in the early 1990s.

He worked as a news reporter for four years before beginning this detailed compendium of the Persian Gulf War. What started as a briefing package for his boss has evolved into what has become known as an authoritative reference on the Gulf War. In fact, his Internet version of this book received more than 90,000 hits during its first nine-month period on the world wide web. Last year, the American War Library named Leyden's work as the Top Military Site on the Internet. He welcomes comments, suggestions, and additions or deletions to this book via email at *andrew@leyden.com*

Leyden holds a B.A. in political science from the University of Illinois and is currently a candidate for J.D. from the University of Notre Dame.

Acknowledgments

I'd like to thank Eric Linhardt, Michael Garrett, J. Marc Wheat, and Derek Utter for assisting me in the logistics of gathering this book. Also, Rolf Dammann and Chris Griffin formerly of Congresswoman Helen Bentley's office for steering me toward some interesting material. Finally, I'd like to thank Weihong Zhao for assisting me with some of the proofreading.

At PSI Research, I'd like to thank Camille Akin for her great work editing this book, Dave Myers for helping me track down some of the more hard-to-locate facts, Steven Burns for turning a mere manuscript into a graphics-rich visual feast, and Emmett Ramey for taking a chance on an unknown author.

In addition, I'd like to thank the nameless folks at the public affairs offices inside the Pentagon, the White House, and the Congress who have replied to my requests in a timely and thorough fashion.

Regional Map

Persian Gulf and Area

Source: U.S. Government Department of Defense

Quick Chronology

Important Events

Pre-Kuwait Invasion

1899	The British sign a treaty with the al Sabah family, putting Kuwait under British protection.
1921	Britain installs Amir Faisal as King of Iraq.
1932	Saudi Arabia is proclaimed by Abd al Aziz. Iraq declares its independence.
1958	The Iraqi monarchy is overthrown in a coup by General Abdul Karim Qassim.
1960	Organization of Petroleum Exporting Countries (OPEC) is founded.
1961	Kuwait is established as an independent nation.
1963	A coup overthrows Qassim. General Abdul Salam Aref is installed into power.
1966	Abdul Rahman Aref succeeds his brother as leader of Iraq.
1968	Baath Party coup occurs. Ahmad Hassan al-Bakr is installed into power. Saddam Hussein becomes his chief deputy.
1977	Sheikh Jaber al-Ahmad al-Jaber, al Sabah becomes the amir of Kuwait.
1979	Saddam Hussein succeeds Bakr as president of Iraq.
1980	Iraq invades Iran on 22 September, starting an eight-year war.
1981	Israel launches air attacks against Iraqi nuclear facilities on 7 June.
1982	King Fahd assumes power in Saudi Arabia on 14 June following the death of King Khalid.
1984	Attacks begin on tankers in the Persian Gulf in April.
1987	Iraq attacks USS *Stark* on 17 May, killing thirty-seven U.S. sailors.
1988	Saddam Hussein orders the use of chemical weapons on the Kurds. Iran-Iraq War ends in August.
1990	Hussein accuses Kuwait on 17 July of oil overproduction and theft of oil from the Rumailia Oil Field.
1990	On 25 July, U.S. Ambassador to Iraq, April Glaspie, tells Hussein that the Iraqi/Kuwaiti dispute is an Arab matter, not one that affects the United States.
1990	Hussein invades Kuwait on 2 August. President Bush freezes Iraqi and Kuwaiti assets. The United Nations calls on Hussein to withdraw immediately.

Quick Chronology

Important Events

Post-Kuwait Invasion

6 August 1990	Economic sanctions are authorized by the United Nations against Iraq and Kuwait.
7 August 1990	Secretary of Defense Cheney visits Saudi Arabia; U.S. military assistance is requested. The 82nd Airborne is dispatched, along with several fighter squadrons.
8 August 1990	Iraq annexes Kuwait.
9 August 1990	The U.N. declares Iraq's annexation of Kuwait invalid.
12 August 1990	The United States announces interdiction program of Iraqi shipping.
22 August 1990	President Bush signs authorization for call up of the Reserves.
25 August 1990	Military interdiction of Iraqi shipping authorized by the United Nations.
14 September 1990	Iraqi forces storm a number of diplomatic missions in Kuwait City.
8 November 1990	Bush orders additional deployments to give "offensive option" to U.S. forces.
20 November 1990	Forty-five Democrats file suit in Washington to have President Bush first seek Congressional approval of military operations. (The suit was eventually thrown out.)
22 November 1990	President Bush and the First Lady visit U.S. troops for Thanksgiving dinner. Speaker of the House Foley, Senate Majority Leader Mitchell, Senate Minority Leader Dole, and Minority Leader of the House Michel also attend.
29 November 1990	U.N. Security Council authorizes force if Iraq does not withdraw from Kuwait by midnight (Eastern Standard Time) 15 January.
30 November 1990	Bush invites Tariq Aziz to Washington and offers to send Secretary of State James Baker to Baghdad.
9 January 1991	Baker and Aziz meet in Geneva. The meeting lasts six hours, but yields no results.
12 January 1991	Congress votes to allow for U.S. troops to be used in offensive operations.
15 January 1991	The deadline established by U.N. Resolution 678 for Iraqi withdrawal.
16 January 1991	First U.S. government statement on Operation Desert Storm made. Marlin Fitzwater announces, "The liberation of Kuwait has begun..." to the press.
16 January 1991	Operation Desert Shield becomes Operation Desert Storm as U.S. warplanes attack Baghdad, Kuwait, and other military targets in Iraq.
17 January 1991	Iraq launches first SCUD missile attack on Israel.

30 January 1991	U.S. forces in the Gulf region exceed 500,000.
6 February 1991	Jordan King Hussein lashes out against American bombardments and supports Iraq.
13 February 1991	U.S. bombers destroy a bunker complex in Baghdad with several hundred citizens inside. Nearly 300 die from this attack.
17 February 1991	Tariq Aziz travels to Moscow to discuss possible negotiated end to the war.
22 February 1991	President Bush issues an ultimatum of 23 February for Iraqi troops to withdraw from Kuwait.
23 February 1991	Operation Desert Storm ground war begins with Marines, Army, and Arab forces moving into Iraq and Kuwait.
25 February 1991	Iraqi SCUD missile hits a U.S. barracks in Saudi Arabia, killing twenty-seven Americans.
26 February 1991	Kuwaiti resistance leaders declare they are in control of Kuwait City.
27 February 1991	President Bush orders a cease-fire effective at midnight Kuwaiti time.
3 March 1991	Iraqi military leaders formally accept cease-fire terms.
4 March 1991	Ten Allied POWs freed, including six Americans.
5 March 1991	Thirty-five POWs released, including fifteen Americans.
8 March 1991	First U.S. combat forces return home.

PART ONE

RECOGNIZING THE FACES, PLACES, AND POLITICS OF WAR...

Military and Diplomatic Background

Chapter One

A Look Overseas

INTERNATIONAL POLITICS

At one level, Saddam Hussein's invasion of Kuwait was merely the end result of a long-running dispute between Iraq and Kuwait. But his action had implications far beyond a mere bilateral disagreement between two nations. International economic interests were affected by the seizure of Kuwaiti oil wells, Arab/Israeli tensions were heightened by Hussein's actions and statements, U.S./U.N. relations were stretched to the limit, and even cold war differences between the Soviets and the United States came back into play. This was clearly an event that called upon all levels of statesmanship by the United States for success.

At the United Nations, a vote was immediately taken in the security council following the invasion condemning Hussein's actions, with only the Arab state of Yemen voting "present." Yemen, which was a temporary member of the security council, defended this decision by saying it wanted to seek an "Arab solution" to the crisis. However, at early meetings of the Arab League, a consensus could not be reached on how to react.

Delicate Diplomacy

As former director of the CIA, ambassador to the United Nations, and vice-president for eight years, George Bush was one of the most qualified men in America to handle the delicate international diplomacy that was required by this invasion. Within hours of the Iraqi tanks crossing the Kuwaiti border, Bush was in contact with many Arab leaders discussing a possible response. The next day, he met with Margaret Thatcher at the Aspen Conference in Colorado, which ironically, was a previously scheduled event at which Bush was to announce his views on a drastically reduced U.S. military following the cold war. Following this meeting, Bush and Thatcher held a press conference in which Bush refused to rule out the use of force to liberate Kuwait — which turned out to be some of the first inklings that military actions were in the works.

Secretary of Defense Dick Cheney and Chairman of the Joint Chiefs of Staff Colin Powell met with the Saudi Ambassador in the United States to give him a "heads up" as to what to expect. The United States was prepared to commit up to 100,000 troops and aircraft to the defense of the Saudi Kingdom. This formal offer was later made in Saudi Arabia directly to King Fahd by Secretary Cheney and General Norman Schwarzkopf.

After the king agreed, Secretary Cheney and General Schwarzkopf flew not only to Egypt to request permission for warships to transit through the Suez Canal, but also to Morocco to avoid offending the North African Arab community. From the very beginning of this crisis, it was clear that diplomatic civilities must be observed and dealt with to ensure a successful coalition.

Bush knew that a solely American or American/European solution would be seen as "Western invaders" in the Gulf region. It was essential that other nations, such as Turkey and Egypt, come on board the alliance to help ensure that the coalition wouldn't be seen as an entirely foreign force. In addition, ensuring an effective sanctions package meant Turkey and Jordan would have to blockade Iraqi trade, something the Jordanian government refused to do.

Following King Fahd's agreement to base U.S. forces in Saudi Arabia, the British government announced its own deployments of fighters and men, along with ships at sea. Prime Minister Thatcher, along with French President François Mitterand, were very effective at securing commitments from many European leaders to enforce the sanctions against Iraq. Other European and Middle Eastern nations agreed to send troops to defend Saudi Arabia and ships to help enforce the United Nations embargo. Those nations that did not send troops, most notably Japan and Germany, were asked to contribute financial resources to help defray the costs of the Allied deployment.

A Resolved United Nations

In the United Nations, the United States was spearheading a drive for sanctions, and more importantly, enforcement resolutions to carry out the sanctions. Although some doubted the United States needed the approval of the U.N. before it acted, the moral weight of U.N. authority was a critical point often cited by defenders of the administration's policies. While it may not have needed the support of the U.N., the United States was glad to have it.

On 29 November 1990, after the United States had started to deploy offensive troops into the Gulf region, the U.N. passed Resolution 678, authorizing the use of force to retake Kuwait if Saddam Hussein did not withdraw by 15 January 1991. The security council vote was 12-2, with Yemen and Cuba opposed to the measure, and China in abstention.

American officials had worked hard for this resolution, and took advantage of the fact that November was the month that the United States was scheduled to preside over the security council. Secretary of State Baker himself flew to New York to oversee the vote, and secure the agreement of the Soviets and other Allies. China, which abstained, was rewarded the next day by a meeting between Bush and the Chinese foreign minister — the first high-level contact between those nations after the crackdown on student demonstrators in Tiananmen Square in 1989.

Following the vote, Bush announced plans to send Secretary of State Jim Baker to Baghdad for one last chance at a diplomatic solution. Throughout December, while Americans were being evacuated from Kuwait, the United States and Iraq argued about what date to meet, with a final agreement eventually being made for Baker and Iraqi Foreign Minister Tariq Aziz to meet on 9 January 1991 in Geneva, Switzerland. This last-minute attempt to solve the crisis diplomatically failed, and it became clear to all who were watching the press conferences following the meetings that war was imminent.

For more information on the many U.N. resolutions passed prior to and during the Gulf War, see chapters 7 and 8.

Maintaining an Alliance

Maintaining the alliance throughout Operation Desert Storm kept American diplomats on their toes. Not only was Saddam trying to bring Israel into the war and fracture the alliance between the United States and the Arab nations, but other countries were pursuing individual acts of diplomacy in the hopes of reaching a negotiated settlement, even after the bombs had started falling.

Most notably, the Soviets undertook their own version of shuttle diplomacy, flying their officials back and forth to meet with the Iraqis to help their former "friends" in Baghdad avoid the devastating onslaught of the Allied ground offensive. Details of the Soviet's attempts at a peaceful solution are included in chapters 7 and 9.

On the ground, there were also smaller incidents of diplomacy that had to be addressed. One of the more cantankerous issues was the participation of the Syrian military in the alliance. Long regarded as a supporter of terrorism, the Syrians were distrusted by most Western Allies (most notably the British) and totally despised by the Israelis and their supporters in the United States. Even some protests were issued when Syrian flags were displayed in victory celebrations in the United States.

At the end of the war, the Allied units returned to their bases in their various nations, and the United States strengthened many ties within the region such that a great opportunity existed for U.S./Arab cooperation on many major issues. The peace movements between the PLO and Israel, and later between Jordan and Israel, can be seen as a result of the American prestige and respect in its dealings with Arab nations in the Gulf Crisis.

The remainder of this chapter helps you get acquainted with the many international faces and foreign places of this critical period of military and diplomatic history.

IRAQ

Formal Name:	Republic of Iraq
Citizens:	Iraqis
Capitol:	Baghdad
Flag:	Three bands; *red over white over black; three green stars in the white band*
Size:	167,925 square miles *(roughly California and Maryland combined)*
Population:	18,800,000 (1990); 3,800,000 in Baghdad
Languages:	Arabic
Ethnic Breakdown:	75% Arab; 20% Kurds; 5% Other
Gross Domestic Product:	$35 billion (US) 1985
Paved Roads:	22,397 km
Railroads:	2,029 km
Ports:	Basra and Umm Qasr
Airports:	Baghdad International; Basra International; 95 other airports (61 with permanent runways)

Following the defeat of the Ottoman Empire in WWI, the United Kingdom put Iraq under British mandate, installing Amir Faisal as king in 1921. The monarchy ruled for several decades, but was eventually overthrown in 1958. This set in motion a decade of coups, countercoups, and the political instability of a country adrift.

In the 1970s, power began to solidify behind the Baath (Arab Socialist Resurrection) Party — partially due to increased spending from oil revenues, partially the result of force. Iraq grew until September of 1980 when Iraqi troops poured over the border into Iran. The bloody, drawn-out battles that lasted the next eight years resulted in the killing of hundreds of thousands (accurate counts are not known) until the war ended much in the same way as it was fought — stalemate.

During the Iran-Iraq War years, Iraq spent considerable sums of money enhancing its military forces. Although most of the weapons were supplied by the Soviets, the Iraqi government also purchased weapons on the international market from France, South Africa, and the United States. Iraq made no secret of its desire to obtain nuclear weapons, although these efforts were seriously set back by an Israeli air raid in 1981 that destroyed Iraqi nuclear facilities.

Iraq had developed several chemical weapons — the "poor man's nuclear bomb" — and became one of the first countries to use them since WWI when it shelled Iranian positions with chemical agents. This increased military spending, coupled with lower oil prices and the devastating costs of the Iran-Iraq War have hindered the economy of Iraq, but dissent has not been easily visible given the authoritarian rule of Saddam Hussein. A biographical sketch on Saddam follows this discussion.

The recent disagreement with Kuwait stems from long-held claims by Iraq to Kuwaiti lands. In 1961, following Kuwait's independence, Iraq made a claim on Kuwaiti lands saying that the Ottoman Empire once considered them one in the same. Kuwait rejected this claim; however, that did not stem Iraq's desire to this land, as clearly evidenced by its 2 August 1990.

Five weeks of Allied bombing caused great damage to the Iraqi military's command, control, and communication network. It also took its toll on the civilian infrastructure of command and control, knocking out bridges and telephone switching centers. Water and power was cut off to several parts of the country. While much of this damage has been repaired, psychological scars still exist from the war and the ostracism of the sanctions that cannot be healed within the Iraqi people.

To compound this difficulty, the United Nations continueș to maintain the embargo on trade with Iraq as long as Saddam Hussein remains in power. Although the sanctions were slightly lifted for humanitarian reasons in May of 1996, considerable damage has already been done to the Iraqi economy and it may be beyond recovery.

In addition, unlike Kuwait which has several billion in foreign assets, much of the money Iraq made over the last ten years has been wasted on a massive military machine that now litters the sands of Kuwait. In fact, the only asset available to Iraq is oil, and with the price of oil stagnating, it is not known whether Iraq will be able to produce petroleum at a level that can sustain its rebuilding efforts.

Militarily, the offensive threat from Iraq was eliminated. Not only have all its weapons been destroyed, but an arms embargo on Iraq is preventing many of the weapons of mass destruction from being rebuilt.

Iraq's industry, especially chemical, nuclear, and biological technology, was devastated by Allied bombers and new safeguards on trade with Iraq should ensure that it is unable to acquire this technology in the future.

Saddam Hussein has restructured some of his war fighting machine, but he lacks the more sophisticated weapons he had prior to the war. The devastation to the Iraqi military has shown Saddam Hussein that even if he did manage to rebuild his military in terms of men and material, he is in desperate need of a reexamining his military's tactics and operations before undertaking additional aggression. In addition, United Nations weapons inspectors are positioned throughout Iraq monitoring its military forces, helping to ensure that Hussein's forces do not attempt to reacquire weapons of mass destruction.

The elimination of Saddam Hussein would be a first step toward resurrecting Iraq, but there are concerns that a weak and disorganized government would be unable to hold Iraq together. Saddam has eliminated so much of the opposition in his country, many feel there is no alternative to the Baath Party, except possibly a coup by the military. Not only are several rebel groups fighting the government, but many of Iraq's neighbors may be interested in land if Iraq is unable to militarily ensure its territorial sovereignty.

Saddam Hussein

Personal

- Born in Takrit, Iraq, 1937
- Married to Miss Tofa
  and known to have at least one mistress
- Four children

Professional

- Cairo University, Egypt
- Al-Mustansariyah University, Baghdad
- Joined the Baath Party, 1956
- Sentenced to death for attempted assassination of General Kassem; fled country and lived in Syria and Egypt, 1959–63
- Member of the 4th Regional Congress and 6th National Congress, 1963
- Arrested for plotting overthrow of President Abdul Salem Aref, 1964
- Played a leading role in the July 1968 Revolution
- Vice-president, Revolutionary Command Council, November 1969
- Attained rank of general, January 1976
- President of the Republic of Iraq, 1979

Saddam Hussein's life has been marked by violence. Beginning in the 1950s, Hussein was an active player in the coups and countercoups that took place in Iraq. He established Iraq's secret police force and has used it effectively to eliminate political opposition to Baath Party rule.

Soon after acceding to the presidency, he invaded Iran and began a bloody war that killed untold thousands and ended in stalemate eight years later. He then turned his military against his own people, the rebellious Kurds, by indiscriminately dropping chemical weapons on civilians. In August 1990, he once again flexed his military muscle by invading Kuwait and systematically destroying that country.

It has been reported that many of the commanders who survived his war with Iran were systematically purged and murdered to eliminate them as a political threat to his rule. Hussein has surrounded himself with a cabinet that supports his every move and, it is believed, had shielded him from many of the facts regarding U.S. and Allied troop strength during the war.

Although not regarded as a religious man, during the war he took a more active interest in Islam and called for a jihad "holy war" against the Allied forces. In addition, he has a large ego common to many dictatorial leaders and attempts at defeating this have been more difficult than defeating his military forces.

At the end of the war, many were speculating that Saddam Hussein's time was short. If he was not killed in a coup by his military, he would be killed by a general civil uprising, be it by the Kurds or by those who suffer the costs of continuing U.N. sanctions. Despite these predictions, he remains in power in Iraq — his grasp on power is as strong as ever.

In 1995, two Iraqi defectors that were married to Saddam's daughters, were brutally murdered by Saddam's "family" members. The message from this incident was clear — do not oppose Saddam Hussein.

KUWAIT

Formal Name:	State of Kuwait
Citizens:	Kuwaitis
Capitol:	Kuwait City
Flag:	Three bands; *green over white over red; black trapezoid on left side*
Size:	6,880 square miles *(slightly smaller than New Jersey)*
Population:	1,976,000 (1989); 225,000 in Kuwait City
Languages:	Arabic and English
Gross Domestic Product:	$17.3 billion (US) 1986
Paved Roads:	3,100 km
Ports:	Shuwaikh and Shuaaba Ports
Airports:	Kuwait International

In 1899, the ruling family of Kuwait drew up an agreement allowing British control of Kuwaiti foreign affairs in exchange for British protection from the Ottoman Empire. Following the collapse of the Turks in WWI, the British redrew the borders between Iraq and Kuwait, giving Iraq additional land but leaving several islands in the hands of the Kuwaitis. In 1961, Kuwait became an independent state, but Iraq claimed the territory and British troops were dispatched to protect the new amir. In 1973, Iraq invaded a strip of coastline in Kuwait, but was forced to remove its troops due to international pressure.

During the 1980s, Kuwait aided the Iraqi government in its war with Iran. However, in July 1990, Iraq accused Kuwait of overproduction of oil which it felt was lowering prices and siphoning oil from the Rumaila Oil Field that stretches through both countries. On 2 August 1990, Iraqi troops invaded Kuwait and set in motion Operation Desert Shield. Kuwait was raped by the occupying forces of Saddam Hussein. Horror stories abound about looting and pillaging at the hands of the Iraqi Army and as the Iraqi troops left the country in hasty retreat, they made sure to leave nothing of value to the advancing Allied armies. Several hundred Kuwaiti nationals were kidnapped by the invading forces, their whereabouts still remain a mystery. The capital of Kuwait City was lit on fire with many of the buildings and factories totally gutted.

In addition, of the 900 oil wells in Kuwait, some 600 were left on fire when the Iraqis retreated and others were booby-trapped with explosives. But these problems have been dealt with. The fires were put out and the houses rebuilt. The scars of the war are still present in some areas, but Kuwait has recovered to at least a level that mirrors the pre-war economy.

In the mid-1980s, the Western-style parliament was disbanded. But in 1992, a Parliament was reformed and elected to bring about democratic change. In 1995, the Parliament issued a major report on the conduct of Kuwaitis, both in politics and in the military during the Gulf War, trying to assess what went wrong and what can be improved.

The royal family has managed to return to power as strong as ever. Kuwait has signed several defense agreements with U.N. Security Council members and maintains strong political and economic ties with the United States. Trade between these two nations is estimated to be about $3 billion annually.

H. H. Sheikh Jaber al-Ahmad al-Jaber, al Sabah

Personal

- Born in Kuwait, 1926
- Muslim

Professional

- Privately tutored
- Director of Public Security Department with jurisdiction over Kuwait Oil Co., 1949–56
- Head of Finance Department, 1959–62
- Minister of Finance and Economy, 1962–65
- Prime Minister, 1965–77
- Designated Crown Prince, 1966
- Amir of Kuwait, 1977–present

The Amir of Kuwait is one of the richest men on the planet — not only because of his oil. The financial ability of the Kuwaiti Kingdom is widely respected by economic analysts around the world and has enabled the government to continue to function despite the loss of its country. Although he has supported many Arab causes, he has been regarded as somewhat "aloof" and disliked by some Arab leaders.

During his exile in Saudi Arabia, he made a number of promises to former members of the Kuwaiti Parliament about the "new" Kuwait that would emerge from the war. The amir promised democratic reforms and now has considerable pressure to enact these reforms. Today, however, the royal family is considered to be extremely strong within Kuwait, despite the predictions of critics of the monarchy.

SAUDI ARABIA

Formal Name:	Kingdom of Saudi Arabia
Citizens:	Saudis or Saudi Arabians
Capitol:	Riyadh
Flag:	Green with Arabic message in white: *"There is no god but God, and Muhamad is the messenger of God;"* horizontal sword (Quintar) beneath message
Size:	839.996 square miles *(roughly Washington, Oregon, Alaska, and Hawaii put together)*
Population:	12,678.000 (1989); 1,380,000 in Riyadh
Language:	Arabic
Gross Domestic Product:	$98 billion (US) 1986
Paved Roads:	22,000 km
Ports:	Ras Tanura; Al Jubayl; Yanbu
Airports:	167 airports, 54 with paved runways

In 1902, Abd al Aziz, an Arab prince, seized Riyadh and set off to reestablish the House of Saud. Abd al Aziz eliminated the Turks from much of the Saudi peninsula in a few decades and in 1932 called the conquered areas the Kingdom of Saudi Arabia. With the discovery of oil, Saudi Arabia was caught between traditional Islamic ways and the urge to modernize to Western methods. These clashes have lasted throughout the last fifty years as Saudi Arabia attempted to modernize to Western ways.

Today's monarch, King Fahd, is regarded as having a pro-Western attitude, but is still faced with continued protest from many more radical fundamentalist Muslims. More on King Fahd is located in the following discussion.

Although virtually untouched and undamaged militarily, Saudi Arabia is facing economic problems. Since the war, the per capita income in Saudi Arabia has been cut in half, due to the nearly $30 billion the Saudis paid for the cost of the war and a stagnant oil market. It is also estimated that nearly 25 percent of the young, the fastest growing segment of the Saudi population, are unemployed with little prospect for work. To compound all these economic difficulties, there are political problems as well. Refer to the following discussion on King Fahd for details on these political problems.

There is also a growing radical Islamic movement within Saudi Arabia, that is thought to have masterminded the two bombing attacks on American servicemen in 1995 and 1996.

H.M. King Fahd Ibn Abdulaziz al Saud

Personal

- Born in 1920
- Muslim

Professional

- Educated by the palace court
- First minister of education
- Second deputy prime minister and minister of interior
- Crowned king after death of King Khalid in June 1982

Under King Fahd (sometimes spelled Fahad), the United States and Saudi Arabia have moved closer together to the point that Saudi Arabia is now one of the top U.S. Allies amongst the Arab nations. Following the devastation of Kuwait by Iraqi troops, he feared losing his kingdom to a possible Iraqi invasion and invited U.S. and Allied forces into his country. He took a great risk in challenging Saddam Hussein and relied on U.S. forces to eliminate any future threat to his kingdom from Iraq.

King Fahd was considered the leader of the Arab coalition that had been constructed for Operation Desert Storm and his future appeared promising. Politically, the future role of Saudi Arabia in the post-war Middle East was very promising.

However, King Fahd is well into his seventies and unlikely to rule for much longer. In 1995, he suffered a stroke from which he has not fully recovered. With a number of "princes" waiting in the wings, and a small but active radical Islamic movement rebelling against "Westerness" in Saudi Arabia, a power struggle for the future of Saudi Arabia could ensue after his reign comes to an end.

ISRAEL

Formal Name:	State of Israel
Citizens:	Israelis
Capitol:	Jerusalem
Flag:	White and light blue, with the Star of David in the center
Size:	8,017 square miles
Population:	4,476,000 (1988)
Language:	Hebrew, Arabic
Religious Breakdown:	81% Jewish (1988); 14% Moslem; 2% Christian
Paved Roads:	12,980 km
Railroads:	575 km
Ports:	Haifa; Ashod; Eilat
Airports:	Ben Gurion, near Tel Aviv

The modern state of Israel was established on 14 May 1948 following years of struggle against British colonial authorities in what was known as Palestine. Arab nations immediately declared war upon Israel, which led to years of fierce conflict in which the Israelis eventually proved triumphant. In 1967, Egyptian and Israeli forces clashed, leading to Jordanian and Syrian attacks on Israel's borders. Within a week, Israel had occupied a large area of land all the way to the Suez Canal and into part of west Jordan. An additional war started in October 1973 when an Egyptian offensive was launched across the Suez Canal and Syrian forces attacked from the Golan Heights. Following a U.N. cease-fire resolution, an eventual disengagement was reached between all parties.

In 1978, at a meeting at Camp David in the United States, President Jimmy Carter helped arrange a peace treaty between Israel and Egypt, which remains in effect to this day. In 1981, Israeli forces launched a massive offensive into Lebanon, which resulted in the removal of many Palestinian terrorists, but ended in a quagmire that forced Israeli troops to withdraw to their northern borders.

During the Gulf War, the highly trained and capable Israeli military was ready to respond to SCUD missile attacks on its country, but restrained under the incredible pressure applied by the United States and the Allies. American Patriot missile batteries were provided to the Israelis, along with American servicemen and servicewomen capable of operating them, until Israeli defense units could be trained to use them. Regardless of the military success of the Patriot, it provided considerable comfort for many Israelis and political cover for both nations. The restraint on the part of the Israelis was surprising given the rather cold relations that existed between the Bush administration and the Likud government that was in power at the time. Prior to the Gulf War, U.S. and Israeli governments were barely speaking to each other, given the Israeli position on a negotiated solution to the Palestinian problem.

Following the Gulf War, the more moderate Labor Party was elected under Yitzhak Rabin. This led to the famous Rose Garden ceremony in which a treaty was signed between Yassar Arafat, head of the PLO and the Israeli government. Rabin was later assassinated by a right-wing extremist. This later led to the Likud Party returning to power with a more "go slow" attitude toward returning the occupied territories to the Palestinians.

Yitzhak Shamir

Personal

- Born in Poland, 1915; died in 1995
- Immigrated to Israel, 1935
- Married
- Two children

Professional

- Active in the Jewish underground movements (Etzel and Lehi), 1937–48
- Businessman, 1948–54
- Held a senior position in the Israeli Intelligence Service (Mossad), 1955–65
- Returned to business, 1966–69
- Joined the Herut political party, 1970
- Elected a member of the Knesset, 1974
- Served as speaker of the Knesset, 1977–81
- Minister of foreign affairs, 1980–83
- Prime Minister of the 20th Government, 1983–84
- Vice-premier and minister of foreign affairs, 1984–86
- Prime minister of the 22nd Government, 1986–88
- Minister of the interior, 1987–88
- Prime minister of the 23rd Government, 1988–90
- Minister of labor and social affairs of the 23rd Government
- Prime minister of the 24th government, June 1990–92

Yitzhak Shamir and his Likud Party were regarded by some as overly stubborn in their dealings with the Arab world. A veteran of the Israeli Revolution and the many wars Israel has endured since then, his views of his Arab neighbors were tainted by the hostility displayed toward the Israeli state. He remained an ally of the United States, but that relationship chilled under the Bush administration given U.S. concerns on the settlement of Soviet émigrés in Jerusalem.

Shamir and the Israeli government maintained a quiet role throughout much of the Gulf Crisis, even in the face of continued attack by Iraqi SCUD missiles. The entry of Israeli forces into the battle would have done little militarily, but could have caused considerable political damage in the efforts to maintain the Arab forces unified against Iraq.

Israel received unprecedented support for its policy of restraint and there was a warming of U.S./Israeli relations to points previously unknown during the Bush administration. During the crisis, President Bush and Secretary Baker were in almost daily contact with the Israeli government.

This communication was in contrast to the previous year in which there was no high-level communication between Washington and Israel. The deployment of U.S. Patriot missiles with U.S. troops and other issues helped to build better U.S./Israeli relations in the years following the war.

Shamir's Likud Party lost in the elections following the Gulf War and was replaced by Prime Minister Yitzhak Rabin, who offered a more moderate policy on negotiations with the Arab world. Rabin was assassinated in 1995, and his successor, Shimon Peres was beaten by the Shamir's Likud Party in 1996. Shamir is now in the role of elder statesmen of the party, with Benjamin Netanyahu as the new prime minister.

EGYPT

Formal Name:	Arab Republic of Egypt
Citizens:	Egyptians
Capitol:	Cairo
Flag:	Three horizontal stripes of red, white, and black, and the national emblem in the center in gold
Size:	386,900 square miles
Population:	52,500,000 (1990)
Language:	Arabic
Gross Domestic Product:	$45.08 billion (1988)
Religious Breakdown:	90% Moslem and 7% Christian
Paved Roads:	21,637 km
Railroads:	4,321 km
Ports:	Alexandria and Port Said
Airports:	Cairo International and 95 other airfields, of which 77 are unusable

Egypt was part of the Ottoman Empire from 1517 until December 1914, when it became a British protectorate. In 1922, it was made an independent monarchy, until the king was overthrown in a revolution led by Abdul Nassar in 1952. Following Nassar's death, his vice-president, Anwar Sadat, took power and led a move toward Westernization in Egypt. Sadat was assassinated in 1981 and was succeeded by current president, Hosni Mubarak.

Egypt is generally considered one of the more moderate Arab states, thanks in large part to the work of Anwar Sadat at the Camp David peace accords with Israel. Despite the fact that Egypt is not at war with the Israelis, Egypt retains a loud and powerful voice in the Arab League. It was thus no surprise that American officials were quick to visit the Egyptian President Hosni Mubarak after the Iraqis invaded Kuwait.

General Schwarzkopf later said that the Egyptians were essential for the operations to succeed. Militarily, their forces spearheaded the Arab units into Kuwait, as they were well equipped with American weapons and had trained with Central Command forces for years. In addition, the Egyptians were experts in Soviet military equipment that made up the backbone of the Iraqi forces, as they themselves had fielded many of the same systems in the same desert climate. For example, they were able to confirm to the intelligence community that a mobile SCUD launcher could be moved within six minutes of firing, a key point for U.S. pilots to remember in the SCUD hunt they undertook.

Politically, Egypt was a bell-weather for how far the Arab League could be pushed in the Gulf Crisis. While it was fairly certain that Arab units would assist in the liberation of Kuwait, their participation in an invasion of Iraq was far more questionable.

OTHER KEY PLAYERS

Besides the nations that were geographically involved, a number of other key international players had a major role in the conduct of the Persian Gulf War. Diplomatic and military actions rendered the leadership of the United Nations, the United Kingdom, and France as some of the major players in the Gulf Crisis. A listing of these leader's backgrounds can help in understanding the conduct of those aligned against Saddam Hussein.

Javier Perez De Cuellar

Personal

- Born in Lima, Peru 19 January 1920
- Married to former Marcela Temple

Professional

- Law Faculty of Catholic University, Lima, Peru, 1943
- Joined Peruvian Diplomatic Service, 1944
- Served in France, the United Kingdom, Bolivia, and Brazil 1944–61
- Director of Legal and Personnel Departments in the Ministry of External Relations, 1961
- Promoted to rank of ambassador, 1962
- Peruvian Ambassador to Switzerland, 1964–66
- Peruvian Ambassador to the Soviet Union and Poland, 1969–71
- Appointed Permanent Representative of Peru to the United Nations, 1971–75
- Special Representative of the Secretary-General in Cyprus, 1975–77
- Peruvian Ambassador to Venezuela, 1977–79
- Appointed U.N. Under-Secretary General Special Political Affairs, 1979–81
- Retired from the Foreign Service of Peru, May 1981
- Appointed U.N. Secretary-General of the United Nations, December 1981
- Reappointed U.N. Secretary-General of the United Nations, October 1986

Javier Perez De Cuellar tried in vain to seek a peaceful solution to the Gulf Crisis for some time before the war began. De Cuellar was involved with conflicts before, including the negotiations on the situation in Cyprus in the 1970s and the Soviet invasion of Afghanistan in the 1980s. Also, under his tenure U.N. peacekeeping forces received the Nobel Peace Prize in 1988.

His understanding of this problem has been evident since his 23 July 1990 statement — one week before the invasion took place — calling for calm as Iraq was massing its troops on the border with Kuwait. In September, he met with Tariq Aziz, but was disheartened by Iraq's intransigence. A last-minute attempt at peace was also launched only days before the 15 January 1991 deadline, but this too fell on deaf ears.

During the war, De Cuellar played a behind-the-scenes role trying to coordinate the many different peace plans that were being floated by a number of countries. De Cuellar's role increased in the post-war Gulf, given the emphasis the Western Allies put on a resolution of other Middle Eastern problems.

In keeping with the precedent set during the escalation of the Gulf Crisis, President Bush used the United Nations as a forum for the discussion of diplomatic solutions to the Arab/Israeli problem. Despite De Cuellar's retirement, the United Nations is still used as a conduit for sending humanitarian aid to the region and conducting the inspections of Iraqi weapons facilities.

King Hussein I of Jordan

Personal

- Born in Amman, Jordan, on 14 November 1935
- Eleven children
- Married former Lisa Halaby of Virginia, now known as Queen Noor, on 15 June 1978

Professional

- Attended the Harrow School in England, 1951
- Proclaimed King of Jordan at 17 years of age on 11 August 1952
- Attended Royal Military Academy in Sandhurst, England, 1953
- Formal accession to the throne on 2 May 1953

King Hussein attempted to serve as a go-between with U.S. and Iraqi governments, but with little success. His country shares a border with Iraq and Israel, along with the major port of Ababa, where many blockade runners were smuggling goods into Iraq prior to the U.S. Navy's interdiction program. Although a personal friend of George Bush, he was unable to sway the president nor his other friend, Saddam Hussein, to settle this disagreement peacefully.

On 6 February 1991, King Hussein was forced to make a speech condemning the Allied bombing of Iraq and, in the eyes of many, put Jordan on the side of Iraq. Public opinion in his country was so overwhelmingly pro-Saddam Hussein that many began to fear the king would fall if he were to continue his stance of neutrality. Following his speech, the king became more popular than ever in his country, ensuring that he would stay in power in the short-term.

In the long-term, King Hussein took a much more moderate stance with the coalition nations and Israel. In late 1994, following the lead of Palestinian Liberation Organization (PLO) leader Yassar Arafat (the only other major Arab figure to support Saddam Hussein), King Hussein of Jordan "made peace" with Israel in a White House Rose Garden ceremony. U.S. military forces now conduct joint exercises with the Jordanian military, and relations, though once strained, now seem on the mend.

In 1962, *Uneasy Lies The Head,* the autobiography of King Hussein, was published in England.

Margaret Thatcher

Personal

- Born in 1925 in Grantham
- Educated at Somerville College, Oxford University, 1947–51; majored in chemistry
- Married Dennis Thatcher, 1951

Professional

- Passed the bar in 1953, becoming a tax lawyer
- Elected to the House of Commons, 1959
- Made Minister of Education and Science, 1970–74
- Elected leader of the Conservative Party and thus leader of the Opposition, 1975
- Led the Conservative Party to victory in 1979, becoming England's first woman prime minister
- Escaped IRA assassination attempt during Conservative Party conference, October 1984
- Resigned as head of party amid controversy over her policy on Europe, November 1990
- Elevated to the House of Lords and became known as Baroness Thatcher of Kesteven, 1992

Paralleling the rise of Reaganism in the United States, Thatcher led the Tories to victory in 1979 as a response to massive union disorder and chronic economic stagnation. Thatcher became a lightning rod for liberal opponents who attacked her efforts at dismantling Britain's large and bloated welfare state. She successfully privatized much of the British economy during the 1980s, selling off large chunks of industry that were until that time controlled by the state. Because of her hard-charging persona, she was given the nickname "the Iron Lady." Thatcher also successfully negotiated the British military effort in the Falkland Islands — a triumph which she cited as helping her develop the necessary skills for dealing with the Iraqi crisis.

Thatcher was one of the first world leaders to meet with Bush following the Iraqi invasion of Kuwait. By chance, both world leaders were scheduled to speak at a foreign affairs conference in Aspen, Colorado, only days after the Iraqi invasion. It was from a hotel room in Colorado that Thatcher ordered the first military movements of the British forces, ordering ships out of Penang and Mombasa to set sail for the Gulf. HMS *York* was already on station in Dubai and was moved into the Gulf.

Thatcher and Bush talked on 2 August, hours after the Iraqi tanks had moved into Kuwait. In her memoirs, Thatcher spoke of two points she hammered through to Bush: 1) aggressors must never be appeased, and 2) Hussein was about to control a large portion of the world's oil reserves should he move into Saudi Arabia. Bush agreed, and the leaders embarked on securing additional Allies throughout the diplomatic community.

While British troops and planes were heading to the Gulf, Thatcher came under incredible domestic pressure not because of her policy toward Iraq, but due to her domestic policy and her views toward a single Europe. Buoyed by the opposition to the so-called "Poll Tax," critics within her own party hammered away at her, forcing her to face an election contest for control of the Conservative Party. Her opponent was Michael Heseltine, and although she beat him on the first ballot by almost fifty votes, she failed to win by the required majority. She resigned rather than face a second ballot, throwing her support to John Major.

John Major

Personal

- Born in 1943
- Educated at Cheam Common Primary School and Rutlish Grammar School, Milton, UK
- Married, with one son and one daughter

Professional

- Appointed Assistant Government Whip, January 1983
- Made Lord Commissioner to the Treasury, September 1984
- Appointed Parliamentary Under-Secretary of State, Department of Health and Social Security, September 1985
- Appointed Minister of State, (Minister for Social Security), Department of Health and Social Security, September 1986
- Appointed Chief Secretary of the Treasury, following the June 1987 election
- Appointed Foreign Secretary, following the July 1989 election
- Appointed Chancellor of the Exchequer, October 1989
- Elected leader of the Conservative Party and appointed prime minister the next day

Major inherited Thatcher's policy in the middle of Operation Desert Shield. British forces were already committed to the Gulf when he took office, and some of his first actions were to reassure the Allied nations that British policy remained steadfast in support of removing Saddam Hussein. Major survived a tough reelection battle following the Gulf War, a battle in which he was not predicted to retain the prime ministership. In 1995, he resigned as head of the Tory Party, only to be quickly re-elected in a move designed to silence some of his critics. However, his next election battle is predicted to be an almost unwinnable fight, with the Conservative Party at record lows in the polls.

François Mitterand

Personal

- Born in Jarnac, France in 1916; died in 1996
- Graduated with a law degree in 1937

Professional

- Ran against DeGaulle in elections for president of France, December 1965
- Became secretary of the Socialist Party, 1971
- Ran for president a second time against Valery Giscard d'Estaing and lost in 1974
- Elected president of France, 1981
- Re-elected to a second term as president, 1988

Despite the traditional view of France's foreign policy — that it marches to its own drummer — François Mitterand was an avid supporter of the Western Allies in the Gulf War. From the opening days of Iraq's invasion, Mitterand pressured a number of his European colleagues to strictly enforce the U.N. economic sanctions and cut ties to the Iraqi regime. France contributed a significant force to the Allied cause, despite some last-minute maneuvers on whether its troops would come under Allied command. France had formally accepted the Allied commanders' authority in the final days prior to the start of the air war, but had repositioned its troops in line with Allied requests long before.

Following the Gulf War, Mitterand continued to rule and in 1992 rallied support for the Maastricht Treaty. This treaty called for a common European currency, borders, and defense. But his failing health put him in the hospital for surgery on his prostate both in 1992 and 1994. He died in early 1996.

Chapter Two
On the Homefront

DOMESTIC POLITICS

Since the end of the Vietnam War, American military overseas deployments have been greeted consistently with a chorus of protests centering around the idea of "no more Vietnams." This refrain, now virtually a cliché, has been voiced about military operations from a small number of military advisors deployed to El Salvador to thousands of Marines in Beirut or Grenada. But the horror of the Vietnam experience haunts many American foreign policy decision-makers and military decision-makers, such that avoiding "another Vietnam" has often taken precedent over other foreign policy goals.

A VERY CLEAR SIGNAL

Battling this stigma in the American psyche was one of the first tasks for President George Bush. Rather than a drawn out, minimal deployment of U.S. forces, leading to a gradual escalation of men and material over time, Bush announced a massive effort to sustain Saudi Arabia from the very beginning. In their first conversations with Saudi ambassador, Prince Bandar Bin Sultan, himself a former fighter pilot with the Saudi Air Force, Secretary of Defense Dick Cheney and Joint Chiefs of Staff Chairman General Colin Powell told the president that nearly 100,000 servicemen and servicewomen would be involved in the first weeks of deployment, eventually to total around 200,000 troops for the defense of Saudi Arabia. In this way, a very clear signal would be sent not only to Saddam Hussein that the United States was serious, but also to the American people that U.S. deployments would be overwhelming and capable of the mission assigned to them.

By jumping forward with such a large deployment of defensive troops, it looked like the troops were going in for a simple defensive operation and that hostilities were not imminent. (Remember, the initial deployments included the 82nd Airborne, which lacked the offensive heavy armor to take on the Iraqis, and some heavy armor and mechanized units of the 24th Mechanized; however, these were not enough to oust Hussein from Kuwait.

In addition, within weeks of the first deployments, the National Guard and National Reserves were called to active-duty service. While there was a very valid military reason for this call-up, as many of the logistical units in the U.S. forces are composed of Guard and Reserve units, there was a not-forgotten side effect of this announcement — that is, rallying of grass-roots support for the president's policy in the Gulf.

Active-duty military families tended to be transient, moving between various military bases across the country and not establishing very deep personal roots to a community at the individual level. National Guardsmen and Reservists have often lived in the same community for decades, knowing "everyone" with a wide network of friends and family. The fact that a neighbor down the street had been called up to active duty resonated much clearer in the minds of many Americans than the fact that a "bunch of troops over at a base" had deployed to the Gulf War. In a sense, the call-up personalized the war for many more Americans and led to greater support for President Bush's policies.

A MUCH MORE VOCAL AND ACTIVE CONGRESS

Back in Washington, the 101st and 102nd Congress, those which were in office during Operation Desert Shield and Operation Desert Storm, were firmly in control of the Democratic Party. While this wouldn't have made a difference forty years ago, as the Congress followed the policy of ending partisanship "at our nation's shores," the Vietnam experience had led to a much more vocal and active Congress in dealing with foreign affairs and national defense. In addition, a large number of extremely liberal members would be hard-pressed to ever support a military deployment of American forces overseas.

On 2 August 1990, Congress passed an economic sanctions bill that merely implemented President Bush's executive order on sanctions into law. The bill was passed by a unanimous vote in both the House and the Senate, thus giving congressmembers a chance to say "We voted for sanctions." Despite this overwhelming support, congressmembers continued to raise objections toward the president's policies. Many spoke up against the use of military force, supporting the concept of letting sanctions take their time. Others voiced concerns about congressional notification of military deployments and actions.

Throughout the fall of 1991, Congress was uneasy with U.S. policy in the Gulf. The unknown length of time that servicemen and servicewomen would be stationed overseas, the costs of the operations, and the always constant threat of military force kept many congressmembers on edge. Supplemental appropriations were needed to fund Operation Desert Shield, and budget ceilings that limited annual defense spending under the Gramm-Rudman Law had to be suspended temporarily.

On the issue of consultations, the administration was rather vague. Sometimes congressmembers would be briefed on operations, sometimes they were kept out of the loop. Some members favored giving flexibility to the president, others wanted a formal notification process to be established for all operations. This issue was left unresolved — or de facto resolved — by the fact that Congress adjourned in October, allowing congressmembers to return home to their districts to seek reelection in November 1990. With Congress not in Washington, the administration was able to deal with a more manageable number of congressional leaders rather than the full chamber of back benchers.

THE BUSH ADMINISTRATION DROPS ITS OWN BOMB

There were few surprises in the election of 1990, with most incumbents easily winning reelection and the Gulf War being not much of an issue. With the economy on so-so ground and a nation in need of strong leadership in Washington, a prevailing "stay the course" attitude affected many Congressional races. However, two days after the election, Bush dropped a bombshell — American forces would now be raised to support an offensive military option. This meant the number of troops deployed would double from 200,000 to nearly 430,000.

This led to widespread criticism from administration opponents and supporters. By moving toward a military solution, many were convinced the administration had no intention of letting sanctions take hold. Others were upset with the administration's decision to act without congressional approval. Fifty-three congressmembers and one senator signed on to a lawsuit against the president that sought an injunction to prevent Bush from ordering U.S. troops in to the Gulf. The injunction in the case, *Dellums vs. Bush*, was denied because only 10 percent of the Congress signed on as a party.

Following the U.S.-inspired Resolution 678 in the United Nations that set up a deadline of 15 January 1991 for military action, Congress was confronted with whether or not to support military actions in line with the U.N. resolution. On 12 January 1991, three days before the deadline, Congress passed Public Law 102-1 Solarz-Michel in support of the president's decision to use force, keeping the operation in line with the requirements of the War Powers Act. (More on Resolution 678 and Public Law 102-1 is found in Chapter 7.)

BUILDING SUPPORT FROM CONGRESS

Despite the strong and vocal left-leaning bloc of Democrats who opposed the use of military force in almost all situations, Bush was able to draw on a quiet, conservative, and southern faction of Democrats, along with a substantial bloc of northeastern liberals (many of whom strongly supported Israel) to build up enough support for his policies in the Gulf.

Congressman Steven Solarz, a Democrat from New York, and by no means a conservative member of the House, was one of the strongest supporters of the president's policy in the Gulf. His efforts on behalf of the president helped ensure the passage of the use of force resolutions in the House. In addition, more conservative southern Democrats occupied high-ranking positions on the House Armed Services Committee or in other committees dealing with foreign policy, and their opinions were respected given their knowledge in these matters. Also, many of the active-duty troops deployed to the Gulf came from the congressional districts of the southern states, leading many of their congressmembers to support the president due to considerable constituent pressure by the families of the servicemen and servicewomen.

Passage of the use of force resolution by the House was surprisingly overwhelming. The House Democrats declared the vote a "conscience vote," meaning that members of the party could vote their conscience without fear of reprisals from the party leadership. (Note: Some votes are tallied by the party bosses as counting toward how well someone tows the party line, a figure sometimes used in leadership contests and committee assignments.) The Gulf War vote was not to be decided on the basis of party interests, but each members' own concerns.

The Senate was a different matter. Protected politically by Senate Armed Services Committee Chairman Sam Nunn's opposition to military action, and lacking a firm liberal spokesperson in favor of military action, the Senate voted on near party-lines (Republicans in support of the president and Democrats opposed to the president) to support the military operations. Overall, ten Democrats voted for and two Republicans against the president's Gulf War policy.

Although it was close for a few tense hours, gradually a number of southern Democrats were convinced to support the president's position. Some of them voiced the concern that it was already too late to really make a difference, as President Bush was going to act unilaterally, with or without Congressional approval. Voting for the resolution was seen as giving moral support to the troops in the war, who would need it as they embarked on their mission. By securing a vote in the United Nations in favor of military action (U.N. Resolution 678), the administration put Congress in the position of voting for military action or taking a position that could be politically portrayed as "weaker" than that of the U.N., not something many congressmembers wanted to explain back in their districts.

During the Gulf War, Congress was relegated to the position of observer. Occasionally a congressmember was called upon to intervene on behalf of a specific serviceman or servicewoman to ensure that an urgent message got through to the front lines or that a servicemember's family was directed to the proper authority in times of crisis. But usually they sat glued to their televisions watching the war just like most Americans. Some even commented that the media coverage via CNN was more accurate than the classified briefings they were receiving from Pentagon officials. For more on the media's role in the Gulf Crisis, see Chapter 8.

Congress passed several resolutions supporting the president's actions to help show unified support for the president after the shooting began.

Congress also passed resolutions to give support to troops who were deployed, such as exemptions from filing income tax forms for those in the Gulf region.

WHEN THE WAR WAS OVER

With the cessation of hostilities, critics remained quiet with the return of the troops, and long-time supporters of the military were boastful of their support for the weapons systems that succeeded in the military campaign. Gradually, as the parades faded and the interest dwindled, critics stepped up their attacks on the administration's pre-war policies toward Iraq and started to contest some of the more outrageous claims that were made about certain weapons, such as the Patriot missile.

Toward the end of the war, President Bush spoke about how the United States had finally cast aside the specter of Vietnam as it relates to future military conflicts. America was more confident about its military, with a greater pride in its armed forces and an important role to play in future world affairs.

America's feelings of confidence in the U.S. military lasted only a few years, until the ill-fated U.S. mission to Somalia led to the deaths of several Americans and the eventual withdrawal of U.S. forces in the face of violent conflicts between feuding warlords.

The rest of this chapter is dedicated to the key people behind the military and diplomacy of the Persian Gulf Crisis. To study the international figures of the Gulf War, refer back to Chapter 1.

George Herbert Walker Bush

Personal

- Born in Milton, Massachusetts, 12 June 1924
- Married former Barbara Pierce, 1945
- Five children: George, Jeb, Neil, Marvin, and Dorothy
- Member of the Episcopalian Church

Professional

- Lieutenant (jg), U.S. Navy, 1942–45
- Distinguished Flying Cross and three Air Medals
- B.A., Yale University, 1948
- Supply Salesman, West Texas and California, 1948–50
- Cofounder, U.S. Overby Development Co., 1951–53
- President and Cofounder, Zapata Off-Shore Co., 1954–66
- Member, U.S. House of Representatives, 1966–70
- U.S. Ambassador, United Nations, 1971–73
- Chairman, Republican National Committee, 1973–74
- U.S. Liaison Officer, People's Republic of China, 1974–75
- Director, Central Intelligence Agency, 1976–77
- Vice-President of the United States, 1980–88
- President of the United States, 1988–92

While in high school, George Bush and his classmates were lectured on the horrors of appeasement by Henry Stimson, who eventually became President Roosevelt's secretary of war. George Bush remembered this lesson and became the youngest Navy pilot in the Pacific while his classmates were at college. The lessons he learned about war and appeasement likely shaped his Gulf War policies.

President Bush received high marks for his management style during the entire crisis. Faced with the toughest test of his life, he performed virtually without flaw in the Persian Gulf Crisis. Although some faulted him for ignoring problems at home, his personal diplomacy aligned the world in its opposition to Saddam Hussein. He appeared at ease with his decision to send in the troops, a decision he reportedly made some time before hostilities broke out. His resolve was demonstrated as he carefully but firmly rejected the last-minute peace opportunities that were designed by the Soviets to give Iraq a face-saving way out of the crisis.

The formation of the coalition and the rallying of world support are widely regarded as a direct result of the president's emphasis on personal diplomacy. In addition, he was able to silence the press "leakers" and in-fighters within his own administration with a no-nonsense directive straight from the Oval Office to those who would speak out of turn. The firing of General Dugan, Air Force Chief of Staff, for his comments on the conduct of the air war sent shock waves throughout the national defense and foreign affairs community in Washington so that everyone knew George Bush was in command.

Bush's management style with the military in this crisis should be regarded as a role model for future presidents. Bush refused to interfere in purely military matters as Lyndon Johnson did in Vietnam, and many attribute this to the professional way in which the war was fought. His one major operational command of the military during the war, the calling of a cease-fire, was done only after he was told it could be done by the military professionals in the Pentagon and in the Gulf.

Politically, Bush seemed unbeatable in 1991. No Democrat could beat him on the national security or foreign affairs platform, but the 1992 election focused more on the economy rather than the successes of the Bush administration's international policies. While at the end of the war, Bush's approval rating was 91 percent, the highest for a president in decades, by the elections in November, Bush garnered only 40 percent of the vote.

That's not to say there were not political successes from the defeat of Saddam Hussein. The Middle Eastern peace initiatives that came to fruition in a number of Rose Garden ceremonies during the Clinton administration were based on a solid foundation of contacts and trust developed during the Gulf War. In addition, Operation Desert Storm demonstrated to many in the military-political community what is required for our defense structure into the next century. While the glow of the Gulf War has faded in eyes of the American public, it will remain one of the most important events in Middle East affairs for the next few decades.

J. Danforth Quayle

Personal

- Born in Indianapolis, Indiana, 4 February 1947
- Married former Marilyn Tucker, 1972
- Three children: Tucker Danforth, Benjamin Eugene, and May Corinne

Professional

- B.A., DePauw University, 1969
- J.D., Indiana University School of Law, 1974
- Served in the Indiana National Guard, 1969–75
- Elected to the House of Representatives, 1976
- Elected to the U.S. Senate, 1980; re-elected 1986
- Vice-President of the United States, 1988–92

Although regarded by many as a "lightweight," especially for his lack of active-duty experience in the military, Vice-President Quayle was present at many of the Presidential National Security Briefings and met with the president on a frequent basis. As second-in-line to the president, he was kept well-informed on the day-to-day operations of U.S. forces in the Gulf and attended the policy-making meetings inside the White House that determined the fate of operations.

Publicly, Quayle was used to drum up support for U.S. policy and rally Americans behind the troops. He traveled to Saudi Arabia during Operation Desert Shield and visited the families of troops during Operation Desert Storm. Unfortunately, any goodwill or respect that developed for the vice-president was lost in the election campaign where he focused on the moral values of the television star *Murphy Brown* and the spelling of the word potato. Today he continues to comment on the decline of family values in books and in the media.

John Sununu

Personal

- Born 2 July 1939
- Married former Nancy Hayes, 1958
- Eight children: Catherine, Elizabeth, Christina, John, Michael, James, Christopher, and Peter

Professional

- B.S., Massachusetts Institute of Technology, 1961; M.S., 1962; Ph.D. 1966
- Founder and Chief Engineer of Astro Dynamics, 1960–65
- President, J.H.S. Engineering Co. and Thermal Research, Inc., 1965–82
- Associate Professor of Mechanical Engineering, 1966–82
- Associate Dean of Engineering, Tufts University, 1968–73
- New Hampshire State Representative, 1973–74
- Governor of New Hampshire, 1983–88
- White House Chief of Staff, 1989–92

John Sununu made a name for himself as the liaison between conservative groups and the more moderate president. Although some regarded him as brash, Sununu had the ear of the president and was one of the few people who met with the president several times a day. His input was essential to the president's decision-making process and he was involved with the day-to-day operations of the Persian Gulf Crisis.

To the public, it appeared that Sununu was nearly invisible during most of the Gulf Crisis. Many attribute this to reports of a flare-up inside the White House that was brought about as a result of Sununu and Office of Management and Budget Director Richard Darman's dismal attempts at arranging a 1990 budget summit. It was also reported that Sununu was "taken to the woodshed" by Bush and his public appearances were reduced considerably. But, behind the scenes, Sununu was considered part of the "Gang of Eight" as described by Colin Powell — that is, those eight policymakers who took part in the major decisions of the Gulf War. (The Gang of Eight consisted of George Bush, Dan Quayle, Jim Baker, John Sununu, Brent Scowcroft, Dick Cheney, Colin Powell, and Bob Gates.)

Shortly after the Gulf War, considerable controversy about the misuse of presidential aircraft and vehicles led to John Sununu's departure from the White House. He was replaced by Sam Skinner, and has recently been hosting the CNN talk show "Crossfire" and writing op-ed articles.

James Addison Baker III

Personal

- Born in Houston, Texas, 28 April 1930
- Married Susan Garrett, 1973
- Eight children

Professional

- Princeton University, 1952
- Lieutenant, Marine Corps
- J.D., University of Texas School of Law at Austin, 1957
- Andrews & Kurth, 1957–75
- Under-Secretary of Commerce, 1975
- National Chairman, President Ford Committee, 1976
- President Reagan's Chief of Staff, 1981–85
- Secretary of the Treasury, 1985–88
- Bush Campaign Chairman, 1988
- Secretary of State, 1988–92

A trusted friend of President Bush, James Baker was called upon not only for his international expertise, but for his own personal feelings on the Gulf Crisis. He was the point man for all diplomatic efforts in bringing the U.N. to support the U.S. position. His style has won high praise and support from leaders around the world.

After the end of the war, Baker took some heat from a politically "hungry" Congress. Baker was rumored to be a possible Republican target of Democratic congressmembers who were seeking a scapegoat for U.S. diplomatic policy with Iraq prior to the crisis. The State Department's handling of U.S./Iraqi relations prior to 2 August 1990 were heavily scrutinized in Congressional hearings and in the media, as were reports of U.S./Iraqi arms deals in the years prior to Operation Desert Storm.

During the election, Baker had to play the role of a very public advisor to President Bush and, at the same time, a skilled diplomat in establishing the basis of the Middle Eastern peace initiative. His diplomatic initiatives convinced the United Nations and other countries to support the U.S. led initiatives against the Iraqis, which created and maintained the fragile coalition.

Dick Cheney

Personal

- Born in Lincoln, Nebraska, 30 January 1941
- Married former Lynne Ann Vincent, 1964
- Two children: Elizabeth and Mary
- Member, United Methodist Church

Professional

- B.A., University of Wyoming, 1965; M.A., 1966; Ph.D. candidate, 1968
- Congressional Fellow, 1968–69
- Special Assistant to the Director of Office of Economic Opportunity, 1969–70
- White House Staff Assistant, 1971
- Assistant Director, Cost of Living Council, 1971–73
- Deputy Assistant to the President, 1974–75
- White House Chief of Staff, 1975–76
- Elected to 96th Congress, 7 November 1978
- Chairman, Republican Policy Committee, 1980–87
- Chairman, Republican Conference, 1987
- Whip, Republican Party, 1988
- Resigned House on 17 March 1989
- Secretary of Defense, 1989–92

Selected as a compromise appointment after the defeat of John Tower for defense secretary, Cheney was well respected and well liked by his former colleagues in the Congress. He oversaw the Pentagon in a no-nonsense way and canceled several major weapons programs due to cost overruns and mismanagement.

One of his first acts as secretary of defense was to discipline a senior general for "violating" civilian defense policy, thus he drew his own "line in the sand" with the top brass. During Operation Desert Shield, he worked with President Bush to fire Air Force Chief of Staff Dugan when the general publicly spoke out about the conduct of the impending air war.

As secretary of defense, he oversaw the day-to-day operations of the war and kept in daily contact with the president to report the status of the battles. With a résumé second only to President Bush, many suspected Cheney to be considered as a possible presidential candidate. However, Cheney, who had several heart operations, opted to skip the 1996 Presidential Campaign.

Brent Scowcroft

Personal

- Born in Ogden, Utah, 19 March 1925
- Married Marian Horner, 1951
- One child: Karen

Professional

- B.S., U.S. Military Academy, 1947
- M.A., Columbia University, 1953; Ph.D., 1967
- 2nd Lieutenant, U.S. Army Air Corps, 1947
- Military Assistant to the President, 1973–75
- Retired as Lieutenant General in the Air Force, 1974
- Deputy Assistant, 1975–77
- Assistant to the President for National Security Affairs, 1977–80
- Member of the President's Special Review Board on Iran Contra (The Tower Commission), 1986–87
- National Security Advisor to President Bush, 1989–92
- Awarded Distinguished Service Medal with two Oak Leaf Clusters, Air Force Commendation Medal, Distinguished Service Medal from Department of Defense, and National Security Medal

Brent Scowcroft was well respected by both Democrats and Republicans as a fair and reasonable man. For this reason, President Reagan selected him to investigate the Iran-Contra weapons deal in 1986.

He went on to serve as the head of the National Security Council and was President Bush's chief advisor on security matters. He had a staff of capable and talented members (mostly military officers) that prepared memorandums and other information for the president on national security matters.

Scowcroft remained out of the public eye during most of Operation Desert Storm, but was relied upon heavily inside the inner-circle of the White House decision-making process. Scowcroft advised the president on opinions and operations of the national security community from the CIA to the Coast Guard and how they would function in Operation Desert Storm. Scowcroft is currently preparing a book on national security with President Bush and is still consulted by many high-level officials as somewhat of an elder statesmen of foreign affairs.

Colin Powell

Personal

- Born in New York City, 5 April 1937; raised in the south Bronx
- Married Alma Vivian Johnson, 1962
- Three children: Michael Kevin, Linda Margaret, and Annemarie

Professional

- B.S., City College of New York, 1958
- Commissioned 2nd Lieutenant, 1958
- Served as an advisor in Vietnam, 1962
- Returned to Vietnam as an executive officer for the 23rd Infantry Division (AMERICAL), 1968
- M.B.A., George Washington University, 1971
- Selected as White House Fellow, 1972
- Commander of 1st Battalion, 32nd Infantry in Korea, 1973
- Commander of 2nd Brigade, 101st Airborne Division, 1976
- Senior Military Assistant to Deputy Secretary of Defense, 1977–80
- Assistant Division Commander for Operations and Training, 4th Infantry Division (Mechanized), 1981
- Senior Military Assistant, Secretary of Defense, 1983–86
- Commander of V Corps, Frankfurt, Germany, July 1986
- President's National Security Advisor, 1987–88
- Commander in Chief, U.S. Forces Command,1989
- Chairman, Joint Chiefs of Staff, 1989–93
- Received the Defense Distinguished Service Medal with two Oak Leaf Clusters, the Distinguished Service Medal (Army), the Bronze Star, the Purple Heart, and other awards

Technically, some viewed the chairman of the Joint Chiefs of Staff as merely an advisor, with the secretary of defense ordering military maneuvers directly through the commanders in chief of the various commands throughout the world. However, with General Powell as the chairman of the Joint Chiefs of Staff (JCS), he communicated daily, if not hourly, with both the policymakers in the White House and the commanders in the field. With President Bush's detached management style, Powell had considerable leeway to plan and execute the strategy the military professionals felt could accomplish the mission set forth by the president. His performance during Desert Storm received high marks from all participants.

Before serving as the chairman of the JCS, Powell spent time as the national security advisor in the White House. This tour of duty was certainly of great help to his handling of the Gulf Crisis, as it exposed him to the intricacies of the political policymaking process and all the nuances that many in the military do not understand. In the same vein, many in the civilian command structure have no concept of how the military planners coordinate and implement their decisions. By having someone with a strong military background, and a working understanding of Washington politics, General Powell was without a doubt, the best individual for this position.

After the war, he suffered a few political attacks following the publication of Bob Woodward's book, *The Commanders*. In this book, it was obvious that Powell had talked with Woodward, as had almost everyone else in Washington. But some in Congress took the chance to criticize the general in a rather petty way. For example, his confirmation hearing was drawn out over two days, and it wasn't until the waning hours of his first tour as chairman that he was reconfirmed.

In September 1993, General Powell retired from the military and began work on his memoirs. Considering himself a Republican, though under fire from the right wing of the party, Powell received poll after poll of data showing he would have a strong candidacy for the White House. While he ruled himself out of the 1996 Presidential Election, some feel this was only a tactical decision before the next election in the year 2000.

Norman Schwarzkopf

Personal

- Born in Trenton, New Jersey, 22 August 1934
- Married Brenda Holsinger
- Three children: Cynthia, Jessica, and Christian

Professional

- B.S., U.S. Military Academy, 1956
- Commissioned 2nd Lieutenant, 1956
- M.S., University of Southern California, 1964
- Two tours-of-duty, Vietnam
- Deputy Director, Operation URGENT FURY (Grenada Invasion), 1983
- Commanding General, I Corps, Fort Lewis, 1986–87
- Awarded Fourth-Star, 1988
- Commander of CENTCOM (Middle East, Southwest Asia, Northeast Africa Command), 1988-92

Norman Schwarzkopf, also known as "Stormin' Norman" and "the Bear," was in charge of all military forces in the Persian Gulf region. Like many American military officers, his views of war were shaped by his combat experiences inside Vietnam and has spoken often of the "obscene nature" of war. In press conferences, he has avoided talking about "kill ratios" and "body counts," seeking to avoid turning Operation Desert Storm into a numbers battle.

His personal style was well liked by the troops and the American public. A gruff and demanding Army man, he still had time to give a word of encouragement to new troops and tell a joke with junior officers. As a child, he spent time in Iran with his father, also a general, and has continued his studies of Arab history along with the tactics of desert conflict. Intelligent and fluent in French and German, General Schwarzkopf was regarded as essential not only to winning Operation Desert Storm, but maintaining the multinational coalition.

There was little room for Schwarzkopf to grow in the military, and it was likely that either the chief of staff of the Army or chairman of the Joint Chiefs of Staff might have been unsatisfying to his own personal desires. On 31 August, General Schwarzkopf retired from the Army.

Following his retirement, he did a number of charity events and continues to work with CBS News as a consultant to showcase stories of human kindness and generosity.

George J. Mitchell

Personal

- Born in Waterville, Maine, on 20 August 1933
- One child: Andrea

Professional

- B.A., Bowdoin College, Brunswick, Maine, 1954
- U.S. Army Counterintelligence Corps, Berlin, 1954–56
- LL.B., Georgetown University Law Center, 1960
- Lawyer, Antitrust Division, Department of Justice, 1960–62
- Executive Assistant, Sen. Edmund Muskie, 1962–65
- Chairman, Democrat State Party, Maine, 1966–68
- Partner, Jensen, Baird, Gardner, Donovan & Henry, Portland, Maine, 1965–77
- U.S. Attorney for Maine, 1977–80
- Appointed U.S. Senator, 1980

- Re-elected to U.S. Senate, 1982, 1988
- Elected Senate Majority Leader for 101st Congress, 1988
- Named U.S.-representative to Northern Ireland Peace Talks, 1996

As senate majority leader, Senator Mitchell was considered one of the most visible elected Democrats in the country. He controlled the order and timing of all legislation on the Senate floor and was one of Bush's chief opponents in the Congress. Although opposed to the use of force, he showed public support for Gulf troops after Operation Desert Storm commenced.

Mitchell, like most in Congress, consigned himself to playing a near-invisible role during operations. He was kept informed of the operations through the president and his staff, but had little role in the conduct of the war.

During Operation Desert Shield, he was part of the leadership of the Congress that refused to bring President Bush's resolution to the floor for a vote until January of 1991.

Before the war, many speculated he would make a good presidential candidate. However, after his retirement from the Senate in 1994, his name virtually disappeared from the radar screen, except for many stories linking him to the then-vacant Major League Baseball commissioner's post.

Most recently he was appointed a special emissary of the president in trying to seek a negotiated end to the political troubles in northern Ireland.

Robert Dole

Personal

- Born in Russell, Kansas, on 22 July 1923
- Married Elizabeth Hanford, former secretary of transportation, secretary of labor, and current President of the American Red Cross
- One child: Robin

Professional

- Attended the University of Kansas
- Platoon leader in the 10th Mountain Division, Italy during World War II
- Wounded and received the Purple Heart, 1945
- Discharged from the Army as a captain, 1948
- B.A., J.D., Washburn Municipal University, Topeka
- Elected to Kansas House of Representatives, 1949
- Russell County prosecuting attorney, 1951–60
- Member of the U.S. Congress, 1960–76
- Republican vice-presidential candidate, 1976
- Elected to the U.S. Senate, 1980, 1986
- Republican presidential candidate, 1988
- Republican Leader of the Senate, 1984–96

Regarded by many as brash and cutting, he was defeated in his bid for the Republican nomination for the presidency by George Bush in 1992. Although both officially deny it, there was a great deal of talk about a "feud" that existed between the White House and Senator Dole. However, during the Gulf Crisis, Bob Dole served as one of most vocal and active supporters of the president.

Dole retired from the Senate in May 1996 to focus all his energy on the presidential election. In June 1996, former President Bush was reported to be working with the Dole campaign to encourage General Colin Powell to undertake a more active role in Dole's election bid, perhaps putting to rest once and for all the talk of bad blood between these two leaders.

Despite all efforts, Dole's campaign never really took off with American voters. He lost to President Clinton, having trailed the president in every poll taken during the 1996 election campaign. Today he is lecturing and appearing on a number of television commentary shows, ranging from Sunday morning political programs to late-night talk shows.

Thomas S. Foley

Personal

- Born in Spokane, Washington, 6 March 1929
- Married Heather Strachan

Professional

- B.A., University of Washington, 1951
- LL.B., University of Washington Law School, 1957
- Deputy Prosecuting Attorney of Spokane County, 1958
- Instructor in Constitutional Law, Gonzaga University Law School, 1958
- Appointed Assistant Attorney General, State of Washington, 1960
- Special Counsel on the Committee on Interior and Insular Affairs, 1961–63
- Elected Congressman from the sixth district, Washington, 1964
- Chairman of Agriculture Committee, 1975–81
- Chairman, House Democratic Caucus, 1976–81
- Whip, House Democratic Party, 1980–87
- Majority Leader, 1987–89
- Speaker of the House, 1989–92

Constitutionally, the speaker of the house is third-in-line for the presidency should the president and vice-president be unable to serve. Politically, Foley was the Democrat's highest ranking elected official and often called upon to give the Democratic response to the president's and the Republican's position. Foley's consent was essential to bring up any legislation regarding the Persian Gulf.

Foley, like many in Congress, was somewhat invisible during the course of the war. Under the established constitutional and legal procedures for the conduct of a war, Foley attended many briefings and discussions with the president, but his input on the day-to-day policy was minimal. Like many Democrats, he did not see any advantage in attacking the president's policy while the war was being conducted. Although prior to hostilities, he was one of the leaders of Congress who refused to bring up the president's war resolution request until the last minute.

Foley made history in 1994 when he became the first sitting speaker of the House of Representatives to lose reelection in nearly a century. Speaker Foley came from a relatively conservative district, and his votes on gun control and opposition to term limits were cited as two factors that caused his loss during the Republican sweep of 1994.

Sam Nunn

Personal

- Born in Perry, Georgia, on 3 September 1938
- Married Colleen Ann O'Brien, 1965
- Two children: Mary Michelle and Samuel Brian

Professional

- Seaman, U.S. Coast Guard, 1959–60
- A.B., LL.B., Emory University, 1962
- Attorney and farmer
- Coast Guard Reserve, 1960–68
- Georgia House of Representatives, 1968–72
- Appointed U.S. Senate, 1972; re-elected 1978 and 1984
- Chairman, Senate Armed Services Committee, 1986

As chairman of the Senate Armed Services Committee, Sam Nunn oversaw all military projects, just as his counterpart Congressman Les Aspin did on the House side. Nunn, a moderate Democrat, was regarded as the Democrats' best chance at winning the presidency, and was encouraged to run in 1988.

He opposed the use of military force on 12 January 1991, but was unable to convince a number of his moderate Democratic colleagues to give sanctions more time. When the war started, however, he closed ranks and called for support of the president. Some in Washington were whispering that his initial opposition to the war may have been for political reasons. By calling for more time with sanctions, Nunn was able to satisfy many of the liberal activists in the Democratic Party and would have been well positioned politically if the tides of war had turned bad. However, many feel his opposition was deeply felt and that the Senator was too classy to say "I told you so" should the war have turned sour.

Regardless of his rationale, Senator Nunn found himself hurt very seriously by this vote. Not only did he have to take the heat for his own vote, but many Democrats who sided with him were upset that he was not more forceful in defending the position he talked them into supporting. The public opinion polls after the war rendered a presidential bid impossible, and Senator Nunn announced that he would not seek Senate re-election after 1996. He later said his vote was a mistake that kept him from the White House.

PART TWO

PREPARING FOR BATTLE...

Armed Forces and Weapons Systems

Chapter Three

The Troops at a Glance

BACKGROUND OF THE TROOPS

Today's all-volunteer military is regarded as the best the United States has ever fielded. Some complain it is overly represented by minorities as compared to the general population. (See Table 3.1 on ethnic breakdown on the next page.) However, military supporters are quick to point out that it is also overly represented by high school graduates as compared to the general population and has fewer criminals and drug users than the general population. Tables 3.2 and 3.3 detailing the education levels and average ages of servicemen and servicewomen are included.

Forces in the Gulf complained about the usual problems that go along with military deployment: the food, the weather, and the boredom. The "hurry-up-and-wait" that troops have always experienced seems to have caused particular problems in the Kuwaiti Theatre of Operations (KTO) as the troops did not know if they would ever be called upon to fight.

Once Operation Desert Shield became Operation Desert Storm, many of the soldiers, especially the younger troops, displayed a "let's-get-this-job-done-and-go-home" attitude toward the operation. However, several of their senior colleagues, especially those who had seen combat before, were more cautious in their assessment of the time it would take to settle the crisis.

Servicewomen in the Gulf

Approximately 37,200 servicewomen were deployed to the Persian Gulf. Of these, 26,000 were Army, 3,700 were Navy, 2,200 were Marines, and 5,300 were Air Force. In addition, 10.3 percent were officers and 10.2 percent were enlisted.

Women in the Gulf were intricately involved in all operations except for combat. Under a Congressional mandate, women were prevented from serving in combat units, but that did not mean they would not see combat. Just as military policewomen in the Panama Invasion "Just Cause" engaged enemy troops, women in the KTO were subject to air raids and missile attacks. In fact, two women were taken prisoner in Operation Desert Storm and several were killed in the SCUD missile attack on a U.S. barracks on 25 February 1991. The performance of females in this operation continues to raise the combat-exclusion debate.

Another issue that developed was the issue of both spouses being deployed to the Gulf at the same time. Congress was undertaking an effort to exempt one of the family members, estimated at around 17,000 people, but the bill eventually died. The administration and the Pentagon had serious objections to removing thousands of troops in the final few days of the preparations for war.

Following the war, Congress and the Pentagon reexamined the issue of women in combat. Despite the fine performance of those women who found themselves in combat situations, a number of objections were raised concerning fraternization between soldiers while on duty in the KTO. While women are still not allowed in ground combat units, a few female pilots have now qualified to fly combat aircraft and are serving in fighter air wings.

TABLE 3.1

SERVICEWIDE ETHNIC BREAKDOWN OF TROOPS – DEPLOYED IN THE GULF

ACTIVE-DUTY FORCES

Group	Army	Navy	USMC	Air Force
Caucasian	62.6/60.9	72.8/68	71.1/71.5	78.1/81.3
African American	28.8/30.4	16/19.3	18.9/18	15.2/13
Hispanic	4.1/4.2	4.3/5.2	1.4/1.5	1.7/1.2
Asian	1.7/1.4	4.3/5.2	1.4/1.5	1.7/1.2
Native American	0.5/0.6	0.5/0.6	0.8/0.9	0.7/0.6
Other	2.4/2.5	0.5/0.5	0.8/0.8	0.8/0.7

RESERVE FORCES

Group	ArmyNG	USAR	USNR	USMCR
Caucasian	75.2/70.8	65.4/63.6	80.2/77.3	72.4/73.7
African American	15.8/23.8	24.7/28.1	10.7/11.7	15.8/14.8
Hispanic	6.2/4.0	5.8/5.4	4.2/4.8	7.5/7.3
Asian	1.3/0.4	2/1.2	1.9/3	2.3/2.2
Native American	0.9/0.5	0.4/0.4	0.8/0.9	0.4/0.5
Other	0.7/0.4	1.7/1.3	2.2/2.4	1.5/1.5

Group	AirNG	USAFR	USCGR	Totals
Caucasian	84.8/88.9	76.9/77	88.1/89.5	74.3/71.6
African American	7.7/6.7	14.8/15	5.1/4.2	16.6/20.7
Hispanic	4.1/2.8	4.6/4.9	0/0	5.5/4.9
Asian	1.8/0.6	1.8/1.4	1.6/1.2	1.7/1.2
Native American	0.9/0.8	0.7/0.6	0.5/0.5	0.7/0.5
Other	0.7/0.2	1.2/1.1	4.8/4.6	1.2/1.0

Numbering the Troops

The exact number of troops and their units can never be perfectly computed. At any one time, for example, there were troops in transit to and from the Gulf region, making any statements of the "exact number" somewhat unrealistic. Most commentators place the number of Allied troops in the Kuwaiti theatre at 540,000. You will find, however, that information available to the public gives a good idea of what the United States and Allied forces amassed in the Gulf area.

Detailed lists of units activated as part of Operation Desert Shield/Storm are included in appendixes A through E. As you read through these lists, keep in mind that some units participated in the conduct of the buildup and war, although they did not deploy to the Kuwaiti Theatre of Operations (KTO).

Additionally, the lists are built on the Pentagon's own accounting, media reports, and hundreds of personal comments relayed via the Internet.

For more specific information on the unit listings, consider obtaining a copy of *Operation Desert Storm/Desert Shield Chronology and Fact Book* by Kevin Hutchinson.

TABLE 3.2

EDUCATION LEVELS OF ACTIVE-DUTY FORCES

OFFICERS	
Below baccalaureate	5%
Baccalaureate only	55%
Advanced degree	35%
Unknown	5%
ENLISTED PERSONNEL	
No high school degree	2%
High school or GED	90%
College (no degree)	1%
Baccalaureate degree	4%
Advanced degree	1%
Other/unknown	3%

TABLE 3.3

AVERAGE AGE OF ACTIVE-DUTY FORCES

STATUS	SEX	GRADE	AGE
Deployed	Male	Enlisted	26
		Officer	32
	Female	Enlisted	26
		Officer	30
Non-deployed	Male	Enlisted	27
		Officer	34
	Female	Enlisted	26
		Officer	32
Average Age:			**28**

UNITED STATES GROUND FORCES

U.S. ground forces formed into three separate groups for Operation Desert Storm. The first group included the 18th Airborne Corps, composed of the 82nd Airborne, the 101st Air Assault, and the 24th Mechanized Infantry. In addition, the 3rd Armored Cavalry Regiment and French forces were attached to this command. Marines made up the second group. The 1st and 2nd Marine divisions were combined in northeast Saudi Arabia. The 1st Marine Division was composed of the 1st, 4th, and 7th Marine expeditionary brigades, and the 2nd Marine Division was comprised of the 5th Marine Expeditionary Brigade.

TABLE 3.4

TOP 20 INSTALLATIONS THAT DEPLOYED FORCES

	Installation	Number
1)	Fort Bragg, NC	33,877
2)	Fort Hood, TX	24,743
3)	Fort Campbell, KY	19,325
4)	Camp Lejeune, NC	17,304
5)	Fort Stewart, GA	15,144
6)	Camp Pendleton, CA	12,307
7)	Fort Bliss, TX	8,624
8)	Fort Riley, KS	8,374
9)	Fort Benning, GA	6,972
10)	Kaneohe Bay, HI	5,801
11)	Fort Sill, OK	5,732
12)	29 Palms, CA	3,365
13)	Fort Eustis, VA	3,287
14)	Fort Lewis, WA	2,600
15)	Eglin AFB, FL	2,170
16)	Fort Knox, KY	2,145
17)	Cherry Point, NC	2,084
18)	Shaw AFB, SC	2,055
19)	El Toro, CA	2,044
20)	Langley AFB, VA	1,783
	Overseas Bases	115,543

The main attack force was the VII Corps, which was recently relocated from Europe. The VII Corps was composed of the 1st and 2nd U.S. armored divisions, the 1st Mechanized Infantry Division, and the 2nd Armored Cavalry Regiment. In addition, the British 1st Armored tank units were attached to this force.

AMERICAN UNIT DEPLOYMENT

Once the movement to Operation Desert Storm commenced, units were activated and moved out from all over the United States to the ports and airfields of Saudi Arabia. While more than 100,000 troops came from overseas bases, mainly units from Germany, a large number of soldiers and sailors deployed from bases within the United States. As can be seen from Table 3.4, Fort Bragg, North Carolina, sent the largest compliment of troops, some 33,000 officers and soldiers of the 82nd Airborne.

Most of the top ten bases that deployed were the locations that housed entire units, such as Fort Stewart, home of the 24th Mechanized, and Fort Campbell, home of the 101st Airborne.

As the troops deployed, huge convoys of vehicles could be seen moving down the nation's highways from the bases to port facilities on the coasts. Throughout the south, which was home to a disproportionate number of the troops that deployed to Operation Desert Storm, huge traffic jams of military vehicles could be seen heading off to war. Train after train of heavy armor passed down the nation's railroads, and a steel bridge was established between the United States and Saudi Arabia composed of American heavy airlift. With the call-up of Guard and Reserve forces, every state witnessed some of its citizens going off to war.

Local communities bore many costs of the deployment. Not only had some of their residents gone off to risk their lives, but many of the small businesses that depended upon military service members for their livelihood fell on hard times, with a few having to close their doors for good. With soldiers away and many military spouses in the workforce, day care centers became clogged up with additional children as two parent households temporarily were run by just one spouse.

Some military families ran up incredible bills trying to keep in touch with the servicemen and servicewomen overseas, oftentimes running up hundreds if not thousands of dollars in phone calls to Saudi Arabia. For many on the homefront, the quick end to the war was a welcome relief, both for peace of mind of their loved ones returning home safely and the financial well-being of families and local businesses.

ALLIED UNIT DEPLOYMENT

Allied contributions took several roles in the Gulf War, all of which were important, though not always recognized as such. Each country was forced to examine its policies and contribute what it could given its own military constraints and domestic political pressures.

The first contribution was ground units. The United Kingdom, Egypt, Syria, and France provided tens of thousands of ground forces and their associated equipment. This entailed a high military cost — shipping tanks and troops to the Gulf was expensive — but also opened a country up for the risk of seeing its servicemen and servicewomen killed in action. This type of risk is a political liability for any nation involved in a war situation.

The second contribution was the naval forces that were sent to the Gulf region to enforce the economic sanctions. While France and the United Kingdom again provided a large number of vessels, other countries like Canada and Italy provided several ships to help enforce the economic embargo on Iraq. This entailed a somewhat lower political cost, as attacks on Allied shipping were far less expensive than attacks on ground soldiers. Further, many nations were simply ill-equipped to supply ocean-going vessels, as many of their own Navies were composed primarily of coastal patrol boats.

The third major contribution came in the form of aircraft, not only strike aircraft, like those contributed by Italy and Canada, but also support aircraft, like the C-130 cargo planes from Argentina, New Zealand, and Australia. The fourth major contribution was support troops, oftentimes in the form of medical personnel or specialized troops. For example, there was a Czech contingent of chemical weapons detectors, and the Polish forces supplied medical personnel. For some, this support was considered as a form of humanitarian assistance and thus helped to silence protesters in the home nations that opposed overseas military deployment.

Finally, there were those nations that provided financial support — most notably Japan and Germany. As a result of post-World War II constitutions drawn up after the Allied victory over the Axis powers, these nations had embarked on a policy of not deploying their troops overseas in any situations. With Japan and Germany being two of the world's leading economies, and major beneficiaries of a free flow of Middle Eastern oil, the pressure on these nations to contribute financially to the Allied forces was considered an essential. Appendix E includes a listing of the Allied troops deployed.

Five Major Units

In broad terms, Allied ground forces were divided into five major units:

1) XVIII Airborne Corps was positioned far to the west, with the 6th French Armored Division along with the 82nd Airborne and elements of the 101st Airborne and the 24th Mechanized Division.

2) VII Corps, which made up the major Allied attack force, included the 1st and 3rd U.S. armored divisions, the 1st Mechanized Infantry Division (Mechanized), the 1st Cavalry Division (Armored), and the 2nd Armored Cavalry Regiment. In addition, the 1st UK Armored Tank units were attached to this force.

3) Joint Forces Command – North, which was composed of the 3rd Egyptian Mechanized Division, the 4th Egyptian Armoured Division, a regiment of Egyptian Rangers, the 9th Syrian Armored Division, a Syrian commando force, the 7th Pakistani Armored Brigade, and the 20th Mechanized Brigade of Saudi Arabia, along with other attached Arab forces. The Egyptian II Corps also operated with JFC–N, which was composed of the 3rd Egyptian Mechanized Division and the 4th Egyptian Armoured Division, a regiment of the Egyptian Rangers.

4) Marine Command, consisting of the First Marine Expeditionary Force and including the 1st and 2nd Marine divisions, and the Second Marine Expeditionary Force. Also with the Marines was the 1st "Tiger Brigade" of the Army's 2nd Armored Division.

5) Joint Forces Command – East, which consisted of the 10th Saudi Infantry Brigade, the United Arab Emirates Motorized Infantry Battalion, and Omani Motorized Infantry Battalion, the 8th Saudi Mechanized Infantry Brigade, a Company of Bahrainian Infantry, a brigade of Kuwaiti soldiers who had escaped the invasion, the Second Saudi National Guard Motorized Infantry Brigade, and a Mechanized Battalion from Qatar.

See Appendix E, Order of Battle, for a detailed list of these units.

Communication and Coordination – Keys to Success

This is not to say that every unit was independent of every other unit. There were Navy gunnery spotters associated with some ground units, and forward air controllers from one service deploying with the forces of another. Cross communication between various forces was considered essential to the success of the integrated war plan, bringing in air, ground, and naval forces against the Iraqi troops.

At sea, U.S. forces composed several distinct forces. The Persian Gulf, Red Sea, and Mediterranean battle forces, composed mainly of aircraft carrier battle groups and naval gunfire support units such as battleships, were used to attack Iraqi positions in Kuwait and Iraq. The U.S. Maritime Interception Force, which was composed of warships on patrol, ensured that the economic sanctions of Iraq were maintained. The Amphibious Task Force was used to support Marine Corps landing forces, including the use of the Marines as a deception.

There were also units assigned to minesweeping, as the Iraqi Navy spent considerable time and effort laying mines in the Persian Gulf. Finally, there were the logistics supply forces, not only those ships that supported other naval ships, but also the critically important sealift vessels that brought most of the Allied equipment to the region. There were also support vessels for the troops, such as the hospital ships and "comfort" vessels that were used to provide rest and relaxation to troops on leave.

In the air, an incredible coordination existed between the various aircraft. To draw distinctions is very difficult as each service — Air Force, Navy, Army, and Marines — had their own aircraft in the theatre. Thus, each had its own specialty under the operational control of the Central Command's Air Staff.

The blueprint for the use of air power first involved heavy lift aircraft bringing in many of the initially deployed troops. This was accomplished by C-5 and C-141 transports of the Military Airlift Command, along with civilian contracted airlines and aircraft mobilized under the Civil Reserve Air Fleet (CRAF). See Chapter 5 for more information on the role of CRAF aircraft. Once in the theatre, Army helicopters handled some of the tactical redeployment along with smaller C-130s. Supporting these aircraft, many of which were from Air Force Reserve units, were a large number of tanker aircraft, both active duty and Reserve.

These tankers were also essential for the day-to-day air strikes that were launched by the "shooters" — those aircraft tasked with air-to-air superiority and close combat support. These were the fighters, such as the F-15, and attack aircraft, such as the F-117 Stealth Fighter, that provided the teeth of the air war. As these aircraft attacked Iraqi positions throughout the KTO, they were joined by heavy B-52 bombers, stationed in the United States and operating from Diego Garcia in the Indian Ocean. Close air support was also in this category, with aircraft like the A-10 proving highly effective in its designed role of destroying Iraqi tanks and vehicles. In addition, Special Operations aircraft provided search and rescue, special forces support and additional combat support, such as the AC-130 gunship.

Not to be forgotten was the important role played by reconnaissance aircraft, including the still under-construction

JSTARs aircraft and the AWACs command and control planes. They were joined by tactical reconnaissance planes, such as the RF-4, which provided ground commanders with current photographs of Iraqi units deployed against them. For more details on these important aircraft, refer to Chapter 5.

To better understand the deployment of U.S. forces and the size of the units involved, it is helpful to have a general idea about a few basic military terms and the associated units that go with them. See the end of this chapter for a list of military unit descriptions. While these figures are approximate — varying from service to service, weapon to weapon, and country to country — they give a basic idea of how forces were organized for service in the Gulf.

COMPARISON OF THE FORCES

When you look at the figures in Table 3.5, the war in the Gulf looked like a fair fight, with both sides rather evenly matched. While the Iraqis may have had more tanks, the Allies had more helicopters, and so on. However, upon closer examination, there were important differences between Iraq's "fourth largest army in the world" and the Allies arrayed against it.

Iraq fielded many high-tech weapons in the Gulf, but these weapons were the exception, not the rule. Twenty- and thirty-year-old weapons systems, mainly of Soviet-design, were commonplace in the Iraqi forces, and those units that did possess top-of-the-line equipment often degraded their combat effectiveness by substandard maintenance and poor training.

A large number of the soldiers that served in the Iraqi Army were draftees. In fact, some of them were reportedly "press-ganged" into service — they were given a rifle and taken to the front against their will. While the Republican Guard was a better motivated, trained, and equipped force, it too suffered from shoddy maintenance and supplies. Iraq had what Americans would consider primitive logistics and command and control capabilities, which further hurt its armed forces. When all of this was added to the onslaught of the massive and overwhelming air

TABLE 3.5

COMPARISON OF U.S., ALLIED, AND IRAQI FORCES IN OPERATION DESERT STORM PRE-WAR TOTALS

	United States	Allies	Iraq
Total troops	500,000	205,000	545,000*
Tanks	2,431	1,285	4,280
Armored personnel carriers	2,700	1,350	2,880
Helicopters	1,700	160	160
Artillery	3,000	442	3,100
Aircraft	1,800	343	550

* 545,000 was the estimated number of troops at the start of hostilities. Following the war, closer examination indicated there were more like 350,000 Iraqis in the KTO at the start of the air war. Accurate figures for Iraqis at the start of the ground offensive are difficult to obtain, due to casualties and desertions that took place as a result of the bombing.

power in the first days of Desert Storm, many Iraqi units were simply degraded into a mere mass of disorganized, starving troops.

American forces possessed an incredible array of high-tech weapons and highly trained troops behind them. For example, one of the oldest weapons in the Gulf War was the B-52 bomber, first designed before many of the current B-52 pilots were born. However, the United States had modified and improved the B-52 from the initial roll-out back in the 1950s, so that the current B-52 is a highly computerized and redesigned aircraft. Many other U.S. weapons, such as the F-15E Strike Eagle were within their first years of service. Specific information on the multitude of primary weapons systems is located in chapters 4 through 6.

In addition, American soldiers took advantage of their months of waiting in the deserts of Saudi Arabia to acclimate themselves and their equipment to fighting in the sand. A considerable number of training exercises were conducted, running through everything from breaching the sand berms of Kuwait to live-fire tank practice in the Saudi desert. The Allies, especially Egypt and Saudi Arabia, contributed valuable intelligence in desert fighting techniques. In fact, one of the most sought after items in all of Saudi Arabia was Saudi-designed desert warfare boots, which were considered much more comfortable than American-issued combat boots.

When American troops smashed through the border in the opening days of the ground war, tens of thousands of Iraqi soldiers fired off a few rounds and then quickly surrendered to the overwhelming onslaught of Allied forces. Interestingly, many American troops reported the Iraqis' rifles and vehicles were in horrible condition. A number of other Iraqis had defected, leaving their vehicles to be hit by Allied air power, and headed north on foot. In the end, while the numbers showed a fair battle, the actual combat indicated a much more lopsided conflict.

A call to action. Many of the armaments used in the Gulf War had been mothballed or had not seen battle for several years. Yet despite their age they proved to still be quite effective. *Source: U.S. Navy*

MILITARY UNIT DESCRIPTIONS

Navy	
Ship	A single vessel usually run by a captain.
Battle group	A group of several vessels usually surrounding a battleship or aircraft carrier.
Task force	Two or more battle groups.
Fleet	A group of several task forces. There are four numbered fleets in the U.S. Navy. For example, the 2nd fleet is the East Coast, the 3rd is the West Coast, the 6th is the Mediterranean and East Atlantic, and the 7th is the Western Pacific to the Indian Ocean.
Air Force	
Flight	Three or four aircraft.
Squadron	Usually two dozen aircraft.
Wing	Approximately seventy-two aircraft.
Army	
Squad	Usually about ten soldiers commanded by a sergeant.
Platoon	Three or four squads commanded by a lieutenant. Armored platoons are four tanks.
Company	A company is 150 to 200 soldiers composed of four platoons.
Battalion	Five companies of approximately 1,000 troops.
Brigade	Two battalions of 1,500 soldiers.
Division	Made up of 4,000 to 10,000 soldiers complete with artillery, aviation, and support troops.
Marines	
Squad	Thirteen soldiers.
Platoon	Forty-five Marines commanded by a lieutenant.
Rifle Company	A rifle company includes 180 Marines and a weapons platoon.
Battalion	A battalion is composed of 850 Marines including headquarters and service.

Chapter Four

Ground Power

INTRODUCTION TO GROUND FORCES

Ground forces deployed by the United States were the result of a massive modernization and reform effort that took place in the late 1970s and 1980s. Designed primarily to defend NATO against a Warsaw Pact invasion, the weapons were designed around the concept of better quality, not quantity. Five major modernizations were started in the 1970s and became active during the 1980s, including the:

- M1-A1 Abrams tank
- Bradley infantry fighting vehicle
- AH-64 Apache attack helicopter
- UH-60 Blackhawk transport helicopter Patriot air-defense missile

The backbone of this new force was the M1 Abrams tank and the mechanized units, which utilized speed and maneuverability to defeat the quantitative advantages of Eastern Bloc forces. The first contracts for the M1 were awarded in 1973, with prototypes tested in 1976 and arriving on active duty in 1980. The tank, which replaced the M-60, was specifically designed to defeat the best Soviet tanks of the day, the same tanks the Iraqi's fielded.

The second system was the Bradley infantry (and cavalry) fighting vehicle. This weapon was designed to fight alongside the M1-A1 and keep up with the Abrams speed, which its predecessor, the M-113 could not. In addition, it offered greater armor protection for the troops and improved firepower from a cannon mounted on the top. The first production models of this system came online in 1981. The AH-64 was designed to replace the AH-1 Cobra, which was found to be too vulnerable to anti-aircraft weapons. In contrast, the AH-64A is considered a flying tank, heavily armed with a mix of missiles and guns, and carrying a highly advanced electronics package. The other helicopter modernization, to replace the UH-1 "Huey," was the UH-60 Blackhawk. This new helicopter could carry a greater number of soldiers or cargo with greater speed than its predecessor.

The last of the major modernizations was the Patriot missile. Initially designed as an anti-aircraft system, the Patriot replaced the Hawk. The Patriot made its name in the Gulf War by its ability to shoot down incoming SCUD missiles, not Iraqi aircraft (as most of these did not fly).

Despite these modernizations, during the Gulf War the United States and the Allied forces utilized all the weapons systems that were "replaced" by the five new systems. These new systems and many of the older ones used against their Soviet-built Iraqi counterparts proved vastly superior. Not only was the technological advantage clear, but the training of soldiers and logistical support for the weapons far outpaced the efforts of the Iraqi Army.

At a policy level, the Gulf War validated the idea of a high-tech military defeating a simpler, but materially larger force. However, many of the gains that were made for this argument in the defense community were diminished by the U.S. mission to Somalia, where lightly armed irregulars utilized sporadic attacks on the American military and U.S. domestic politics to "defeat" the technologically superior U.S. forces. While it appears the high-tech argument continues to hold sway, this debate is certain to be echoed throughout the weapon's decisions that will be made in the next decade.

TANKS

M1-A1 Abrams Tank

Length:	**32 feet, 3 inches**
Width:	**12 feet**
Height:	**8 feet**
Weight:	**134,000 lbs**
Maximum Speed:	**41 mph**
Fuel Capacity:	**500 gallons**
Cross-country Speed:	**30 mph**
Range:	**279 miles (cruising); 289 miles (cruising without nuclear, biological, chemical protection); 127 miles (working)**
Crew:	**Four (4)**
Main Gun:	**M256 120 mm smooth bore cannon**
Ammunition:	**M829/A1 Armor Piercing Fin Stabilized Sabot (SABOT); M830 High Explosive Anti-Tank Multi-Purpose (HEAT)**
Main Gun Load:	**40 rounds**
Other Weapons:	**One M2 .50 caliber machine gun; two M240 7.62 mm machine guns**
Power:	**1,500 hp gas turbine; 4-speed automatic transmission**
Contractor:	**General Dynamics Land Systems Division**

M1-A1 Abrams. The M1 tank had an outstanding 90 percent operational readiness rate during the Gulf Crisis. *Source: U.S. Government Department of Defense*

Background

The Abrams tank was the backbone of the U.S. armored forces in the Gulf. The more modern M1-A1 and M1-A1(HA), which were sent to the Kuwaiti Theatre of Operations (KTO) from Europe, include an NBC cooling system to allow the tanks to operate in a chemical warfare situation. The M1 is also equipped with night vision, automatic fire suppression systems and, in some cases, reactive armor to defeat armor-piercing weapons, although reactive armor wasn't used on the M1 in Operation Desert Storm. Because of the tank's size, a C-5 Galaxy transport plane can only carry one of these tanks at a time, making overseas shipment of these tanks by ships necessary.

Iraqi Counterpart

Iraq had a considerable array of tanks, most of them based on Soviet designs. The T-72, of which Iraq owned close to 500, had a 125 mm gun and was equipped with chemical weapons protection. Considered one of Iraq's best tanks, it is still regarded as inferior to the M1 and comparable to the M60 tank used by the U.S. Marine Corps. Specifications of the T-72 are listed below:

T-72

Length:	**30 feet, 4 inches**
Width:	**11 feet, 10 inches**
Height:	**7 feet, 9 inches**
Weight:	**90,405 lbs (combat loaded)**
Maximum Speed:	**50 mph**
Operational Speed:	**37 mph**
Range:	**434 miles (with external fuel tanks)**
Crew:	**Three (3)**
Main Gun:	**125 mm smooth bore main gun**
Other Weapons:	**One 7.62 mm machine gun; one 12.7 mm machine gun**
Power:	**780 hp diesel**

In addition, Iraq had a number of earlier Soviet models, such as the T-62 and T-54/T-55, both of which were developed in the 1960s. Both of these tanks are also regarded as inferior to the M1 Abrams. Iraq was thought to possess as many as 1,600 T-62s and 700 T-54/T-55s, but exact figures are difficult to obtain given the eight years of war with Iran. Iraq was also suspected of having a small inventory of British Chieftain tanks. During the Iran-Iraq War, tanks were converted to fixed artillery pieces by commanders who dug them into the ground for fear of losing them to enemy attack. The same practice in Operation Desert Storm made them easy targets for air-to-ground attacks by coalition warplanes.

Action in Desert Storm

A total of 1,178 M1-A1s and 594 M1-A1 Heavy Armor (HA) tanks were deployed, utilizing depleted uranium armor. Of the 2,300 M1-A1s deployed, 528 were placed in operationally ready float status and war reserve stocks. The Marine Corps used sixteen M1-A1s and sixty M1-A1(HA) tanks.

U.S. tanks spearheaded the operations across Iraqi fortifications and engaged enemy tanks whenever and wherever possible. Because of Iraq's use of tanks as fixed artillery pieces, digging them into the ground and preventing their quick movement, Allied air power smashed approximately 50 percent of Iraq's tank threat before Allied units moved across the border. The highly advanced M1-A1 took out a number of Iraqi tanks that did manage to go mobile. One report indicated that American thermal sights were unhampered by the clouds of thick black smoke over the battlefield that were the result of burning Kuwaiti oil wells. Such was not the case with the sights in the Iraqi tanks, which were being hit from units they could not even see. Concerns about the M1-A1's range were eliminated by a massive resupply operation that will be studied for years as a model for operations.

Bradley fighting vehicle. Bradleys kept up with and sometimes led the advancing columns. *Source: U.S. Government Department of Defense*

Bradley Fighting Vehicle (M2 and M3)

Length:	21 feet, 6 inches
Width:	10 feet, 6 inches
Height:	9 feet, 9 inches
Weight:	50,000 lbs; 66,000 lbs with add-on armor tiles
Maximum Speed:	41 mph
Operational Speed:	30–35 mph ("swim" speed is 4.4 mph)
Fuel Capacity:	175 gallons
Range:	300 miles (cruising)
Crew:	M2 has a 9-man infantry squad; M3 has a 5-man scout section
Main Gun:	M242 25 mm cannon
Other Weapons:	TOW anti-tank missile; M240 C7.62 coaxial machine gun
Power:	500 hp (A1) Cummins Diesel; 600 hp (A2) Cummins Diesel
Contractor:	FMC Corporation

Background

In 1981, the Army accepted the first Bradley into service and continues to procure this vehicle to supplement the M113 armored personnel carrier. The Bradley disembarks troops by lowering a door in the rear and protects them with a wide variety of armaments. During testing, many questions were raised about the survivability of the Bradley after taking a hit from an anti-tank missile. In response to these concerns, reactive armor is being considered for extra protection.

The M2 Bradley is called the infantry fighting vehicle, carrying a nine-man squad (three people are considered a crew). The M3 is the cavalry fighting vehicle, carrying a five-man scout section (three people are considered a crew).

Iraqi Counterpart

Iraq had a number of Soviet-made BRDM-2 and other scout vehicles that it used extensively in desert warfare. The BRDM-2 is a wheeled vehicle equipped for chemical weapons warfare and a favorite of many Third World countries. It contains a similar size gun as the Bradley and can be equipped with anti-tank missiles.

The Iraqis also had nearly 1,000 Soviet-made tracked BMPs, which were developed in the 1950s. The BMP carries a troop load of eight and is armed with a 73 mm gun and a launcher for an anti-tank missile. The BMP is in extensive use throughout the Third World. In addition, the Iraqis also possess a large number of Soviet BTR-50s and BTR-60s, Soviet-made armored personnel carriers designed in the 1960s and armed with 7.62 mm guns. The BTR-60 is a wheeled personnel carrier that can carry up to sixteen troops. In the Soviet military, which the Iraqi military tends to mimic, the BMPs are linked with the tank divisions and the BTR-50s and BTR-60s are linked to motorized infantry.

Action in Desert Storm

Bradleys, M113s, and Marine LAVs supplied the armored personnel carrier needs of U.S. forces in the region. Linking up with tank units, Bradleys kept up with and sometimes led the advancing columns. Only a few Bradleys were taken out by Iraqi units, although some Bradleys were destroyed by Allied aircraft in friendly-fire incidents. While the Bradley was not able to defeat tank rounds from the T-72, it did provide protection to troops from fire from smaller arms. There were no reports of the Bradley's armor "burning" from flash fire, as some had predicted during the survivability debates of the mid-80s. Further, a "mid-crisis crisis," in which some claimed the transmission would fail in the Bradley, passed by with less than a dozen vehicles with transmission problems. More Bradleys were lost to friendly fire than to enemy fire.

Initial deployments were with the more basic A1 model. Although 692 newer A2 versions were shipped during Operation Desert Shield to help modernize the forces in the theatre. The A2 had enhanced survivability with add-on armor, a larger engine, and improved ammunition storage. Overall, 2,200 Bradleys were in the theatre and maintained an operational readiness rate of more than 90 percent.

ARTILLERY

Multiple Launch Rocket System (MLRS)

Length:	**21 feet, 6 inches**
Width:	**10 feet, 6 inches**
Height:	**9 feet, 9 inches**
Weight:	**55,420 lbs**
Engine:	**500 hp diesel**
Maximum Speed:	**40 mph**
Range:	**298 miles (cruising)**
	M77 rocket
Length:	**155 inches**
Weight:	**675 lbs**
Range:	**32 km**
Warhead:	**644 M77 bomblets; anti-tank mines; and radar-guided munitions**
	ATACMS rocket
Length:	**13 feet**
Range:	**20–28 miles**
Propulsion:	**Solid**
Crew:	**Three (3)**
Contractor:	**LTV Aerospace and Defense Company**

Background

The MLRS is a tracked vehicle containing twelve missiles designed to deliver a large quantity of munitions into an area in a short time. Its primary mission is the suppression of enemy air defenses and counterfire against fixed targets. The MLRS is used by a number of European Allies in their military forces. It fires an M77 rocket in a six-round pod. The rocket warhead contains 644 full-purpose grenades for lightly armored systems and personnel. One MLRS M77 rocket can dispense its grenades over four to five acres. If the launcher was to fire all its load of twelve rockets, the target area coverage would be thirty acres. It can also fire the Army Tactical Missile System (ATACMS) which is used as a deep strike against soft, stationary, and semi-fixed targets.

Iraqi Counterpart

The BM-21 is a multiple rocket launching system based on a variety of chassis but most often seen on a cross-country truck. It carries forty missiles with a small warhead and has a range of about twelve miles. Its range and payload, however, are vastly outclassed by the MLRS. The Iraqis also used the Astros II multiple rocket launcher with a larger range.

Action in Desert Storm

The MLRS was used in preparatory attacks on Iraqi front-line units before the ground war. Using a variety of munitions, including scatterable anti-tank mines, the MLRS was in operation with U.S. and British units. The MLRS was also used to suppress enemy artillery that caused problems for Allied front-line troops prior to the ground war. The ATACMS rocket was used against air-defense sites.

Multiple Launch Rocket System (MLRS). Iraqi prisoners referred to the MLRS as "steel rain." *Source: U.S. Government Department of Defense*

The psychological effect of a massive MLRS strike was devastating. Iraqi prisoners referred to the weapon as "steel rain." Nearly 189 MLRS were deployed to the theatre, firing a total of 9,660 rockets.

M109 self-propelled Howitzer. The M109's tracked chassis helped it sift through the desert sands of the KTO. *Source: U.S. Government Department of Defense*

M109 Self-Propelled Howitzer (Paladin)

Length:	**29.9 feet**
Width:	**10.3 feet**
Height:	**10.8 feet**
Weight:	**64,000 lbs**
Speed:	**33 mph**
Range:	**23.5 km with rocket assisted projectile; 18.1 km unassisted; 220 miles (cruising)**
Main Armament:	**M284 155 mm cannon at four rounds per minute for three minutes; one round per minute sustained**
Other Weapons:	**.50 caliber M2 machine gun**
Crew:	**Six (6)**
Contractor:	**BMY, York, Pennsylvania**

Background

The M109, first fielded in the early 1960s, is an air-transportable system — the via C-5 Galaxy — and is based on a tracked chassis. The M109 is capable of firing all types of munitions — conventional, chemical, and nuclear. An improvement program that is currently underway will include night vision, a new cannon, and nuclear, biological, and chemical (NBC) protection for the crew.

Iraqi Counterpart

It was in the area of artillery that the Iraqis were thought to hold a slight edge. Iraq had several thousand artillery pieces, some of which were of the self-propelled variety. The Iraqi Army fielded the Soviet M-1973 with a 152 mm gun and even a small quantity of American M109s.

Artillery was very important to the Iraqi military and they had a wide variety of towed pieces. Like much of the Iraqi military, Soviet-made weapons played a leading role. One such weapon, the 122 mm gun named the D-30, was the primary artillery piece in the Soviet military and had a range of about ten miles. The Iraqis also had a number of D-74 122 mm Howitzers; these had a range of more than twenty miles.

Action in Desert Storm

During much of the air war, the only enemy activity (besides SCUDs) was artillery duels between Iraqi and coalition forces. Iraqi artillery, believed to be some of the best in the world, was surprisingly inaccurate in a number of attacks and allowed Allied units to return fire safely and effectively. The M109 artillery system and other self-propelled guns, benefited from their tracked chassis in the sifting sands of the desert. In some cases, Iraqi towed artillery was reportedly stuck in the sand and mud. This caused a delay in repositioning and made the system vulnerable to air attacks. Overall, 642 Howitzers were deployed.

INFANTRY

M-16 Rifle

Caliber:	5.56 mm
Type of Fire:	Semi-automatic, three-round bursts
Weight:	8.9 lbs
Range:	550 yards
Magazine Capacity:	30 rounds
Attachments:	M7 bayonet and an M203 grenade launcher

Background

Developed for use in Vietnam, the M-16A2 is now the primary combat rifle used by the U.S. military and many of its Allies around the world. This weapon was seen everywhere in Operation Desert Shield/Storm as all U.S. troops in Saudi Arabia were under standing orders to carry their weapons at all times. Saudi and Kuwaiti forces were also armed with M-16s.

Iraqi Counterpart

The Iraqis were armed with the standard Eastern Bloc weapon, the AK-74 and the AK-47. This weapon is a favorite of many Third World guerrilla groups and is made under a variety of names by other Eastern Bloc and communist countries. This weapon carries thirty rounds of 5.45 mm ammunition and weighs about eight pounds. Its performance is similar to the M-16.

Action in Desert Storm

Operation Desert Storm reemphasized that the soldier behind the weapon is just as important, if not more important than the weapon he is using. In Operation Desert Storm, this was

M-16 rifle. U.S. troops were under standing orders to carry their M-16s at all times. *Source: U.S. Government Department of Defense*

demonstrated by the care and quality of the soldier's rifle. Fighting off the sand and the grit proved difficult for even the most cautious soldier, but U.S. forces took extreme pride in keeping their weapons in optimum operating condition by cleaning and protecting their M-16s from the elements. A number of the Iraqi AKs were found to be poorly maintained and, in some cases, not operable at all, giving a good indication of the state of the Iraqi Army.

High Mobility Multipurpose Wheeled Vehicle (HMMWV) (*cargo/troop version)

Length:	**80–203 inches**
Width:	**85 inches**
Height:	**72–105 inches**
Weight:	**5,200–7,180 lbs**
Speed:	**65 mph**
Range:	**300 miles**
Payload:	**2,149–3,177 lbs**
Crew/Cab:	**Two to four**
Towing Capacity:	**3,400 lbs**
Contractor:	**AM General**

Background

The HMMWV — also known as the Hummer or HUMVEE — replaced the jeep as the standard vehicle in the U.S. motorpool for all U.S. forces and Guard units. Based on a common one and one-quarter ton chassis, the HMMWV can be configured for a variety of different uses from TOW missile carrier to ambulance. The HMMWV was introduced in the 1980s.

HMMWV. Nearly 20,000 of the Army's 59,883 HUMVEEs were deployed to the Gulf War.
Source: U.S. Government Department of Defense

Iraqi Counterpart

There are several Iraqi counterparts, including a variety of Soviet, British, Japanese, and American light trucks. Most of these were bought on the open market and converted to military use.

Action in Desert Storm

HUMVEEs were used in all facets of Operation Desert Storm. Besides operating in a transport mode, a number of TOW-equipped HUMVEEs were used to eliminate Iraqi armor during the ground war. Other HUMVEEs were used in medical evacuation and as communications vehicles. The deserts of Kuwait provided the HMMWV with a successful combat test for a system that should be in the U.S. inventory for several more decades. The only major complaint was that the hard seat was uncomfortable.

Overall, 20,000 of the Army's 59,883 HUMVEEs were deployed to the Gulf War with a 90 percent operational readiness rate. As a result of the popularity of the vehicle during the war, the contractor released a civilian version called the HUMMER.

MISSILES

Patriot Air-Defense Missile

Length:	**17 feet, 5 inches**
Diameter:	**1 foot, 4 inches**
Weight:	**221 lbs high explosive**
Range:	**43 miles**
Speed:	**Mach 3**
Altitude:	**78,000 feet**
Contractor:	**Raytheon**

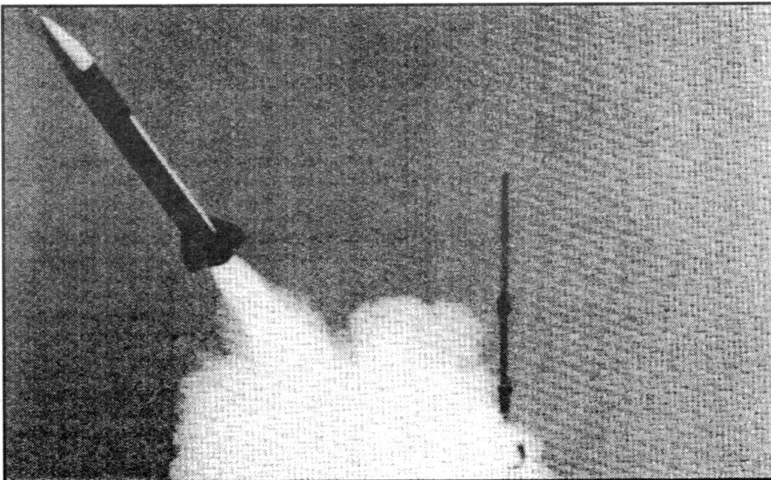

Patriot missile. Although the overall effectiveness of the Patriot was in question, it was a valuable weapon for knocking out some SCUDs. *Source: U.S. Government Department of Defense*

Background

The Patriot system surrounded many of the air bases and troop locations in the Gulf region to protect them from incoming Iraqi missiles and aircraft. A Patriot battery included up to eight launchers, each with four MIM-104 missiles and support equipment, including radars and power plants. Completely computerized, the system is activated when a launch is detected. Missiles are launched when the highest probability of a kill is obtained.

Iraqi Counterpart

There is no comparable weapon to the Patriot air-defense missile.

Action in Desert Storm

No other weapon received more attention than the Patriot during Operation Desert Storm. President Bush, Israel, and the families of the servicemen and servicewomen in the Gulf owed a great deal to this anti-missile defense system that intercepted and destroyed dozens of incoming SCUD missiles. Patriots used an elaborate early warning system which gave controllers about six minutes warning prior to interception of the incoming missile.

Twenty-one batteries (132 launchers) were deployed to Saudi Arabia. Two U.S. and two Dutch batteries were sent to Turkey, and seven batteries (48 launchers) were used in Israel. A total of 158 missiles were fired at Iraqi SCUDs.

Just as the SCUD caused more political headaches than military ones, the Patriot also found itself engaged in conflict far from the battlefield. Given the lack of information or imagery from the actual impact of a Patriot and a SCUD — most standard televisions were too slow in terms of frames per second to properly record — it was difficult to assess the actual effective rate of the missiles. In addition, some Patriots never launched until after the SCUD missiles had started their final dissent, often accompanied by junk and debris. Congressional hearings into the effectiveness of the system were inconclusive, with both sides claiming the evidence supported their point of view.

Nonetheless, during the war, the Patriot served a military value in knocking out some SCUDs, a political value in assisting our relations with Israel during their SCUD attacks, and a psychological value in assuring troops and their loved ones that coalition forces were under an umbrella of protection from incoming Iraqi missiles.

SCUD missiles. Although fairly inaccurate, the SCUD managed to cause several political headaches for the Allies during the war. *Source: U.S. Government Department of Defense*

SCUD Missile (Iraq)

Length:	**37 feet, 4 inches**
Diameter:	**2 feet, 9 inches**
Weight:	**1,000 lbs warhead (Al Hussein); 650 lbs warhead (Al Abbas)**
Range:	**400 miles (both the Al Hussein and the Al Abbas)**

Background

The SCUD missile, like the V-1 and V-2 of World War II, is properly described as a terror weapon. Its military value is extremely limited given its inaccuracy and small warhead.

Action in Desert Storm

Launched either from fixed or mobile launchers, Iraqi missiles caused problems for the troops in Operation Desert Storm. It was feared Saddam Hussein would use this weapon with a chemical warhead against U.S. forces and Israeli civilians. Refer to Chapter 12 for more information on chemical weapons. In Saddam Hussein's first counterattack of the war, he used SCUD missiles with conventional warheads against Israel and Saudi Arabia, causing minimal damage. U.S. Patriot missiles intercepted the SCUDs on many occasions, but due to the large size of the SCUDs, many pieces of debris fell to the ground and caused damage. His two modifications of the SCUD, the Al Hussein and Al Abbas, were designed with longer range capabilities to enable attacks against Tehran in the Iran-Iraq War.

The elimination of Iraq's SCUD threat became a priority with commanders in Operation Desert Storm, not so much because of the military threat it posed, but the political and psychological value of the weapon. SCUDs almost brought the Israeli military into the war, jeopardizing the Arab contributions to the coalition. Further, millions of Israeli and Saudi citizens were subjected to nightly terror attacks by these weapons.

Iraq was believed to have thirty-three mobile launchers, but this figure is considered drastically low. Some estimates put the number of mobile launchers at around 200, but the Iraqis were known to use numerous decoys. At the end of the war, nineteen launchers were known to have survived the combat. Almost 2,500 sorties were launched against the SCUD missiles, along with a British SAS team operating in enemy territory searching for mobile launchers.

Overall, eighty-eight SCUDs were fired during the Persian Gulf War — forty-two at Israel and forty-six at Saudi Arabia. More than

230 people were injured by these weapons. The most serious damage came when a SCUD landed on a barracks full of American servicemen, killing 28 and wounding nearly 100 in just one attack.

TOW anti-tank missile. Coalition forces used TOWs to combat Iraqi tanks during the Battle of Khafji. *Source: U.S. Government Department of Defense*

TOW Anti-Tank Missile

Length:	**3 feet, 10 inches**
Diameter:	**6 inches**
Weight:	**204 lbs (launcher); 56.65 lbs (missile)**
Range:	**Four-fifths of a mile**
Speed:	**620 mph**
Warhead:	**7–13 lbs**
Operating Crew:	**Three (3)**
Contractor:	**Hughes**

Background

The tube-launched, optically-tracked, wire-command (TOW) missile is the primary anti-tank weapon used by the infantry. It is mounted on the Bradley infantry fighting vehicle, the Humvee, and the AH-1 Cobra helicopter along with a ground-launched version. The TOW is guided to its target merely by the gunner keeping the cross-hairs on the target. Corrective information is sent to the missile by two thin wires that deploy in flight. Several advanced versions exist, including a thermal night sight and an improved warhead variant.

Iraqi Counterpart

Iraqi forces used a wide variety of anti-tank systems bought from the international arms market. Although not as technologically advanced as the TOW, these weapons have proved effective in many wars around the Third World. One such example is the shoulder-launched RPG-7, which is in service virtually everywhere in the world where there is warfare. The RPG-7 launches an 85 mm grenade about 540 yards and can penetrate light armor. The Iraqis also fielded the Soviet-made SPG-9, which has twice the range of the RPG-7 and is launched from a tripod mount.

Iraq had also purchased and used the MILAN anti-tank, wire-guided missile. Made in France, the weapon has a range of about 1.2 miles and was used extensively in Iraq's eight-year war with Iran.

Action in Desert Storm

The TOW was plagued by problems when it first arrived in the Persian Gulf, many of them due to the climatic conditions in the desert. After some adjustments, TOWs were successfully used in the invasion against Iraqi tanks and vehicles without the predicted casualties amongst the users. In the battle over the Saudi town of Khafji, coalition forces used TOWs with a great deal of success against Iraqi tanks. Arab forces advancing along the coast during the ground war reported great success with the TOW against Iraqi armor. Iraq's anti-tank missile efforts were essentially useless against heavily armored American armor, with several vehicles having had reported hits, but few destroyed.

The helicopter variant of the TOW costs $15,000.

HAWK Missile System

Length:	**16 feet, 6 inches**
Diameter:	**1 foot, 2 inches**
Weight:	**1,382 lbs**
Range:	**3 miles**
Speed:	**Mach 2.5**
Contractor:	**Raytheon**

Background

The HAWK is a medium-range air-defense missile developed during the 1960s and improved several times in the last thirty years. Units with HAWK missiles are teamed with acquisition radar, a command post, a tracking radar, an Identification Friend or Foe (IFF) system, and three to four launchers with three missiles each. A proximity fuse is used to detonate its warhead. The HAWK is used by several U.S. Allies and was the weapon delivered to Iran as part of the Iran-Contra scandal.

Iraqi Counterpart

The SA-6 Gainful contains three missiles on a tracked vehicle and has an effective range of about fifteen miles. In addition, Iraq had a number of U.S. Hawk missiles which it seized from Kuwait when it invaded in August 1990. U.S. planners made destruction of Iraqi anti-air missiles and their command centers a priority in the initial days of Operation Desert Storm.

Besides missiles, Iraq maintained an incredible array of anti-aircraft guns, numbering as high as the tens of thousands. Although U.S. pilots had little to fear from one or two of these weapons, when hundreds were fired at one aircraft, the amount of "flak" in the air could have been devastating. One such system was the ZSU-23 anti-aircraft gun mounted on a tracked chassis. It has an accurate range of less than two miles and has been used extensively throughout the Third World.

HAWK missile. The HAWK is used in coordination with an Identification Friend or Foe (IFF) system. *Source: U.S. Government Department of Defense*

Action in Desert Storm

With no Iraqi aircraft operating over friendly positions, Allied anti-aircraft were not put to the test in Operation Desert Storm as some had envisioned. The Iraqis on the other hand, used their full armada of anti-aircraft weaponry against American pilots. American pilots over Baghdad, some of which participated in the bombing of Vietnam, called the flak in Iraq some of the worst they had ever seen.

However, much of this was unguided anti-aircraft artillery and missiles launched without the benefit of radar systems. If the Iraqis had turned on the radar, their systems would have been destroyed by F-4 Wild Weasel aircraft with high-speed, anti-radiation (HARM) missiles designed to seek out radars and neutralize them. With one of the first targets of the air war being the air-defense system, Allied commanders were effective in eliminating coordinated anti-aircraft throughout the country, forcing Iraq to operate only at the local unit level.

Chapter Five

Air Power

INTRODUCTION TO AIR FORCES

Following the same arguments as the modernization of ground forces that took place in the 1970s, the air forces of the United States were drastically improved during the 1970s and 1980s, with several new systems coming into service during this period and many others undergoing dramatic renovations. The emphasis on technology is clear as many of these warplanes contain the most advanced avionics in the world.

U.S. air power in the Gulf was primarily the responsibility of the Air Force, but the Navy and Marines provided valuable assistance and cooperation in all phases of the air and ground wars. When first deployed, obtaining air superiority was a major concern of Allied planners. A number of air superiority fighters, such as the F-15 and F-16, were some of the first aircraft to arrive in Saudi Arabia. Also of vital importance in the first days were tank killing A-10s designed to blunt an Iraqi tank attack should one occur while Allied forces were still deploying. Naval planners sent their carrier-based F-14s and F-18s to accomplish a similar air superiority and attack function. Additional attack planes, such as the F-111 and the F-117 Stealth fighter, and bombers, such as the B-52, were eventually deployed to give Allied commanders an offensive option.

Although overlooked once the fighting commenced, the valuable role of air transport and refueling was the key to the entire Desert Shield and Desert Storm operations. Before the first fighters were even in the air, the arrangements were made for tanker aircraft to meet the fighters on their transit across the Atlantic. Joining the fighters as they flew to Saudi Arabia were the huge C-141 and C-5 airlifters carrying over the initial troops and equipment of the 82nd Airborne and other troops.

Once the initial deployments were complete, airlifters filled the valuable role of deploying immediately needed spare parts to the theatre from supply depots in the United States. Tactical airlifters, such as the C-130, assisted in the redeployment of troops throughout Saudi Arabia up until the final hours before the start of the ground war. Overall, air deployment transport missions by aircraft looked something like this:

- 3,980 for the C-5s;
- 9,085 for the C-141s;
- 1,193 for the C-130s; and
- 395 for the KC-10s

In addition, the Civil Reserve Air Fleet (CRAF) program was activated, putting all U.S. and Foreign airlines into military service. A total of 3,813 air deployment missions were flown by CRAF planes. Table 5.1 shows the top ten airline carriers with the most missions. When all was said and done, these missions transported 509,129 passengers and 594,730 tons of cargo.

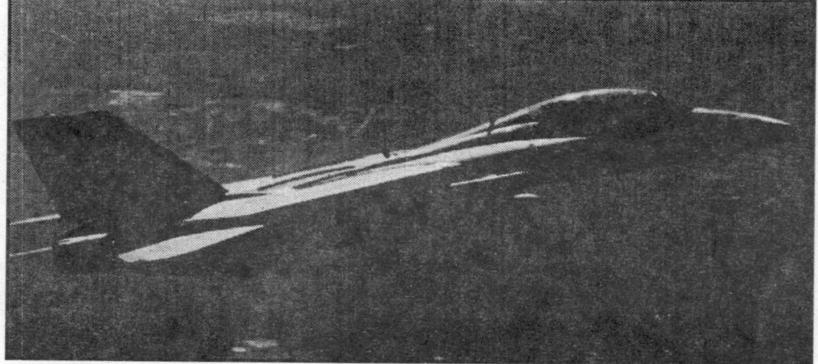

F-14 Tomcat. No F-14s were lost in air-to-air combat during the Persian Gulf War. *Source: Grumman Aerospace*

COMBAT AIRCRAFT

F-14 Tomcat

Wingspan:	64 feet, 2 inches open; 38 feet, 2 inches swept
Length:	62 feet, 8 inches
Height:	16 feet
Weight:	72,935 lbs (maximum)
Speed:	1,544 mph (maximum); 576 mph (cruise)
Ceiling:	56,000 feet
Range:	500 miles (combat air patrol); 2,000 miles (with drop tanks)
F-14 Power:	Two Pratt and Witney TF30-P414 turbofan engines with afterburners and 20,900 lbs static thrust
F-14B/D Power:	Two F110-GE-400 augmented turbofan engines with afterburners and 23,600 lbs static thrust
F-14A Power:	Two PW TF30-P-414As rated at 28,000 lbs
Armament:	One M61A1 Vulcan 20 mm cannon and a mix of the following depending on the mission: AIM 54 Phoenix; AIM 7 Sparrow; AIM 9 Sidewinder
Crew:	Two (2)
Service:	Navy
Contractor:	Grumman Aerospace

TABLE 5.1		
MOST CRAF MISSIONS FLOWN IN OPERATION DESERT SHIELD AND DESERT STORM		
CARRIER	PASSENGER MISSIONS	CARGO MISSIONS
Federal Express	29	576
American Trans Air	494	0
Pan Am	335	69
Northwest	268	117
Connie Kalitta	0	370
Evergreen International	0	347
World	188	149
Hawaiian	263	0
Southern Air Transportation	0	252
Rosenbalm	0	249

Background

Selected in the late 1960s to replace the F-4, the Tomcat has become the standard carrier-based combat aircraft in the Navy. Considered one of the best fighters in the world, F-14s were involved in the downing of Libyan planes in the Gulf of Sidra and in the apprehension of the Achille Lauro kidnappers in the Mediterranean. It is also known for its role in the movie *Top Gun*.

Iraqi Counterpart

Iraq had no carrier-based aircraft, but the F-14s faced a similar threat as that posed to the F-15 from the MIG-21, MIG-25, MIG-29, and the French-built Mirage F-1.

Action in Desert Storm

Both the F-14A and F-14B models were deployed in Operation Desert Storm. As an air-to-air fighter, the F-14 did not get to see much of the Iraqi Air Force due to its destruction and the Iraqi's desire not to fly. Only one aircraft, an Iraqi helicopter, was destroyed by an F-14. One F-14 was downed by enemy ground fire, however, no F-14s were taken out in air-to-air combat. One possible problem was the lack of an Identification Friend or Foe (IFF) interrogator given the danger of fratricide over land areas of Kuwait for the maritime-based fighter.

Overall, 99 F-14s flew 4,182 sorties for a total of 14,248 flight hours — the most of any Navy fixed-wing aircraft. The sixteen F-14s configured to carry a tactical air reconnaissance pod system that flew a total of 2,552 flight hours. Five of the six carriers in the KTO carried F-14s and the mission capable rate was 77 percent.

F-15 Eagle. F-15Cs were responsible for 33 of the 38 air-to-air kills in Operation Desert Storm. *Source: McDonnell-Douglas*

F-15 Eagle

F-15C

Wingspan:	42 feet
Length:	63 feet
Height:	18 feet, 5 inches
Weight:	68,000 lbs (maximum)
Speed:	1,650 mph (about Mach 2.5)
Ceiling:	60,000 feet
Range:	330–720 miles (combat)
Power:	Two Pratt and Whitney F100-PW-100 turbofan engines thrust
Armament:	One M61A1 Vulcan 20 mm cannon and a mix of the following depending on the mission: AIM-7 Sparrow; AIM-9 Sidewinder
Crew:	One (1)
Service:	Air Force
Contractor:	McDonnell-Douglas

F-15E

Wingspan:	42 feet, 10 inches
Length:	63 feet, 8 inches
Height:	18 feet, 5 inches
Weight:	73,000 lbs (maximum)
Speed:	2,100 mph
Ceiling:	63,000 feet
Range:	960 miles (combat)
Power:	Two Pratt and Whitney F100-P220 turbofan
Armament:	One M61A1 Vulcan 20 mm cannon and a mix of the following depending on the mission: 500 lb MK-82 general purpose bomb; 2,000 lb MK-84 general purpose bomb; 500 lb GBU-12 laser-guided bomb; 2,000 lb GBU-10 laser-guided bomb; CBU-89 anti-personnel cluster munitions; CBU-52 anti-armor cluster munitions
Crew:	Two (2)
Service:	Air Force
Contractor:	McDonnell-Douglas

Background

The Air Force designed the F-15 Eagle as an air superiority fighter, but found it was effective for use as an attack plane as well. A later version of the F-15, designated as the F-15E, is designed and equipped for all-weather and night operations.

Iraqi Counterpart

Iraq's number one air superiority fighter was the advanced MIG-29, codenamed Fulcrum by NATO. Highly maneuverable and well designed, the MIG-29 is a serious threat when flown in the right hands. However, Iraq had a limited number of these aircraft and, with the embargo of spare parts by the Soviet Union, a number of these planes did not fly in the war. Initial reports showed half the planes were destroyed by American aircraft, and the others fled to the sanctuary of Iranian airbases.

The other fighters that engaged in air combat were the French Mirage F-1, MIG-21, and MIG-25. Of these, the F-1 was considered the most serious threat. The Mirage is extremely popular in the Third World, and both Kuwait and the Arab state of Qatar have purchased a number of these F-1s. Some Iraqi F-1s were designed to give air support to ground troops, but the Iraqi air forces were more content to stay in their hangars than support their troops.

Action in Desert Storm

The F-15Cs of the 1st Tactical Fighter Wing were in Saudi Arabia in less than 24 hours after President Bush ordered troops to be deployed. From the first day of the air war, F-15Cs were used to secure air superiority, including F-15s flown by the Saudi Air Force.

A total of 118 F-15Cs were deployed, flying 4,480 sorties during Operation Desert Storm. The F-15Cs achieved thirty-three of the thirty-eight air-to-air kills in Operation Desert Storm. No F-15Cs were lost. Other F-15s flown by the Saudis were successful in bringing down several of Iraq's best fighters in air-to-air combat. F-15Es were used in an attack role against Iraqi ground positions. Using sophisticated night-fighting equipment called Low-Altitude

F-15 in pursuit. The F-15E can easily handle all-weather and night operations. *Source: U.S. Department of Defense*

Navigation and Target Infrared for Night (LANTIRN), the F-15E was credited with a number of successful kills on enemy airfields and communications systems. Overall forty-eight F-15Es were in place at the start of hostilities and flew more than 2,200 missions. Two F-15Es were lost during combat.

F-16 Falcon. Nearly sixty F-16s were involved in the 19 January raid on the Baghdad Nuclear Research Center — the largest single raid of the war. *Source: U.S. Air Force*

F-16 Falcon

Wingspan:	**31 feet**
Length:	**49 feet**
Height:	**16 feet, 8 inches**
Weight:	**42,300 lbs (maximum)**
Speed:	**More than 1,320 mph (maximum)**
Ceiling:	**More than 53,000 feet**
Range:	**340 miles (combat); 2,415 miles (transit)**
Power:	**One F110-GE-100 augmented turbofan engine with afterburners or a Pratt and Whitney F100-P-220 turbofan**
Armament:	**One M61A1 Vulcan 20 mm cannon and a mix of the following depending on the mission: AIM-9 Sidewinder; 500 lb MK-82 general purpose bomb; 2,000 lb MK-84 general purpose bomb; 500 lb GBU-12 laser-guided bomb; 2,000 lb GBU-10 laser-guided bomb; CBU-89 anti-personnel cluster munitions; CBU-52 anti-armor cluster munitions**
Crew:	**One (1)**
Service:	**Air Force**
Contractor:	**General Dynamics**

Background

The F-16 is a small and agile fighter in use by the Air Force for air combat and attack roles. A new version of the F-16 is being considered a replacement to the A-10 to provide close air support to ground troops. The F-16 is an international fighter with many other countries, including Israel who uses it as its standard fighter. The F-16 is no stranger to Iraq as Israel used several F-16s in its 1981 attack on the Iraqi nuclear reactor at Osirak.

Iraqi Counterpart

Iraq had three major types of dual-role aircraft — about 100 French Mirage F-1s in various configurations and Soviet-built SU-20s and SU-24s. The SU-20 is an export version of the SU-17 "Fitter-C" jet in the Soviet arsenal. Iraq was estimated to have about seventy of these 1960s-era aircraft. The SU-24, on the other hand, entered service in the Soviet Union in the mid-1970s as an attack aircraft capable of Mach 2. However, Iraq was estimated to have barely a dozen of these aircraft in its arsenal and Iraq undoubtedly fell victim to a spare parts shortage.

Action in Desert Storm

F-16s were used in an attack role against Iraqi fortifications in the KTO. One squadron of F-16s was used primarily as "spotter" aircraft, flying into an area and identifying targets for other aircraft to attack. F-16s were also used for combat air patrols early in Operation Desert Shield, but given the Iraqi's unwillingness to fly against American planes, they did not engage many Iraqi planes. Overall, 251 F-16s participated in Operation Desert Storm. F-16s were used in an attack role against a variety of Iraqi military targets. On 19 January 1991, fifty-six F-16s attacked the Baghdad Nuclear Research Center in the largest single raid of the war. Five F-16s were lost in combat.

F/A-18 Hornet

Wingspan:	**37 feet, 7 inches**
Length:	**56 feet**
Height:	**15 feet, 3 inches**
Weight:	**23,050 lbs (empty); 51,900 lbs (maximum)**
Speed:	**1,189 mph (Mach 1.8)**
Ceiling:	**50,000 feet approximately**
Range:	**440 miles (fighter mission); 500 miles (attack mission); 662 miles (attack mission with drop tanks); 2,300 miles (transit)**
Power:	**Two General Electric F404-GE-400 turbofan engines with 16,000 lbs static thrust**
Armament:	**One M61A1 Vulcan 20 mm cannon and a mix of the following depending on the mission: AIM7 Sparrow; AIM9 Sidewinder; AGM-84 Harpoon anti-ship missile; Cluster bombs; AGM-88 HARM missile; AGM-65 Maverick missile**
Crew:	**One (1) in the A and C models; Two (2) in the D model**
Service:	**Navy and Marines**
Contractor:	**McDonnell-Douglas**

Background

The Hornet joined the service in 1983. Its roots are traced to the YF-17, the unsuccessful contender with the YF-16 (F-16) in the Air Force fighter competition. The Hornet was designed to replace the

Navy's F-4 and A-7 aircraft. It is now the standard fighter in the Navy and Marine Corps and is also flown by the Blue Angels flight demonstration team. CF/A-18s were also used by the Canadian forces in the Persian Gulf.

Iraqi Counterpart

Iraq had a few dozen Soviet SU-7s "Fitter-A" that were used in a ground attack mode, as the F-18 can be utilized. The SU-7 was designed in the 1950s and is not regarded as much of a match for the high-tech F-18. The F-18 also faced the advanced SU-25s and SU-29s in an air combat role when they were airborne.

Action in Desert Storm

Joining the A-6 in an attack role from carriers, the F-18 was used extensively in attacks on Iraqi positions. Marine Corps pilots also used the F-18 for close air support missions as they moved up through Kuwait. The F-18 was the first plane downed, but overall losses were considerably low throughout the conflict. The loss of this first aircraft is now believed to be the result of air-to-air combat, the only such loss to U.S. forces.

The Navy deployed ninety F/A-18 A/Cs from four aircraft carriers. The Marines deployed thirty-six F/A-18As and thirty-six F/A-18Cs. The aircraft was used in both an attack and fighter role. Three USMC F/A-18s were damaged by anti-aircraft missiles and one by anti-air artillery, but all returned to their bases and were back in service within two days. One Navy F/A-18 was lost in air-to-air combat. The Marines also deployed twelve F/A-18Ds, with two sustaining battle damage, but both returning. These aircraft were used as tactical air coordinators and airborne forward control roles.

U.S. Navy F/A-18. This Hornet is carrying MK-83 bombs on a ground attack mission. For protection from enemy fighters, the F-18 keeps its radar-guided Sparrow and heat-seeking missiles when it attacks. *Source: McDonnell-Douglas*

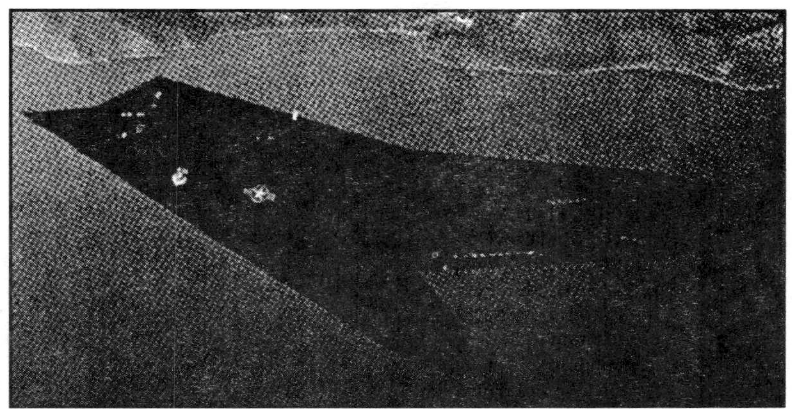

F-117 Stealth. Overall, the Stealth flew 3 percent of the total missions but destroyed more than 43 percent of the total targets.
Source: Lockheed Aircraft

F-117 Stealth

Wingspan:	**43 feet, 4 inches**
Length:	**66 feet**
Height:	**12 feet, 5 inches**
Weight:	**52,500 lbs**
Speed:	**Subsonic**
Ceiling:	**52,500 feet**
Range:	**540–720 combat radius**
Power:	**Two GE F404-GE-F102 turbojets Armament: Two laser-guided bombs**
Crew:	**One (1)**
Service:	**Air Force**
Contractor:	**Lockheed Aircraft**

Background

The F-117 was designed in the 1980s as a "black project" — meaning "heavily classified." Many of the exact specifics remain shrouded in secrecy. Its existence was suspected for years, but not until the late 1980s did the Air Force even acknowledge this plane existed. Today it is a popular attraction at air shows around the country and has seen combat action in Panama with mixed reviews. Given its radar-evading ability, the Stealth fighter has been used in attacks deep behind enemy lines. It is said that the first Iraqi anti-aircraft weapons to be fired were after bombs from the F-117s hit their targets.

Iraqi Counterpart

There is no comparable aircraft to the F-117 Stealth anywhere in the world.

Action in Desert Storm

F-117s were the first aircraft to strike Baghdad in the opening minutes of the air war. Footage from the on-board cameras showed a number of 2,000 lb bombs from F-117s scoring direct hits on Iraqi strategic targets and mobile missile launchers. Air Force commanders reported that the F-117 flew three percent of the total missions (about 1,788 sorties), but destroyed more than 43 percent of the total targets. With no reported losses, Stealth supporters will cite the success of the F-117 Stealth fighter when arguing for the production of the B-2 Stealth Bomber.

A-10 Thunderbolt. The Warthog provided cover to downed pilots while rescue crews worked to save them. *Source: Grumman Aerospace*

A-10 Thunderbolt (Warthog)

Wingspan:	**57 feet, 6 inches**
Length:	**53 feet, 4 inches**
Height:	**14 feet, 8 inches**
Weight:	**51,000 lbs maximum takeoff**
Speed:	**437 mph**
Ceiling:	**30,500 feet**
Range:	**2,455 miles (transit); 250 miles (combat)**
Power:	**Two General Electric TF-34-GE-100 turbofans, 9,000 lbs thrust each**
Armament:	**One 30 mm GE GAU-8/A Gatling Gun and 16,000 lbs of a mix of bombs and missiles depending on the mission**
Crew:	**One (1)**
Service:	**Air Force**
Contractor:	**Fairchild Republic Company**

Background

The slow-moving, high-surviving A-10 is designed as a tank killer and for close air support of troops on the ground. It is designed to take multiple hits from enemy fire and still continue flying. The A-10 is also used to support rescue operations of downed pilots. The A-10 entered service in the mid-1970s and is scheduled to be replaced in the future.

Iraqi Counterpart

Iraq had the SU-25 Frogfoot in its arsenal for close air support. A Soviet-designed aircraft, the SU-25 is slightly faster than the A-10 and carries a similar mix of weapons. In addition, French-built Mirage fighters also played a close air support role.

Action in Desert Storm

The A-10 was the ugly duckling of Operation Desert Storm. Even though pilots of A-10s were mocked for flying a "slow" aircraft, and the plane's physical appearance was best described by its nickname "Warthog," the A-10 did an excellent job in attacking and destroying Iraqi armor positions, including dug-in and fortified units. In one attack on fleeing Iraqi units, two A-10s teamed up to destroy some twenty-three tanks using a variety of missiles and the cannons in the noses of these aircraft. A-10s also provided cover to downed pilots while rescue crews worked to save them. Although it is going to be phased out in some units, there are many ground soldiers who would like to see the A-10 kept in service for several more years.

A total of 136 A-10s and 12 OA-10s were deployed to Southwest Asia. The aircraft flew 8,077 sorties, often for anti-air defense missions and for hunting SCUD missiles. Ten of the fifteen aircraft damaged returned to action. Six others were shot down and lost.

A-6 Intruder

Wingspan:	53 feet
Length:	54 feet, 9 inches
Height:	16 feet, 2 inches
Weight:	58,660 lbs (maximum)
Speed:	1,544 mph (maximum); 576 mph (cruise)
Ceiling:	42,400 feet
Range:	1,077 miles (combat); 3,100 miles (transit)
Power:	Two Pratt and Whitney J52 P-8A turbojets
Armament:	18,000 lbs in a mix of bombs, rockets, and missiles depending on the mission
Crew:	Two (2)
Service:	Navy and Marines
Contractor:	Grumman Aerospace

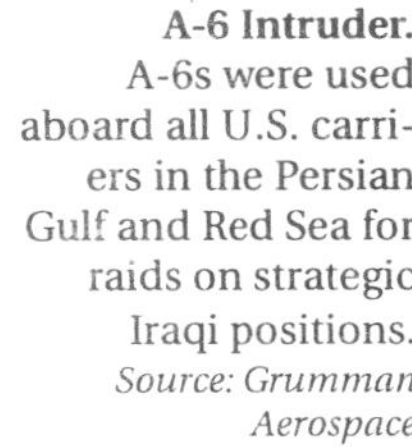

A-6 Intruder. A-6s were used aboard all U.S. carriers in the Persian Gulf and Red Sea for raids on strategic Iraqi positions. *Source: Grumman Aerospace*

Background

The A-6 Intruder was the primary attack aircraft aboard U.S. carriers in the Persian Gulf. The Intruder had seen action in both Vietnam and in Libya in 1986 and provided close air support for Marine operations in Operation Desert Shield/Storm. The A-6 was to be replaced by the A-12 Stealth attack fighter, but given cost overruns and mismanagement, Secretary Cheney canceled the A-12 giving the A-6 several more years in operation.

Iraqi Counterpart

Iraq possessed no carrier aircraft but had many similar ground-based attack fighters, such as the SU-20, SU-24, and the French-built Mirage aircraft.

Action in Desert Storm

A-6s were used extensively in attacking strategic targets inside Iraq. Launched from carriers in the Red Sea and the Persian Gulf, A-6s were used in both day and night raids on strategic Iraqi positions inside the KTO. The aircraft was also used in air defense suppression missions with anti-radiation missiles.

Overall, ninety-five Navy A-6s flew 4,045 sorties. The Marines deployed twenty A-6s flying 854 missions from land bases. Five A-6s were lost or damaged in combat — two early in the war during low-altitude attacks. This was the highest loss rate of any U.S. aircraft type.

A variant of the A-6, the EA-6B Prowler, was used to clear the way for Navy strike aircraft. The EA-6B is an electronic counter measure aircraft, complete with jamming equipment and HARM anti-radiation missiles. Prowlers flew 1,632 combat sorties, totaling 4,600 flying hours with no losses. More than 150 HARM missiles were fired from this aircraft.

AV-8 Harrier. The Harrier helped breach the Iraqi Army defenses once the ground war began. *Source: McDonnell-Douglas*

AV-8 Harrier

Wingspan:	**30 feet, 3 inches**
Length:	**46 feet, 4 inches**
Height:	**11 feet, 7 inches**
Weight:	**31,000 lbs maximum**
Speed:	**630 mph**
Range:	**506 miles (combat); 2,015 miles (transit)**
Power:	**1 Rolls-Royce Pegasus II F-402-RR-406 vectored thrust turbofan engine**
Armament:	**25 mm cannon and a mix of the following depending on mission: AIM-9 Sidewinder; AGM-65E Maverick; MK-80 series bomb; CBU-72 fuel air explosives**
Crew:	**One (1)**
Service:	**Marines**
Contractor:	**McDonnell-Douglas**

Background

The Harrier "jump-jet" is a vertical takeoff and landing aircraft that was designed by the British over a decade ago. U.S. Marines use this plane to support their forces on the ground and also in a fighter role against enemy aircraft. The U.K. variant of the Harrier is a combat veteran of the Falklands War of 1982, which proved essential to the British victory.

Iraqi Counterpart

The Iraqi military had no comparable aircraft to the U.S. military's AV-8 Harrier.

Action in Desert Storm

In close air support missions, the Marines found the Harrier to be a capable aircraft, effective in eliminating the menacing artillery barrages that were launched in the early days of Operation Desert Storm. When the ground war began, Harriers were used to help breach the defenses of the Iraqi Army.

Operating from off-shore amphibious vessels and from small runways and land strips inside Kuwait, the AV-8 attacked Iraqi tanks and artillery while Marines took Iraqi POWs. The AV-8 was essentially combat tested in the Falklands, but Operation Desert Storm certainly showed many American commanders the capabilities of a vertical takeoff attack aircraft. Eighty-six AV-8Bs were deployed in support of Operation Desert Storm. Aircraft were based on the USS *Nassau,* USS *Tarawa,* and at a Saudi Naval base. Harriers flew 3,342 sorties in more than 4,317 flight hours.

B-52 Stratofortress. An amazing sixty-two B-52Gs dropped more than 54 million pounds of bombs without a single combat loss.
Source: U.S. Government Department of Defense

B-52 Stratofortress

Wingspan:	**185 feet**
Length:	**161 feet**
Height:	**40 feet, 8 inches**
Weight:	**488,000 maximum**
Speed:	**595 mph**
Ceiling:	**55,000 feet**
Range:	**5,016 miles on internal fuel (worldwide with refueling)**
Power:	**Eight 13,750 lbs Pratt and Witney J57-P-43WB turbojets**
Armament:	**50,000 lbs in a mix of weapons**
Crew:	**Six (6)**
Service:	**Air Force**
Contractor:	**Boeing**

Background

Designed as the U.S. main strategic bomber in 1950s, the B-52 has been on active duty since 1954. It has seen action in Vietnam where it dropped thousands of tons of munitions. Six B-52s can clear an area two miles long and five-eighths of a mile wide. The B-52 was scheduled to be replaced by the B-2 Stealth or some other bomber in the future, but given the cost of the B-2, the B-52 may be around for several more years.

Iraqi Counterpart

Iraq had about a dozen or two strike bombers, the TU-16 Badger and TU-22 Blinder. Their range is less than that of the B-52, as is their bomb capacity. The TU-22 is a fast aircraft compared to the B-52, capable of Mach 1.4, but none of these penetrated U.S. interceptors to reach their targets, and several fled to Iran.

Action in Desert Storm

The B-52 was used for massive bombing operations against Republican Guards and other front-line targets. Launched from bases in the United States, Diego Garcia, and England, the B-52s would carpet-bomb Iraqi tanks and armored columns in Iraq and Kuwait. Besides the tremendous physical destruction caused by the B-52, there was also a great amount of psychological damage when a formation of these planes attacked a concentration of enemy forces. One B-52 was lost to mechanical difficulty while returning from a combat mission.

During Operation Desert Storm sixty-eight B-52Gs were deployed. They delivered more than 54 million pounds of bombs without a combat loss. In addition, several B-52s from Louisiana were used to launch cruise missiles prior to the start of the air war, flying thirty-five hours over 14,000 miles — the longest combat mission in history. B-52Gs, which comprised only three percent of combat aircraft, delivered 30 percent of the total tonnage of air munitions.

HELICOPTERS

AH-64A Apache

Length:	**49 feet**
Weight:	**14,445 lbs**
Rotor Diameter:	**48 feet**
Cruise Speed:	**184 mph**
Endurance:	**1.8 hours**
Armament:	**Hellfire missiles, Hydra 70 rockets, and 30 mm chain guns**
Range:	**360 miles (transit); 162 miles (combat)**
Crew:	**Two (2)**
Contractor:	**McDonnell-Douglas Helicopter**

Background

Known as "flying tank," the Apache was designed to destroy invading Soviet tank columns in Europe. It is fully equipped for night fighting and is the primary attack helicopter in the Army. Early on it was plagued by technical problems at home, but commanders in Operation Desert Storm reported a much higher readiness rate than they experience during peacetime.

Iraqi Counterpart

Iraq flew a number of attack helicopters under the Army Air Corps, but the primary system was the MI24 HIND, which was designed by the Russians and used effectively in Afghanistan. The HIND carried built-in machine guns along with a wide variety of missiles and rockets. It also transported eight combat troops. Iraq had a number of French-built Gazelles and American-designed Hughes 500s, although these were not as well armed as the AH-64.

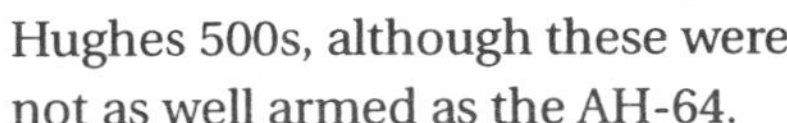

AH-64A Apache. In a single attack, two Apaches forced 400 Iraqis to surrender just before the ground war started. *Source: McDonnell-Douglas*

Action in Desert Storm

In Operation Desert Storm, the Apache was called on to perform its primary mission of tank killing and did so with tremendous success. In the first attacks of the air war, Apaches attacked Iraqi command and control centers for air defenses twenty miles inside Iraqi territory. Using the laser-guided Hellfire missile, Apaches destroyed a number of tank and armor units prior to the ground invasion. In one of the more interesting attacks of the air war, two Apaches were successful in forcing some 400 Iraqi prisoners to surrender just prior to the start of the ground war. When the ground war commenced, Apaches provided close air support to advancing Allied forces, destroying a considerable number of Iraqi tanks. On the downside, Apaches were also involved in the first friendly-fire casualties of the ground war.

In all, 274 AH-64s were deployed to the KTO. This represented 45 percent of the Army's AH-64 fleet at the time. AH-64s flew more than 18,700 hours with a readiness rate of over 90 percent. One AH-64 was lost to enemy fire, but its crew was recovered. Sand was a major enemy of the aircraft, causing serious problems with auxiliary power units, environmental controls, and shaft-driven compressors.

AH-1 Cobra. U.S. Marines used Cobras to support advancing Allied forces during the Battle of Khafji. *Source: McDonnell-Douglas*

AH-1 F/J/W/T "Cobra"

Length:	**58 feet**
Weight:	**14,750 lbs (loaded)**
Rotor Diameter:	**48 feet**
Speed:	**141 mph**
Endurance:	**2.5 hours**
Armament:	**20 mm chain gun, eight TOW anti-tank missiles, and two 70 mm rocket launchers**
Range:	**140 miles (combat radius)**
Crew:	**Two (2)**
Contractor:	**Bell Helicopters**

Background

Noticeable because of its unique profile, the Cobra was used extensively in Vietnam. The Marines use a version of this helicopter as its attack helicopter. It is also used to escort transport helicopters in and out of hostile landing zones and provides air support to troops on the ground. Together with the AH-64 Apache, the Cobra gave U.S. commanders flexibility in air attacks on Iraqi forces.

Iraqi Counterpart

Iraq primarily used the MI24 HIND as its attack helicopter. See the description under AH-64 Apache in the previous discussion.

Action in Desert Storm

The AH-1 was used in many similar missions to those conducted by the AH-64. The Cobra was used by the Marines in the Battle of Khafji to support advancing Allied forces. The Cobra also supported the Marines in the breach of Iraqi barriers on the Kuwaiti border. Besides anti-tank and close air support, a number of Cobras were used in an escort role around transport helicopters as they ferried men and equipment to the front lines.

In anti-armor and armed reconnaissance missions, AH-1Ws reportedly took out 97 tanks and 104 armored personnel carriers. The older AH-1Js were used for combat escort and armed reconnaissance for helicopter assault operations.

The Marine Corps deployed four of six active squadrons (fifty AH-1Ws) and two reserve squadrons (twenty-six AH-1Js). In addition, three AH-1Ts were aboard USS *Nassau* (LHA4). USMC squadrons flew 8,278 hours. Overall, the Army deployed 145 AH-1Fs to the KTO and flew more than 10,000 hours.

UH-60 Blackhawk

Length:	**57 feet, 3 inches**
Weight:	**22,000 lbs (maximum gross)**
Rotor Diameter:	**53 feet, 9 inches**
Cruise Speed:	**165 mph**
Endurance:	**2.3 hours**
Propulsion:	**Two T700-GE-700 C engines**
Payload:	**8,000 lbs external (or eleven combat troops)**
Armament:	**Two M60 7.62 mm machine guns**
Range:	**396 miles**
Crew:	**Two (2) pilots, 1 crew chief/gunner**
Contractor:	**Sikorsky Helicopter**

UH-60 Blackhawk. Although affected by the KTO's desert sand and surface heat, the Blackhawk had a mission capable rate of 82 percent. *Source: U.S. Department of Defense*

Background

Replacing the UH-1 Huey — the workhorse of Army air power — was a difficult task. But the UH-60 Blackhawk certainly measured up well. With its ability to carry a full squad of eleven men, and its ability to carry a 105 mm Howitzer, the UH-60 plays an important role in any mobile force. The Blackhawk is used servicewide, from a Navy version called the "SeaHawk" to a special VIP version called "Marine 1," a VH-60 which was used by President Bush when he needed a helicopter outside Washington, D.C. The Blackhawk is airmobile itself as it can fit inside U.S. cargo aircraft for rapid deployment to any area of the world.

Iraqi Counterpart

Iraq's main transport helicopter was the Soviet-made MI-8 HIP, which carried up to twenty-four troops or nearly 9,000 pounds. This aircraft, in service since the 1960s, was combat-proven in Afghanistan and many other Third World nations.

Action in Desert Storm

Blackhawks performed well in Operation Desert Storm by transporting troops to and from front-line units and providing emergency medical evacuation. The Blackhawk experienced many of the same problems that other helicopters did in Operation Desert Storm, such as sand and surface heat, yet came out with minimal losses.

Several variants of the Blackhawk saw service in the Gulf. The Navy used the SH-60 Seahawk during its patrols for enemy shipping. Special forces units used the MH-60A and MH-60K for rescue and special operations missions. Even the president used his VH-60 when he visited the troops in the Gulf for Thanksgiving.

Blackhawks took part in the 300 helicopter raid conducted by the 101st Airborne during the first day of the ground war. Although a few were reported as crashed during the crisis, given the incredibly poor flying conditions, Allied commanders were pleased with the performance of these helicopters. By comparison, most Iraqi helicopters never got off the ground, given the air superiority achieved by the Air Force.

Overall, 489 Blackhawks were deployed, representing 46 percent of the total inventory. Eighteen UH-60 assault companies, along with MEDEVAC, cavalry squadrons, maintenance companies, and special operations units were deployed. The Blackhawk had a mission capable rate of 82 percent. More than 44,000 flight hours were logged in the UH-60. One UH-60 was lost in a training incident during Operation Desert Shield, which injured five people.

CH-53E Super Stallion

Length:	**99 feet**
Weight:	**33,228 lbs**
Rotor Diameter:	**79 feet**
Speed:	**173 mph**
Propulsion:	**Three G.E. T64/65 416 turboshafts**
Payload:	**18 tons (or 50 troops)**
Armament:	**None**
Range:	**257 miles**
Crew:	**Three (3)**
Contractor:	**United Technologies Sikorsky Aircraft**

Background

A large transport helicopter, the Stallion is used for a wide variety of missions from transport to special operations. Later versions are capable of air-to-air refueling and may be used for long-range commando raids or rescue missions. A special operations version, the MH-53E, is capable of minesweeping operations and other difficult missions. This helicopter is also used for transport of heavy equipment, such as artillery and recovery of downed aircraft.

Iraqi Counterpart

Iraq's heavy air transport helicopter was the MI-6 Hook, which is capable of carrying seventy troops. First flown in the late 1950s, the Hook also is capable of carrying artillery and vehicles. However, Iraq had a very limited number of this aircraft.

CH-53E **Super Stallion.** The 20th Special Operations Squadron used a modified MH-53J to help liberate the U.S. Embassy in Kuwait City. *Source: U.S. Department of Defense*

Action in Desert Storm

One of the main missions of the Stallion was mineclearing operations in the Persian Gulf. Using towed sleds, a minesweeping variant, the MH-53E, was called upon to clear paths for a possible amphibious operation. Six Stallions were in the theatre for this purpose. Modified MH-53J Pave Lows were used in special operations missions, including the "liberation" of the U.S. Embassy in Kuwait City by the 20th Special Operations Squadron.

With the slow development of the V-22 by the military and the combat performance of this helicopter in the KTO, it is predicted that the CH-53 will continue to be the main workhorse of the armed services helicopter fleet.

CH-47 Chinook

Length:	**50 feet, 8 inches**
Weight:	**50,000 lbs (maximum gross)**
Rotor Diameter:	**60 feet**
Cruise Speed:	**165 mph**
Endurance:	**2.2 hours**
Propulsion:	**Two Auco Lycoming T55-L-712 turboshafts**
Payload:	**15,873 pounds (or 33 combat troops)**
Range:	**155 miles (loaded); 1,279 (transit)**
Crew:	**Two (2) pilots, 1 crew chief**
Contractor:	**Boeing Vertol**

Background

The Chinook was designed in the 1950s and used extensively in Vietnam. This twin-engine, tandem rotor cargo helicopter is used not only to carry troops, but also can carry large equipment from Howitzers to bulldozers. A modernization is underway to extend the service life of this helicopter into the next century.

Iraqi Counterpart

Iraq's helicopter that is most similar to the Chinook was the M1-6 Hook. Refer to the description under CH-53E Super Stallion above.

Action in Desert Storm

The Chinook and Blackhawk provided the lift utilized in the 300 helicopter attack by the 101st Airborne. This raid, the largest heliborne operation ever undertaken, was successful in establishing a resupply base deep inside Iraq that allowed Allied forces to continue their remarkable success without running out of fuel. By the end of the first day, four teams of CH-47s lifted 131,000 gallons of fuel to keep the offensive alive.

Chinooks were also used to transport a number of enemy prisoners from front-line units that captured them to the rear where they were put in POW camps. Further, the CH-47 was used for rapid redeployment of artillery pieces.

Overall, ten companies, with 163 CH-47s, were deployed — which represented about 47 percent of the total inventory. The mission capable rate was 85 percent during Operation Desert Storm and the CH-47 flew more than 13,700 hours. No aircraft were lost to enemy gunners.

SUPPORT AIRCRAFT

C-130 Hercules

Wingspan:	**132 feet, 7 inches**
Length:	**97 feet, 9 inches**
Height:	**38 feet, 1 inch**
Weight:	**155,000 lbs maximum**
Speed:	**345 mph**
Ceiling:	**42,000 feet**
Range:	**5,300 mile (transit)**
Power:	**Four Allison T56-A-15 turboprop engines**
Crew:	**Four (4)**
Service:	**Navy, Marines, Air Force, and Coast Guard**
Contractor:	**Lockheed**

Background

The C-130 is the workhorse of air transport for dozens of countries and many private companies. The C-130 has seen action in Vietnam, Grenada, and Panama and is essential to resupply operations to the front lines. There are several versions of this aircraft — from a special operations plane to a Coast Guard long-range rescue plane. An attack version of this aircraft, the AC-130 is heavily armed with a 20 mm cannon and other weapons designed to destroy an enemy-held area.

C-130 Hercules. Although primarily used for transport and refueling, C-130s dropped 15,000 pound bombs over enemy territory. *Source: Lockheed*

Iraqi Counterpart

Iraq had several transport aircraft, but none with very long-range capability. The AN-12 "Cub" is probably the closest to the C-130, but Iraq had only a dozen or so of this aircraft. Iraq also had several older transport planes, such as the AN-24 and the IL-14.

Action in Desert Storm

C-130s were used for several missions in Operation Desert Storm. Using highways as landing strips, C-130s transported material to the front-line troops just prior to the ground invasion. They were also used for refueling operations, including missions over hostile territory. Transport and refueling were two of the main missions during Operation Desert Storm.

Some of the special tasks performed by the C-130 included special operations. During the attack on Khafji, one AC-130 gunship assigned to the Special Forces was lost with its crew of fourteen. Other C-130s were used to drop 15,000 pound bombs over enemy territory. Because of the tremendous size and weight of these weapons, the C-130 was used instead of a conventional bomber.

KC-10A Extender

Wingspan:	**165 feet, 4 inches**
Length:	**181 feet, 7 inches**
Height:	**58 feet, 1 inch**
Weight:	**590,000 lbs (maximum)**
Speed:	**619 mph**
Range:	**4,400 miles (with cargo)**
Power:	**Three General Electric CF-6-50C2 turbofans**
Crew:	**Four (4)**
Service:	**Air Force**

Background

The KC-10A has two roles with the Air Force: a primary mission of aerial refueling, but also a secondary task of delivering up to twenty-seven pallets of cargo or up to seventy-five troops to a war zone. Based on the commercial DC-10, the KC-10A supplements the KC-135 as the main air-to-air refueling craft of the U.S. Air Force. The KC-10A can also refuel from a large aerial refueling boom, or use a hose and drouge refueling system for Navy and Allied aircraft.

Iraqi Counterpart

The Iraqis have converted some Il-76s into a tanker variant, but the Il-76 remains primarily a cargo aircraft with the Iraqis.

Action in Desert Storm

Forty-six KC-10s were used in both cargo and aerial refueling missions during the Gulf War. Because of its boom and hose system, the KC-10 was used to refuel not only U.S. Air Force planes, but also refueled U.S. Navy and coalition fighter aircraft. The KC-10 — and its older colleague the KC-135 — conducted about 51,700 separate refueling operations and delivered 125 million gallons (475 million liters) of fuel without missing a single scheduled rendezvous.

C-141 Starlifter. Nicknamed the "Desert Express," the C-141 ferried urgently needed replacement parts to the Gulf on an overnight basis. *Source: U.S. Air Force*

C-141 Starlifter

Wingspan:	**160 feet**
Length:	**168 feet, 4 inches**
Height:	**39 feet, 4 inches**
Weight:	**343,000 lbs maximum**
Speed:	**566 mph**
Range:	**More than 6,390 miles (worldwide when refueled)**
Power:	**Four Pratt and Whitney TF33-P-7 turbofan engines**
Crew:	**Four (4)**
Service:	**Air Force**

Background

The C-141 was first operational in the early 1960s as a longer-range compliment to the C-130. The C-141 saw action throughout Vietnam and is capable of carrying up to 150 troops. However, age and strain is starting to force a number of these aircraft into retirement.

Iraqi Counterpart

The Iraqis had an unknown number of Il-76 cargo aircraft that could carry about 140 troops or paratroopers. Iraq had also converted some Il-76s into airborne early warning systems and may have modified some planes to a tanker variant.

Action in Desert Storm

The C-141, like the C-5, deserves much of the credit for the airlift success of Operation Desert Shield and the buildup of U.S. forces in the region. After ferrying in many of the troops, the planes were used to bring in essential spare parts from the United States to the KTO. C-141s were also used to transport injured servicemen and servicewomen from Saudi Arabia to the United States when they required further care. The C-141 is scheduled to be replaced by the C-17 in the next decade.

Overall, C-141s flew more than 8,322 missions — 53 percent of the total — transporting 355,955 short tons of cargo and 93,126 passengers. In addition, a special C-141 was on standby daily. Nicknamed the "Desert Express," it was utilized to ferry urgently needed replacement parts to the Gulf on an overnight basis. There were more than 135 of these missions launched during Operation Desert Shield/Desert Storm.

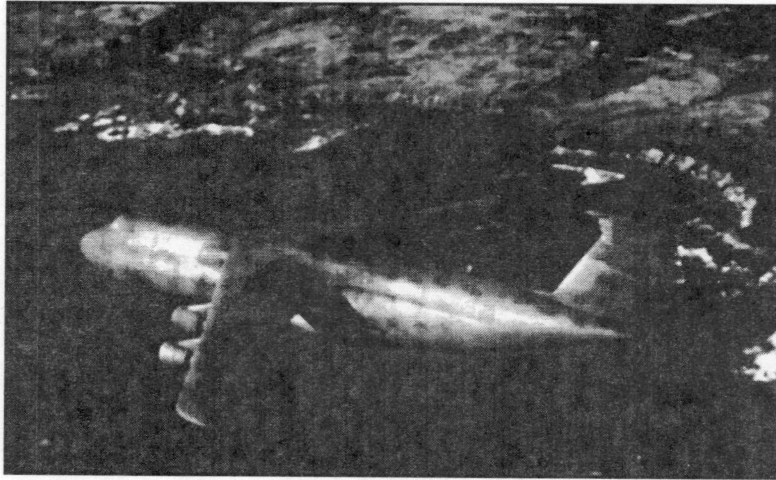

C-5 Galaxy. C-5s landed every ten minutes in Saudi Arabia bringing in everything from helicopters to toothbrushes. *Source: Lockheed*

C-5 Galaxy

Wingspan:	**222 feet, 8 inches**
Length:	**247 feet, 9 inches**
Height:	**65 feet, 1 inch**
Weight:	**837,000 lbs maximum**
Speed:	**564 mph**
Ceiling:	**35,750 feet**
Range:	**3,434 miles with full load (worldwide when refueled)**
Power:	**Four 43,000 lbs thrust GE TF39-GE-1C turbofan engines**
Crew:	**Five (5)**
Service:	**Air Force**
Contractor:	**Lockheed**

Background

The C-5 Galaxy was, until a recent Soviet aircraft based on the C-5 design, the largest aircraft in the world. It is capable of carrying more than 300 troops and poured millions of tons of equipment into Operation Desert Shield/Storm.

Iraqi Counterpart

There is no comparable aircraft to the C-5 Galaxy.

Action in Desert Storm

The C-5 was a major factor in the success of the initial military airlift portion of Operation Desert Shield. With their enormous carrying capacity, C-5s were used to bring in everything from helicopters to toothbrushes to supply the forces defending Saudi Arabia. The landing of C-5s and C-141s every ten minutes in Saudi Arabia certainly sent a message to Saddam Hussein that the United States was in this operation on a large scale. With Congress debating whether or not to purchase a new transport aircraft — the C-17 — or produce a number of new C-5s, the C-5 should have some advantage now that it has demonstrated combat capability.

A total of 3,773 missions were flown by the C-5 and these aircraft carried most of the cargo of the deployment — (42 percent of the airborne cargo). More than 222,024 short tons of cargo and 1,111 passengers flew into Operation Desert Storm via the Galaxy. Thirty-three percent of the aircraft were deemed unavailable on average. Overall, 118 of 126 U.S. C-5s supported Operation Desert Shield/Storm.

E-3 Sentry (AWACs). U.S. E-3s and Saudi E-3s teamed up to help keep Iraqi fighters away from Allied aircraft.
Source: Boeing

E-3 Sentry (AWACs)

Wingspan:	130 feet, 10 inches
Length:	145 feet, 6 inches
Height:	41 feet, 9 inches
Weight:	325,000 lbs maximum
Speed:	530 mph
Range:	11 hour endurance
Ceiling:	29,000 feet
Power:	Four 21,000 lbs Pratt and Whitney TF33-P-100 turbofans
Crew:	Four (4) in aircraft; 16 in AWACs
Service:	Air Force
Contractor:	Boeing

Background

The AWACs aircraft is easily identifiable by the large, saucer-shaped radar protruding out of its fuselage. This plane is designed to oversee all aircraft in an operating area, identify friend or foe, and then dispatch an appropriate response to deal with threats. Saudi Arabia also possesses a number of these aircraft which the United States sold to them in the early 1980s.

Iraqi Counterpart

The Iraqis are said to have had a number of Il-76 Candid aircraft built by the Soviets and retooled by Iraq into what the Iraqis call the Adnan1 and Adnan2. This aircraft has a similar appearance and electronic capability as the AWACs aircraft, but without proper fighter cover, was vulnerable to U.S. attack.

Action in Desert Storm

AWACs played an invaluable role in the success of the air war. With thousands of sorties a day, and sometimes hundreds in one specific area, it is a tribute to the skill of the AWACs that there were no mid-air collisions. During the Battle of Khafji, there were so many planes in one sector that the pilots had to wait fifteen minutes to get clearance from the AWACs to make their runs. AWACs also played an important role in keeping Iraqi fighters away from Allied aircraft. Since Saudi Arabia already had a number of these aircraft, the coordination between the United States and the Saudis was made much easier in this crisis.

The Iraqi AWACs were not called upon in an air defense role. With the lack of Iraqi air power, there was little need for the plane and a number of them reportedly flew to Iran for safe haven. Eleven U.S. aircraft were deployed in Saudi Arabia and three others in Turkey.

E-8 JSTARS

Wingspan:	**146 feet**
Length:	**145 feet**
Weight:	**325,000 lbs (combat)**
Speed:	**480 mph (cruise)**
Range:	**3,000 miles**
Power:	**Four TF-33 turbofan engines**
Crew:	**Four (4) flight crew (or 17 to 25 mission specialists)**
Contractor:	**Grumman Aerospace**

Background

JSTARS is a joint Army/Air Force development program designed to provide near real time surveillance and targeting information to ground commanders. In short, it is to the ground commander what the AWACs is to the flight commander. JSTARS has the capability to detect, precisely locate, and track thousands of fixed and mobile targets on the ground over an area larger than 20,000 square kilometers from a stand-off distance in excess of 250 kilometers. Targets it can detect include fighting vehicles, helicopters, low-speed aircraft, missile launchers, rotating antennas, ships, barges, tanks, trucks, and convoys.

Iraqi Counterpart

Iraq has no aircraft similar to the E-8 JSTARS.

Action in Desert Storm

Two E-8 JSTARS were deployed to Riyadh and started flying on 14 January 1991. JSTARS was still in design and testing during the Persian Gulf War, but was brought into the battlefield for real time experience. The information it provided on ground

E-8 JSTARS. JSTARS can detect ground targets over a 20,000 square kilometer area from a distance of more than 250 kilometers. *Source: Grumman Aerospace*

unit movements was of extreme importance to the commanders in locating targets for both the air and the ground war. The massive retreat out of Kuwait City was spotted by the JSTARS and the information relayed to tank and Air Force units, which then created the "Highway of Death" — the term used to describe when Allied planes decimated retreating Iraqi units.

TACTICAL MISSILES

Exocet Missile (Iraq)

Length:	**15 feet, 5 inches**
Diameter:	**1 foot, 1 inch**
Weight:	**1,444 lbs; 363 lbs (warhead)**
Range:	**43 miles**
Speed:	**708 mph**
Contractor:	**Aérospatiole**

Background

Fired from planes or boats, the Exocet is regarded as one of the deadliest anti-ship missiles in the world. Made famous by its devastating impact in the Falklands War and in the tanker battles during the Iran-Iraq War, the Exocet was also used in the Persian Gulf, including an Iraqi attack against USS *Stark* in 1987 that was claimed as an accident.

Although the Exocet is highly effective against smaller vessels, some doubt it would be able to penetrate the 16-inch armor of a battleship or larger vessel. Allied countermeasures to the Exocet included chaffe — small metallic fragments designed to confuse its radar and Phalanx anti-missile guns to blow the Exocet out of the sky.

U.S. Counterpart

The Harpoon AGM-84D is the United States over-the-horizon, anti-ship missile produced by McDonnell-Douglas. It is capable of being launched from surface ships, submarines, or aircraft against other naval targets. With Iraqi shipping confined mainly to small patrol vessels, the Harpoon's unique requirements were not needed.

Harpoon AGM-84D (U.S.)

Length:	**12 feet, 7 inches (air launched); 15 feet (surface launched)**
Speed:	**645 mph**
Range:	**608 miles**

Action in Desert Storm

Some commanders feared sending the larger U.S. warships into the Persian Gulf because they feared they would become vulnerable to Iraqi Exocets. Defending against missile attack was a priority for many escort vessels and Navy aircraft on combat air patrol. One report after the war said nearly half the planes on each carrier were dedicated to protecting the ships from the Iraqis. Several Iraqi aircraft and ships armed with Exocets were destroyed before they were able to launch their weapons against Allied ships in the Persian Gulf. One aircraft was able to launch two missiles, but the first missed its target (USS *Missouri*) and the second was shot down by a Sea Dart anti-missile fired by HMS *Gloucester*.

Tomahawk Cruise Missile (U.S.)

Length:	**20 feet, 8 inches**
Diameter:	**20 inches**
Weight:	**3,200 lbs**
Range:	**1,550 miles**
Speed:	**500 mph**
Engine:	**Solid propellant for boost, turbofan for cruise**
Warhead:	**1,000 lbs high explosive (TLAM-C); 166 BLU 97/B bomblets in twenty-four packages (TLAM-D)**
Contractor:	**McDonnell-Douglas; General Dynamics**

Background

The Tomahawk cruise missile was designed to deliver nuclear weapons into the Soviet Union from aircraft and ships off the shore. It is a highly accurate system that uses on-board computers to guide it to its target.

An air-launched version of the Tomahawk is also available and is used with the B-52. The TLAM-C drops a 1,000 lbs warhead on larger targets, with the TLAM-D being used for armor-piercing and fragmentation attacks.

Tomahawk missile. A total of 333 Tomahawks were fired at a cost of $380,300,000. *Source: Grumman Aerospace*

Action in Desert Storm

Initial reports of Operation Desert Storm indicated a success rate of almost 90 percent. The Tomahawk was primarily used from ships in the Gulf against hard, non-moving targets. Some of the first Allied hits on Baghdad were Tomahawk cruise missiles launched from USS *Wisconsin* in the Persian Gulf. These highly accurate weapons were targeted against Iraqi fixed positions, such as command and control centers and military industry. Within two weeks, the Navy had launched more than 200 Tomahawks — a number of them coming from submarines — with a devastating success rate. Both the submarines USS *Louisville* and USS *Pittsburgh* launched these weapons. Although the Iraqis claimed to have shot down a number of missiles, this was never confirmed by independent observers.

By the end of the war, 282 of 288 Tomahawks were successfully launched from sixteen surface ships and two submarines. Of these, 64 percent were launched in the first forty-eight hours of the war. Thirty-five air launched missiles were fired, all on the first day of the air war. Each Tomahawk cost $1.1 million and the air launched version cost $1.3 million. Between the Air Force and Navy, a total of 333 were fired, costing $380,300,000.

Tomahawks were also used in June 1993 by President Clinton in retaliation for the foiled Iraqi assassination plot against President Bush.

Chapter Six
Sea Power

INTRODUCTION TO SEA FORCES

During the 1980s, the United States Navy embarked on a policy of a 600-ship Navy, designed both to project power into any area of the world and to protect a resupply operation of Europe should a conventional land battle erupt with the Soviets. To meet this goal, new ships were built, and several older vessels were modernized or brought out of mothballs.

American forces were designed around the carrier battle group. This consisted of an aircraft carrier, a cruiser, and several frigates, destroyers, and support vessels. These battle groups were designed to go on six-month patrols around the world, with at least one carrier always on duty in the Mediterranean or Gulf region. These forces were designed to use their attack aircraft against hostile shipping or to attack inland targets from the safety of the open seas. The surface ships were capable of protecting the carriers from attack, from the land, sea, or air forces of a hostile nation. In addition, they could provide naval gunfire support to units on land close to the shore.

Also during the 1980s, World War II-era battleships were brought out of the reserve fleet and formed into battle groups. Not only did these vessels possess the same 16-inch guns that shelled the islands of the Pacific, but they also were modified to include the Tomahawk cruise missile, giving them the capability to strike deep into the heart of enemy territory.

Although designed for combat with the Soviets, the United States also modernized its undersea forces — the world of submarines. The Los Angeles Class attack submarine was designed to knock out Soviet ballistic missile submarines before they launched their nuclear weapons on the United States. Without such a threat in the Gulf War, these vessels were used as Tomahawk cruise missile launching platforms and for intelligence use to track incoming and outgoing shipping from Iraq.

The United States also deployed a formidable amphibious group to the Persian Gulf. These helicopter and landing craft-carrying vessels were used to support U.S. Marines fighting on-shore, serving as a launching base for close air support aircraft. In addition, these vessels helped coordinate the anti-mine operations that were undertaken in the Gulf to clear the sea lanes for Allied vessels enforcing the U.N. economic embargo.

Last, but in no way least, were the support and logistic vessels that delivered most of the weapons used in the Persian Gulf. During the 1980s, the United States constructed several expensive and fast sea-lift vessels, which were intended to deploy American-based units to Europe at a high speed should an invasion take place. These ships, along with many other slower vessels, deployed everything from tanks to bandages to the Gulf region, providing the United States with the heavy equipment it needed for the ground war. In addition, prepositioned ships in Guam and Diego Garcia — support vessels already loaded with tanks and other heavy equipment — were sent to the Gulf region within hours of the initial deployment of U.S. troops. When American forces deplaned in Saudi Arabia, they were matched up with equipment deployed from these prepositioned vessels.

There were several Coast Guard Port Defense Units deployed that helped provide port security in Saudi Arabia. In addition, Coast Guard Law Enforcement Detachments were embarked on board ships in the Persian Gulf to help conduct searches of vessels trying to break the Allied blockade. The Coast Guard crews were quite adept at searching the ships, given their long-standing experience searching for drug smuggling.

Nimitz Class aircraft carrier in the Persian Gulf. Carriers in the KTO emerged unscathed despite fears of anti-ship missiles. *Source: U.S. Navy, Scott Rebman*

AIRCRAFT CARRIERS

Nimitz Class: *CVN-71 Theodore Roosevelt*

Displacement:	96,358 tons
Length:	1,040 feet
Beam:	134 feet
Speed:	30 knots
Power Plant:	Two nuclear reactors supplying four steam turbines that produce a total of 280,000 shaft horsepower through four shafts
Aircraft:	Ninety (90)
Armament:	Sea Sparrow missiles; four Phalanx anti-missile guns
Crew:	5,300

Forrestal Class: *CV-60 Saratoga, CV-61 Ranger*

Displacement:	75,900 tons
Length:	1,063 feet
Beam:	129 feet
Speed:	33 knots
Power Plant:	Eight boilers, four steam turbines, four shafts, and 280,000 shaft horsepower
Aircraft:	Ninety (90)
Armament:	Sea Sparrow missiles; three Phalanx anti-missile guns
Crew:	5,180

Background

Aircraft carriers are the ultimate in "power projection" weapons. Operating from international waters, a carrier can place ninety aircraft off a country's border in a short amount of time. In the Persian Gulf, carriers were used as platforms to launch attacks on Iraqi forces and provide air support to the fleet in the Persian Gulf.

Iraqi Counterpart

The Iraqi military had no comparable vessel to the U.S. military's carriers.

Action in the Gulf

"Where are the carriers?" is the first question most presidents ask when confronted with a military crisis. Within an hour of the Iraqi invasion of Kuwait, carriers were being repositioned into the Persian Gulf and Red Sea. The French used a carrier as well, the *Clemeanceau,* but only as a helicopter transport to ferry French forces to the region and then return to France.

Around 20 percent of the sorties launched by U.S. air power came from the carriers in the Gulf and the Red Sea. The carriers on station were used to launch a variety of raids against strategic and tactical targets, along with support and command operations for Navy and Marine aircraft in the theatre. Despite fears of anti-ship missile attack, the carriers emerged from the battle unscratched. A carrier presence will be maintained in the Gulf region for several years to come.

BATTLESHIPS

Displacement:	**58,000 tons**
Length:	**887 feet**
Beam:	**108 feet**
Speed:	**35 knots**
Power Plant:	**Eight boilers supplying four turbines that produce a total of 212,000 shaft horsepower through four shafts**
Aircraft:	**Unmanned Aerial Vehicle (UAV) used for spotting**
Armament:	**Nine 16-inch MK7 guns; twelve 5-inch MK28 guns; four Phalanx anti-missile guns; Tomahawk cruise missiles; and Harpoon anti-ship missiles**

Background

Both the *Missouri* and *Wisconsin,* which saw service in Operation Desert Storm, were originally laid down during World War II. After actions in the Pacific, they were retired until the Korean War when they were recalled for service. The *New Jersey,* also of the Iowa Class, was recalled for duty in Vietnam. These ships have been mothballed several times and were recommissioned when needed because they cost too much to maintain during peacetime. On 19 April 1989, forty-seven crewmembers were killed due to a turret explosion on board USS *Iowa.*

Iraqi Counterpart

Iraq had no vessel comparable to an American battleship.

U.S. battleship. Retired since the Korean War, BB-64 *Wisconsin* was recalled for duty during the Gulf War. *Source: U.S. Navy, Scott Rebman*

Action in the Gulf

Iowa Class battleships used their 16-inch guns to provide naval gunfire support to troops ashore. Each gun (there are nine) can fire one 2,700 pound armor-piercing shell more than 20 miles every 30 seconds. During Operation Desert Storm, 1,102 16-inch rounds in 83 different missions were fired.

Fire missions could be called in from ground observers or through the use of Unmanned Aerial Vehicles (UAVs). In one highly publicized incident, a UAV on a spotting mission "took prisoners," with Iraqi troops attempting to surrender to the pilotless craft. In addition to the 16-inch guns, the Iowa Class battleships were used as launching platforms for Tomahawk cruise missiles. Overall, 282 Tomahawks were launched from sixteen surface ships and two submarines. Of these, 64 percent were in the first 48 hours of the war.

Upon return to the United States, both battleships — *Missouri* and *Wisconsin* — were again mothballed for cost-savings.

CRUISERS

Ticonderoga Class (CG47-60)

Displacement:	**9,600 tons**
Length:	**563 feet**
Beam:	**55 feet**
Speed:	**More than 30 knots**
Power:	**Four gas turbines producing 80,000 shaft horsepower through two shafts**
Aircraft:	**Helicopter platform**
Armament:	**Two, 5-inch guns; two triple torpedo tubes; two Phalanx anti-missile guns; Tomahawk cruise missiles; and Harpoon anti-ship missiles**
Crew:	**358**

Background

The Ticonderoga Class cruiser employs the AEGIS Radar and Defense System which is rated one of the best in the world. However, one AEGIS cruiser, *Vincennes,* was responsible for downing an Iranian civilian airliner in 1988. This incident was attributed to user error, not computer malfunction. In the Persian Gulf, the cruisers used their AEGIS radar to oversee the skies in an escort role for the carriers and were called upon to provide naval gunfire support to troops on the shore.

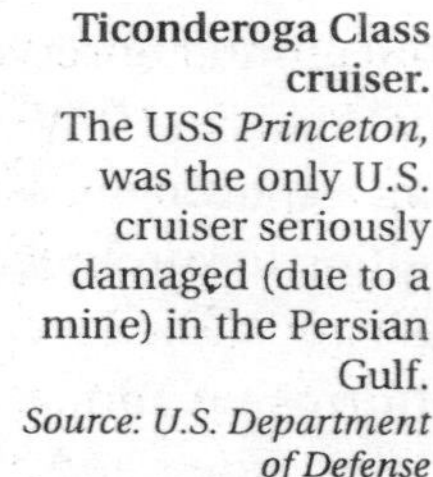

Ticonderoga Class cruiser. The USS *Princeton,* was the only U.S. cruiser seriously damaged (due to a mine) in the Persian Gulf.
Source: U.S. Department of Defense

Iraqi Counterpart

Iraq had no comparable vessel to the U.S. military's cruisers.

Action in Desert Storm

Cruisers in the Gulf were successful in their primary role of protecting the fleet from air attack. Coordinating all incoming intelligence from their own radar and from other surface ships, the AEGIS cruisers were central to the fact that no U.S. ships were lost to enemy attack from the air, despite the dreaded threat of Iraqi anti-ship missiles. However, one cruiser, USS *Princeton,* one of the newest ships in the fleet, was seriously damaged by a mine and had to be towed out of the region for repairs. Cruisers also played a major role in the blockade of Iraqi shipping, stopping hundreds of suspect vessels. The USS *San Jacinto,* an AEGIS cruiser, fired the first Tomahawk cruise missiles of the war, followed by the USS *Bunker Hill.*

DESTROYERS

Spruance Class (DD)

Displacement:	7,800 tons
Length:	563 feet
Beam:	55 feet
Speed:	33 knots
Power Plant:	Four gas turbines producing 80,000 shaft horsepower through two shafts
Aircraft:	Platform for SH-60 Seahawk helicopter
Armament:	Two 5-inch guns; two Phalanx anti-missile guns; Tomahawk cruise missiles; Harpoon anti-ship missiles; and two triple torpedo tubes
Crew:	296

Farragut Class (DDG-37/DDG-46)

Displacement:	**6,000 tons**
Length:	**512 feet**
Beam:	**52 feet**
Speed:	**33 knots**
Power:	**Four boilers supplying four steam turbines that produce 85,000 shaft horsepower through four shafts**
Aircraft:	**None**
Armament:	**One 5-inch gun; Harpoon anti-ship missiles; and two triple torpedo tubes**
Crew:	**360**

Iraqi Counterpart

Iraq had no destroyers, but did maintain an extensive fleet of much smaller patrol craft. These ships — some estimates put the number above fifty — posed a threat when used for minelaying operations or when armed with anti-ship missiles, such as the Exocet. With Iraq's limited number of ports, these ships were easy targets for U.S. warships operating in the Gulf region.

Action in Desert Storm

U.S. destroyers played an important role in the interception and interrogation of enemy and unfriendly shipping in the Persian Gulf region. With the elimination of the Iraqi Navy's smaller patrol boats, U.S. destroyers were able to operate without much fear of being taken out by an anti-ship missile. As a platform for Tomahawk missiles, destroyers were also on hand for cruise missile attacks on Iraq if the larger battleships became engaged in other action.

DD-966 *Hewitt* out of Mayport, Florida. American destroyers like the *Hewitt* continually intercepted and interrogated enemy and unfriendly shipping in the Gulf region. *Source: U.S. Department of Defense*

The role of a U.S. frigate. Frigates like FFG-54 *Ford* were used to intercept merchant vessels to uphold U.N. economic embargo sanctions. *Source: U.S. Government Department of Defense*

FRIGATES

Oliver Hazard Perry Class (FFG)

Displacement:	**4,400 tons**
Length:	**445 feet**
Beam:	**49 feet**
Speed:	**29 knots**
Power Plant:	**Two gas turbines producing 40,000 shaft horsepower through one shaft**
Aircraft:	**Platform for SH-60 Seahawk helicopter**
Armament:	**One 76 mm gun; six torpedo tubes; one Phalanx anti-missile gun; Harpoon anti-ship missiles; and the SM-1 (MR) missile system**
Crew:	**206**

Iraqi Counterpart

Iraq had four frigates of the Italian-made, Lupo Class. However, the delivery of the frigates to Iraq was held up because of the war. They were slightly smaller than the Oliver Hazard Perry Class, but came fully armed with anti-ship missiles, torpedoes, and a 127 mm deck gun. Iraq also had one other Yugoslavian-made frigate, which it used for training purposes. The frigate *IBN Khaldun* was destroyed during the Gulf War.

Action in the Gulf

Two Oliver Hazard Perry Class vessels, the USS *Stark* and USS *Samuel B. Roberts,* were damaged in the Persian Gulf during Kuwaiti tanker reflagging operations in 1987. *Samuel B. Roberts* struck a mine and *Stark* was hit by an Iraqi-fired Exocet missile, which killed thirty-seven Americans. Despite the inability of the Iraqi Navy and Air Force to fight, frigates were called on to escort larger ships and defend them from attack. Several frigates, including USS *Curts* and USS *Nicholas* did undertake offensive operations, attacking Iraqi oil platforms and ships and capturing a number of enemy prisoners of war. Frigates also played a large role in the interception of merchant vessels.

AMPHIBIOUS CRAFT

Tarawa Class

Displacement:	**39,000 tons**
Length:	**820 feet**
Beam:	**106 feet**
Speed:	**24 knots**
Power Plant:	**Two boilers supplying two steam turbines producing 70,000 shaft horsepower through two shafts**
Aircraft:	**CH-53, CH-46 Sea Knight, and other helicopters, along with AV-8A Harriers that operate off the flight deck**
Crew:	**950 (1,703 Marines)**

Iwo Jima Class

Displacement:	**18,000 tons**
Length:	**602 feet**
Beam:	**84 feet**
Speed:	**23 knots**
Power Plant:	**Two boilers supplying one steam turbine producing 22,000 shaft horsepower through one shaft**
Aircraft:	**CH-53, CH-46 Sea Knight, and other helicopters**
Crew:	**684 (1,703 Marines)**

Background

Amphibious assault ships are used to place Marines ashore via air or sea. Each ship can accommodate a number of smaller landing craft. Assault vessels such as these have been used as a platform for the rescue of civilians from hostile areas in Liberia (1990) and, most recently, in Somalia (1991).

Amphibious vessel. Amphibious assault ships were used to feint Iraqi forces into believing an amphibious operation was imminent. *Source: U.S. Department of Defense*

Iraqi Counterpart

Iraq had three landing ships (the Polinocny D Class) from the Eastern Bloc that had been modified to handle helicopters and to lay mines. However, they were much smaller than the American ships — they carried only 180 Marines and six tanks. The Iraqi amphibious ships were named *Atika, Nouh,* and *Jawada,* all of which were destroyed.

Action in Desert Storm

Amphibious assault vessels played a large role in diversionary actions — for example, in feinting Iraqi forces into believing an amphibious operation was imminent. These ships loaded and launched many landing craft and helicopters, giving the impression that the Marines would be coming ashore on the Kuwaiti coast. In the end, the invasion did not come, but these ships were essential resupply bases for Marines and other units inland.

In addition, AV-8 Harrier jump-jets used these ships as platforms for carrying out close air support attacks on Iraqi forces. One ship, USS *Tripoli,* was seriously damaged by a mine in the northern Persian Gulf, but remained on station until the end of hostilities.

PART THREE

HEEDING A CALL TO ACTION...

The War Against Saddam Hussein

Chapter Seven
Operation Desert Shield

It is hard to pick a specific reason for the invasion of Kuwait by the Iraqis. Some cited the British indifference to Middle East traditions when the United Kingdom carved up the present day Arab world. Others point to the Kuwaitis flaunting of their wealth in the face of many poorer neighbors. Still others see it as a natural result of Saddam Hussein's "bully-like" nature. Nevertheless, there are a few specific events that took place in mid-1990 that are important in understanding Operation Desert Shield and Operation Desert Storm.

17 JULY 1990

On 17 July 1990 Saddam Hussein accused Kuwait and the United Arab Emirates of flooding the world oil market. In addition, he singled out Kuwait for the production of oil from a disputed supply, the Rumaila Oil Field which ran beneath both countries. To bolster his threats, Iraqi military units were placed on alert and moved toward the Kuwait border. While many saw this as merely a negotiating ploy, U.N. Secretary General Javier Perez De Cuellar recognized the possibility for war and called on all sides to calm down and demobilize their forces. For a time, it appeared as if there would be no invasion. Nonetheless, on 24 July, General Colin Powell called General Norman Schwarzkopf, commander of Central Command (CENTCOM) and ordered him to prepare a response to Saddam's threatening actions.

25 JULY 1990

On 25 July, the now famous meeting took place between U.S. Ambassador April Glaspie and Saddam Hussein. Throughout the conflict, many opponents of U.S. policy said Glaspie's response at this meeting led to the invasion by Iraqi forces. However, after the war, Glaspie testified she informed Saddam Hussein that the United States would not sit idly if a military operation was undertaken. However, the United States did not have much of an opinion in "Arab-Arab" conflicts, like the disagreement with Kuwait. Apparently, Saddam Hussein misjudged this, as he would many other things, as a signal the United States would not interfere in an Iraqi invasion of Kuwait. On this same day, Kuwaiti military units were mobilized.

1 AUGUST 1990

Talks between Iraq and Kuwait collapsed on 1 August. General Schwarzkopf briefed Secretary of Defense Cheney that he anticipated an attack. On 2 August, at 0100 Kuwaiti time (1700, 1 August, Washington time), three divisions of the Republican Guard forces attacked Kuwait. At 0130, special operations forces attacked Kuwait City. Commandos — many of whom had infiltrated Kuwait prior to the invasion — attacked government buildings in the city and the amir's palace. The amir was forced to flee into Saudi Arabia in exile, and his brother was killed in the assault on the palace.

The Republican Guard forces linked with the special forces units in Kuwait City at 0530 and had control of the city by 1900. Later that night, the forces headed south toward the Saudi Arabian border. By 6 August, the forces were dug in and elements of eleven Iraqi divisions were on their way to Kuwait, which Saddam Hussein proclaimed as the "19th Province of Iraq."

Worldwide condemnation of the Iraqi action rang out from the capitals of the world, but it was too late to change the course of Iraqi action. The Kuwait known to the world as a rich and prosperous moderate Arab country was now gone.

EXECUTIVE ORDER 12722
Blocking Iraqi Government Property and Prohibiting Transactions with Iraq

2 August 1990

By the authority vested in me as President by the Constitution and the laws of the United States of America, including the International Emergency Economic Powers Act (50 U.S.C. 1701 et seq.), the National Emergencies Act (50 U.S.C. 1601 et seq.), section 301 of title 3 of the United States Code.

I, George Bush, President of the United States of America, find that the policies and actions of the Government of Iraq constitute an unusual and extraordinary threat to the national security and foreign policy of the United States and hereby declare a national emergency to deal with that threat.

Section 1. All property and interests in property of the Government of Iraq, its agencies, instrumentalities and controlled entities and the Central Bank of Iraq that are in the United States, that hereafter come within the United States or that are or hereafter come within the possession or control of United States persons, including their overseas branches, are hereby blocked.

Section 2. The following are prohibited, except to the extent provided in regulations that may hereafter be issued pursuant to this order:

(a) The importation into the United States of any goods or services of Iraqi origin, other than publications and other informational materials;

EXECUTIVE ORDER 12722 (continued)

(b) The exportation to Iraq of any goods, technology (including technical data or other information controlled for export pursuant to Section 5 of the Export Administration Act (50 U.S.C. App. 2404), or services from the United States, except publications and other informational materials, and donations of articles intended to relieve human suffering such as food, clothing, medicine and medical supplies intended strictly for medical purposes;

(c) Any transaction by a United States person relating to transportation to or from Iraq; the provision of transportation to or from the United States by any Iraqi person or any vessel or aircraft of Iraqi registration; or the sale in the United States by any person holding authority under the Federal Aviation Act of 1958, as amended (49 U.S.C. 1514), of any transportation by air which includes any stop in Iraq;

(d) The purchase by any United States person of goods for export from Iraq to any country;

(e) The performance by any United States person of any contract in support of an industrial or other commercial or governmental project in Iraq;

(f) The grant or extension of credits or loans by any United States person to the Government of Iraq, its instrumentalities and controlled entities;

(g) Any transaction by a United States person relating to travel by any United States citizen or permanent resident alien to Iraq, or to activities by any such person with Iraq, after the date of this order, other than transactions necessary to effect such person's departure from Kuwait, or travel for journalistic activity by persons regularly employed in such capacity by a news-gathering organization; and

(h) Any transaction by any United States person which evades or avoids, or has the purpose of evading or avoiding, any of the prohibitions set for in this Order.

For purposes of this Order, the term "United States person" means any United States citizen, permanent resident alien, juridical person organized under the laws of the United States or any person in the United States.

Section 3. This order is effective immediately.

Section 4. The Secretary of the Treasury, in consultation with the Secretary of State, is hereby authorized to take such actions, including the promulgation of rules and regulations, as may be necessary to carry out the purposes of this order. Such actions may include prohibiting or regulating payments or transfers of any property or any transactions involving the transfer of anything of economic value by any United States person to the Government of Iraq, its instrumentalities and controlled entities, or to any Iraqi national or entity owned or controlled, directly or indirectly, by Iraq or Iraqi nationals. The Secretary may redelegate any of these functions to other officers and agencies of the Federal Government. All Agencies of the Federal Government are directed to take all appropriate measures within their authority to carry out the provisions of this Order, including the suspension or termination of licenses or other authorizations in effect as of the date of this Order.

This Order shall be transmitted to the Congress and published in the Federal Register.

George Bush

(Executive Order 12723 is identical to 12722, with the substitution of "Kuwait" for "Iraq.")

2 AUGUST 1990

President Bush immediately took action to protest the invasion. Warships currently on station in the Persian Gulf were bolstered and U.S. forces were put under a higher state of alert. On 2 August, within one hour of the initial attack, the USS *Independence* CVN-62 battle group was dispatched from Diego Garcia to the Gulf of Oman. The USS *Dwight Eisenhower* CVN-69 was ordered to sail from the eastern Mediterranean Sea to prepare to enter the Red Sea. The 82nd Airborne Division's Ready Brigade was also alerted.

Using emergency powers, the president signed two executive orders — Executive Order 12722 and Executive Order 12723 — freezing Iraq's and Kuwait's assets, and later modified this measure to bar trade between U.S. companies and the Iraqis. See the previous page for exact wording of these two critical executive orders.

5 AUGUST 1990

Bush dispatched his top foreign affairs and defense advisors to the capitals of the world. Secretary Cheney and Secretary Baker were sent overseas to work on developing a cohesive and unified world response to the Iraqi invasion of Kuwait. President Bush went so far as to say "this aggression will not stand." Table 7.1 below lists a summary of the twelve executive orders President Bush signed during the Persian Gulf Crisis.

TABLE 7.1

EXECUTIVE ORDER SUMMARY

12722 – 2 August 1990. Froze Iraqi assets and prohibited transactions with Iraq.	**12742** – 8 January 1990. Gave the president the power to direct industry to produce necessary war-related goods over domestic products.
12723 – 2 August 1990. Froze Kuwaiti assets and prohibited transactions with Kuwait.	**12743** – 18 January 1991. Allowed the president to call up the reserves for up to twenty-four months if needed.
12724 – 9 August 1990. Strengthened the previous orders freezing assets and prohibiting trade with Iraq.	**12744** – 21 January 1991. Designated the Persian Gulf region as a war zone for the purpose of the troops tax extensions and exemptions.
12725 – 9 August 1990. Strengthened the previous orders freezing assets and prohibiting trade with Kuwait.	**12750** – 14 February 1991. Designated the Persian Gulf region as the Persian Gulf Desert Shield area for tax purposes.
12727 – 22 August 1990. Ordered to active duty selected elements of the Reserves.	**12751** – 14 February 1991. Authorized the secretary of veterans' affairs to provide health care for wounded personnel from the Gulf Crisis.
12728 – 22 August 1990. Allowed the president to suspend promotions, retirement, or separation of members from the Armed Services.	
12734 – 14 November 1990. Allowed the president to redirect military construction funds to priority projects in the Gulf.	

While in Saudi Arabia, Secretary Cheney presented Saudi King Fahd with evidence the Iraqis were massing on his country's border for a possible invasion against his oil fields. Some reports indicated that Iraqi tanks had actually crossed over the border, which is not hard to believe when the only territorial division is a line on a map in some library, not a demarcation in the sand. The Saudis, who have been purchasing American military equipment for the last decade, were well equipped, but not militarily capable of defending themselves against the overwhelming Iraqi forces. They would need help, and in a big way. On 7 August, Saudi Arabia formally requested assistance from the United States. In a formal statement, King Fahd communicated to his people the need to defend the kingdom. See below for his speech.

Secretary Cheney proposed a massive deployment of U.S. forces — with the 82nd Airborne and the 24th Mechanized Infantry to start, along with several air wings of U.S. planes. These forces were the remnants of the Carter designated "Rapid Deployment Force." They could be on the way in hours and on station in a matter of weeks. The size of this movement would convince the Saudis and Iraqis that the United States was serious about helping its ally in the Gulf.

Secretary Baker met with Soviet Foreign Minister Gromyko to hammer out a diplomatic response between the two superpowers. The United States was successful in obtaining the Soviet's opposition to the Kuwait invasion, and a joint communiqué was issued calling for action against the Iraqis. President Bush, delivering what was to be the first

KING FAHD'S SPEECH
Defending the Kingdom

9 August 1990

In the name of God, the Merciful, the Compassionate. Thanks be to God, Master of the Universe and Prayers of Peace be upon the last Prophets Mohammed and all his kinfolk and companions.

Dear brother citizens, may God's peace and mercy be upon you.

You realize, no doubt, through following up the course of regrettable events in the Arab Gulf region during the last few days the gravity of the situation the Arab Nation faces in the current circumstances. You undoubtedly know that the government of the Kingdom of Saudi Arabia has exerted all possible efforts with the government of the Iraqi Republic and the State of Kuwait to contain the dispute between the two countries.

In this context, I made numerous telephone calls and held fraternal talks with the brothers. As a result, a bilateral meeting was held between the Iraqi and Kuwaiti delegations in Saudi Arabia with the aim of bridging the gap and narrowing differences to avert any further escalation.

A number of brotherly Arab kings and presidents contributed, thankfully, in these efforts based on their belief in the unity of the Arab Nation and the cohesion of its solidarity and cooperation to achieve success in serving its fateful causes.
However, regrettably enough, events took an adverse course to our endeavors and the

KING FAHD'S SPEECH (continued)

aspirations of the People's of the Islamic and Arab nation, as well as peace-loving countries.

Nevertheless, these painful and regrettable events started in the pre-dawn hours of Thursday 11 Muharram 1411H., corresponding to 2nd August A.D. 1990. They took the whole world by surprise when the Iraqi forces stormed the brotherly state of Kuwait in the most sinister aggression witnessed by the Arab nation in its modern history. Such an invasion inflicted painful suffering on the Kuwaitis and rendered them homeless.

While expressing its deep displeasure at this aggression on the brotherly neighbor Kuwait, the Kingdom of Saudi Arabia declares its categorical rejection of all ensuing measures and declarations that followed that aggression, which were rejected by all the statements issued Arab leaderships, the Arab League, the Islamic Conference Organization, and the Gulf Cooperation Council, as well as all Arab and international bodies and organizations.

The Kingdom of Saudi Arabia reaffirms its demand to restore the situation in the brother state of Kuwait to its original status before the Iraqi storming as well as the return of the ruling family headed H. H. Sheikh Jaber al-Ahmad, al-Jaber, al Sabah, the Amir of Kuwait and his government.

We hope that the emergency Arab summit called by H.E. President Mohamad Hosni Mubarak of sisterly Egypt will lead to the achievement of the results that realize the aspirations of the Arab nation and bolster its march towards solidarity and unity of opinion.

In the aftermath of this regrettable event, Iraq massed huge forces on the borders of the Kingdom of Saudi Arabia. In view of these bitter realities and out of the eagerness of the Kingdom to safeguard its territory and protect its vital and economic potentials, and its wish to bolster its defensive capabilities and to raise the level of training of its armed forces — in addition to the keenness of the government of the Kingdom to resort to peace and non-recourse to force to solve disputes — the Kingdom of Saudi Arabia expressed its wish for the participation of fraternal Arab forces and other friendly forces.

Thus the governments of the United States, Britain and other nations took the initiative, based upon the friendly relations that link the Kingdom of Saudi Arabia and these countries, to dispatch air and land forces to sustain the Saudi armed forces in performing their duty to defend the homeland and the citizens against any aggression with the full emphasis that this measure is not addressed to anybody. It is merely and purely for defensive purposes, imposed by the current circumstances faced by the kingdom of Saudi Arabia.

It is worth mentioning in this context that the forces which will participate in the joint training exercises with the Saudi armed forces are of a temporary nature. They will leave the Saudi territory immediately at the request of the Kingdom.

We pray to Almighty God to culminate our steps towards everything in which lie the good of our religion and safety of our homeland, and to guide us on the right path.

May God's peace and blessing be upon you.

in a series of addresses on how to draw down the military, met with British Prime Minister Margaret Thatcher.

At the United Nations, the first two resolutions — Resolution 660 and Resolution 661 — condemning the Iraqi invasion and instituting a trade embargo on Iraq, were quickly passed through the U.N. Security Council. See the following pages for details on these resolutions.

In previous decades, the Soviet veto of these measures would have ended any hope of international pressure to pull the Iraqis out of Kuwait. But given the new relationship between the Soviet Union and the United States, it was possible to forge an alliance against Saddam Hussein. Table 7.2 shows the U.N. members at the time of the Gulf Crisis.

RESOLUTION 660
United Nations Security Council

2 August 1990 The Security Council,

Alarmed by the invasion of Kuwait of 2 August 1990 by the military forces of Iraq,

Determining that there exists a breach of international peace and security as regards the Iraqi invasion of Kuwait,

Acting under Articles 39 and 40 of the Charter of the United Nations,

1) Condemns the Iraqi invasion of Kuwait;

2) Demands that Iraq withdraw immediately and unconditionally all its forces to the positions in which they were located on 1 August 1990.

3) Calls upon Iraq and Kuwait to begin immediately intensive negotiations for the resolution of their differences and supports all efforts in this regard, and especially those of the League of Arab States;

4) Decides to meet again as necessary to consider further steps to ensure compliance with the present resolution.

VOTE: 14 for, 0 against, 1 abstention (Yemen)

TABLE 7.2

U.N. SECURITY COUNCIL

1990	1991
China	China
United Kingdom	United Kingdom
United States	United States
France	France
Soviet Union	Soviet Union
Canada	Austria*
Colombia	Belgium*
Cuba	Cuba
Ethiopia	Ecuador*
Finland	India*
Malaysia	Zimbabwe*
Cote d'Ivorie	Cote d'Ivorie
Romania	Romania
Yemen	Yemen
Zaire	Zaire

*Indicates new membership as of 1 January 1991

RESOLUTION 661
United Nations Security Council

6 August 1990 The Security Council,
Reaffirming its resolution 660 (1990) of 2 August 1990,

Deeply concerned that resolution has not been implemented and that the invasion by Iraq of Kuwait continues with further loss of human life and material destruction,

Determined to bring the invasion and occupation of Kuwait by Iraq to an end and to restore the sovereignty, independence and territorial integrity of Kuwait,

Noting that the legitimate Government of Kuwait has expressed its readiness to comply with resolution 660 (1990),

Mindful of its responsibilities under the Charter of the United Nations for the maintenance of international peace and security,

Affirming the inherent right of individual or collective self-defense, in response to the armed attack by Iraq against Kuwait, in accordance with Article 51 of the Charter,

Acting under Chapter VII of the Charter of the United Nations,

1) Determines that Iraq so far has failed to comply with paragraph 2 of resolution 660 (1990) and has usurped the authority of the legitimate Government of Kuwait;

2) Decides as a consequence, to take the following measures to secure compliance of Iraq with paragraph 2 of resolution 660 (1990) and to restore the authority of the legitimate Government of Kuwait;

3) Decides that all States shall prevent:

(a) The import into their territories of all commodities and products originating in Iraq or Kuwait exported therefrom after the date of the present resolution;

(b) Any activities by their nationals or in their territories which would promote or are calculated to promote the export or transshipment of any commodities or products from Iraq or Kuwait; and any dealings by their nationals or their flag vessels or in their territories in any commodities or products originating in Iraq or Kuwait and exported therefrom after the date of the present resolution, including in particular any transfer of funds to Iraq or Kuwait for the purposes of such activities or dealings;

(c) The sale or supply by their nationals of or from their territories or using their flag vessels of any commodities or products, including military equipment, whether or not origination in their territories but not including supplies intended strictly for medical purposes, and in humanitarian circumstances, foodstuffs, to any person or body in Iraq or Kuwait or to any person or body for the purposes of any business carried on, in, or operated from Iraq or Kuwait, and any activities by their nationals or in their territories to promote such sale or supply of such commodities or produces;

4. Decides that all States shall not make available to the Government of Iraq or to any commercial, industrial or public utility undertaking in Iraq or Kuwait, any funds or any other financial or economic resources and shall prevent their nationals and any persons within their territories from removing from their territories or otherwise making available to that Government or to any other such undertaking any such funds or resources and from remitting any other funds to persons or bodies with Iraq or Kuwait,

RESOLUTION 661 (continued)

except payments exclusively for strictly medical or humanitarian purposes and in humanitarian circumstances, foodstuffs;

5. Calls upon all States, including States non-members of the United Nations, to act strictly in accordance with the provisions of the present resolution notwithstanding any contract entered into or license granted before the date of the present resolution;

6. Decides to establish, in accordance with rule 28 of the provision rules of procedure of the Security Council, a Committee of the Security Council consisting of all the members of the Council, to undertake the following tasks and to report on its work to the Council with its observations and recommendations:

(a) To examine the reports on the progress of the implementation of the present resolution which will be submitted by the Secretary-General;

(b) To seek from all States further information regarding the action taken by them concerning the effective implementation of the provisions laid down in the present resolution;

7. Calls upon all States to cooperate fully with the Committee in the fulfillment of its task, including supplying such information as may be sought by the Committee in pursuance of the present resolution;

8. Requests the Secretary-General to provide all necessary assistance to the Committee and to make the necessary arrangements in the Secretariat for the purpose;

9. Decides that, notwithstanding paragraphs 4 through 8 above, noting the present resolution shall prohibit assistance to the legitimate Government of Kuwait, and calls upon all States:

(a) To take appropriate measures to protect assets of the legitimate Government of Kuwait and its agencies;

(b) Not to recognize any regime set up by the occupying Power;

10. Requests the Secretary-General to report to the Council on the progress of the implementation of the present resolution, the first report to be submitted within thirty days;

11. Decides to keep this item on its agenda and to continue its efforts to put an early end to the invasion by Iraq.

VOTE: 13 for, 0 against, 2 abstentions (Cuba and Yemen)

A show of thanks and support. President Bush and the First Lady joined troops stationed in Saudi Arabia for Thanksgiving dinner. *Source: U.S. Government*

U.N. resolutions also allowed the coalition naval forces to commence boarding operations of Iraqi shipping. Table 7.3 provides a summary of the U.N. Security Council's resolutions concerning the Persian Gulf Crisis.

TABLE 7.3

U.N. SECURITY COUNCIL SUMMARY OF RESOLUTIONS

Resolution 660	2 August 1990 Condemned the invasion of Kuwait and demanded Iraq's withdrawal.
Resolution 661	6 August 1990. Imposed economic sanctions on Iraq and Kuwait.
Resolution 662	9 August 1990. Rejected Iraq's annexation of Kuwait.
Resolution 664	18 August 1990. Called on Iraq to assist the departure of foreign nationals in Iraq and Kuwait.
Resolution 665	25 August 1990. Allowed the use of force to enforce economic sanctions.
Resolution 666	13 September 1990. Defined humanitarian aid that could be exempted from sanctions.
Resolution 667	16 September 1990. Condemned Iraqi attacks on diplomatic personnel in Kuwait.
Resolution 669	24 September 1990. Asked for economic aid to countries harmed by sanctions on Iraq.
Resolution 670	25 September 1990. Called for an embargo of air traffic into Iraq.
Resolution 674	29 October 1990. Called on Iraq to stop mistreating and oppressing the nationals of Kuwait.
Resolution 677	28 November 1990. Demanded that Iraq not destroy the population and census records of Kuwait.
Resolution 678	29 November 1990. Set a 15 January deadline for Iraq's withdrawal from Kuwait, and authorized military action to enforce this.
Resolution 686	2 March 1991. Established the guidelines for the reconciliation of hostilities.

7 AUGUST 1990

Speaking before the nation on 8 August, President Bush announced his decision to dispatch troops and planes to defend the Saudi Kingdom. This powerful speech made by the president is on the following page. As he spoke, elements of the 82nd Airborne were already on planes for the long flight overseas. The carrier battle group headed by USS *Independence* continued to steam from the Indian Ocean to the Persian Gulf, and USS *Enterprise* and USS *Saratoga* with their support groups were ordered to steam toward the Gulf region. At Langley Air Force Base in Virginia, the 1st Tactical Fighter Wing was alerted and dispatched to Saudi Arabia in the opening minutes of the now codenamed "Operation Desert Shield." These initial deployments were supported by Marine units from around the world.

In the next few days, the old axiom "amateurs talk tactics, professional talk logistics" demonstrated the skill and professionalism of the American military. The Military Airlift Command, and later the sealift forces, began the most incredible and massive transport operation ever conducted. More than 90 percent of the U.S. military long-range airlift was in use and all eight of the Navy's fast sealift, plus dozens of other navy vessels pressed into transport service. The Marine Corps prepositioned *(text continued on page 118)*

GEORGE BUSH'S SPEECH
Sending in the Troops...

8 August 1990

In the life of a nation, we're called upon to define who we are and what we believe. Sometimes these choices are not easy. But today as president, I ask for your support in a decision I've made to stand up for what's right and condemn what's wrong — all in the cause of peace.

At my direction, elements of the 82nd Airborne Division, as well as key units of the United States Air Force are arriving today to take up defensive positions in Saudi Arabia. I took this action to assist the Saudi Arabian government in the defense of its homeland.

No one commits America's Armed Forces to a dangerous mission lightly. But after perhaps unparalleled international consultation and exhausting every alternative, it became necessary to take this action. Let me tell you why.

Less than a week ago, in the early morning hours of August 2nd, Iraqi armed forces, without provocation or warning, invaded a peaceful Kuwait. Facing negligible resistance from its much smaller neighbor, Iraq's tank stormed in *blitzkrieg* fashion through Kuwait in a few short hours. With more than 100,000 troops, along with tanks, artillery, and surface to surface missiles, Iraq now occupies Kuwait. This aggression came just hours after Saddam Hussein specifically assured numerous countries in the area that there would be no invasion. There is no justification whatsoever for this outrageous and brutal act of aggression.

A puppet regime imposed from the outside is unacceptable. The acquisition of territory by force is unacceptable. No one, friend or foe, should doubt our desire for peace; and no one should underestimate our determination to confront aggression.

Four simple principles guide our policy. First, we seek the immediate, unconditional, and complete withdrawal of all Iraqi forces from Kuwait. Second, Kuwait's legitimate government must be restored to replace the puppet regime. And third, my administration, as has been the case with every president since President Roosevelt to President Reagan, is committed to the security and stability of the Persian Gulf. And fourth, I am determined to protect the lives of American citizens abroad.

Immediately after the Iraqi invasion, I ordered an embargo of all trade with Iraq and, together with many other nations, announced sanctions that both freeze all Iraqi assets in this country and protect Kuwait's assets. The stakes are high. Iraq is already a rich and powerful country that possesses the world's second largest reserves of oil and over a million men under arms. It's the fourth largest military in the world. Our country now imports nearly half the oil its consumes and could face a major threat to its economic independence. Much of the world is even more dependent upon imported oil and is even more vulnerable to Iraqi threats.

We succeeded in the struggle for freedom in Europe because we and our allies remain stalwart. Keeping the peace in the Middle East will require no less. We're beginning a new era. This new era can be full of promise, an age of freedoms.

Appeasement does not work. As was the case in the 1930s, we see in Saddam Hussein an aggressive dictator threatening his neighbors. Only 14 days ago, Saddam Hussein promised his friends he would not invade Kuwait. And 4 days ago, he promised the world he would withdraw. And twice we have seen what his promises mean: His promises mean nothing.

GEORGE BUSH'S SPEECH (continued)

In the last few days, I've spoken with political leaders from the Middle East, Europe, Asia, and the Americas; and I've met with Prime Minister Thatcher, Prime Minister Mulroney, and NATO Secretary General Woerner. And all agree that Iraq cannot be allowed to benefit from its invasion of Kuwait.

We agree that this is not an American problem or a European problem or a Middle East problem: it is the world's problem. And that's why soon after the Iraqi invasion, the United Nations Security Council, without dissent, condemned Iraq, calling for the immediate and unconditional withdrawal of its troops from Kuwait. The Arab world, through both the Arab League and the Gulf Cooperation Council, courageously announced its opposition to Iraqi aggression. Japan, the United Kingdom, and France, and other governments around the world have imposed severe sanctions. The Soviet Union and China ended all arms sales to Iraq.

And this past Monday, the United Nations Security Council approved for the first time in 23 years mandatory sanctions under chapter VII of the United Nations Charter. These sanctions, now enshrined in international law, have the potential to deny Iraq the fruits of aggression while sharply limiting its ability to either import or export anything of value, especially oil.

But we must recognize that Iraq may not stop using force to advance its ambitions. Iraq has massed an enormous war machine on the Saudi border capable of initiating hostilities with little or no additional preparation. Given the Iraqi government's history of aggression against its own citizens as well as its neighbor, to assume Iraq will not attack again would be unwise and unrealistic.

And therefore, after consulting with King Fahd, I sent Secretary of Defense Cheney to discuss cooperative measures we could take. Following those meetings, the Saudi Government requested our help, and I responded to that request by ordering U.S. air and ground forces to deploy in the Kingdom of Saudi Arabia.

Let me be clear: The sovereign independence of Saudi Arabia is of vital interest to the United States. This decision, which I shared with the congressional leadership, grows out of the long-standing friendship and security relationship between the United States and Saudi Arabia. U.S. forces will work together with those of Saudi Arabia and other nations to preserve the integrity of Saudi Arabia and to deter further Iraqi aggression. Through their presence, as well as through training and exercises, these multinational forces will enhance the overall capability of Saudi Armed Forces to defend the Kingdom.

I want to be clear about what we are doing and why. America does not seek conflict, nor do we seek to chart the destiny of other nations. But America will stand by her friends. The mission of our troops is wholly defensive. Hopefully, they will not be needed long. They will not initiate hostilities, but they will defend themselves, the Kingdom of Saudi Arabia, and other friends in the Persian Gulf.

We are working around the clock to deter Iraqi aggression and to enforce U.N. sanctions. I'm continuing my conversations with world leaders. Secretary of Defense Cheney has just returned from valuable consultations with President Mubarak of Egypt and King Hassan of Morocco. Secretary of State Baker has consulted with his counterparts in many nations, including the Soviet Union, and today he heads for Europe to consult with President Ozal of Turkey, a staunch friend of the United States. And he'll then consult with the NATO Foreign Ministers.

GEORGE BUSH'S SPEECH (continued)

I will ask oil-producing nations to do what they can to minimize any impact that oil flow reductions will have on the world economy. And I will explore whether we and our allies should draw down our strategic petroleum reserves. Conservation measures can also help; Americans everywhere must do their part. And one more thing: I'm asking the oil companies to do their fair share. They should show restraint and not abuse today's uncertainties to raise prices.

Standing up for our principles will not come easy. It may take time and possibly cost a great deal. But we are asking no more of anyone than of the brave young men and women of our Armed Forces and their families. And I ask that in the churches around the country prayers be said for those who are committed to protect and defend America's interests.

Standing up for our principles is an American tradition. As it has so many times before, it may take time and tremendous effort, but most of all, it will take unity of purpose. As I've witnessed throughout my life in both war and peace, America has never wavered when her purpose is driven by principle. And on this August day, at home and abroad, I know she will do no less.

Thank you, and God bless the United States of America.

Holding his ground. President Bush was instrumental in developing a unified world stance on the Iraqi invasion of Kuwait. *Source: U.S. Navy*

EXECUTIVE ORDER 12724
Blocking Iraqi Government Property and Prohibiting Transactions with Iraq

9 August 1990 By the authority vested in me as President by the Constitution and the laws of the United States of America, including the International Emergency Economic Powers Act (50 U.S.C. 1701 et seq.), the National Emergencies Act (50 U.S.C. 1601 et seq.), section 301 of title 3 of the United States Code, and the United National Participation Act (22 U.S.C. 287c), in view of United Nations Security Council Resolution No. 661 of August 6, 1990, and in order to take additional steps with respect to Iraq's invasion of Iraq and the national emergency declared in Executive Order No. 12722,

I, George Bush, President of the United States of America, hereby order:

Section 1. Except to the extent provided in regulations that may hereafter be issued pursuant to this order, all property of the Government of Iraq that are in the United States, that hereafter come with the possession or control of United States persons, including their overseas branches, are hereby blocked.

Section 2. The following are prohibited, except to the extent provided in regulations that may hereafter be issued pursuant to this order:

(a) The importation into the United States of any goods or services of Iraqi origin, or any activity that promotes or is intended to promote such importation;

(b) The exportation to Iraq, or to any entity operated from Iraq, or owned or controlled by the Government of Iraq, directly or indirectly, of any goods, technology (including technical data or other information), or services either (i) from the United States, or (ii) requiring the issuance of a license by a Federal agency, or any activity that promotes or is intended to promote such exportation, except donations of articles intended to relieve human suffering, such as food and supplies intended strictly for medical purposes;

(c) Any dealing by a United States person related to property of Iraqi origin exported from Iraq after August 6, 1990, or property intended for exportation from Iraq to any country, or exportation to Iraq from any country, or any activity of any kind that promotes or is intended to promote such dealing

(d) Any transaction by a United States person relating to travel by any United States citizen or permanent resident alien to Iraq, or to activities by any such person with Iraq, after the date of this order, other than transactions necessary to effect (i) such person's departure from Iraq, (ii) travel and activities for the conduct of official business of the Federal Government or the United Nations, or (iii) travel for journalistic activity by person regularly employed in such capacity by a news-gathering organization;

(e) Any transaction by a United States person relating to transportation to or from Iraq; the provision of transportation to or from the United States by an Iraqi person or any vessel or aircraft of Iraqi registration; or the sale in the United States by any person holding authority under the General Aviation act of 1958, as amended (49 U.S.C. 1301 et seq.), of any transportation by air that includes any stop in Iraq;

(f) The performance by any United States person of any contract, including a financing contract, in support of an industrial, commercial, public utility, or government project in Iraq;

(g) Except as otherwise authorized herein, any commitment or transfer, direct or indirect, of funds, or other financial or economic resources by any United States person to the Government of Iraq or any other person in Iraq.

EXECUTIVE ORDER 12724 (continued)

(h) Any transaction by any United States person that evades or avoids, or has the purpose of evading or avoiding, any of the prohibitions set forth in this order.

Section 3. For the purposes of this order:

(a) the term "United States person" means any United States citizen, permanent resident alien, juridical person organized under the laws of the United States (including foreign branches), or any person in the United States, and vessels of U.S. registration.

(b) the term "Government of Iraq" includes the Government of Iraq, its agencies, instrumentalities and controlled entities, and the Central Bank of Iraq.

Section 4. This order is effective immediately.

Section 5. The Secretary of the Treasury, in consultation with the Secretary of State, is hereby authorized to take such actions, including the promulgation of rules and regulations, as may be necessary to carry out the purposes of this order Such actions may include prohibiting or regulation payments or transfers of any property or any transactions involving the transfer of anything of economic value by any United States person to the Government of Iraq, or to any Iraqi national or entity owned or controlled, directly or indirectly, by the Government of Iraq or Iraqi nationals. The Secretary of the Treasury may redelegate any of these functions to other officers and agencies of the Federal Government. All Agencies of the Federal Government are directed to take all appropriate measures within their authority to carry out the provisions of this order, including the suspension or termination of licenses or other authorizations in effect as of the date of this order.

Section 6. Executive Order No. 12722 of August 2, 1990, is hereby revoked to the extent inconsistent with this order. All delegations, rules, regulations, orders, licenses, and other forms of administrative actions made, issue, or otherwise taken under Executive Order No. 12722 and not revoked administratively shall remain in full force and effect under this order until amended, modified, or terminated by proper authority. The revocation of any provision of Executive Order No. 12722 pursuant to this section shall not affect any violation of any rules, regulations, orders, licenses, or other forms of administrative action under that order during the period that such provision of that order was in effect.

This order shall be transmitted to the Congress and published in the Federal Register.

George Bush

(Executive Order 12725 is identical to 12724, substituting "Kuwait" for "Iraq.")

USS *Enterprise* and its battle-group alerted. As President Bush announced his plans to dispatch armed forces to defend Saudi Arabia, military units were already en route. *Source: U.S. Navy*

ship program — materials and munitions in ships ready to be sent anywhere in the world — was activated from bases in Guam, Diego Garcia, and Virginia to meet the Marines who were coming in by air.

9 AUGUST 1990

The 1st Tactical Fighter Wing from Langley Air Force Base arrived after flying fourteen hours with seven aerial refuelings. By 9 August, these planes were flying combat air patrols along the border, supported by RC-135 Rivet Joint reconnaissance platforms that had just deployed from Europe and E-3 Airborne Warning and Control aircraft from the United States. Additionally, the first elements of the ready brigade of the 82nd Airborne arrived to establish a perimeter around the Saudi airport at Dhahran. By 13 August, the entire brigade was in position and a second brigade was on the way.

On the diplomatic side, President Bush issued another executive order (12724) to further strengthen the U.S. position regarding Iraqi trade. In addition, the United Nations passed Resolution 662, which formally rejected Iraq's annexation of Kuwait.

RESOLUTION 662
United Nations Security Council

9 August 1990 The Security Council,

Recalling its resolutions 660 (1990) and 661 (1990),

Gravely alarmed by the declaration by Iraq of a "comprehensive and eternal merger" with Kuwait,

Demanding, once again, that Iraq withdraw immediately and unconditionally all its forces to the positions in which they were located on 1 August 1990,

Determined to bring the occupation of Kuwait by Iraq to an end and to restore the sovereignty, independence, and territorial integrity of Kuwait,

Determined also to restore the authority of the legitimate Government of Kuwait,

1. Decides that annexation of Kuwait by Iraq under any form and whatever pretext has no legal validity, and is considered null and void;

2. Calls upon all States, international organizations and specialized agencies not to recognize that annexation, and to refrain from any action or dealing that might be interpreted as an indirect recognition of the annexation;

3. Further demands that Iraq rescind its actions purporting to annex Kuwait;

4. Decides to keep this item on its agenda and to continue its efforts to put an early end to the occupation

VOTE: Unanimous (15-0)

The scope and size of Operation Desert Shield soon became apparent. Some 225,000 U.S. troops were to be deployed in a test of the U.S. military's ability to rapidly deploy forces into a region. F-15s, F-16s, F-111s, and F-117s were sent to the region along with a variety of support and other aircraft. Marines and firefighters, cooks and anti-aircraft batteries were called upon from around the world to support the largest U.S. deployment since Vietnam. During the height of the movement, planes were landing every ten minutes in Saudi Arabia, forming what controllers called an "aluminum bridge" between two countries. In a matter of weeks, the airlift of U.S. forces into the Gulf passed the tonnage figures for the Berlin Airlift of 1949.

16 AUGUST 1990

By 16 August, the United States had a Naval force in place of such a size that interceptions could begin to enforce U.N. resolutions on the embargo of trade with Iraq. The next day (17 August in the United States, 18 August in the Gulf), two U.S. warships intercepted and interrogated an Iraqi vessel on its cargo and destination. This was the first of thousands of interceptions, some of

An aluminum bridge. The massive airlift into the Gulf was just one element that demonstrated the true scale of Operation Desert Shield. *Source: Department of Defense*

EXECUTIVE ORDER 12727
Ordering the Selective Reserve of the Armed Forces to Active Duty

22 August 1990

By the authority vested in me as President by the Constitution and the laws of the United States of America, including sections 121 and 673b of title 10 of the United States Code, I hereby determine that it is necessary to augment the active armed forces of the United States for the effective conduct of operational missions in and around the Arabian Peninsula. Further, under the stated authority, I hereby authorize the Secretary of Defense, and the Secretary of Transportation with respect to the Coast Guard when the latter is not operating as a service in the Department of the Navy, to order to active duty units and individuals, of the Selected Reserve.

This order is intended only to improve the internal management of the executive branch, and is not intended to create and right or benefit, substantive or procedural, enforceable at law by a party against the United States, its agencies its officers, or any person.

This order shall be published in the Federal Register and transmitted promptly to the Congress.

George Bush

which led to U.S. and Allied ships forcing Iraqi and other vessels to return to their ports. At one point, an Iraqi tanker (*Khanaqin*) refused a challenge by U.S. naval forces, so the USS *Reid FFG-30* fired the first warning shot of the war across her bow. By the end of the war, some 964 ships had been boarded and more than 7,500 challenged.

17 AUGUST 1990

By 17 August, a number of units were on the move toward the Gulf. The 101st Airborne, the 1st, 2nd, 4th and 7th marine expeditionary brigades, the 1st Cavalry Division, the Tiger Brigade of the 2nd Armored Division, the 3rd Armored Cavalry, USS *Wisconsin,* and dozens of wings of fighters, bombers, and transports were heading to the Gulf. Some who questioned U.S. policy in the Gulf felt this deployment was overkill, but General Norman Schwarzkopf had learned from Vietnam the problems of gradual escalation. Also on 17 August, the military activated Stage 1 of the Civil Reserve Air Fleet (CRAF) and some thirty-seven civilian airliners pressed into military service.

Inside Iraq and Kuwait, a number of American civilians were being held by the Iraqis to discourage the use of military forces. These hostages, called "human shields," were placed at several strategic military bases around the country so that they would be killed by U.S. bombs. The release of these hostages came at a slow pace with many famous personalities traveling to

EXECUTIVE ORDER 12728
Delegating the President's Authority to Suspend Any Provision of Law Relating to the Promotion, Retirement, or Separation of Members of the Armed Forces

22 August 1990

By the authority vested in me as President by the Constitution and the laws of the United States of America, including sections 673c of title 10 of the United States Code and section 301 of title 3 of the United States Code, I hereby order:

Section 1. The Secretary of Defense, the Secretary of Transportation with respect to the Coast Guard when it is not operating as a service in the Department of the Navy, are hereby designated and empowered to exercise, without the approval, ratification, or other action of the President, the authority vested in the President by section 673c of title 10 of the United States Code (1) to suspend any provision of law relating to promotion, retirement, or separation applicable to any member of the armed forces which are essential to the national security of the United States.

Section 2. The authority delegated to the Secretary of Defense and the Secretary of Transportation by this order may be redelegated and further subdelegated to subordinates who are appointed to their offices by the President, by and with the advice and consent of the Senate.

Section 3. This order is intended only to improve the internal management of the executive branch and is not intended to create any right or benefit, substantive or procedural, enforceable at law by a party against the United States, its agencies, its officers, or any person.

George Bush

Iraq and leaving with a few hostages here and there. In fact, it was not until 6 December that all hostages were released, the result of an order issued by Saddam Hussein.

22 AUGUST 1990

On 22 August, the president implemented the first call-up of Guard and Reserve forces since the Vietnam War by signing executive orders 12727 and 12728. The specifics in these resolutions can be found on the previous pages.

This action was made necessary by the Pentagon's policy of integrating essential units in wartime with a mix of active and reserve components. The military had designed this policy to ensure that any war we would enter into would require a massive mobilization and support.

Inside Kuwait tales of horror and tragedy were slowly coming to public light. The Iraqis were reportedly destroying the Kuwaiti infrastructure, torturing citizens on the streets, and looting and pillaging the riches of the conquered Arab kingdom. As economic sanctions began to take hold, food became more difficult to acquire.

Throughout the first months, Allied intelligence showed a marked increase in enemy forces in the Kuwaiti Theatre of Operations. The initial invasion force had been doubled in a matter of weeks and by October, some 400,000 Iraqis were facing off against a U.S. force of about 240,000. Refer to Chapter 3 for details of the comparison between U.S., Allied, and Iraqi forces.

American forces in the Gulf used this time to prepare and train for the eventual battle. Air force units practiced refueling missions and desert environment flying tactics. Ground forces worked on breaching exercises to cross over the Iraqi defenses that had been established. Some units were required to retrain with new equipment, such as the Army units that obtained more advanced M1-A1s upon arrival to the Gulf.

Preparing for the storm. During the fall of 1990, Armed forces prepared with critical maneuvers such as this refueling of a KC-135. *Source: U.S. Navy*

8 NOVEMBER 1990

On 8 November, President Bush moved to change the face of the Gulf Crisis. He announced that U.S. forces in the region would be nearly doubled to give American commanders the "offensive" option should it become necessary to enforce the U.N. sanctions. This additional deployment relied heavily on U.S. forces in the European theatre, bringing in the 7th Corps, along with the 1st Armored Division stationed in Kansas. Appendixes A through E provide listings of units deployed.

EXECUTIVE ORDER 12734
National Emergency Construction Authority

14 November 1990

By the Authority vested in me as President by the Constitution and the laws of the United States of America, including the International Emergency Economic Powers Act (50 U.S.C. 1701 et seq.), the National Emergencies Act (50 U.S.C. 1601 et seq.) and 3 U.S.C. 301, I declared a national emergency by Executive Order No. 12722, dated August 2, 1990, to deal with the threat to the national security and foreign policy of the United States caused by the invasion of Kuwait by Iraq. To provide additional authority to the Department of Defense to respond to that threat, and in accordance with section 301 of the National Emergencies Act (50 U.S.C. 1631), I hereby order that the emergency construction authority at 10 U.S.C. 2808 is invoked and made available in accordance with its terms to the Secretary of Defense and, at the discretion of the Secretary of Defense, to the Secretaries of the military departments.

This order is effective immediately and shall be transmitted to the Congress and published in the Federal Register.

George Bush

Additionally, Bush signed Executive Order 12734 on 14 November, allowing redirection of military construction funds for priority projects in the Gulf.

The United States was not interested in a unilateral declaration of war against the Iraqis. President Bush, a former ambassador to the United Nations, recognized the value of U.N. support for American actions. The U.N. had passed eleven resolutions condemning the Iraqi invasion and Bush began work on one more. He dispatched top-level American officials to the nations of the security council to secure their support for the wording of a resolution that would set up a formal deadline for the removal of Iraqi forces from Kuwait.

29 NOVEMBER 1990

The all-important U.N. Resolution 678 was passed on 29 November and called for the Iraqis to withdraw by midnight 15 January 1991. The vote was 12 to 2 (Cuba and Yemen), with one abstention (China). The deadline was now set and it was up to Allied commanders to back up militarily this threat.

Matching the initial deployments in speed and effectiveness was the second round of shutting Allied forces into the region. American tanks from Europe and additional U.S. fighter wings were being rushed overseas to give credibility to the offensive option. Hundreds of thousands of Reservists were activated, some for duty in the Gulf and some taking the place of active-duty servicemen and servicewomen who were deployed. The idea that some of the troops would soon be rotated out of the Gulf and be home for Christmas was gone for good.

In Congress, there was considerable concern for the president's actions. Bush reportedly asked the leadership of the Congress to approve U.N. Resolution 678 a day after it was passed, but Congress refused. Many on Capitol Hill believed that sanctions should be given more time, but some speculated it was "politics as usual," with the Democrats unwilling to support a Republican president unless absolutely necessary. On a daily basis, many of the rank and file congressmembers took to the floor to denounce the administration for not seeking a diplomatic solution.

9 JANUARY 1991

To satisfy his critics, President Bush made one last attempt at a diplomatic solution by offering to send Secretary of State Baker to Baghdad and receiving the Iraqi Foreign Minister in Washington. For weeks this offer

RESOLUTION 678
United Nations Security Council

29 November 1990

The Security Council,

Recalling its resolutions 660 (1990), 661 (1990), 662 (1990), 664 (1990), 665 (1990), 666 (1990), 667 (1990), 670 (1990), 674 (1990), and 677 (1990),

Noting that despite all efforts by the United Nations, Iraq refuses to comply with its obligation to implement Resolution 660 (1990) and subsequent resolutions, in flagrant contempt of the Council,

Mindful of its duties and responsibilities under the Charter of the United Nations for the maintenance and preservation of international peace and security,

Determined to secure full compliance with its decisions,

Acting under Chapter VII of the Charter of the United Nations,

1. Demands that Iraq comply fully with Resolution 660 (1990) and all subsequent relevant resolutions and decides, while maintaining all its decisions, to allow Iraq one final opportunity, as a pause of goodwill, to do so;

2. Authorizes member States cooperating with the Government of Kuwait, unless Iraq on or before 15 January 1991, fully implements, as set forth in paragraph 1 above, the foregoing resolutions, to use all necessary means to uphold and implement the Security Council Resolution 660 and all subsequent relevant Resolutions and to restore international peace and security in the area;

3. Requests all states to provide appropriate support for the actions undertaken in pursuance of paragraph 2 of this resolution; and

4. Requests the states concerned to keep the Council regularly informed on the progress of actions undertaken pursuant to paragraphs 2 and 3 of this resolution;

5. Decides to remain seized of the matter.

VOTE: 12 for, 2 against (Cuba and Yemen), 1 abstention (China)

remained unanswered, although Saddam Hussein went out of his way to speak to other people who showed up in the Iraqi capital. Finally, on 9 January, Baker and Tariq Aziz agreed to a last-minute meeting in Geneva to discuss the situation in the Gulf. This was regarded as the last chance at averting a war. Throughout the meeting, the media reported that progress was being made. However, in the end, everything fell apart. A personal letter (included below) from President Bush to Saddam Hussein was not even accepted as the Iraqi government demonstrated its intransigence at peacefully ending the Gulf Crisis. War seemed more imminent now than ever.

12 JANUARY 1991

On Capitol Hill, the congressional leadership finally relented to the president's request and held a debate on a resolution in support of U.N. Resolution 678. Although this was not a declaration of war, it did fall within the

LETTER FROM PRESIDENT BUSH TO SADDAM HUSSEIN
(This letter was not accepted by the Iraqi government.)

5 January 1991 We stand today at the brink of war between Iraq and the world. This is a war that began with your invasion of Kuwait; this is a war that can be ended only by Iraq's full and unconditional compliance with U.N. Security Council Resolution 678.

I am writing you now, directly, because what is at stake demands that no opportunity be lost to avoid what would be certain calamity for the people of Iraq. I am writing as well, because it is said that you do not understand just how isolated Iraq is and what Iraq faces as a result.

I am not in a position to judge whether this impression is correct; what I can do, though, is try in this letter to reinforce what Secretary of State Baker told your Foreign Minister and eliminate any uncertainty or ambiguity that might exist in your mind about where we stand and what we are prepared to do.

The international community is united in its call for Iraq to leave all of Kuwait without condition and without further delay. This is not simply the policy of the United States; it is the position of the world community as expressed in no less than twelve Security Council resolutions.

We prefer a peaceful outcome. However, anything less than full compliance with U.N. Security Council Resolution 678 and its predecessors is unacceptable.

There can be no reward for aggression. Nor will there be any negotiation. Principle cannot be compromised. However, by its full compliance, Iraq will gain the opportunity to rejoin the international community.

More immediately, the Iraqi military establishment will escape destruction. But unless you withdraw from Kuwait completely and without condition, you will lose more than Kuwait.

What is at issue here is not the future of Kuwait — it will be free, its government will be restored — but rather the future of Iraq. This choice is yours to make.

The United States will not be separated from its coalition partners. Twelve Security Council resolutions, twenty-eight countries providing military units to enforce them, requirements of the War Powers Act and would authorize the president to commence offensive operations to eject Iraq from Kuwait.

After several days of debate, Congress finally voted on 12 January — three days before the deadline in the U.N. resolution — to allow the president to militarily eject Iraqi forces from Kuwait. Public Law 102-1 (H. J. Res. 77). This important action by Congress is on the next page.

From 12 January to 15 January 1991, all the world watched as the clock ticked down and no sign of withdrawal was seen. Iraqi statements continued to claim Kuwait as the 19th Province of Iraq and that they would never be separated. In the United States, the country heard President Bush state that offensive operations would take place "sooner rather than later" following the midnight deadline on 15 January. The deadline passed and all eyes turned to 16 January for the start of hostilities.

LETTER FROM PRESIDENT BUSH TO SADDAM HUSSEIN (continued)

more than 100 governments complying with sanctions — all highlight the fact that it is not Iraq against the United States, but Iraq against the world.

That most Arab and Muslim countries are arrayed against you as well should reinforce what I am saying. Iraq cannot and will not be able to hold on to Kuwait or exact a price for leaving.

You may be tempted to find solace in the diversity of opinion that is American democracy. You should resist any such temptation. Diversity ought not to be confused with division. Nor should you underestimate, as others have before you, America's will.

Iraq is already feeling the effects of the sanctions mandated by the United Nations. Should war come, it will be a far greater tragedy for you and your country.

Let me state, too, that the United States will not tolerate the use of chemical or biological weapons or the destruction of Kuwait's oil fields and installations. Further, you will be held directly responsible for terrorist actions against any member of the coalition.

The American people would demand the strongest possible response. You and your country will pay a terrible price if you order unconscionable acts of this sort.

I write this letter not to threaten, but to inform. I do so with no sense of satisfaction, for the people of the United States have no quarrel with the people of Iraq.

Mr. President, U.N. Security Council Resolution 678 establishes the period of January 15 of this year as a 'pause of goodwill' so that this crisis may end without further violence.

Whether this pause is used as intended, or merely becomes a prelude to further violence, is in your hands, and yours alone. I hope you weigh your choice carefully and choose wisely, for much will depend upon it.

George Bush

PUBLIC LAW 102-1 (H.J. RES. 77)
Solarz-Michel

12 January 1991 (The vote — 250-183 in the House and 52-47 in the Senate — is regarded as the key vote in the conduct of the Gulf Crisis.)

To authorize the use of United States Armed Forces pursuant to United Nations Security Council Resolution 678.

Whereas both the House of Representatives (in H. J. Res. 658 of the 101st Congress) and the Senate (in S. Con. Res. 147 of the 101st Congress) have condemned Iraq's invasion of Kuwait and declared their support for international action to reverse Iraq's aggression; and

Whereas, Iraq's conventional, chemical, biological, and nuclear weapons and ballistic missile programs and its demonstrated willingness to use weapons of mass destruction pose a grave threat to world peace; and

Whereas the international community has demanded that Iraq withdraw unconditionally and immediately from Kuwait and that Kuwait's independence and legitimate government restored; and

Whereas the U.N. Security Council repeatedly affirmed the inherent right of individual or collective self-defense in response to the armed attack by Iraq against Kuwait in accordance with Article 51 of the U.N. Charter; and

Whereas, in the absence of full compliance by Iraq with its resolutions, the U.N. Security Council in Resolution 678 has authorized member states of the United Nations to use all necessary means, after 15 January 1991, to uphold and implement all relevant Security Council resolutions and to restore international peace and security in the area; and

Whereas Iraq has persisted in its illegal occupation of, and brutal aggression against Kuwait: Now, therefore, be it

Resolved by the Senate and House of Representatives of the United States of America in Congress Assembled,

Section 1. Short Title.
This joint resolution may be cited as an "Authorization for Use of Military Force Against Iraq Resolution."

Section 2. Authorization for use of United States Armed Forces.

(a) Authorization. The President is authorized, subject to subsection (b), to use United States Armed Forces pursuant to United Nations Security Council Resolution 678 (1990) in order to achieve implementation of Security Council Resolutions 660, 661, 662, 664, 665, 666, 667, 669, 670, 674, and 677.

(b) Requirement for determination that use of military force is necessary. Before exercising the authority granted in subsection (a), the President shall make available to the Speaker of the House of Representatives and the President pro tempore of the Senate his determination that

(1) the United States has used all appropriate diplomatic and other peaceful means to obtain compliance by Iraq with the United Nations Security Council resolutions cited in subsection (a); and

(2) that those efforts have not been and would not be successful in obtaining such compliance.

(c) War powers resolution requirements.

(1) Specific Statutory Authorization. Consistent with section 8 (a)(1) of the War Powers Resolution, the Congress declares that this section is intended to constitute specific statutory authorization within the meaning of section 5(b) of the War Powers Resolution.

2) Applicability of other requirements. Nothing in this resolution supersedes any requirement of the War Powers Resolution.

Section 3. Reports to Congress.
At least once every 60 days, the President shall submit to the Congress a summary on the status of efforts to obtain compliance by Iraq with the resolutions adopted by the United Nations Security Council in response to Iraq's aggression.

Chapter Eight

Operation Desert Storm

Weeks One through Three

PLANNING THE AIR CAMPAIGN

While the first units were in the air and on their way to Saudi Arabia, the Air Staff at Central Command began planning for the conduct of the Gulf War air campaign under the codename "Instant Thunder." Under the command of Brigadier General Buster C. Glosson, the Air Staff set up shop in a basement storage room at the headquarters of the Royal Saudi Air Force. Glosson and his commander, Lieutenant General Charles Horner were veterans of Vietnam and vowed not to have a similar package of air strikes that they flew in Southeast Asia.

Instant Thunder was different from the gradual escalation that surrounded the "Rolling Thunder" air campaign in Vietnam during the 1960s. Instead, Instant Thunder was designed to destroy eighty-four strategic targets within the first week of the war. On 25 August, the plan was presented to Secretary of Defense Cheney with four broad phases.

- **Phase I.** A strategic air campaign against Iraq.
- **Phase II.** A Kuwait air campaign against Iraqi air forces in the KTO
- **Phase III.** A ground combat power attrition to neutralize the Republican Guards and isolate the Kuwait battlefield.
- **Phase IV.** A ground attack, to eject Iraq from Kuwait.

For the next few months, this plan was refined and details added. Even lawyers were consulted to clarify what targets constituted "cultural" relics and could not be attacked under international law. The eighty-four strategic targets would require six days of good weather and about 700 sorties. As planning continued, the list of strategic targets moved to 600 with 300 eventually being added to the target list. The attacks on Iraqi ground forces, Phase III, was run through a series of computer simulations. It was suggested that it would take a month of air attacks to destroy 75 to 80 percent of the Iraqi armor, vehicles, trucks and artillery of the Regular Army in Kuwait. Phase III, the attacks on the Republican Guards, was moved up to coincide with the

Phase I, and the Republican Guards were thought to enforce loyalty amongst the Regular Army.

As planning continued, five objectives were sought, with twelve target sets attacked to secure those objectives.

- **OBJECTIVE 1.**
  Isolate and incapacitate the Iraqi Regime.

  Target Set 1
  Leadership and command facilities;

  Target Set 2
  Crucial electrical facilities powering military facilities; and

  Target Set 3
  Telecommunications facilities and C3 systems.
- **OBJECTIVE 2.**
  Gain air superiority.

  Target Set 4
  Strategic air-defense systems, including radars and missiles; and

  Target Set 5
  Air forces and airfields.
- **OBJECTIVE 3.**
  Destroy nuclear, chemical, and biological (NBC) warfare capability.

  Target Set 6
  Known NBC research, production, and storage facilities.
- **OBJECTIVE 4.**
  Destroy Iraq's offensive military capability.

  Target Set 7
  Military production and storage sites;

  Target Set 8
  SCUD missile launchers, production, and storage sites;

  Target Set 9
  Oil refining and distribution facilities; and

  Target Set 10
  Naval forces and port facilities.
- **OBJECTIVE 5.**
  Collapse Iraqi Army and mechanized forces.

  Target Set 11
  Railroads and bridges used by the military; and

  Target Set 12
  Army units, including the Republican Guards.

A Master Attack Plan (MAP) was formulated which was a single, concise plan consolidating all aspects of the battle. This plan focused around the twelve target sets and the best weapons system to achieve the desired effect against a target was chosen. This plan was modified as bomb damage assessment arrived and other factors, like weather and intelligence, were factored in. The original MAP for the first day was only twenty-one pages. It contained the sequence of attachés for a 24-hour period and included the time on target, target number, description, number, and type of weapons systems and supporting systems for each package.

An Air Tasking Order (ATO) was then issued giving details and guidance to the aircrews. Things like target assignments, routes, altitudes, refueling tracks, fuel offloads, call signs, IFF codes, and other details were included in the ATOs. These were prepared on a laptop computer, printed out (around 100 to 300 pages) and checked for accuracy. After the corrections were made, they were electronically distributed to the different units via the Computer Assisted Force Management System (CAFMS).

On a day-to-day basis, there were three big events:

- The day's attacks
- The ATO for tomorrow
- The MAP formulation for the day after tomorrow

Intelligence shortcomings and slow bomb damage assessment hampered the creation of the next MAPs, but planners merely improvised to complete their mission.

To help separate air strike elements and prevent the inefficiency of striking the same target, air planners developed the kill box system. This system centered around 30 by 30 mile grids drawn over the KTO and subdivided into four quadrants. Then, each quadrant was assigned a flight for a specific period of time where aircraft operating were allowed to locate and attack targets of opportunity.

PLANNING THE GROUND WAR

As early as 25 August, General Schwarzkopf had an outline for a four-phase campaign ending with a ground campaign. In mid-September, the Army assembled a group of officers to develop a course of action for the ground offensive. These officers — called the "Jedi Knights" — were graduates of the Army School of Advanced Military Studies (SAMS) at Fort Leavenworth, Kansas.

The planners came to several conclusions and operational imperatives that would become central planning tenets throughout the offensive. First, the air campaign would have to reduce Iraqi combat effectiveness in the KTO by half for the ground campaign to be successful. Second, coalition forces would need to engage enemy units necessary to achieve coalition objectives while bypassing other enemy forces. Third, tactical battlefield intelligence would be required so that fire power could be placed on target quickly before the target could move.

Clearing a path. The AH-64 Apaches' initial objective was to destroy as many front-line radar and command centers as possible. *Source: U.S. Government Department of Defense*

On 6 October, the planners presented a course of action calling for one corps leading a frontal attack into Kuwait from Saudi Arabia. The objective was to get to the high ground of the Mutla Pass and Ridge near Kuwait City. General Schwarzkopf judged this plan as risky, in that it could lead to high casualties and cause the Republican Guards to escape. He briefed Powell and Cheney that success could not be guaranteed with the existing balance of forces. He received guidance from Cheney to look at an "envelopment" by two Army Corps of Iraqi forces. The VII Corps in Germany was the logical choice given its proximity to the theatre and modern equipment. To give the Corps more mobility, the 1st Infantry Division from Fort Riley, Kansas, was also deployed. Planning also continued for an amphibious assault on Kuwait, although no such invasion was used in the eventual operation.

The plan that was to become the "Hail Mary" sweeping motion and envelopment of the Iraqi military forces was presented to the secretary of defense in extensive briefings on 19 December and 20 December. The logistics buildup to the ground war would take two weeks, repositioning of forces another two weeks. The actual ground offensive was to take two weeks, mopping up operations another four weeks. The secretary approved the plans, but determined it would require the president's approval before actual operations could commence.

WEEK ONE

Day 1

Thursday, 17 January 1991 (16 January 1991 EST)

A great deal of activity in the Persian Gulf War took place in the early morning hours Saudi Arabia time, which were the late afternoon hours in the United States. Thus, while something could have occurred on say a Tuesday in the Gulf, Americans watching the evening news would learn about it on a Monday. This has caused some confusion in compiling a record of the day-by-day chronology of the Gulf War. This book attempts to provide the most accurate timing possible.

Military

Throughout the day, rumors were rampant of imminent military action. The deadline set by U.N. Resolution 678 of midnight EST, 15 January had passed and indications from the administration were that military actions would commence "sooner rather than later." However, Washington was filled with rumors, and those who truly knew when the operations were to begin were not talking to anyone.

Unbeknownst to all but a select few in the military and the White House, the decision to go to war was made the day before, on Tuesday, 15 January when President Bush signed a national security directive authorizing the use of force unless some last minute diplomatic settlement was reached or Iraqi forces withdrew in mass from Kuwait. He then told Secretary Cheney he was authorized to sign the "execute" order that would be passed to the military National Command Authority after the U.N. deadline passed. It was then up to the command structure to implement the plan that they had worked so many months to create. Wednesday morning, National Security Advisor Brent Scowcroft informed Cheney that there was no change in plans and he should proceed as previously directed.

On the morning (Eastern Standard Time) of 16 January 1991, B-52 bombers took off from Louisiana carrying conventionally armed air-launched cruise missiles. These missiles were launched approximately two hours before "H-Hour." About ninety minutes before H-Hour, additional Tomahawks were launched from USS *San Jacinto* in the Persian Gulf and moments later from USS *Bunker Hill* in the Red Sea.

Around midnight in the Gulf (1630 EST, 16 January), the first fighter aircraft

Destination Baghdad. After a path through the Iraqi anti-aircraft systems had been made, fighters such as these Tornadoes headed to the capital. *Source: French Government*

were launched from Saudi Arabia and off U.S. carriers in the region. These were joined by tankers, electronic warfare, and command and control aircraft. Helicopter "extraction" units were alerted should a pilot have gone down and have needed to be rescued from behind enemy lines. Their targets had been decided upon months ago by Air Force planners, and an Aircraft Tasking Order (ATO) had been issued, specifying which units would attack which targets at what times. Table 8.1 lists Day 1 targets.

TABLE 8.1
DAY 1 TARGETS IN BAGHDAD
Directorate of Military Intelligence
Five telephone switching stations
Ministry of Defense National Computer Complex
Electrical transfer station
Ministry of Defense Headquarters
Ashudad highway bridge
Railroad yard
Muthena Airfield
Air Force Headquarters
Iraqi Intelligence Service
Secret Police compound
Army storage depot
Republican Guard Headquarters
New Presidential Palace
Electrical power station
SCUD assembly building
Baath Party headquarters
Government conference center
Ministry of Industry and Military Production
Ministry of Propaganda
TV transmitter
Two communication relay stations
Jumhuriya highway bridge
Government Control Center South
Karada (14 July) highway bridge
Presidential Palace Command Center
Presidential Palace Command Bunker
Secret Police Headquarters
Iraqi Intelligence Service Regional Headquarters
National Air Defense Operations Center
Ad Dawrah Oil Refinery
Electrical power plant

The first aircraft to penetrate Iraqi airspace were MH-53J Pave Low special operations helicopters from the 1st Special Operations Wing (SOW) along with AH-64 Apaches of the 101st Airborne. Their mission was to eliminate many of the front-line anti-aircraft radar and command centers. They attacked just as the first EF-111 Raven radar jamming aircraft came into radar coverage. The aim of Allied planners was to decimate the country-wide system of anti-aircraft and force each Iraqi unit to act independent of other Iraqi forces. Through this breach flew EF-111 Ravens, electronic warfare aircraft, and F-4G Wild Weasel air defense suppression jets — clearing a path through the anti-aircraft systems straight into Baghdad. These were followed by F-117 Stealth aircraft, F-15E Strike Eagles, and GR-1 Tornadoes.

At 0235 on 17 January, Baghdad time, CNN reporters described the scene of anti-aircraft fire arching into the sky and of large explosions coming from the outskirts of Baghdad. At first, they were unsure if they were really under attack or this was merely an accidental firing on the part of Iraqi air defense systems. But a large bomb blast heard over reporters' telephone lines confirmed that the war had begun. Back home, millions of Americans called their friends and family telling them to watch their televisions. This was the beginning of the first "live" television war.

The first wave. F-18s assisted in leading the strike on the primary objectives of the initial strike on Iraq. *Source: U.S. Air Force*

As Allied bombs continued to drop, the central telephone exchange was knocked out of service. With it went most of the major American networks covering the war from Baghdad, but CNN had a special "four-wire" telephone link to the United States that ran through a separate facility. Thus, CNN fascinated the world by staying on live throughout the first night of attacks.

Around 0244 on 17 January, Baghdad time, F-117 Stealth fighters dropped their bombs on several targets in and around Baghdad. Priority targets were command and control functions that could control the Iraqi military's response. The telephone exchange, communications centers, and many of Iraq's military command headquarters were taken out in this first wave of Operation Desert Storm. The first wave of attackers was actually three separate groups, including thirty F-117s and fifty-four Tomahawk cruise missiles. These attacks, and attacks elsewhere in the KTO, were joined by Tomahawk cruise missiles launched from ships in the Persian/Arabian Gulf and other aircraft such as the F-15Es and F-18s from the carrier forces. Free Kuwait, Saudi Arabian, and British forces also joined in these initial air attacks.

Later that night, Washington time, nearing the dawn of the 17th, Baghdad time, A-10s and F-16s commenced attacks on Iraqi ground forces and radar sites in Kuwait and Iraq. USMC strikes were launched against Iraqi air bases and armor units. USAF F-15Es attacked permanent SCUD missile launch sites, but mobile launchers were still operational. Nuclear, chemical, and biological (NBC) sites were also attacked on the opening day.

As the reports came in, it was discovered only one U.S. aircraft, a Navy F-18 Hornet had been lost. The aircraft, based on USS *Saratoga,* was originally listed as hit by an anti-aircraft missile, and its pilot, Lieutenant Commander Michael Scott Speicher, was listed as missing — later declared killed in action. Later evidence pointed out that it was shot down in a dogfight with an Iraqi MIG-25PD, which, as it would turn out, was the only such American loss during the entire war. The F-18 was flying a Suppression of Enemy Defense Mission (SEAD) when its wingman encountered a MIG. The MIG disengaged and Lieutenant Commander Speicher launched his HARM at his target. But, in doing so, he likely indicated his position to the Iraqi MIG which shot him down, probably with an AA-6 missile. A French Jaguar and a Kuwaiti A-4KU were also downed. For a detailed list of coalition air losses, see Appendix F.

Surprisingly, Iraq's highly-regarded Air Force was nowhere to be seen. With the exception of minor artillery shelling of a small Saudi border town called Khafji, Iraq offered no defense and no retaliation. Its Air Force remained on the ground and anti-aircraft weapons were fired without guidance and haphazardly, hoping to hit an attacking aircraft. More than 200 HARM anti-radar missiles were fired on this first night, along with a number of tactical air-launched decoys (TALDs). These TALDs confused Iraqi defenders and may have led to Saddam's erroneous statements that nearly eighty attacking warplanes were shot down, when in reality they were simply crashing decoys. Nearly 700 U.S. combat aircraft entered Iraqi airspace.

Diplomatic

Under the resolution passed by the House and Senate a few days before, Congress had effectively taken itself out of the day-to-day operations in the Gulf. Nevertheless, President Bush chose to notify Congressional leaders of his decision early Wednesday morning. The leadership of the Congress and the military-related committees were told to find "secure" phones and await a phone call from the president. They were then informed that the attack would come that evening.

Bush then made his way through the coalition forces, sometimes contacting leaders directly and sometimes allowing Secretary of State James Baker to inform their ambassadors of the pending action. After the planes were launched, the Soviet foreign minister was informed of the attack, and he immediately relayed this message to President Gorbachev. Gorbachev called Bush to see if he could relay a message to Saddam to pull out, but his message was not delivered until after the first bombs began dropping.

Domestic

Around the country, heartbeats sped up and tears were shed as the first reports of military action trickled in over the television. The bombing had made CNN — the only network with a feed into Baghdad — the number one source of news. Smaller independent stations, even the British Broadcasting Corporation (BBC), dumped their evening programming and broadcast CNN all night. Even some of the cable movie stations broadcast written messages across their screens so that their viewers could change the channel and watch the news.

At 0300 on 17 January, Baghdad time, Marlin Fitzwater walked into the White House briefing room to deliver a brief statement on the initiation of hostilities. Had it not been for the instant satellite coverage, his words would have been the first to indicate that the battle had begun. Instead, he merely restated what was obvious to anyone watching television, and gave the country a new codename to memorize: Operation Desert Storm. The name was suggested months earlier by General Schwarzkopf after hearing the codename Operation Desert Shield.

At 2100 EST, President Bush addressed the country with a speech he had been working on for some time. It was not a long speech, but in it he assured the nation that this battle was just, and that he fully intended to bring the troops home as soon as it was possible to do so. One other statement that brought cheers from many veterans of the Vietnam War was the president's assurance that this war "would not be fought with one hand tied behind our back."

Bush finished his remarks and returned to his office to follow the course of the battle. His statement became the most watched event in television history, with

GEORGE BUSH'S SPEECH
Commencement of Ground War in Operation Desert Storm

23 February 1991

Good evening. Yesterday, after conferring with my senior national security advisers, and following extensive consultations with our coalition partners, Saddam Hussein was given one last chance — set forth in very explicit terms — to do what he should have done more than 6 months ago: withdraw from Kuwait without further condition or further delay, and comply fully with the resolutions passed by the United Nations Security Council.

Regrettably, the noon deadline passed without the agreement of the Government of Iraq to meet demands of United Nations Security Council Resolution 660, as set forth in the specific terms spelled out by the coalition to withdraw unconditionally from Kuwait. To the contrary, what we have seen is a redoubling of Saddam Hussein's efforts to destroy completely Kuwait and its people.

I have therefore, directed General Norman Schwarzkopf, in conjunction with coalition forces, to use all forces available, including ground forces, to eject the Iraqi Army from Kuwait. Once again, this was a decision made only after extensive consultations within our coalition partnership.

The liberation of Kuwait has now entered a final phase. I have complete confidence in the ability of the coalition forces to swiftly and decisively accomplish their mission.

Tonight, as this coalition of countries seeks to do that which is right and just, I ask only that all of you stop what you are doing and say a prayer for all the coalition forces, and especially for our men and women in uniform who this very moment are risking their lives for their country and for all of us.

May God bless and protect each and every one of them. And may God bless the United States of America. Thank you very much.

George Bush

nearly 80 percent of the television viewers watching his speech. Bush's speech is located on the previous page.

Outside the White House, a handful of demonstrators showed up to protest the advent of war, but the situation was so fluid that few people could tear themselves away from their televisions; no one wanted to leave their homes. Many people stayed up late into the early morning hours watching the television coverage, hoping for more information about the war. When early polls were released, they showed that nearly 80 percent of the American people supported the president's actions.

Day 2
Friday, 18 January 1991
(Thursday, 17 January 1991 EST)

Military

Allied military strikes continued against Iraq with aircraft striking Iraqi command and control facilities along with attacks against the Iraqi Air Force. Reports later indicated that the Iraqis offered some resistance on the second day of fighting. There were a number of Iraqi combat air patrols operational and U.S. forces engaged some aircraft in air-to-air combat, downing eight Iraqi aircraft in dogfights. See Chapter 11 for a list of the exact air-to-air kills. The target packages for the second day included many of the same types of targets hit on the first day — air defenses, biological and chemical facilities, and enemy airfields.

Joining the attacks today were B-52 bombers which were used to attack the Republican Guard units stationed in Northern Kuwait and Southern Iraq. These thirty-year-old bombers, launched from bases inside Saudi Arabia and the island of Diego Garcia, had been upgraded many times since their original construction and delivered devastating loads of explosives on enemy forces.

Attack packages were created to hit the Republican Guard divisions in Kuwait. Three armored divisions were targeted and hit, including:

- Tawakalna Mechanized Infantry; which consisted of ninety F-16s, eight F/A-18s, and three B-52s;
- Hammurabi Armored Division, consisting of sixteen F/A-18s and three B-52s; and
- Al-Madinah Armored Division, including twenty-four F-16s and three B-52s.

Naval aircraft and warships continued their attack, concentrating on naval installations and coastal facilities. Half of the initial strikes from the Persian Gulf naval forces were against Iraqi naval facilities, oil platforms, and coastal defense sites. RAF Tornadoes continued their attacks against Iraqi airfields and runways. Eight coalition aircraft were downed today, four of them U.S. Several of the pilots were captured and taken as prisoners of war.

Near the border of Iraq and Jordan and the border of Iraq and Kuwait, the Iraqi military was preparing a response to the air attacks. Mobile SCUD missile launchers were being readied to launch their weapons against Saudi Arabia and Israel, in an attempt to bring the Jewish country into a war with the Arab world. These missiles, which have similar characteristics to the German V-2 in World War II, were not considered effective against military targets as their guidance system was not that advanced, and served only as a threat to civilian populations.

Domestic

In the United States, a feeling of euphoria and confidence swept the country. Thousands of sorties had been launched, and only one American pilot had been lost. Chairman Powell claimed that 80 percent of the sorties were rated as effective in delivering their ordnance on target. Some commentators were beginning to talk of a "one week air war." But that evening, the Iraqis effectively dashed these hopes.

Once again, the evening news began the best conduit for intelligence out of the region. Correspondents in Israel were breaking in to regular news coverage to bring news of air raid sirens in Tel Aviv and Jerusalem. Moments later, the reporters in Saudi Arabia were reporting the same. The news anchors in Washington could do little but watch as their counterparts in the region quickly donned gas masks and moved into sealed rooms for fear of a chemical attack. SCUD missiles had been launched against both countries, and there was concern that they would carry chemically armed warheads. One missile was launched against Saudi Arabia and seven were sent toward Israel.

The missiles against Saudi Arabia were intercepted in what would become a common occurrence. An American Patriot missile, originally designed for an anti-aircraft role, had been recently modified to intercept short-range ballistic missiles. The Patriot hit the SCUD and debris fell over Dhahran harmlessly. The seven missiles over Israel were not intercepted and landed in Tel Aviv and Haifa, causing extensive damage and injuring at least seven.

Day 3
Saturday, 19 January 1991
(Friday, 18 January 1991 EST)

Military

In an effort to prevent the Israelis from retaliating, the United States promised to make SCUD missile launchers a priority target. A large portion of Allied sorties were redirected to hunt and kill Iraq's many mobile SCUD launchers. On Day 3, approximately eleven mobile SCUD launchers were engaged, and Allied commanders were hopeful this would lessen the threat from these psychologically damaging weapons. Despite these attacks, Iraq again launched SCUD missiles toward Israel. This time three SCUDs fell on Tel Aviv, causing about ten injuries and major property damage. Again Israel remained silent, acceding to U.S. wishes that it not retaliate for these attacks.

For the first time, air attacks came from air bases inside Turkey. These attacks by F-111s were concentrated in northern Iraq and were significant not because of their military value, but because clearly put Turkey on the side of coalition forces. Despite the Turkish people's opposition to the war, President Ozal allowed the attacks from Turkish soil in what many observers felt was his desire to move more toward the Western world. In addition, Iraq had about 150,000 troops on the Turkish border that were threatening Turkey.

On the ground, the minor artillery duel between Iraqi and Allied forces near the border town of Khafji intensified slightly with U.S. Marines returning fire and calling in air strikes on the Iraqi positions. The Iraqi battery was reported as "silenced" but later artillery duels continued in the same area.

Throughout Saudi Arabia, Allied ground units were in transit toward the Kuwaiti border. Media sources in the region reported seeing convoys of hundreds of vehicles heading north toward the border. Despite the reporters' claims of an imminent ground war, Allied military briefers went out of their way to make it known the war would take a long time.

A new priority target. SCUD attacks into Saudi Arabia and Israel prompted the U.S. forces to destroy as many mobile SCUD launchers as possible. *Source: U.S. Government Department of Defense*

At sea, the Navy engaged three enemy patrol boats operating in the northern Persian Gulf. Iraq's Navy — a number of small coastal patrol craft — was considered a minimal threat, but some of its craft were capable of minelaying operations and a few had the capability of launching the ship-killing Exocet missile. It became clear, the destruction of Iraqi naval forces would need to be accomplished before any amphibious operations could commence.

Also at sea, USS *Louisville,* a Los Angeles class attack submarine, launched five TLAM cruise missiles into Iraq from the Red Sea. This was the first combat for a U.S. submarine since World War II. Additional Tomahawk missiles were fired by warships.

Back in the United States, President Bush declared a national emergency and authorized an additional mobilization of reserve and guard troops for an additional twelve months. This action was made official in Executive Order 12743. The following page contains the exact wording of this order. In addition, Secretary Cheney activated Stage II of the Civil Reserve Air Fleet, which placed additional civilian aircraft into service.

Diplomatic

Suffering from several SCUD missile attacks, many believed that Israel would finally be brought into this conflict. All indications were that the Israeli government was fully prepared to attack Iraq. Some reports even claimed

EXECUTIVE ORDER 12743
Ordering the Ready Reserve of the Armed Forces to Active Duty

18 January 1991 By the authority vested in me as President by the Constitution and the laws of the United States of America, including the National Emergencies Act (50 U.S.C. 1601 et. seq.), and section 301 of title 3 of the United States Code; in furtherance of Executive Order 12722, dated August 2, 1990, which declared a national emergency to address the threat to the national security and foreign policy of the United States posed by the invasion of Kuwait by Iraq; and, in accordance with the requirements contained in section 301 of the National Emergencies Act, 50 U.S.C. 1631, I hereby order as follows.

Section 1. To provide additional authority to the Department of Defense and the Department of Transportation to respond to continuing threat posed by Iraq's invasion of Kuwait, the authority under section 673 of title 10, United States Code, to order any unit, and any member not assigned to a unit organized to serve as a unit, in the Ready Reserve to active duty (other than for training) for not more than 24 consecutive months, is invoked and made available, according to its terms, to the Secretary concerned, subject, in the case of the Secretaries of the Army, Navy and Air Force, to the direction of the Secretary of Defense. The term "Secretary concerned" is defined in section 101(8) of title 10, United States Code, to mean the Secretary of the Army with respect to the Army, the Secretary of the Navy with respect to the Navy, the Marine Corps and the Coast Guard when it is operating as a service in the Navy; the Secretary of the Air Force, with respect to the Air Force; and, the Secretary of Transportation with respect to the Coast Guard when it is not operating as a service in the Navy.

Section 2. To allow for orderly administration of personnel within the armed forces, the authority vested in the President by section 527 of title 10, United States Code, to suspend the operation of sections 523-526 of title 10, United States Code, regarding officer strength and officer distribution in grade, is invoked to the full extent provided by the terms thereof.

Section 3. To allow for the orderly administration of personnel within the armed forces, the authority vested in the President by section 644 of title 10, United States Code, to suspend the operation of any provision of law relating to the promotion, involuntary retirement, or separation of commissioned officers of the Army, Navy, Air Force, or Marine Corps, is invoked to the full extent provided by the terms thereof.

Section 4. The Secretary of Defense is hereby designated and empowered, without the approval, ratification, or other action by the President, to exercise the authority vested in the President by section 527 and 644 of title 10, United States Code, as invoked by sections 2 and 3 of this order, to suspend the operation of certain provisions of law.

Section 5. The authorities delegated by sections 1 and 4 of this order may be redelegated and further subdelegated to civilian subordinates who are appointed to their offices by the President, by and with the advice and consent of the Senate.

Section 6. This order is intended to improve the internal management of the executive branch, and is not intended to create any right or benefit, substantive or procedural, enforceable at law by a party against the United States, its agencies, its officers, or any person.

Section 7. This order is effective immediately, and shall be transmitted to the Congress and published in the Federal Register.

George Bush

it had aircraft in the air, but the United States would not give them the Identification Friend or Foe (IFF) codes that would enable them to fly safely through Allied anti-aircraft. In addition, several Arab countries refused Israel overflight rights through their airspace on the way to Iraq.

Besides these practical considerations, President Bush and Secretary Baker were engaged in a diplomatic offensive with the Israeli government. This was a change from the frigid relations the United States had with Israel during the previous two years because of a dispute over the occupied territories. Now, the U.S. administration was on the phone constantly trying to secure assurances that Israel would not enter the war and cause possible problems in the Arab coalition. With the arrival of Patriot missiles, and the assurances of the United States that SCUD hunting would remain a major priority, Israel stated it would not attack at this time.

Day 4
Sunday, 20 January 1991
(Saturday, 19 January 1991 EST)

Military

Given the apparent success of the Patriot missile system in Saudi Arabia, and the desire of the United States to maintain Israeli's restraint, the United States sent Patriot units to Israel along with American crews to operate the system. Although Israel had agreed to buy the system from the United States earlier, it insisted that Israeli Defense Forces (IDF) troops man the batteries. As the IDF had not finished its training with the system, it became necessary for the first time to have American combat troops provide protection to the people of Israel. Israel's military troops were put on an accelerated training schedule to eventually take over the Patriot.

To supplement the Patriots, Allied warplanes increased their attacks on mobile SCUD sites throughout Iraq. Also, unknown to most, British Special Air Services (SAS) and American special forces launched a series of daring raids in enemy territory to knock out the launchers.

In the northern Persian Gulf, the frigate USS *Nicholas,* along with the Kuwaiti fast-attack craft *Istiqlal,* conducted the first surface action of the war. They attacked an Iraqi position on an off-shore oil platform. The platform was being used as a base for anti-aircraft fire that American aircraft considered a threat. The *Nicholas* attacked the platform, and then Navy special forces seized the facility, taking twenty-three Iraqi soldiers prisoner. Five Iraqis were killed in the attacks. Also at sea, two Marine task forces of assault ships moved into the Gulf.

Allied forces reported more vigorous defenses from Iraqi troops. Six Iraqi aircraft were downed, bringing the total downed Iraqi aircraft to fourteen. SCUD missile sights remained a priority along with power plants and telephone exchanges in the city of Baghdad. By the end of the day, the Pentagon claimed "air superiority" and indicated it would change its attack strategy from Iraq's command and control to direct attacks on Iraqi troops in Kuwait.

On the ground, Allied forces again came under attack from Iraqi artillery units. Marine units, linking up with A-10 Thunderbolts and attack helicopters, attacked these positions and destroyed several artillery pieces. Four Marines were wounded by Iraqi artillery — one seriously. There were additional reports of ground skirmishes between Allied patrols and Iraqi forces.

Inside Saudi Arabia, troop deployments continued toward the border, including the 101st and 82nd airborne units moving forward, accompanied by elements of the British "Desert Rats" and the French Foreign Legion. These units were being positioned for the coming ground offensive and to spread out Allied forces from possible counterattacks.

Later in the day, Secretary of Defense Cheney authorized the call-up of an additional 170,000 Reservists. This notification was done under new authority that extended the Reservist's time on active duty from three months to one year. Many of these Reservists were from the Individual Ready Reserve — former soldiers and sailors who retired and remained in the Reserves.

The Patriot counterattacks. A Patriot battery includes up to eight launchers, each with four MIM-104 missiles and support equipment. *Source: U.S. Government Department of Defense*

WEEK TWO
Day 5
Monday, 21 January 1991
(Sunday, 20 January 1991 EST)

Military

The SCUD war continued on this day with the Patriot system having its most successful test. Ten missiles were launched at Saudi Arabia — nine were intercepted by Patriots, and one fell harmlessly into the Persian Gulf. Although Americans were in awe of the Patriot's ability to track and intercept these multiple in-bound missiles, American military planners were dismayed by the fact that their concentrated efforts at the SCUD launchers were still not entirely successful. After the war, the success of the Patriot was brought into question. But many servicemen and civilians were in awe of it apparent success.

American air raids continued to strike deep into Iraq and it was confirmed that Iraq's four primary nuclear power plants had been disabled. Iraq had been attempting to build a nuclear weapon for some time and, with the help of the Soviet Union and France, built several reactors and research facilities capable of producing the necessary materials for a bomb. The bombing of these facilities, along with Saddam's chemical weapons plants, indicated to some that the United States was not merely interested in evicting

Iraq from Kuwait, but assuring the region and the world that Iraq was incapable of mounting a serious threat for some time to come.

Monday's losses were considered relatively heavy. Three American aircraft were downed, making this the highest loss of aircraft in one day for the first week of operations. To date, nine American aircraft had been shot down, one crashed because of mechanical difficulty, and one was rendered nonoperative upon returning to its carrier. Despite these losses, Allied commanders were pleased to see such limited losses after flying 7,000 sorties.

An American F-14A was shot down over Iraq, but for the first time, American extraction units were able to rescue the pilot. The pilot was on the ground for nearly eight hours while two A-10 Thunderbolts circled him and arranged for helicopter transportation to get him out. Refueling several times, the A-10s maintained a constant vigil against enemy units that might have threatened the life of the downed pilot. Just as the helicopters approached, an Iraqi truck drove on the scene, which was destroyed by the A-10s. With Allied pilots seeing their captured colleagues on television, the rescue of this downed pilot was a great morale boost.

Some air losses. Day 5 saw three downed American aircraft. Despite this, Allied commanders were still encouraged considering 7,000 sorties had been flown to date. *Source: U.S. Navy*

The main story of the day was when Iraqi television showed broadcast interviews with seven Allied servicemen taken as prisoners of war — three of them Americans. The airmen, shot down throughout the Kuwaiti Theatre of Operations, appeared injured with several bruises on their faces. Although many Americans suspected torture, no one was able to discern if these wounds came from their planes crashing or at the hands of their captors. The captured flyers spoke slowly, identifying themselves, their units, and then adding "statements" about the war "against the peaceful people of Iraq." These statements were not regarded as credible, and in one case, it appeared if one pilot was reading from a cue card. A detailed POW list is included in Appendix F.

There were no indications of Iraqi ground maneuvers or artillery but as a result of earlier fighting, the first Purple Heart was awarded. Navy medic Clerence Conner of Hemet, California, was stationed with a Marine unit that came under fire near Khafji during the opening days of the war. The 19-year-old medic received a shrapnel wound with a jagged piece of metal wounding his right shoulder.

Diplomatic

In Israel, American Deputy Secretary of State Lawrence S. Eagleburger met with government officials to solidify Israeli restraint in the face of continued Iraqi SCUD attacks. Eagleburger sought to mend the rift between the United States and Israel that had developed during the previous year over settlement of Soviet Jews in occupied lands. With the crisis under way, President Bush and Secretary Baker broke from their policy of virtually ignoring the Israeli government to frequent contact and consultation with Yitzhak Shamir.

Domestic

The pictures of American POWs on television galvanized support behind the president and against the Iraqi government. Many former POWs from Vietnam recognized the fear that the new POWs showed and felt sympathy for their plight. The families of the new POWs identified their loved ones, but questioned their use of language and suggested they were being told what to say by their Iraqi captors.

In New York, 10,000 Jewish Americans rallied in support of the troops and against Saddam Hussein. This was the first public reaction of many in the American Jewish community, voicing private feelings of concern for the fate of Israel under attack by Saddam Hussein. Many Americans found comfort in helping Israel while it was under attack by heading to Israel and doing whatever they could.

Day 6
Tuesday, 22 January 1991
(Monday, 21 January 1991 EST)

Military

The air war against Iraq continued but was hampered by a foreseen but uncontrollable factor: the weather. Throughout the opening week, low-level clouds prevented many aircraft from locating and identifying their targets. Under orders to prevent civilian casualties — also known as collateral damage — Allied planes returned to bases with their armaments under their wings, indicating they were unused during their missions.

The cloud cover also hampered "bomb damage assessment" — whether or not a weapon accomplishes its goal of destroying its target or renders it inoperable. Although figures were released of 80 percent effectiveness of Allied weapons, these were the result of "gun camera footage" and pilot reports.

Still of concern to many was the fate of the Allied POWs. Although happy to hear that they were alive, the families and the Pentagon began to express the desire for a "war crimes" tribunal for Saddam Hussein after the cessation of hostilities. Iraq announced that the POWs would be stationed at industrial and military facilities as "human shields" against Allied bombing. This, along with the parading of POWs on television and the failure to notify the International Red Cross of their capture, were considered direct violations of the Geneva Convention for the holding of prisoners of war. Even President Bush expressed "outrage" at the brutal parading of the Allied pilots. When asked if Hussein would be held accountable for this action, Bush responded: "You can count on it."

Four more SCUDs were launched toward Saudi Arabia, but they did not cause any significant damage. One was intercepted by a Patriot, one splashed into the Gulf, and two others landed in deserted areas of Saudi Arabia. Israel enjoyed its second night without air raids.

Diplomatic

Lawrence Eagleburger remained in Israel to work on U.S/Israeli relations, but the best indication of the warming between the two countries was not in the meeting rooms but on the streets of Tel Aviv. Israeli citizens cheered for American servicemen manning the Patriot missile batteries. Eagleburger was also cheered when he toured a SCUD landing site. He expressed satisfaction that Israel would restrain from attacking Iraq for the launching of SCUDs and was able to smooth over other differences while in Israel.

Domestic

The American public's support for the war remained high with polls putting it around 80 percent. The videotape of the Allied POWs had an uncertain effect on Americans, but many suspected it would anger the American population and move them to support the efforts of President Bush. Although the support for Bush remained unchanged, a majority of the American public expressed the opinion that the war would last several months and would cause considerably more casualties.

EXECUTIVE ORDER 12744
Designation of Arabian Peninsula Area, Airspace, and Adjacent Waters as a Combat Zone

21 January 1991

By the Authority vested in me as President by the Constitution and the laws of the United States of America, including section 112 of the Internal Revenue Code of 1986 (26 U.S.C. 112), I hereby designate, for purposes of that section, the following locations, including the airspace above such locations, as an area in which Armed Forces of the United States are and have been engaged in combat:

- the Persian Gulf
- the Red Sea
- the Gulf of Oman
- that portion of the Arabian Sea that lies north of 10 degrees north latitude and west of 68 degrees east longitude.
- the Gulf of Aden
- the total land area of Iraq, Kuwait, Saudi Arabia, Oman, Bahrain, Qatar, and the United Arab Emirates.

For the purposes of this order, the date of the commencing of combatant activities in such zone is hereby designated as January 17, 1991.

George Bush

In a little noticed move, President Bush issued an executive order — Executive Order 12744 — that designated the KTO as a "combat zone." See the previous page for exact wording of this order. While this was obvious to everyone, the order officially exempted troops in the region from having to pay income tax on their military pay. In addition, it gave the troops a three-month extension for the filing of their income taxes.

Day 7
Wednesday, 23 January 1991
(Tuesday, 22 January 1991 EST)

Military

SCUD missiles again caused headlines with one missile landing in Tel Aviv and causing considerable casualties. Three were reported killed and ninety-six injured when a SCUD slammed into a row of apartment buildings in downtown Tel Aviv. The SCUD was hit by a Patriot missile, but the impact did not destroy the SCUD and the debris fell along with the warhead.

Six SCUDS were launched at Saudi Arabia, but three landed in uninhabited areas and three others were intercepted by Patriot missiles. Portions of one missile landed in the streets of Riyadh, Saudi Arabia, but damage was considered minimal.

In Kuwait, reports and aerial photos showed a number of oil wells and storage tanks on fire. The rationale for doing this was unknown, but some speculated the smoke could be used to shroud possible targets from Allied bombers. The massive clouds of black smoke could hinder optically guided smart bombs and the fires on the ground were thought to cause problems with heat-sensitive munitions. It was also possible that the bombing of these fields could have been caused by errant American strikes that hit the facilities by accident. American and Allied officials pledged to watch these fires to see what impact they would have on the battlefield.

Diplomatic

This most recent attack by Iraq on Israel brought fears that this would finally prompt the Israelis to action. But, with Secretary Eagleburger still in the country and considerable U.S. pressure not to move, the Israelis again demonstrated restraint. Even as Israeli television showed the casualties being pulled from the rubble of a Tel Aviv apartment building, Israeli public opinion continued to support the policy of restraint and caution.

The Israeli government asked for more aid from the United States. The more than $13 billion request was the largest ever received from the Israelis and led many to believe some sort of deal was struck to keep Israel out of the war by paying it a large amount of foreign aid. However, when examining the figure, almost $10 billion was requested as part of the Soviet Jewry immigration which had reached incredible proportions. The other $3 billion would be used to pay for the heightened state of the Israeli military during the war and for losses to the economy by the Persian Gulf Crisis. This money was in addition to the $3 billion a year in economic and military aid the United States already gives to Israel.

Day 8
Thursday, 24 January 1991
(Wednesday, 23 January 1991 EST)

Military

After one week of military operations, Allied commanders were excited and confused by the lack of Iraqi opposition. With minimal threat from Iraqi aircraft, additional Allied planes could shift from air-to-air roles to participating in the hunt for SCUD missiles. During a briefing, General Colin Powell emphasized that Allied air power, which had now flown 12,000 sorties, would concentrate on Iraqi air defense systems and early warning systems, along with a vigorous policy of finding and destroying SCUD launchers. The countries now participating in the air war included Britain, Canada, France, Italy, Kuwait, Saudi Arabia, and Qatar.

When asked for his policy on eliminating the Iraqi Army, General Powell said "First, we're going to cut it off, and then we're going to kill it." There was one incident of ground skirmishing when soldiers from the 3rd Armored Cavalry Regiment encountered an Iraqi patrol and exchanged fire, taking six prisoners with no losses.

Attacking Qurah. Navy SEALs were essential in taking control of the small island of Qurah, which became the first liberated part of Kuwait. *Source: U.S. Navy*

The SCUD war continued with Iraq launching four SCUDs toward Saudi Arabia and one toward Tel Aviv. For the first time, the missile heading toward Israel was intercepted and destroyed. The Israeli Cabinet issued a statement that Israel would not retaliate for the previous day's SCUD attack and felt confident with the U.S. Patriots.

At sea, two Iraqi minelayers were attacked by Navy aircraft — one was sunk and the other ran into its own mine. Nearly twenty-two Iraqi sailors jumped into the water, but were later picked up by U.S. forces and interned as POWs. While attacking these vessels, U.S. helicopters came under fire from a small Island called Qurah. This island was then attacked and twenty-nine POWs were taken captive by Navy SEALs. This island became the first liberated part of Kuwait.

Domestic

After the initial bombing of Iraq, all Western journalists, with the exception of CNN's Peter Arnett, were expelled. One of Arnett's reports concerned a "baby milk factory" which was destroyed by Allied bombers. The packages on the ground said "baby milk" in English, and file footage of the plant showed workers with clothing that also said "baby milk factory" in English. The White House claimed this site was bombed because it was a chemical/biological weapons facility hidden behind the guise of a baby milk factory. It then went on to question all reports being filed from Iraq as "propaganda" and many people, including several members of Congress, began to question Arnett's patriotism. The exact purpose of the "baby milk" plant is still being debated, but in Arnett's book, *Live from the Battlefield,* he claims that he grabbed some of the packages and fed them to children hiding in the bomb shelter of his hotel. Whether or not there were chemical or biological weapons in the plant may never be known, but there certainly was some baby milk formula.

Day 9
Friday, 25 January 1991
(Thursday, 24 January 1991 EST)

Military

At sea, three Iraqi vessels, including a hovercraft, were attacked and destroyed. These vessels were believed to be engaged in mine warfare activities. To date, twenty-five free-floating mines had been found and destroyed by Allied forces in the Gulf.

Iraqi forces launched what was believed to be their first air attack against Allied vessels. Two Iraqi Mirage F-1s flew down the Saudi coast armed with Exocet missiles on their way to the Allied fleet. They were intercepted by two Saudi F-15Cs flying combat air patrol. Captain Ayedh, a Saudi Air Force pilot, brought down both airplanes in the same engagement, garnishing considerable media attention.

Several SCUDs were launched today. Along with the SCUDs from the previous evening, a total of ten SCUDs were fired in twenty-four hours. This barrage

THE MEDIA IN OPERATION DESERT STORM

During the Vietnam War, many blamed the media coverage for the lack of popular support for our policy in southeast Asia. Although studies since then by both the media and the military found that the coverage did not cause our "defeat," there are many who still believe the press corps slanted and distorted the horrors of war before the eyes of the American public.

In Operation Desert Storm, the military constrained the reporting by the media to unprecedented levels. Besides protecting information about troop movements and battle plans, the Pentagon restricted information thought to be "detrimental to our policy" in the Gulf. Everything filmed by the journalists in Saudi Arabia was reviewed by U.S. military personnel and certain information was withheld by these censors. Media wishing to cover a story had to first receive permission from the military and then were assigned to a "media pool" of several reporters to cover the story, who must have given the story to any journalist who requested it.

Coverage of the war, despite the restrictions, was massive. In the opening days, CNN took advantage of its large staff and international capabilities to bring out the first dispatches direct from Baghdad, along with numerous other exclusives, the other three networks could not obtain. As the war progressed, the "big three" networks began to regroup and dispatched large teams into the Gulf region, but the initial defeat by CNN established the 10-year-old network as the main source of news to many concerned about Operation Desert Storm. In fact, for some time the only western reporter allowed in Baghdad was

was the highest number of missiles fired in one day during the war.

Domestic

Four CBS journalists, headed by veteran Middle East correspondent Bob Simon, were reported missing after they were seen heading toward Kuwait. Many media personnel experienced difficulty operating under the guidelines established by the military and the CBS crew was no exception.

The crew was later found to be in Iraqi hands in Baghdad and released after the cease-fire agreement. The spotlight below discusses the security constraints put on the media and the overwhelming desire of the media to report from the front lines.

Day 10
Saturday, 26 January 1991
(Friday, 25 January 1991 EST)

Military

Militarily, there was little departure from previous days attacks. Allied air attacks continued with 2,000 sorties and one additional country participating in actions — Bahrain began flying defensive missions. U.S. officials also announced that 236 Tomahawk cruise missiles had so far been fired, including several from submarines in the KTO. This was the first successful launch of submarine cruise missiles in combat. Also, one Iraqi ship was destroyed at sea and four more were attacked while in port. The SCUD war continued with seven fired at Israel and two at Saudi

THE MEDIA IN OPERATION DESERT STORM (continued)

Peter Arnett. CNN's coverage is now watched for information not only by our own military, but by Saddam Hussein as well.

Many reporters broke off from the media pool to bring stories from the front lines unedited by military censors once the ground war commenced. CBS News was in Kuwait City before the Allied troops and was able to scoop all other networks with live footage of the liberation. The military was preoccupied with the massive ground operation and, given the remarkable success of the campaign, did not track down those reporters who broke the rules.

While some reporters found it was easiest to operate without the pool, four journalists from CBS who broke out of the pool were abducted by the Iraqis and taken back to Baghdad as prisoners. The four, led by CBS reporter Bob Simon, were repeatedly beaten and malnourished by their captors, proving the point that the military repeatedly emphasized the dangers of the battlefield to members of the media. The four were released following the cease-fire agreement.

At home, the debate about the controls over the media will continue well after the war, thanks in part to the attention given it by the media. Polling data suggests that most Americans understood and did not mind the constraints that were placed on the reporting of the war. However, a growing segment of the population is concerned that the censorship may be hiding the facts necessary for a democracy to function.

Arabia. Patriot missiles intercepted the incoming SCUDs, but debris did land in Israel killing one and injuring approximately sixty.

The major new development in the conflict was the announcement of a gigantic oil spill heading from Kuwait toward Saudi Arabia. The Allies said that millions of barrels of oil were being dumped into the Persian Gulf from the Sea Island Terminal off Kuwait's refinery at Mina al Ahmadi and from tankers that were in port there. The exact size of the slick became subject to debate later on, but initial reports put it several times larger than the Exxon Valdez spill in Alaska back in 1989.

The oil slick caused considerable ecological damage and raised concerns about the desalinization plants that provide water to Saudi Arabia, its people, and Allied forces. Militarily, administration officials said the oil slick would have minimal to no effect on U.S. plans, but a special team of Coast Guard, Environmental Protection Agency, and National Oceanographic and Atmosphere Administration employees were called in to advise the Saudi government with a response. For more information on the environmental damage of the war, see Chapter 12.

Day 11
Sunday, 27 January 1991
(Saturday, 26 January 1991 EST)

Military

The oil slick doubled in size overnight with estimates on its size ranging between thirty to seventy miles long. The United States and other Allied countries began to rush oil clean-up equipment and experts to the region to consult with military leaders and figure out a way to solve the problem. Military forces also took part. U.S. F-111s attacked the facility pumping oil into the Persian Gulf using smart weapons. (These weapons were often guided to their targets by utilizing small television cameras located on the warheads. The footage of these missiles streaking toward their targets made good filler coverage on many evening newscasts.) Two bombs were dropped on the manifolds of the pipelines leading out to the loading terminal. These manifolds were regarded as the "hub" of the spill, a place where the oil could be turned off without further environmental damage. The offshore loading facility was set afire in a separate action when Allied naval vessels engaged Iraqi patrol boats.

Six SCUD missiles were launched, but all were intercepted by Patriots and no damage was reported. The air war continued with the number of sorties crossing the 20,000 mark and Allied planes emphasizing Iraqi troop concentrations near the front.

The big air war story dealt with desertions on the part of the Iraqi Air Force. At least two dozen Iraqi warplanes and transports, including their most sophisticated fighters, had fled to Iran and landed. The Teheran government, reaffirming its neutrality, said the planes would not leave Iran until after the war was over. The United States, after seeing the Iraqi Air Force flee, and concentrating their attacks on hardened Iraqi aircraft hangers, declared air supremacy — where the enemy is incapable of effective interference — a formal declaration of what had been in effect since the first day. Three Iraqi planes were shot down, bringing the number of coalition air-to-air kills up to nineteen.

Domestic

In Washington D.C., the largest anti-war demonstration to date took place when 75,000 protesters marched to protest the bombing and call for a cease-fire. Although the majority of the protesters were composed of the very liberal section of American society, there were a few relatives of troops who wanted to see their sons and daughters brought home. Despite the claims of organizers, this event was not the "start" of bigger protests, but more like a finale. After this event, the anti-war crowd essentially faded from view.

Mixed messages. Persian Gulf anti-war demonstrators did not receive as much media coverage or general support from the public as protesters from past U.S. conflicts did. *Source: Alex Sobie*

THE ANTI-WAR MOVEMENT

One of the benefits of living in a democracy is that not all sides agree on a particular issue or belief. Although public opinion polls indicated widespread support for the president and his policy, a quick look at the television during Operation Desert Storm showed an occasional protest around the country.

Commentators were quick to recognize the similarities between these protests and the ones during the Vietnam era. One reason for this is that many of the Gulf War protesters were protesters during Vietnam. Although some families of troops deployed and some younger persons were out expressing their points of view, the majority of the demonstrators were extremely liberal, even radical members of society.

The numbers of protesters and the public opinion polls were far different from the dissent we experienced during the Vietnam War. During the height of the Vietnam protests, U.S. public support was at least evenly divided in those who supported and those who opposed the war. During Operation Desert Storm, the protest community remained relatively small and the poll numbers overwhelmingly in support of the president.

In late January, the anti-war movement held its largest, and last major event — a rally in Washington D.C. with 75,000 marchers. It received considerable media attention, but following this event, the anti-war movement essentially "died."

The anti-war coalition of groups, a collection of dozens of special interests, were never able to come up with a solid plan or message that could be relayed to the American public. "No blood for oil" or "cease-fire now" were easy to shout, but left the United States with no policy to

WEEK THREE
Day 12
Monday, 28 January 1991
(Sunday, 27 January 1991 EST)

Military

The war against the Iraqi Navy, a compilation of patrol boats and minelayers, intensified when it was learned that some ships may have been carrying Exocet anti-ship missiles. To date, eighteen Iraqi ships had been destroyed.

The air war experienced the most intense dogfight to date when two U.S. F-15s destroyed a total of four Iraqi aircraft — three MIG-23s and one Mirage — raising the count to twenty-three shot down in air-to-air combat. As for the rest of the Iraqi Air Force, the number of Iraqi aircraft in Iran continued to climb with almost forty on the ground to date. Explanations ranged from the obvious — that Saddam Hussein was seeking to save his air power for a later day — to the more complex idea that the Iraqi Air Force was fleeing Saddam's terror. Unsubstantiated communiqués out of the Soviet Union indicated that Saddam had killed his Air Defense Chief of Staff and was furious with his Air Force's cowardliness. After the war, Iraqi defectors testified that Saddam executed a number of his top-level military leaders.

Air force planners began to shift their attacks to Republican Guard divisions. Several bridges were destroyed and the traffic tie-ups behind them became lucrative targets for Allied planes flying overhead.

In recognition of his outstanding work, and due to practical necessities, Major General Gus Pagonis, the man who was coordinated all the logistics in the Gulf, was promoted to lieutenant general (three silver-stars). What normally would have taken a few months to accomplish was personally shepherded through the Senate by General Colin Powell. General Schwarzkopf and Captain Gus Pagonis — the general's oldest son — gave the three stars a few weeks earlier in a desert ceremony. General Pagonis later wrote a book, *Moving Mountains*, which chronicles the incredible buildup of Allied forces.

THE ANTI-WAR MOVEMENT (cont.)

pursue, and, if enacted, could have caused considerable military problems for U.S. forces. Stuck with this same message, and offering no other solution to the problem of Saddam Hussein, the anti-war movement was never able to broaden its appeal to the masses. It was effective at mobilizing its core constituency — the extremely liberal segment of society but failed to make the slightest inroads into the mainstream. With the exception of banging on drums, which went on outside the White House, the anti-war movement had little impact on the conduct of Operation Desert Storm.

Years after the war, a hard-core group of anti-war protesters continues to protest American involvement in the Middle East. Former Attorney General Ramsey Clark wrote a book detailing American "war crimes" in the region during the Gulf War. Additional complaints are launched about the environmental damage caused by the war and the debris of the war including depleted uranium shells which some claim have toxic effects.

Diplomatic

In Israel, the cabinet reaffirmed its position that restraint was the best course of action, alleviating some commander's fears of a possible breakup of the Arab coalition. As a result of this policy of restraint, Israel received considerable praise in the world community. To aid in the defense of Israel, additional Patriot batteries were deployed.

Day 13
Tuesday, 29 January 1991
(Monday, 28 January 1991 EST)

Military

The air war topped 25,000 sorties with clear weather allowing better bomb damage assessment and giving Allied pilots a clearer view of their targets. Also taking advantage of the clear weather was Iraq's Air Force by flying an additional forty planes to Iran for safe-haven. Eighty planes were now in Iran and the government in Tehran announced that it would confiscate the planes. Allied forces announced they would not attack the planes that had fled, but would try to intercept additional aircraft making a dash for Iran. One MIG-23 was shot down, totaling twenty-four downed in air-to-air combat.

Two SCUDs — were fired — one each on Israel and Tel Aviv, but Patriot batteries intercepted the incoming missiles. To date, fifty-one SCUDs were launched.

Diplomatic

The scheduled summit between President Bush and Soviet President Gorbachev was postponed today, indefinitely because of the war in the Gulf. Although Operation Desert Storm was said to be taking up too much of President Bush's time, many suspected the summit was also delayed because of the Soviet crackdown in the Baltic republics and suspicion of the Soviet's true intentions in the most recent arms-control negotiations.

Domestic

Peter Arnett, scoring the first "scoop" of the war, was able to interview Saddam Hussein on camera for CNN. The first question asked, and the one most troops wanted to hear answered, was whether or not Iraq intended to use chemical weapons. The response, guarded in careful language, was that Iraq would use "whatever force was used against it." This did little to calm the fears of American servicemen and servicewomen and their families. Hussein also defended his use of POWs as human shields and he responded it was hypocritical of the Western Allies to complain about POWs while Britain was holding Iraqi students at a military base in England. Arnett's entire interview ran several times and was labeled propaganda by both the U.S. government and those who believed Peter Arnett to be a traitor.

Unlike Vietnam, the administration resisted criticizing the anti-war protesters of the previous day. During the Nixon years, Vice-President Agnew frequently turned on the anti-war crowds with intense verbal assaults, questioning everything from their patriotism to their personal lifestyles. During Operation Desert Storm, Vice-President

Quayle attacked the protesters only once, and then backed away when President Bush offered respectful comments toward those opposing his policy.

Day 14
Wednesday, 30 January 1991
(Tuesday, 29 January 1991 EST)

Military

The first major ground operation took place today when four separate incursions were launched by Iraqi troops. Described by Allied commanders as probing operations and not as an offensive, the Iraqis moved into Saudi Arabia in four separate thrusts until they were repulsed by U.S. and coalition forces. In one battle near the Kuwaiti/ Saudi border, two U.S. Marine Corps vehicles were hit, killing eleven Marines inside. It was later reported seven of these Marines died from friendly fire launched by American aircraft and four more from a TOW missile fired by other Marines. A total of thirteen Marines perished in the first ground casualties of Operation Desert Storm.

A systematic destruction of the Iraqi military. Numerous Iraqi vehicles were "peppered" with shrapnel from smart bombs dropped by the Allied forces. *Source: Andy Lee Johnson*

One column, heading toward the Saudi town of Khafji, managed to beat back the Saudi and Marine defenders and occupied the town. The Khafji thrust took place when several hundred tanks from the Iraqi 5th mechanized and 3rd armored divisions moved forward — some with their turrets turned toward the rear — the understood sign for surrender. When the Iraqis came across Saudi and Qatari forces guarding Khafji, they turned their guns around and began to attack, pushing the Allied forces into retreat. They eventually halted in Khafji where they dug in for the night. Two U.S. Army soldiers from a transportation battalion, including a U.S. female, were reported missing and believed to have been captured near Khafji.

In the air war, Marine Corps Harriers and other warplanes came across a convoy of Iraqi vehicles and caused considerable damage. In this raid, some twenty-four tanks were destroyed, along with a number of armored personnel carriers and trucks. This attack was called the largest loss of Iraqi forces in one engagement to date. One more MIG-23 was destroyed, the twenty-fifth Iraqi plane shot down to date.

The Iraqi military reported that one of the Allied POWs was killed by Allied bombing raids overnight. The Iraqis had stated they would be placing captured flyers in strategic and military targets to use as human shields, but some suspected they they made this claim simply to force Allied bombers to be more selective in their targeting. After the war, no proof of this claim could be found.

Diplomatic

Almost overshadowing the president's State of the Union was a joint statement issued by U.S and Soviet officials calling for a diplomatic solution to the war. The joint statement called on the Iraqis to take immediate and concrete steps toward complying with the U.N. resolutions and made vague references to talks in the future on "other Middle East issues," such as the Palestinian problem in Israel. This "linkage" of the Gulf Crisis to the Israeli Crisis was something the administration has vigorously rejected in the past, and the release of this statement caused confusion about U.S. policy. Secretary of State Jim Baker eventually reaffirmed U.S. opposition to any linkage and his spokesperson attributed the release of the memo to "shoddy staff work" and not official U.S. policy.

Domestic

President Bush addressed a joint session of Congress for his State of the Union address and spent half of his speech on the Gulf War. Enjoying near unanimous support from Congress and from the American public, the president tried to explain why the United States had to bear so much of the burden. Bush said "Among the countries of the world, only the United States of America has had both the moral standing and the means to back it up."

President Bush's speech was well received and even the Democrats response, by Senator George Mitchell, supported his efforts to bring the war to a "swift and decisive" end. Congress gave a standing ovation for the troops when the president singled out its efforts in Operation Desert Storm.

Day 15
Thursday, 31 January 1991
(Wednesday, 30 January 1991 EST)

Military

The battle of Khafji continued with Saudi, Qatari, and U.S. forces teaming up to retake the captured border town. Air power played an important role with a steady stream of coalition aircraft taking out Iraqi armor units. One AC-130 (a special forces gunship) crashed just off the coast, which killed fourteen. Iraqi forces, estimated to number around 500 troops and forty tanks, had captured the town the night before and fought off at least two counterattacks by Saudi forces late into the night.

U.S. forces in the theatre crossed the 500,000 mark on this day and General Schwarzkopf took time out from directing the war to hold a press conference to sum up the battle. He reported that to date the Allies had flown 30,000 sorties and had destroyed:

- 38 of 44 target airfield;
- 33 of 66 targeted bridges;
- 31 of 31 targeted nuclear, biological and chemical facilities;
- One-fourth of all electrical plants; and
- One-third of Iraq's command, control, and communications facilities.

While the numbers were impressive, Schwarzkopf cautioned that the Iraqi military remained a formidable fighting machine. He then went on to credit the technology of the U.S. Air Force in the attacks, but backed off from putting all

FRIENDLY-FIRE INCIDENTS

As General Schwarzkopf pointed out in his book, *Norman Schwarzkopf, the Autobiography: It Doesn't Take a Hero,* the term "friendly fire" is really a misnomer. Once a bullet is fired, it is no longer friendly, no matter who is the shooter.

Nearly one in four U.S. combat deaths in Operation Desert Storm were caused by friendly fire from U.S. forces, the highest in our nation's history. Of 148 U.S. troops killed in action, 35 died by friendly fire, 21 of them Army and 14 Marines. Of these, 25 of the 28 separate accidental incidents occurred on the ground. Two others involved ships, while a third involved a surface-to-air missile launched at a fighter, which missed the target. In fact, of the 34 pieces of American armor destroyed, 27 were done so by friendly fire. In addition, a large number of British soldiers were killed in several incidents where U.S. forces shot at British armored units.

29 January

- Four Marines from the 1st Marine Division were killed by a TOW missile in Khafji, Saudi Arabia.
- Seven Marines from the 1st Marine Division were killed when a missile fired by an A-10 malfunctioned.

2 February

- One Marine was killed by a 500 pound bomb dropped from a Marine Corps A-6E.

17 February

- Two soldiers were killed from the 1st Infantry Division when a Hellfire missile from an AH-64 Apache struck their Bradley fighting vehicle.

23 February

- One Marine was killed when a HARM missile struck his radar unit.

24 February

- One Marine was killed when his convoy was attacked by a tank.

24 February

- Three soldiers from the 2nd Armored Cavalry Regiment were killed by machine gun fire from a tank.
- One soldier from the 3rd Armored Division was killed by a premature burst of an artillery round.
- Two soldiers were killed from the 3rd Armored Division when their Bradley was shot by an M1-A1 tank.

27 February

- Six soldiers were killed from the 2nd Armored Division when M1-A1 tanks fired on them.
- Two soldiers from the 24th Infantry Division were killed when their Bradley was fired on by an M1-A1.
- One soldier was killed from the 1st Armored Division when M1-A1s fired upon his Bradley fighting vehicle.
- Two soldiers were killed from the 3rd Armored Division when hit by an M1-A1 tank.
- One soldier was killed from the 1st Armored Division when shot by machine gun fire.
- Nine Britons were killed when A-10s attacked their armored personnel carrier.

his faith in technology. Further, in the SCUD war, Iraq launched another missile at Israel, but it fell harmlessly in the occupied West Bank, causing no injuries nor property damage.

Day 16
Friday, 1 February 1991
(Thursday, 31 January 1991 EST)

Military

Early in the morning, Saudi and Qatari forces reentered the town and rescued twelve U.S. Marines who had been trapped behind enemy lines. Baghdad radio hailed the seizure of Khafji as a great military success, personally planned by Saddam Hussein. But Allied General Norman Schwarzkopf said it was military suicide and referred to it as important as a "mosquito on an elephant."

By midday on the 31st Persian Gulf time (very early in the morning on the 31st in the United States), the town of Khafji was liberated and Iraqi forces were destroyed. At sea, the U.S. Navy reported more than sixty Iraqi naval vessels had been destroyed to date.

Diplomatic

Senior Iraqi officials flew to Iran to meet with French, Algerian, and Yemenese representatives to discuss ways to end the war. Although no one claimed to be negotiating, Iran's new interest in the war — including its acceptance of nearly 100 Iraqi airplanes — caused concern in many Western capitals. With Saddam Hussein out of power, Iran would accomplish two objectives: revenge for the eight-year war and a leading role in the post-war Middle East.

Day 17
Saturday, 2 February 1991
(Friday, 1 February 1991 EST)

Military

The six-month anniversary of Iraq's invasion passed with little fanfare as the air war continued hammering Iraqi front-line positions. There were no major ground operations on this day, but instead, an examination of the events that unfolded at the previous battle for border town of Khafji.

At sea, the United States reported the Iraqi Navy had been effectively eliminated as a threat to the Allied fleet. Although never regarded as a serious foe, the small patrol boats were capable of carrying Exocet anti-ship missiles which could have caused considerable damage to some smaller U.S. ships. All the Iraqi boats were reportedly damaged, except for one which fled to Iran.

Domestic

President Bush flew to three military bases for a morale boosting trip — both for himself and for the dependents of the troops. The president delivered a few speeches, but spent most of his time wading into the crowds of supporters shaking hands and having his picture taken.

Bush also met with the families of several servicemen who were listed as missing in action.

Day 18
Sunday, 3 February 1991
(Saturday, 2 February 1991 EST)

Military

Another Marine died on Saturday, this time the suspected victim of friendly fire. He was killed by a 500 pound Allied cluster bomb dropped by an A-6E that exploded near his convoy and two other soldiers were wounded. For more information on the numerous friendly-fire incidents that occurred during Operation Desert Storm, see the spotlight on page 154.

Air activities continued with concentration being given to attacking the Republican Guards and other front-line units in Kuwait and southern Iraq. To date, some 37,000 sorties had been launched with fifteen U.S. and seven Allied planes lost to hostile fire. The twenty-sixth air-to-air kill was recorded when an F-15C shot down a IL-76 Iraqi transport. As for SCUDs, two more missiles were launched at Israel and one at Riyadh, Saudi Arabia. The Israeli-bound SCUDs exploded harmlessly in the West Bank and a Patriot intercepted the missile over Saudi Arabia.

Chapter Nine

Operation Desert Storm

Weeks Four through Six

WEEK FOUR
Day 19
Monday, 4 February 1991
(Sunday, 3 February 1991 EST)

Military

The first B-52 was reported lost in Operation Desert Storm on this day. The huge bomber was returning to its base on the island of Diego Garcia in the Indian Ocean when it experienced mechanical difficulties and had to put down at sea. Three of the crewmen from the plane were rescued, but three others were listed as missing — one of which was later reclassified as killed in action.

The Red Cross reported today that it had visited more than 300 Iraqi prisoners of war held by the coalition.

Day 20
Tuesday, 5 February 1991
(Monday, 4 February 1991 EST)

Military

The battleship *Missouri* was brought into action for the first time since the Korean War. Its 16-inch guns pounded an Iraqi command bunker near the Kuwaiti coast and reportedly destroyed it with its one-ton shells.

Intelligence estimates today revealed that the amount of supplies reaching Iraqi forces in the KTO were far below the level needed to sustain combat operations. Forty of the fifty-four bridges across the Tigris and Euphrates rivers, along with railroad yards and truck convoys, were pounded by Allied aircraft. The remaining traffic was forced into long delays behind the remaining bridges, and "plinked" by aircraft while trying to flee.

Diplomatic

An offer to mediate the Persian Gulf War came from Iran with Iranian President Rafsanjani saying any negotiations without Iran would jeopardize "genuine security" in the region. Rafsanjani's actions were announced following a three-day visit by Iraqi officials who discussed the war with Iran and representatives of several other countries. Iran reiterated its neutral stance, even though nearly 100 Iraqi aircraft were in their country. The official U.S. reaction was described as "cool" with State Department Spokesperson Margaret Tutwiler asking "what's to mediate?" She did leave the option open for Iran to continue its efforts, but only if it could get Saddam Hussein to comply with all twelve U.N. resolutions.

Day 21
Wednesday, 6 February 1991
(Tuesday, 5 February 1991 EST)

Military

Allied air planners shifted their focus from strategic targets and Republican Guard forces to direct attacks on Iraqi forces in the KTO. Large 15,000 pound BLU-82 bombs were dropped on Iraqis by MC-130 aircraft. Just about every three hours, U.S. bombers pounded the Iraqi Republican Guard forces.

USS *Missouri* was replaced by USS *Wisconsin* which took over shelling operations off the coastline. This was the first time *Wisconsin's* giant 16-inch guns had been fired in combat since the Korean War.

Missouri's fury. The USS *Missouri* had been in active offshore shelling in the Persian Gulf, but was relieved on Day 21 to perform other critical operations. *Source: U.S. Navy*

Day 22
Thursday, 7 February 1991
(Wednesday, 6 February 1991 EST)

Military

In an effort to alleviate casualties, Allied forces had begun spreading some 14 million leaflets — also called Safe Conduct Passes — instructing Iraqi troops on the proper procedure for surrender. The leaflets, in Arabic and English, contained instructions and cartoons asking Iraqis to give themselves up and avoid being killed by the massive air strikes. The instructions from one leaflet read: *"If you want to escape the killing, be safe, and return to your families, do the following things: 1- Remove the magazines from your weapons; 2- Put your weapon over your left shoulder with the barrel pointed down; 3- Put your hands over your head; 4- Approach military positions slowly. Note: Beware of the minefields sown along the border. Now, use this safe conduct pass. The Iraqi soldiers who are carrying this pass have indicated their desire for friendship, to cease resistance, and to withdraw from the battlefield. You must take their weapons from their hands, afford them proper treatment, provide food and water, and render any needed medical treatment."*

Although it may be difficult to prove that the leaflets brought over deserters, a number of Iraqis taken as prisoners had the papers folded and kept in their pockets should their surrender become necessary. Samples of these leaflets are included below.

Five Iraqi aircraft were downed today, raising the total to thirty-one destroyed in air-to-air combat.

Diplomatic

Nowhere had the economic sanctions and anti-imperialism feelings been felt harder than in Jordan. King Hussein —

"Safe conduct pass" samples. The idea behind these passes was to reduce casualties and to encourage surrender amongst the Iraqi forces. *Source: U.S. Government Department of Defense*

long considered an ally and personal friend of President Bush — bowed to overwhelming pressure on the part of the Jordanian people and forcibly condemned the American air war and civilian casualties. Sharing a large border with Iraq, Jordan lost considerable economic trade as a result of the U.N. sanctions. Since the people of Iraq considered the war against Saddam Hussein to be a war against all Arabs, it pledged considerable assistance to the Iraqi government. In some cases, pieces of shot down Allied planes were auctioned off in the Jordanian capital of Amman for thousands of dollars to be given to Iraqi war relief. With this sort of support for Iraq, many Western analysts felt King Hussein would have to support Saddam Hussein or face a possible revolt by his own people.

Day 23
Friday, 8 February 1991
(Thursday, 7 February 1991 EST)

Military

The air war continued with Allied commanders stating that more concentration would not be given to Iraqi forces in Kuwait. Although these units had been targeted since the early days of the war, this new emphasis was seen as a precursor to the coming ground war. This was made evident as Allied air power sought out and destroyed individual Iraqi tanks and vehicles instead of concentrating on large command and control targets.

Another five aircraft were destroyed in the air war, including a helicopter shot down by two F-14A Tomcats — making this the first air-to-air kill for the Navy's premier fighter. This raised the total of downed Iraqi planes to thirty-six.

In Texas, a number of Louisiana National Guard members were declared absent without leave (AWOL) from their training at Fort Hood. As part of the total force concept, Reservists were to fill in the gaps in active-duty combat units to round out the force. This "desertion," along with problems with other Guard and Reserve units, caused some in the Congress to question the policy of using Guard and Reserve units for combat purposes.

Diplomatic

President Bush ordered a review of foreign aid to Jordan following King Hussein's support of Iraq. The United States previously gave Jordan approximately $50 million a year. Rumors that Jordan was going to break relations with the United States were quickly discounted in Amman, leading many to believe that Jordan did not want to ruin long-term relations with the United States.

Day 24
Saturday, 9 February 1991
(Friday, 8 February 1991 EST)

Military

The air war continued over Iraq with sorties now totaling more than 55,000. U.S. officials, who had been reluctant to talk about the damage inflicted by the air war, reported at least 600 tanks had been destroyed by Allied air power since the beginning of the war. Briefers also reported supplies to the Iraqis in Kuwait had been cut by 90 percent thanks to the destruction of several key bridges on the supply line to Kuwait. Iraq's Air Force continued fleeing the battle with almost 140 planes now in Iran.

Day 25
Sunday, 10 February 1991
(Saturday, 9 February 1991 EST)

Military

Secretary of Defense Cheney and General Colin Powell met with the Allied military command for nine hours to discuss the progress of the war and necessity of a ground war. At the briefing, Cheney and Powell were given dozens of scenarios for a U.S. attack and possible reactions from Saddam Hussein. Although given a positive briefing on the state of the air war, Allied commanders reportedly asked for a few more days of air raids to continue weakening the Iraqi defenders.

U.S. officials increased their estimate of Iraqi tank damage to 750 tanks, 600 armored personnel carriers, and 650 artillery pieces destroyed. Allied commanders added that captured Iraqi prisoners had indicated "execution battalions" were active in Kuwait to deter or kill possible deserters. Most of the air attacks on this day were directed against Iraqi front-line troops and the port city of Basra in southern Iraq. Navy aircraft reported taking out a Silkworm missile site that could have threatened the Allied fleet in the northern Gulf. Iraq's only offensive action was another SCUD toward Israel. The missile was hit by a Patriot, but debris landed in a Tel Aviv neighborhood, injuring twenty-six and causing considerable damage.

Diplomatic

Iraq formally cut ties with the United States today. Since the United States had previously expelled most of the Iraqi embassy staff for fears of terrorism, and due to the presence of Iraqi diplomats at the United Nations should the United States need to negotiate, the practical effect was minimal.

Some concern was given to a speech by Soviet President Gorbachev that the

Air combat continues successfully. Two F-14A Tomcats proved themselves by destroying five Iraqi aircraft on Day 23. This was the first air-to-air kill of the war. *Source: U.S. Navy*

Offshore Tomahawk defense. Tomahawk missiles proved to be highly beneficial for keeping Iraqi artillery attacks neutralized. *Source: U.S. Navy*

air war may be "going to far." This statement was brought about by the obvious attempt of Allied bombers to destroy the entire Iraqi Army, much of it Soviet-supplied and trained, in the process of liberating Kuwait.

Gorbachev appealed to Saddam Hussein to remove his forces from Kuwait, but many saw this statement as a clear backing off from the Allied military policy. Analysts speculated that his statement was made necessary by the growing strength of the military in his own country and the positive relations the Soviet Union had, and wished to maintain in the Arab world. The Soviets also dispatched diplomats to Iran to seek a negotiated settlement to the crisis.

WEEK FIVE

Day 26
Monday, 11 February 1991
(Sunday, 10 February 1991 EST)

Military

The air war took advantage of clear weather and the Allies launched almost 2,800 missions against the Iraqis. U.S. B-52s were launched for the first time from bases in Fairford, England, where Prime Minister John Major gave permission for the United States to use British soil to launch combat operations. The constant bombardment on the well-entrenched foot soldiers brought another seventy-five deserters across the Saudi border. To date, 1,000 deserters and POWs were in Saudi detention camps.

Day 27
Tuesday, 12 February 1991
(Monday, 11 February 1991 EST)

Military

Secretary Cheney and General Powell returned to Washington to report their findings to the president. Both suggested that the air war continue as Allied commanders reported they still had a number of targets to attack. The coalition had destroyed approximately 20 percent of the Iraqi armor in the KTO, although 50 percent was considered the desirable number before land operations would commence. Both men also noted — barring some diplomatic solution — a ground war would become a necessity. Military officials said no date had been set for the ground war to commence.

Emerging from the meeting, President Bush spoke to reporters in the Rose Garden and said "the air campaign had been very effective and would continue for awhile." Bush went on to state that the war was being fought on "our timetable" and he would not be pressed into a ground offensive before his military commanders recommended it as a necessity.

In the KTO, three SCUDs were launched, two at Israel and one at Saudi Arabia. The Patriot system intercepted the one bound for Riyadh, but falling debris injured several civilians. Another air-to-air kill — number thirty-seven — was recorded as a result of an F-15C that fired Sparrow missiles.

Diplomatic

Israeli Defense Minister Moshe Arens spoke with President Bush on the damage being caused by the SCUD missile attacks. Arens reminded Bush of the tremendous pressure put on Israel because of its restraint, and the president reportedly extended his thanks for Israel's policy and urged the Israelis to continue standing up in the face of Iraqi aggression. Arens also met with Secretary of Defense Cheney and Vice-President Quayle.

In Baghdad, a Soviet emissary met with Saddam Hussein to press for a diplomatic solution to the war. The Soviets called on Hussein to withdraw, assuring him he would not suffer retribution if he were to pull out. But spokesmen were not hopeful Saddam Hussein would accept this plan.

Day 28
Wednesday, 13 February 1991
(Tuesday, 12 February 1991 EST)

Military

Demonstrating close coordination, elements of the 1st Marine Division combined their fire with U.S. air strikes and sea bombardments to hit Iraqi positions in Kuwait. The Allies hit the Iraqis for several hours, but upon cessation of the attack, the Iraqis began to return fire, albeit undirected. Later in the day, the 2nd Marine division teamed up with USS *Missouri* and Saudi artillery to attack the Iraqi artillery that was firing on its position and effectively neutralized it. Inside Kuwait, reports came of Iraqi forces igniting oil wells and some fifty were noticed aflame on U.S. reconnaissance photos of the area.

Diplomatic

Finishing meetings with the Soviet representative, Saddam Hussein spoke on Baghdad radio and said he was willing to work with the Soviets, but vowed to keep fighting until the "aggressors" were destroyed. Gorbachev's emissary returned to Moscow where the Soviet government, although discouraged, was still committed to negotiating some agreement.

Day 29
Thursday, 14 February 1991
(Wednesday, 13 February 1991 EST)

Military

The war's toll on the innocents was reinforced in a graphic event. An F-117

Stealth bomber dropped a 2,000-pound smart bomb on what the United States called a "command bunker" in Baghdad. CNN camera crews, along with many other journalists, brought out photos of hundreds of dead civilians who were using the facility as a bomb shelter.

U.S. officials, citing intelligence information obtained from the builders of the bunker, stated the building was once a civil defense structure, but was later modified for use as a command center. The roof was reinforced, the communications equipment was specially designed to withstand a nuclear attack, and there were several military vehicles present at the scene. U.S. commanders acknowledged that they did not desire additional civilian casualties, but that in war, they were likely to happen. CNN reported about 200 casualties, the Iraqi government claimed 500. The United States and other coalition members blamed Saddam Hussein for placing civilians in a military target. Following this tragedy, the number of attacks in downtown Baghdad began to decrease.

Oil fires raged out of control. It is speculated that oil fires were ignited by gunfire, as well as from intentional lighting, to make combat more difficult. *Source: Michael Lawson*

The United States also claimed that the hotel where the Western journalists were staying was also a major military communications facility, but that the United States would not be targeting it nor bridges in Baghdad. To date, four of the six bridges in Baghdad had been destroyed and the United States did not want to cause further civilian casualties by attacking the other two.

At a press conference, Secretary Cheney pointed out that the Iraqis had begun to place military equipment in residential and historical places because of the U.S. policy of not bombing these areas. Cheney mentioned that two MIG-21 fighters had been positioned near a pyramid in the city of Ur — a valuable archeological city. Lieutenant General Thomas Kelly — one of the Pentagon's chief briefers — said somewhere between 50 and 100 Iraqi fighters had been repositioned in residential neighborhoods.

Diplomatic

The Soviet special envoy to Iraq, Yevgeny Primakov, was quoted as saying there was a "cause for hope" for a negotiated end to the war. Soviet spokesmen refused to go into detail, except to add that Tariq Aziz would be coming to Moscow for further discussions.

At the United Nations, a special session of the security council was demanded by the Yemenese and other North African nations to discuss the bombing of the Baghdad shelter. The United States and its coalition Allies on the council were successful in having the meeting take place in private, out of the eye of the media. The session was scheduled to take place the next day.

Day 30
Friday, 15 February 1991
(Thursday, 14 February 1991 EST)

Military

The United States raised the estimate of Iraqi armor destroyed, bringing the number closer to the 50 percent level desired by some commanders as the minimum required for the initiation of a ground offensive. To date, 1,300 tanks, 1,100 artillery pieces, and 800 armored personnel carriers were destroyed — approximately 30 percent of Saddam Hussein's fighting force.

These claims of Iraqi attrition were the subject of a fierce, but quiet debate between the Central Intelligence Agency (CIA) and the Defense Intelligence Agency (DIA). CIA officials reported far less attrition than Central Command estimates. While the evidence used in this debate remained highly classified, selected portions were leaked to the media to help bolster the claims of one side or the other.

Diplomatic

The closed session of the U.N. Security Council began today to discuss the bombing of the Baghdad bunker. Many smaller countries, in opposition to the secretiveness of the hearing, opted not to speak in protest, but the case was made that the Allies were not being careful in their selection of targets.

In Washington, President Bush said U.S. bombing policy would not change "one iota," but officials in the Pentagon

EXECUTIVE ORDER 12750
Designation of Arabian Peninsula Area, Airspace, and Adjacent Waters as the Persian Gulf Desert Shield Area

14 February 1991

By the authority vested in me as President by the Constitution and the laws of the United States of America, including section 7508 of the Internal Revenue Code of 1986 (26 U.S.C. 7508), I hereby designate, for purposes of that section, the following locations, including the air space above such locations, as the Persian Gulf Desert Shield area in which any individual who performed Desert Shield services (including the spouses of such individual) is entitled to the benefits of section 7508 of the Internal Revenue Code of 1986.

- The Persian Gulf
- The Red Sea
- The Gulf of Oman
- That portion of the Arabian Sea that lies north of 10 degrees north latitude and west of 68 degrees east longitude
- The Gulf of Aden
- The total land area of Iraq, Kuwait, Saudi Arabia, Oman, Bahrain, Qatar, and the United Arab Emirates

George Bush

said more attention would be paid to targets that might have a mixed-use — that is, both a military and civilian purpose. The United States concluded that the bunker was a military target, and considered its investigation into the matter closed.

Additionally, President Bush signed two more executive orders — 12750 and 12751 — today relating to the Persian Gulf Crisis. These are included on the previous page and below.

EXECUTIVE ORDER 12751
Health Care for Operation Desert Storm

14 February 1991

By the authority vested in me as President by the Constitution and the laws of the United States of America, including the National Emergencies Act (50 U.S.C. 1601 et seq.), section 5011A of title 38 of the United States Code, and pursuant to the national emergency declared with respect to Iraq in Executive Order No. 12722 of August 2, 1990, it is hereby ordered that, in the event that the Department of Veterans Affairs is requested by the Department of Defense to furnish care and services to members of the United States Armed Forces on active duty in Operation Desert Storm, the Secretary of Veterans Affairs may, pursuant to this order, enter into contracts with private facilities for the provision of hospital care and medical services for veterans to the fullest extent authorized by section 5011A(b)(1)-(2) of title 38 of the United States Code.

George Bush

Day 31
Saturday, 16 February 1991
(Friday, 15 February 1991 EST)

Military

In preparation for a ground offensive, U.S. Marine units were reported to be heading toward the front in great numbers. Although the president had put a ground offensive on hold for the time being, General Schwarzkopf headed to the front today to confer with senior Marine officials on the plan of attack once the ground war began. The Marines were followed by convoys of supplies and other equipment necessary to sustain offensive operations.

Also, unknown to the public, a major redeployment continued inside the KTO on today. With a ground war imminent, Schwarzkopf began a massive logistical effort to move forces west to the Saudi/Iraqi border. Prior to this time, these forces had been all aligned in Kuwait. But, in what was later called the "Hail Mary" play, Schwarzkopf moved U.S. forces so that they could outflank their Iraqi defenders in a ground war.

In the air, the Allied attacks continued at the same pace with the total number of sorties nearing 73,000. Officials in Saudi Arabia acknowledged that the planes had begun to use a bomb called a fuel-air explosive. This bomb created a fine mist of fuel and then ignited the "cloud" causing a tremendous fireball and a powerful concussion. By using these explosives over vast areas of the desert, Allied forces were able to clear a path through enemy minefields in preparation for ground operations.

In the air, the last air-to-air kill of Operation Desert Storm was recorded when an A-10 shot down an Iraqi helicopter. This brought the total to thirty-eight aircraft destroyed in air-to-air combat, with only one possible air-to-air loss of an F/A-18 on the first day of the war.

Diplomatic

In a statement read on Baghdad radio, the Iraqi Revolutionary Council — the eight-member group that runs Iraq and is controlled by Saddam Hussein — announced that Iraq would withdraw from Kuwait, thus complying with one of the demands of the United Nations. The initial reaction around the world was that of jubilation, with citizens in Iraq dancing in the streets and firing weapons into the air in celebration. Upon further review of the translation of the statement, the hopes of many were dashed as it was discovered the offer contained many preconditions.

The Revolutionary Council issued an incredible list of things that had to be met before the withdrawal could take place. Included among these demands were:

- An immediate cease-fire;
- An Israeli pullout of occupied territories;
- Removal of all Allied forces from the KTO; and
- Payment of reparations to Iraq for war damage.

In a speech a few hours after the Iraqi statement, President Bush referred to the Iraqi proposal as a "cruel hoax." He announced that the "linkage" to the other problems in the Gulf, along with some of the extreme conditions, made the entire package unacceptable to the Allied forces. Opposition to the Iraqi plan was also expressed in the capitals of coalition countries, with each condemning Iraq for raising hopes and then dashing them. However, in the Soviet Union, Soviet Foreign Minister Alexander Bessmertnykh welcomed the Iraqi proposal and called it "encouraging." The Soviets planned a major negotiating session with Iraqi Foreign Minister Tariq Aziz for the day after tomorrow and many analysts saw the Soviet's comments as an attempt not to poison the upcoming talks.

Domestic

President Bush traveled to Andover, Massachusetts, to meet with a crowd of workers at the Raytheon Company. Raytheon developed the Patriot missile and its workers had been working overtime to ensure a steady supply of the anti-SCUD weapon to the forces in the Gulf. The president used this rousing reception to call on the Iraqi people to end the war by rising up and overthrowing Saddam Hussein. Apparently, the administration was buoyed by the scenes of Iraqi civilians in Baghdad celebrating what many believed to be the end of the war.

Day 32
Sunday, 17 February 1991
(Saturday, 16 February 1991 EST)

Military

The coalition forces continued operations today with little change in mission structure. Two SCUD missiles were launched toward Saudi Arabia, one intercepted and the other allowed to land in a deserted part of Saudi

Arabia. Two Allied planes were shot down in northern Kuwait, raising the total combat losses of U.S. planes to approximately twenty.

Two U.S. soldiers from the 1st Infantry Division were killed when their armored personnel carrier was hit by an American Hellfire missile, fired by an American Apache helicopter. This latest case of friendly fire resulted in the dismissal of an American commander several days later.

Diplomatic

The Soviet Union joined the Allies on Saturday in rejecting the conditions put forward in the so-called peace plan. The Soviets were initially guarded in their comments about the statement released by the Iraqi Revolutionary Council, but closed ranks with the United States and the Allies in assuring their support for the full implementation of the U.N. resolutions. The situation inside the Soviet Union was being watched by many analysts who felt the right-wing military leaders would use the imminent Iraqi defeat to drive Gorbachev from power.

WEEK SIX
Day 33
Monday, 18, February 1991
(Sunday, 17 February 1991 EST)

Military

Speculation intensified about an imminent ground war when reports came from the front of "aggressive patrols" being launched by U.S. and Allied forces into Kuwait. American commanders were sending in small units, supported by artillery, Navy ships, and air cover to seek out weaknesses in the Iraqi lines and destroy any units discovered. All in all, there were seven clashes between Allied and enemy forces on the Saudi/Kuwait border.

Domestic

Although the anti-war movement had suffered a lack of inertia, there were still isolated cases of Americans expressing opposition to the fighting. In Kennebunkport, Maine, where President Bush was enjoying a weekend church service, a protester interrupted services to speak out against the bombing. John Schuchardt, who has a long history of civil disobedience,

A great concern to Allied naval forces. One of the greatest tasks for naval ships was maneuvering through mine-infested waters. *Source: U.S. Navy*

was quickly escorted out of the church by Secret Service and taken away by Kennebunkport police.

Diplomatic

Iraqi Foreign Minister Tariq Aziz arrived in Moscow to discuss possible peace options.

Day 34
Tuesday, 19 February 1991
(Monday, 18 February 1991 EST)

Military

On the ground, U.S. forces continued border skirmishes, hoping to engage Iraqi forces and then call in air and naval gunfire to destroy them. Also, battlefield preparation began with Allied bulldozers tearing down sand walls called berms that Iraq had built as a first line of defense around Kuwait.

One of the greatest concerns to Allied naval forces was the threat of Iraqi mines strewn throughout the Persian Gulf. To substantiate that fear, two U.S. warships struck mines, damaging both and forcing one to be taken out of action. At 0436, USS *Tripoli,* a helicopter assault ship, which ironically was the flagship for anti-mine operations, hit a mine and suffered a 16 by 20 foot hole in its hull. Four crewmembers were injured, but none were serious. Damage control efforts were successful and the ship stabilized.

Three hours later, another vessel, USS *Princeton,* an AEGIS cruiser, set off an influence mine, damaging its propellers and causing a considerable crack in its main deck. The influence mine did not cause a hole, but the damage was so serious the ship had to be towed out of the area and was considered out of action. USS *Beaufort,* a tug, and USS *Adroit,* a minesweeper, maneuvered through an uncharted minefield to reach the damaged *Princeton* and tow the cruiser to a Gulf port. To date, some eighty mines had been destroyed by Allied forces, but Navy commander said the area where these two ships were hit appears to be more heavily mined than expected.

Diplomatic

Tariq Aziz left the Soviet Union today with a new peace proposal in hand. The plan, details of which were not released, was later revealed to call for:

- Unconditional withdrawal from Kuwait;
- Protection for Iraqi territorial integrity;
- No punishment of Saddam Hussein or other Iraqi leaders; and
- Talks about other Middle Eastern problems.

Domestic

Tragedy struck the anti-war movement when a protester died in Amherst, Massachussetts. The man, carrying a peace sign, doused himself in flammable liquid and ignited himself. The protester was later identified as Gregory Levy, 30 the son of two *Boston Globe* columnists.

Day 35
Wednesday, 20 February 1991
(Tuesday, 19 February 1991 EST)

Military

Throughout the war, General Norman Schwarzkopf was uneasy about commenting on Iraqi losses in Kuwait. For one, he did not want to give the Iraqis a clear picture of how much damage was being inflicted upon their forces and inform them of the capabilities of Allied intelligence. Second, General Schwarzkopf said early on that he did not want to get involved in body counts as his superiors did in Vietnam. It came as a surprise to many when he made comments to the *Los Angeles Times* saying Iraq's Army was on the verge of collapse.

Schwarzkopf claimed that Allied forces were destroying upwards of 100 Iraqi tanks per day and that many of their troops were on the verge of deserting. He cautioned his statements, not wanting to appear overly optimistic as his predecessors did in Vietnam. But there was little hiding the fact that early beliefs that the Iraqi military was a strong and competent fighting force were probably in error.

Diplomatic

Commenting for the first time on the Gorbachev proposal, President Bush said it "fell well short." Many looked at the plan as a last-ditch attempt by the Soviets to reestablish themselves as a player in Middle Eastern politics. The British government also rejected the Soviet proposal. It was now rather clear that the United States no longer desired a negotiated end to the Gulf War and was ready to settle the matter on the battlefield.

Iraqi berms. Coalition forces would destroy as many berms as they could to further weaken Iraqi ground defenses. *Source: Andy Lee Johnson*

Day 36
Thursday, 21 February 1991
(Wednesday, 20 February 1991 EST)

Military

A helicopter raid was launched against an Iraqi bunker complex in Kuwait, snaring a surprisingly high 420 prisoners of war, including twenty officers. The attack began when two AH-64 Apaches, guided by two OH-58 Kiowa scout helicopters, began destroying a web of Iraqi bunkers in Kuwait. The attack was called "extremely violent" by American briefers and the Iraqi forces came out of the bunkers waving white flags. CH-47 transport helicopters and their troops flew into Kuwait and captured the Iraqis while the Apaches stood guard. The POWs were loaded aboard the transports and all aircraft returned safely to base.

Air sorties against the Iraqis concentrated on Republican Guard emplacements and attacks on Baghdad. A flight of B-52s attacked the area where a SCUD missile was fired the previous night. Pilots of the B-52s reported a number of secondary explosions indicating a hit on their targets. Two other SCUDs were destroyed by A-10s in western Iraq.

In air attacks on Iraqi troops, approximately 300 vehicles were attacked by U.S. air forces sixty miles from the Saudi border. Initial reports indicated at least twenty-eight tanks were destroyed along with three ammunition bunkers. The attacks lasted several hours and no aircraft were reported lost.

One U.S. casualty resulted when a company from the Army's 5th Cavalry was killed in his vehicle by Iraqi forces. His unit, engaged in a firefight, reported five enemy tanks destroyed and seven enemy prisoners of war taken.

Domestic

One of the biggest complaints heard in the conduct of the war was the media's opposition to the censorship on the part of the military. The military had made no claim to the contrary, and the American public had overwhelmingly supported the restrictions placed on the media by the Pentagon. Nonetheless, the Governmental Affairs Committee of the Senate decided to hold hearings on the role of the media and the military and the Department of Defense's chief spokesperson Pete Williams was called in to testify.

Williams acknowledged a *New York Times* report that some commanders had denied reporters access to areas if they wrote critical stories on military operations. Williams claimed there were reports of this happening and pledged to do what he could to correct the situation. Williams was followed by former CBS anchor Walter Cronkite who argued the media should be given unlimited access to the battlefield but also suggested he would support a return to the policy of World War II — indicating heavy delays in the reporting of various war stories.

The result of air attacks. This is one of the twenty-eight Iraqi tanks that were destroyed during air attacks. *Source: Andy Lee Johnson*

Another issue causing some concern in Congress was exemptions for parents who were stationed in the Gulf. Approximately 17,500 military parents had been sent to the KTO and many felt they should be reassigned to positions outside of the combat area. The Pentagon insisted that its protections against undue hardship were already in place and that a massive shift of thousands of troops during the middle of operations would have been devastatingly disruptive. In the end, the Senate rejected the proposal 38-54 and passed a non-binding resolution calling on the Pentagon to work out a new policy on parents in uniform.

Day 37
Friday, 22 February 1991
(Thursday, 21 February 1991 EST)

Military

Air operations continued as usual, with most of the day's excitement coming in the diplomatic community. The air war focused more on front-line troops, with at least 1,000 sorties against targets in southern Iraq and Kuwait. Helicopter units launched several more incursions into Kuwait, returning to the bunker they had attacked the previous day and capturing another fourteen prisoners, several weapons, and a number of intelligence documents. From these documents it was learned that Iraqi commanders were requiring their troops to take "loyalty oaths" and holding commanders directly responsible if there were any desertions from a unit.

Ground operations intensified with some of the heaviest artillery barrages against Iraqi positions on the Kuwaiti/Saudi border. Multiple launch rocket systems (MLRS) of the United States and Britain teamed up on an attack on a ten-mile stretch of the desert. More than 1,300 rounds were launched against the Iraqi forces from the MLRS and 72 British Howitzers.

GULF WAR MEDALS

Several medals and ribbons were created to commemorate the Gulf War and the people that risked their lives. Primarily, these honors were commissioned from national, state, and Allied governments.

A.

B.

A. United States
Department of Defense
Gulf War Civilian Service Medal

B. United States
National Defense Service Medal

C. Saudi Arabia
Liberation of Kuwait Medal

C.

Military discipline was demonstrated today when an American commander was relieved of his command for violating operational restrictions and killing two Americans in friendly fire — which happened on Day 33 of the war. The commander of an Army Apache helicopter battalion flew into combat, despite a First Infantry Division prohibition on commanding officers from participating in battle. The attack on a group of trucks was carried out by launching 100 Hellfire missiles. This misuse of weapons led General Schwarzkopf to issue a blunt statement against using the $50,000 weapons on "a fly" and ordered commanders to use appropriate force when they attacked enemy columns.

There were no aircraft sorties by Iraqi forces, but four SCUDs were launched against Saudi Arabia, including two during the daytime. All were intercepted by Patriot missiles and damage was not reported. In addition, Iraqi forces launched two shorter-ranged FROG missiles into Saudi Arabia. One of the missiles landed and injured a number of soldiers from Senegal.

At home, the Pentagon authorized the National Defense Service Medal (pictured) to all U.S. service personnel on active duty after 2 August 1990 in special recognition of "outstanding performance during Desert Shield and Desert Storm." This award was granted to all troops — at home and in the KTO.

Diplomatic

Saddam Hussein issued a statement early in the morning that was regarded as belligerent and unyielding. In this speech, he rejected the idea of surrender and criticized Allied forces for seeking to destroy Iraq. Many analysts regarded this speech as another in a long line of bellicose ravings from Hussein. And, coupled with Tariq Aziz's mission to Moscow, some people began to believe this speech was merely propaganda for the Iraqi people, as Iraq was acting much differently in the world arena than it did in statements to its own people.

This theory gained credibility when the Soviet Union announced the details of a major peace plan that was worked out as a result of a meeting between Gorbachev and Aziz. The plan consisted of eight main points:

- Iraq would announce the full and unconditional withdrawal of troops from Kuwait.
- Withdrawal would begin two days after a cease-fire.
- The withdrawal would be completed on a fixed schedule to be determined.
- U.N. economic sanctions would cease to be in effect after two-thirds of Iraqi troops had withdrawn.
- All other U.N. resolutions would lapse after Iraq forces left Kuwait.
- All POWs would be released immediately after the cease-fire.
- The U.N. would compose a commission to monitor this pull-out designating countries not involved in the conflict.
- Additional details would be settled as the agreement was implemented.

President Bush, who was in contact with Gorbachev, publicly stated "serious reservations" about the plan. He called a meeting of his top staff and they discussed the matter. Bush then went to a play at Ford's Theater in Washington while his aides continued their analysis; later he returned to the White House to decide on the U.S. response. After a late night meeting, the administration declared the Soviet plan was unacceptable because it amounted to a "conditional withdrawal."

While this plan was a great step forward from previous Iraqi demands, the United States had reservations due to the fact that a good percentage of the Iraqi military machine would be allowed to retreat and be saved for another day. Although the U.N. resolutions made it clear that the liberation of Kuwait was the goal, American commanders made no secret of the fact that the destruction of Iraq's military was necessary for this to be achieved.

Domestic

This day was the "International Day of Student Action against the War." Around the country, students at a number of campuses held demonstrations against U.S. policy in the Gulf, complete with teach-ins, panel discussions, and civil disobedience. Despite the coordination of a national office and number of anti-war groups, turnout was disappointing and, in many areas, nonexistent. The anti-war movement's fade into obscurity was apparent to even the most committed activist.

Day 38
Saturday, 23 February 1991
(Friday, 22, February 1991 EST)

Military

Black smoke billowed over Kuwait today, the result of hundreds of oil well fires lit by the Iraqis to deter air attacks. Despite the smoke, Allied planes flew a record number of missions over the Kuwaiti theatre in preparation for the ground offensive. On the ground, one Marine was killed by Iraqi artillery and five others were wounded.

Diplomatic

Responding to the Soviet plan with a plan of his own, President Bush set down a U.S. policy with an ultimatum dictating exactly what the United States would require to forestall a ground offensive. The plan was direct and short and included the following three issues:

- Pull-out to begin by noon EST Saturday (Sunday in the KTO.)
- Pull-out must be completed in one week.
- Iraq must be out of Kuwait City in forty-eight hours and allow the Kuwaiti government to return.

Other conditions called for the return of POWs and Iraqi removal of the thousands of mine and booby traps set in Kuwait. The United States seven-day withdrawal was designed to give the Iraqis little chance of recovering most of their equipment stationed in Kuwait, making it nearly impossible to bring out stockpiled supplies.

The Soviet Union, still trying to maintain its friendship with Iraq and its new friendship with the United States, modified its earlier proposal to bring it closer to U.S. demands. In this new proposal, Iraqi forces were to withdraw in twenty-one days and all POWs would be released in three days. This proposal was explained to President Bush in a ninety-minute phone call by President Gorbachev, but the U.S. ultimatum remained.

Day 39
Sunday, 24 February 1991
(Saturday, 23 February 1991 EST)

Military

The first Iraqi Silkworm missile attack on coalition ships occurred today when two missiles were fired at USS *Missouri.* The first landed harmlessly in the sea, but the second was shot down by an anti-missile Sea Dart missile from HMS *Gloucester.* A-6Es were then sent in to the launch facility in Kuwait, which dropped twelve cluster bombs to destroy the launching site.

In mid-afternoon, it was reported that General Schwarzkopf had been given the authorization to begin a ground war. This was later acknowledged, but clarified in that Schwarzkopf had the authority to start the war for some time, barring a major diplomatic solution. President Bush reportedly gave the approval to a war plan that would begin at 2000 on Saturday, 23 February, as much as ten days before the actual operation began. Throughout the week approaching this invasion, the president and his top aides were quoted as saying "everything was on schedule," an obvious reference to this previously unknown plan. Throughout the day, Allied air power clobbered Iraqi positions, flying a record 1,200 missions over Kuwait for a total of 2,900 sorties for the day.

Chapter Ten

The 100-Hour War

THE GROUND WAR FINALE

The exact moment of the ground war is difficult to determine, as special operations units and patrols were engaging in reconnaissance missions into Iraq for days. But by 2000 (0400 24 February, Kuwaiti time), it was obvious that U.S. forces were on the move. All television networks interrupted their programming and reports from the border indicated intense bombardments of Iraqi positions. Allied forces were on the move in mass and the long-awaited ground offensive had begun.

For weeks, military commentators had speculated on the direction of the ground attack. All seemed to agree that a frontal assault against Iraqi positions would be devastating and recommended a wide, flanking maneuver to encircle and trap Iraqi forces. Many newspapers and magazines carried graphics and maps of a possible U.S. invasion, which were chillingly realistic when the actual battle plan was released.

Attacks on Saturday night were designed as a feint to make the Iraqis think the main U.S. thrust would be right up the middle of Kuwait. During the buildup, the United States positioned all Allied units just south of the Saudi/Kuwaiti border, to give the appearance that a major invasion would come through the southern border of Kuwait. However, General Schwarzkopf had no intention of giving the Iraqis the slugfest they desired. After air superiority was obtained (blinding Iraqi reconnaissance missions), Schwarzkopf ordered what he later called the "Hail Mary" play, shifting the bulk of his forces westward to the Saudi/Iraqi border for the ground war.

First Shots Fired

Late Saturday night, Sunday morning Saudi time, the first shots were fired in the ground war. Combined attacks were launched against Iraqi forces at three points. In the far west, the French 6th Armored Division, along with the 2nd Brigade of the 82nd Airborne, moved north into Iraq toward the Iraqi city and airfield called As-Salman. This thrust would be the farthest west of all Allied units, forming a defensive line against any units trying to attack from Baghdad or repositioning at the Turkish border. The 101st Airborne Division (Air Assault) conducted a massive air and ground operation to help secure the flank.

A Classic Breaching

In Kuwait, the U.S. 1st Marine divisions crossed over the Kuwaiti border headed into Kuwait on a path toward Kuwait City. These units were divided into several different task forces composed of the 1st Marines, 3rd Marine Regiment, 4th Marines, 7th Marines, and 1st Light Armored Infantry. The opening hours of this offensive against the well-designed but poorly defended Iraqi trenches were later described by General Schwarzkopf as a "classic breaching" of enemy positions that would be "studied for years." As a result of the air war, front-line Iraqi units had deteriorated to the point that they had lost more than 50 percent of their pre-war strength. Marines crossed over the mines and barbed wire and immediately engaged enemy tanks, which surrendered shortly after the fighting began.

GEORGE BUSH'S SPEECH
Commencement of Ground War in Operation Desert Storm

23 February 1991

Good evening. Yesterday, after conferring with my senior national security advisers, and following extensive consultations with our coalition partners, Saddam Hussein was given one last chance — set forth in very explicit terms — to do what he should have done more than 6 months ago: withdraw from Kuwait without further condition or further delay, and comply fully with the resolutions passed by the United Nations Security Council.

Regrettably, the noon deadline passed without the agreement of the Government of Iraq to meet demands of United Nations Security Council Resolution 660, as set forth in the specific terms spelled out by the coalition to withdraw unconditionally from Kuwait. To the contrary, what we have seen is a redoubling of Saddam Hussein's efforts to destroy completely Kuwait and its people.

I have therefore, directed General Norman Schwarzkopf, in conjunction with coalition forces, to use all forces available, including ground forces, to eject the Iraqi army from Kuwait. Once again, this was a decision made only after extensive consultations within our coalition partnership.

The liberation of Kuwait has now entered a final phase. I have complete confidence in the ability of the coalition forces to swiftly and decisively accomplish their mission. Tonight, as this coalition of countries seeks to do that which is right and just, I ask only that all of you stop what you are doing and say a prayer for all the coalition forces, and especially for our men and women in uniform who this very moment are risking their lives for their country and for all of us.

May God bless and protect each and every one of them. And may God bless the United States of America. Thank you very much.

George Bush

To the west of the 1st Marine Division, the 2nd Marine Division and the Army's Tiger Brigade from the 2nd Armored Division moved across the border. These attacks were designed as a feint, giving the Iraqis the impression this would be the main Allied attack. By midnight, the Marines had moved approximately twenty miles in Kuwait. Along the coast of Kuwait, Saudi tank forces began to attack Iraqi positions and moved northward into Kuwait City.

Fighting was reportedly light with most of the Iraqis deciding to surrender instead of fighting. By the time most Americans went to bed, some 5,000 enemy prisoners of war had been taken, but Allied commanders warned the most serious fighting was yet to come.

Back in the United States

The commencement of ground operations was a mixed blessing for most Americans. On the one hand, it was feared due to the increase in casualties that was expected from the land war. But on the other, it signified that Allied military operations had entered the final phase and soon the troops would be home. Across the country, Americans again gathered around their television sets to watch the battles.

Around 2100 EST, President Bush returned aboard *Marine 1* to the White House from Camp David, where he had been spending the weekend with his top advisors. The president came into the press briefing room forty-five minutes later and made a statement saying "The liberation of Kuwait has entered a final phase." To read this statement, see the opposite page.

The president was very concerned about the reports of Iraqi atrocities being committed in Kuwait — fires were being started, hostages taken, and executions of Kuwaiti citizen were being conducted in the streets. Many suspected Bush's decision to invade may have been hastened by the reports of these assaults.

Following the president, Secretary Cheney addressed the press with a message many Americans understood and many media folks dreaded: the Pentagon was going to have to suspend briefings and press conferences during the initial phases of the ground offensive. Citing the need to protect the troops, the secretary informed the press that it would have to wait for reports from the front lines, which didn't sit well with many in the media. In the Gulf region, a number of reporters broke off from the pool system, figuring the Allied "censors" would be too busy to track them down. Cheney's press conference offered little news on the status of operations and concentrated on the structure of the operations and the initiation of the invasion order.

DAY 1 OF THE GROUND WAR
Day 40
Monday, 25 February 1991
(Sunday, 24 February 1991 EST)

Military

By the time most American's awoke, Allied forces were underway on all fronts of the campaign. The units that launched the earliest assaults were all meeting their objectives for the opening hours of the war.

The battlefield was divided into different commands. The XVIII Airborne Corps was out to the west, along with the French 6th Armored and 24th Infantry (Mechanized). Their mission was to block additional reinforcements from Baghdad coming to assist the Kuwaiti defenders. Next to them was the main U.S. attack force — the VII Corps — which would smash into southern Iraq, paralleling the Kuwait/Iraq border, and then turning toward the sea, trapping all the Iraqis trying to retreat to Kuwait.

Next to them, heading straight through Kuwait was Joint Forces Command – North, composed of Egyptian, Syrian, and Saudi forces. Their right flank was protected by the Marines Central Command, composed of the 1st Marine Expeditionary Brigade which encompassed the 1st Marine Division, the 2nd Marine Division, the 3rd Marine Aircraft Wing, and the 1st UK Armoured Division. Their mission was to smash up from Saudi Arabia heading toward Kuwait City. Finally, along the coast, Joint Forces Command – East was composed of Saudi and other Arabian units that would head up the shore to Kuwait City. Liaisons between the various commands were placed with each unit to advise on close air and naval gunfire support. For a detailed listing of the order of battle, refer to Appendix E.

The French 6th Armored and the 82nd Airborne had captured the Iraqi city of As-Salman (some ninety miles over the border) and continued northward. Less than seven hours later, these forces had secured the left flank of operations.

Just after midnight EST (0800 KTO time), the 101st Airborne, in the largest helicopter invasion ever launched, moved some seventy miles into Iraq and established a support base for future operations. This assault, which utilized 300 helicopters carrying 2,000 troops, secured a refueling base for helicopters carrying out operations near the Iraqi Republican Guards and prevented their resupply by road. By the end of the day, the unit was met by some 700 support vehicles carrying fuel

Striking force. This U.S. Howitzer was placed outside of Kuwait and used during the "head-on invasion" of Kuwait. *Source: Andy Lee Johnson*

and several thousand additional troops. As a result, 100,000 gallons of helicopter fuel were put in position to support air operations in the Euphrates River area.

With the success of the French 6th Armored's and 101st Airborne's assault, the 24th Mechanized crossed the lines five hours ahead of schedule. Moving sometimes at a speed of 25 to 30 mph, the 24th Mechanized was 75 miles into Iraq by the end of the evening, encountering only light opposition.

In Kuwait, the Marines 1st and 2nd divisions were successful in their breaching operation and began to take a huge number of Iraqi prisoners. Saudi tank forces reported similar success in their trek up the Kuwaiti coast. Additional pan-Arab forces launched operations in Kuwait as a further diversionary tactic to make Iraq think the bulk of operations would be inside Kuwait.

With Iraqi forces now alerted to a "head-on invasion" in Kuwait, a massive force moved north into Iraq led by the VII Corps and composed of the:

- 1st Armored Division;
- 3rd Armored Division;
- 2nd Armored Cavalry Regiment;
- 1st Infantry Division (Big Red One); and
- 1st Cavalry.

They were joined in Iraq by the British 1st Armoured Division, including the famous "Desert Rats" of the 7th Armoured Brigade. This massive force made up the main striking force against the Iraqis, concentrating their attacks on Republican Guard Forces.

The VII Corps crossed the border about seventy miles west of the Saudi/Kuwaiti border some fifteen hours ahead of schedule. Moving through the breaches created by the engineering units, the 1st Infantry Division poured into Iraq. As these units crossed over the border, they began to take prisoner thousands of starving and frightened Iraqi soldiers.

The plan was that the VII Corps would parallel the attacks of the French and Airborne units to their left, and then make a massive right turn once deeply into Iraq to trap all retreating units from Kuwait. The 1st Cavalry Division launched a limited attack on the left to cause the Iraqis to think the main attack would come from that direction. To their right was the 2nd Armored Cavalry Regiment which breached the lines, followed by the 1st and 3rd armored divisions.

In the middle of the VII Corps attack was the 1st Infantry Division, trailed by the 1st UK Armoured Division. By the time the 1st Infantry crossed the line of departure, the 1st and 3rd armored divisions were already thirty kilometers into Iraq. The 1st Infantry consolidated and prepared to allow the 1st UK Armoured Division to pass through and attack.

In his book, General Schwarzkopf was critical of the VII Corps movements during the first days. While VII Corps reached its objectives and then prepared for an Iraqi counterattack, Schwarzkopf was afraid the war was moving too fast and that VII Corps would never engage the enemy. As Iraqis fled from the impending invasion, VII Corps wasn't moving fast enough to catch them. Later, upon re-election, Schwarzkopf tempered his criticism of the movements of the corps.

In western Kuwait, the Joint Forces Command – North moved out at 1600 Kuwait time (0800 EST), headed by the 3rd Egyptian Mechanized Division. They were followed by the 4th Egyptian Armored and the 3rd Egyptian Mechanized. The 9th Syrian Armored Division followed as the reserve force. The Egyptians, fearful of an Iraqi counterattack, set up defensive positions for the night within Kuwait short of their first day objective. Like VII Corps, they were moving according to the original battle plan, and not reacting quickly to the rapidly changing battlefield.

In Kuwait, the 1st Marine Expeditionary Force headed north into Kuwait. Here it met some stiff resistance from the bulk of the Iraqi defenses. However, Iraqi commanders misidentified the true threat to their defense. While concentrating on this Marine attack, they were oblivious to the real threat of the VII Corps moving northward to the west.

Having succeeded in the deception, the Marines then concentrated on moving forward into Kuwait. By 1400 (0600 EST), the Marines had achieved their objective for the day and prepared for an Iraqi counterattack. By day's end, the Marines had eliminated the better part of three infantry divisions.

At 0800 (2400 EST), the 8th and 10th Saudi mechanized brigades, farther to the east by the Gulf, headed north as well, receiving fire support from the 16-inch guns from USS *Missouri* and USS *Wisconsin*. The Joint Forces Command – East secured its respective objectives during the initial attack.

All along the front lines, Iraqi forces were surrendering in mass to Allied forces. Some of the first pool video released showed captured Iraqis kissing their captors, so happy were they to have their lives spared. In fact, the massive amount of POWs caused some

Remains of a downed SCUD. This SCUD was shot down by Allied forces near Kuwait. *Source: Andy Lee Johnson*

commanders to fear the care and guarding of these men would slow down the Allied columns.

Iraqi resistance was offered by some of the second-tier forces — regular Army units with some armor. However, Allied commanders reported the battles with these units were rather one-sided, as Allied forces quickly overwhelmed and destroyed the defending units.

Secretary Cheney's suspension of media briefings lasted less than a day. The reports from the front were so encouraging that the military wanted to share them as soon as possible. Briefing the press in Saudi Arabia, Schwarzkopf told the media that 10,000 prisoners had been taken with Allied forces suffering "extremely light casualties." It was later revealed that only four Americans had been killed in the opening day of ground operations. Schwarzkopf said all attacking units had reached their first day objectives with little resistance.

Destroyed trucks. This Iraqi cargo truck was destroyed by American airpower in the final days of the Ground War. *Source: Andy Lee Johnson*

Diplomatic

The support for ground operations rang out in the capitals of the coalition countries with all calling for the Iraqis to give up or face a certain fate. Queen Elizabeth of Britain, in her first wartime broadcast, told her country's citizens that the war would be as swift "as it was certain." In France, President Mitterand said Saddam Hussein had chosen "a kind of political and military suicide." However, in many Arab countries, support for Saddam Hussein was expressed at massive rallies against the Allied action. The protesters in these crowds hung on every word of Baghdad radio reports of the war, which were slanted toward a major Iraqi military victory.

DAY 2 OF THE GROUND WAR
Day 41
Tuesday, 26 February 1991
(Monday, 25 February 1991 EST)

Military

Before dawn, the 4th Marine Expeditionary Brigade — off the coast of Kuwait in amphibious assault ships — feinted an invasion from the sea. Navy SEALs detonated charges along the beaches and Naval Special Warfare units entered Kuwait City to link up with Kuwaiti resistance fighters. These deceptions kept additional Iraqi divisions tied up defending the coastlines. As the battle continued, it became apparent the Iraqi forces were combat ineffective, having been devastated by the Allied air strikes and lacking the command, control, and communications capabilities to "see" the entire battlefield and understand the military threat with which they were faced.

In the west, the XVIII Airborne Corps continued its northward march in Iraq and Kuwait to establish bases near the Euphrates River Valley. At the western edge of advancing forces, the French 6th Armored Division followed by the 82nd Airborne had established a defense to prevent the Iraqis from reinforcing their units with troops from Baghdad or the west. To the east of the French, the 24th Mechanized continued to race northward, having pushed nearly 100 miles.

The XVIII Airborne Corps worked feverishly to take control of highways and airports in its sector to prevent any fleeing Iraqis from returning to Baghdad. The 101st Airborne (Air Assault) sent its 3rd Brigade on the deepest air assault in military history, moving some 175 miles north to occupy observation and blocking positions on the banks of the Euphrates River. The 24th Infantry Division (Mechanized) moved forward, encountering limited opposition and hundreds of Iraqi prisoners.

The main Allied attack continued with VII Corps moving northward to take up position west of the Republican Guards. The 1st UK Division had passed through the breaches opened by the 1st Infantry Division and turned east, engaging the 52 Iraqi Armored Division. This attack started nearly continuous combat for the "Desert Rats" during the next two days.

By the end of the day, 25,000 prisoners had been taken and seven Iraqi divisions destroyed. Allied intelligence reported that the Republican Guards were oriented to attack southward of their positions, directly into the Marines feint as planned. The existence of VII Corps remained a mystery to them. This was a tragic error on their part.

In Kuwait, Joint Forces Command – North continued its advance. Joint Forces Command – East moved forward on the coast with little resistance.

The Marines continued moving forward, encountering the heaviest resistance of

Pushing to the north. The coalition forces feverishly captured over 25,000 Iraqi prisoners and destroyed seven Iraqi divisions on Day 41. *Source: U.S. Government Department of Defense*

the ground offensive. The 2nd Marine Division was met by an Iraqi counterattack, but it was beat back by the 6th Marine Regiment which utilized artillery, close air support, tanks, and TOW missiles. The Army's Tiger Brigade joined the attack of the 2nd Marine Division. The M1-A1s of the Tiger Brigade were successful in eliminating the Iraqi armor and caused thousands of enemy soldiers to surrender.

The Marines 1st Division moved toward the Jaber airfield in central Kuwait and began some heavy fighting with Iraqi forces. A strong Iraqi counterattack was beat back in a massive tank battle, which led to the destruction of 100 Iraqi armored vehicles. By the end of the day, the Marines were within ten miles of Kuwait City.

DAY 3 OF THE GROUND WAR
Day 42
Wednesday, 27 February 1991
(Tuesday, 26 February 1991 EST)

Military

Having raced northward, this became the day of the "turn." The VII Corps had penetrated by following its objectives in Iraq and now headed east to engage Iraqi Republican Guards. Units continued to seize unbelievable numbers of enemy prisoners and destroyed a considerable number of Iraqi Army units.

Many Iraqi troops were pushed back toward Kuwait City by the Marines and the Joint Forces Command – East. The Iraqis began looting and stealing any available transport they could for a massive retreat up a four-lane highway north out of Kuwait City.

The XVIII Airborne had established a defense line with the French 6th Armored and the 82nd Airborne protecting the western front. Inside this closed area, the 101st Airborne and the 24th Mechanized Infantry were raiding enemy bases and cutting off Iraqi supply lines. By the end of the day, soldiers from the 101st were flying over the Euphrates River and establishing bases in the river valley.

This area, now seized by the Allies from the French 6th Armored to the Kuwaiti border, contained a considerable amount of Iraq's oil production capability. When questioned about the "coincidence," U.S. officials interjected "it was no coincidence."

VII Corps continued its deep envelopment mission into Iraq, encountering some of the best Iraqi units it had fought thus far. Once completing this turn, the VII Corps was spread out, with the 1st Armored Division on the left (north), the 3rd Armored in the center, and the 2nd Armored Cavalry Regiment and 1st Infantry Division on the right (south). Farther south, the 1st UK Armoured turned as well and continued its attacks.

In what became one of the "classic" battles of the war, certain to be studied at war colleges for some time, the 2nd Armored Cavalry Regiment moved into a well-fortified Iraqi position at a map reference known as "73 Easting." The 2nd Armored Cavalry was outnumbered and outgunned by two Iraqi divisions — the 12th Armored and the Republican Guard Tawakalna Division. Finding a seam between the two units, the Americans poured in and commenced a tank battle, where coalition forces destroyed 29 tanks and 24 armored personnel carriers and captured 1,300 prisoners in a timespan of twenty-three minutes.

In Kuwait, the Allied forces advanced on Kuwait City. From the south along the coast, Saudi and Arab forces moved toward Kuwait City. For diplomatic and political reasons, it was decided that some of the first troops to liberate Kuwait should be Arab forces instead of U.S. Marines. The elements of Joint Forces Command – North moved forward through the Marines positions and headed into the city.

The Marines continued northward with their objective of capturing the Kuwait International Airport. The Marines were seeking to control the escape options of the Kuwaiti forces in Kuwait City. The Tiger Brigade moved to the high ground northwest of Al-Jahara to the Al-Mutla Ridge. The U.S. then controlled the highest point for hundreds of miles in any direction. Teamed up with air strikes, the Tiger Brigade destroyed vehicles of all types on the roads, resulting in the "Highway of Death."

The rest of the Marines in the 1st Division moved toward the airport, encountering heaving resistance from Iraqi forces. In a major battle, where Iraqis chose to fight with their backs against the wall, some 250 tanks and 70 armored vehicles were destroyed near the airport.

By nightfall EST, the first elements of the Marines reconnaissance groups had entered Kuwait City. American television crews reported live from the outskirts of the city where dozens of Kuwaiti citizens, many of them heavily armed as part of the "Kuwaiti resistance," were praising the Allied forces for liberating their homeland.

At the end of the ground war's third day, thirty-three Iraqi divisions were assessed by the Defense Intelligence Agency (DIA) as combat ineffective.

DAY 4 OF THE GROUND WAR
Day 43
Thursday, 28 February 1991
(Wednesday, 27February 1991 EST)

Military

Today was the final day of destruction for the Iraqis. The VII Corps moved due east from its positions in Iraq, flanked by the XVIII Airborne Corps to the north and the Marine forces to the south in Kuwait. Beginning the night before and throughout this final day, Allied tanks conducted a series of running battles with the Iraqi forces. To accomplish this, Allied forces called in close air support to destroy hundreds of Iraqi tanks, many of them still dug into the ground.

The XVIII Airborne Corps turned eastward to close in the remaining Iraqi forces. The 24th Mechanized cleared the way by taking two airports that were held by the Iraqis, although it had to solve a minor problem of lack of fuel. Because of the rapid advance, the 24th Mechanized had outrun its fuel tankers, and when the first supply vehicles arrived, their tanks were less than full. After some creative efforts on the part of the 24th Mechanized officers, the units were refueled and the attack continued against retreating units with limited resistance.

VII Corps rolled east, conducting a massive attack against three mechanized Republican Guard Divisions. Spreading out all of its power, VII Corps pounded the remaining Iraqi defenders and retreating units from Kuwait. In a massive assault, much of the Republican Guards were destroyed. Later reports claimed that these were merely "rear guards" while the main body of the Republican Guards were escaping North through the Iraqi city of Basra due to the premature cessation of hostilities. While some units certainly did get out of Iraq prior to the cessation of the war, Allied commanders later stated that the level of attrition in these units was so devastating that they were no longer combat effective. Continued bombing of these units would have resulted in the law of diminishing returns — the Republican Guards would have lost a few more tanks, but the Allies would also have lost a few more men. The VII Corps continued its advance eastward until the war was declared over.

In Kuwait City, the lead elements of the pan-Arab forces entered to the cheering and thanks of thousands of Kuwaiti citizens. People were out on the streets waving Kuwaiti and American flags and firing weapons into the air in celebration. Many Americans likened the reception to what Allied forces received after liberating Paris in 1944. The Marine units

GEORGE BUSH'S SPEECH
Suspension of Offensive Operations by Allied Forces

27 February 1991

Kuwait is liberated. Iraq's army is defeated. Our military objectives are met. Kuwait is once more in the hands of the Kuwaitis, in control of their own destiny. We share their joy, a joy tempered only by our compassion for their ordeal.

Tonight the Kuwaiti flag once again flies above the capital of a free and sovereign nation. And the American flag flies above our embassy. Seven months ago, America and the world drew a line in the sand. We declared that the aggression against Kuwait would not stand. And tonight, America and the world have kept their word.

This is not a time of euphoria, certainly not a time to gloat. But it is a time of pride: pride in our troops; pride in the friends who stood with us in the crisis; pride in our nation and the people whose strength and resolve made victory quick, decisive, and just. And soon we will open wide our arms to welcome back home to America our magnificent fighting forces.

No one country can claim this victory as its own. It is not only a victory for Kuwait, but a victory for all the coalition partners. This is a victory for the United Nations, for all mankind, for the rule of law, and for what is right.

After consulting with Secretary of Defense Cheney, the Chairman of the Joint Chiefs of Staff, General Powell, and our coalition partners, I am pleased to announce that at midnight tonight eastern standard time, exactly 100 hours since ground operations commenced and 6 weeks since the start of Desert Storm, all United States and coalition forces will suspend offensive combat operations. It is up to Iraq whether this suspension on the part of the coalition becomes a permanent cease-fire.

GEORGE BUSH'S SPEECH (continued)

Coalition political and military terms for a formal cease-fire include the following requirements:

Iraq must release immediately all coalition prisoners of war, third country nationals, and the remains of all who have fallen. Iraq must release all Kuwaiti detainees. Iraq also must inform Kuwaiti authorities of the location and nature of all land and sea mines. Iraq must comply fully with all relevant United Nations Security Council resolutions. This includes a rescinding of Iraq's August decision to annex Kuwait, and acceptance in principle of Iraq's responsibility to pay compensation for the loss, damage, and injury its aggression has caused.

The coalition calls upon the Iraqi government to designate military commanders to meet within 48 hours with their coalition counterparts at a place in the theatre of operations to be specified, to arrange for military aspects of the cease-fire. Further, I have asked Secretary of State Baker to request that the United Nations Security Council meet to formulate the necessary arrangements for this war to be ended.

This suspension of offensive combat operations is contingent upon Iraq's not firing upon any coalition forces and not launching SCUD missiles against any other country. If Iraq violates these terms, coalition forces will be free to resume military operations.
At every opportunity, I have said to the people of Iraq that our quarrel was not with them but instead with their leadership and above all, with Saddam Hussein. This remains the case. You, the people of Iraq, are not our enemy. We do not seek your destruction. We have treated your POWs with kindness. Coalition forces fought this war only as a last resort and look forward to the day when Iraq is led by people prepared to live in peace with their neighbors.

We must now begin to look beyond victory and war. We must meet the challenge of securing the peace. In the future, as before, we will consult with our coalition partners. We've already done a good deal of thinking and planning for the postwar period, and Secretary Baker has already begun to consult with our coalition partners on the region's challenges. There can be, and will be, no solely American answer to all these challenges. But we can assist and support the countries of the region and be a catalyst for peace. In this spirit, Secretary Baker will go to the region next week to begin a new round of consultations.

This war is now behind us. Ahead of us is the difficult task of securing a potentially historic peace. Tonight though, let us be proud of what we have accomplished. Let us give thanks to those who risked their lives. Let us never forget those who gave their lives. May God bless our valiant military forces and their families, and let us all remember them in our prayers.

Good night, and may God bless the United States of America.

George Bush

linked up with the Joint Forces Command – North and Joint Forces Command – East units as they entered into Kuwait City.

Having been briefed on the Allied success, President Bush telephoned General Schwarzkopf with what many say was his only military request: stop the killing. Bush wanted to know if a cease-fire was possible and he was told yes. Iraq's Republican Guards had been defeated, its Army had surrendered, and Allied forces were engaged in mopping up operations throughout the region.

It was later determined that of the forty-two divisions of Iraqi troops, all had been effectively destroyed, with stragglers making up about one division widely spread throughout the entire region. It had been a 100-hour war, with unbelievably low casualties among Allied forces.

The ground campaign had achieved the results desired by General Schwarzkopf, these include:

- Control of critical lines of communication;
- Ejection of Iraqi forces from Kuwait;
- The securing of Kuwait International Airport and crossroads of Kuwait City;
- The flanking and destruction of Republican Guard forces; and
- The liberation of Kuwait City.

Diplomatic

Bush addressed the world at 2100 EST with a simple message. (His speech can be found on pages 185 and 186.)

Effective at 2400 EST, all offensive operations would cease. Iraq would have to agree to specific military conditions for a temporary cease-fire, to be followed upon later by a U.N. resolution setting forth the terms of a permanent cessation of hostilities. One condition put forth forcefully was the immediate release of all POWs from

Captured rifles. A U.S. soldier gathers AK47s — the Iraqi equivalent of the U.S. Army's M60 rifle. *Source: Andy Lee Johnson*

Iraqi custody as the president wanted to avoid prolonging the crisis. Throughout the capitals of the coalition countries, there was support for the president's actions. In several Arab nations, many believed that Saddam Hussein had beaten the United States, but the television footage eventually dismissed these beliefs.

Domestic

The cease-fire announcement took many by surprise. For months, commentators and professional pundits in the media had predicted a ground offensive of weeks, even months, at a cost of thousands of casualties. When it was all done, 100 hours had passed with a miraculously low number of Americans killed. Refer to Appendix F for lists of casualties.

Despite any initial surprise, across the country a euphoria was spreading. Although President Bush said in his statement it "was not a time to gloat," American flags were displayed everywhere and the countdown to the return of American forces began. The families of the servicemen and servicewomen were finally able to sleep better as they now knew their loved ones were coming home.

PART FOUR

LOOKING BACK ON THE VICTORIES AND DEFEATS...

Post-War Reflections

Chapter Eleven

End-of-the-War Report

THE POST-WAR YEARS
1 MARCH 1991 AND BEYOND

Although the war "ended" with the cessation of offensive operations by the Allies, there were isolated incidents that took the lives of a number of Allied troops. Land mines and pockets of resistance killed several American men and women and the Kuwaiti theatre remained a very dangerous place.

On 3 March, General Schwarzkopf sat down with his defeated counterparts and dictated the terms for the cease-fire. Originally, he wanted the negotiations to happen on USS *Missouri,* where the surrender of Japan took place in World War II; but the logistics of this were impossible. His next choice was also a problem as Allied forces did not physically occupy the land where the peace treaty was signed due to some miscommunication within VII Corps. Nevertheless, the area was taken (after the cessation of hostilities) and the generals on both sides sat down and discussed the Iraqi surrender.

Allied forces would remain in defensive positions in the area of Iraq that they currently occupied. Iraqi forces would be allowed to leave this area, but could not take any of their equipment or supplies. In addition, no aircraft were allowed to operate in an area near the U.S. forces and other flights were strictly limited. This did not include helicopters, which Schwarzkopf later said was a mistake because Iraq used helicopters to put down Kurdish rebels.

PRIORITY ONE – RELEASE OF POWS

A full accounting of the POWs, which was never given during the course of the war, was requested, and the Iraqis provided the Allies with a list. Included were several airmen previously listed as missing in action. The first ten POWs, including an American woman, were released on 4 March and thirty-five more were released on 5 March. According to the Iraqis, they had only held forty-five POWs.

PRIORITY TWO – THE ARAB-ISRAELI CONFLICT AND BRINGING THE TROOPS HOME

On 6 March, President Bush addressed Congress and announced that the liberation of Kuwait was complete. He then called on a settlement to the Arab-Israeli conflict and pledged to work with the Operation Desert Storm Allies to hammer out a solution to that long-standing conflict. He also announced that the first U.S. combat troops would be removed from the theatre and brought home as soon as possible. He cautioned American expectations of a quick pullout by stating it would take several months for a full withdrawal. But the first elements of U.S. forces touched American soil for the first time in months on 8 March.

A NEW CRISIS – REBELLIONS

In Iraq, a new crisis was developing as disgruntled Army troops moved into the Iraqi city of Basra and began to take out their aggression against Saddam Hussein. Although these rebellions in Basra were reportedly crushed by Iraqi Republican Guard forces, the rebels gained strength from Shiite fundamentalists and Kurdish rebels in northern Iraq — which began a possible state of civil war in Iraq.

Allied responses to the uprising were muted. Although the Allies could hardly resume military operations against Iraqi forces, as there remained little organized Iraqi defense, there were incidents of combat between the cease-fire parties. Iraqi airplanes, which were being used to attack rebel forces, were shot down by American planes flying patrol over Iraq. This did not include helicopters, which were used rather effectively in attacking Kurdish positions. American forces eventually moved in to assist Kurdish refugees in Operation Provide Comfort, but this was merely a humanitarian operation.

Homecoming parade in Washington D.C. President Bush is saluted by General Norman Schwarzkopf and the returning troops from the Persian Gulf War. *Source: U.S. Government*

WELCOMING HOME THE TROOPS

Throughout March, homecomings took place at military bases around the country. U.S. forces were being pulled out in order of their time spent with the longest serving units being brought home first. Many of the lightly armed infantry troops, such as the 82nd Airborne, were to be out of the theatre by April, with the heavy armor units taking several more months. Allied air forces were brought out in a similar fashion, with the longest serving units flown out in the early part of March. At sea, several carrier groups were sent home in early March, but they were replaced by recently deployed units from the United States.

A U.S. PRESENCE IN THE GULF

Secretary of Defense Cheney and many other American military leaders announced that the United States would maintain a presence in the Gulf region for several years to come. Although forward positioning of troops on Arab soil is something that will be kept to a minimum, with more emphasis placed on joint training and prepositioning of supplies in the region.

A U.S. presence has been maintained in the Kuwaiti theatre ever since the end of the war. At times, American warplanes have shot down Iraqi fighters that violated the no-fly zone in northern and southern Iraq. There have also been tragedies as part of this protection.

In April 1994, two Army Blackhawks were shot down due to a series of errors between U.S. AWACs and F-15C fighters on patrol as part of the no-fly zone. Twenty-six people were killed including fifteen Americans, six British, French, and Turkish officers, and five Kurdish leaders.

Today, Allied aircraft still patrol over southern Iraq and United Nations inspection teams scour the Iraqi countryside, finding evidence of nuclear, chemical and biological warfare plants all over the country. Some 20,000 troops, over 200 warplanes and more than 20 warships are assigned to the Kuwait area along with 100 Tomahawk missiles. Prepositioned equipment is now in Saudi Arabia and Qatar enabling American forces to quickly return to the theater and commence operations in a matter of days. At sea, the U.S Navy has designated the ships assigned to this region as the "Fifth Fleet" and put those forces under Central Command's control.

The United States made a number of strong and valuable Allies during the conduct of Operation Desert Storm. In addition, older alliances, such as those with England, France, and Israel were strengthened. The United States is now in a better position than any time in its history to bring peace to the Middle East, but it remains to be seen if the 2,000 years of conflict will end in this century.

END-OF-THE-WAR STATISTICS

At the end of the war, reports showed that:

- 112,000 sorties had been conducted.
- 148 Americans were killed in action (KIA).
- 141 Iraqi aircraft were held in Iran.
- More than 70,000 Iraqis were held as POWs.
- 88 SCUDs were launched.

IRAQI EQUIPMENT DEGRADATION

The degradation and virtual destruction of the Iraqi military was more than evident. For example. at the start of the war, Iraq was said to have 4,280 tanks, 2,880 armored personnel carriers, and 3,100 artillery pieces. The number of Iraqi tanks destroyed prior to the ground war (100-Hour War) was 2,435. An additional 1,443 armored personnel carriers and 1,649 artillery pieces were destroyed. A daily accounting of the Iraqi equipment degradation is found in Table 11.1 below.

The devastation to the Iraqis at sea was also great. All Iraqi naval bases and ports were damaged. All northern Persian Gulf oil platforms were searched and secured. A total of 143 Iraqi vessels were destroyed or damaged, including:

- 11 anti-ship missile boats
- 2 anti-ship missile boats
- 3 Poinocny Class amphibious vessels
- 1 *IBN Khaldun* frigate
- 1 Bogomol PCF patrol boat
- 116 small craft
- 9 minelayers

All of this occurred without attacks from Iraqi surface vessels against coalition forces. Further, a number of Iraqi air power was defeated. In fact, the United States lost only one aircraft in air-to-air combat, while the United States took out thirty Iraqi aircraft. In addition, no U.S. ground troops were attacked by Iraqi aircraft. To give you a better idea of the downed Iraqi aircraft, refer to Table 11.2 on page 195.

THE STORY BEHIND MUNITIONS

Although the evening news was filled with high-tech imagery of precision-guided munitions snaking their way downward at the controls of American pilots, smart bombs were not the most commonly used munitions by Allied pilots. Dumb weaponry — also known as gravity bombs, because gravity and inertia play a major role in deciding their course — were used tens of thousands of times to devastate Iraqi soldiers and materials in the KTO.

Where the so-called smart bombs made a difference was in areas such as Baghdad, with military targets existing side-by-side to civilian areas.

TABLE 11.1

IRAQI EQUIPMENT DEGRADATION IN THE KTO

Date	Tanks	Armored Personnel Carriers	Artillery
22 Jan	14	0	77
27 Jan	65	50	281
01 Feb	476	243	356
06 Feb	728	552	535
11 Feb	862	692	771
16 Feb	1,439	879	1,271
21 Feb	1,563	887	1,428
23 Feb	1,688	929	1,452
24 Feb	1,772	948	1,474
28 Feb	2,435	1,443	1,649

TABLE 11.2

AIR-TO-AIR KILLS

Date	Aircraft	Service	Unit	Downed	Weapon
17 Jan	F-15C	USAF	1st TFW	Mirage F1	AIM-7
	F-15C	USAF		Mirage F1	Ground
	F-15C	USAF	33rd TFW	Mirage F1	AIM-7
	F-15C	USAF	33rd TFW	MIG 29	AIM-7
	F-15C	USAF	33rd TFW	MIG 29	AIM-7
	F-15C	USAF	33rd TFW	MIG-29	AIM-7
	F/A-18C	USN	VFA-81	MIG-21	AIM-9
	F/A-18C	USN	VFA-81	MIG-21	AIM-9
19 Jan	F-15C	USAF	33rd TFW	MIG-25	AIM-7
	F-15C	USAF	33rd TFW	MIG-25	AIM-7
	F-15C	USAF	33rd TFW	MIG-29	Ground
	F-15C	USAF	33rd TFW	MIG-29	AIM-7
	F-15C	USAF	36th TFW	Mirage F1	AIM-7
	F-15C	USAF	33rd TFW	Mirage F1	AIM-7
24 Jan	F-15C	RSAF	13 Squadron	Mirage F1	AIM-9
	F-15C	RSAF	13 Squadron	Mirage F1	AIM-9
26 Jan	F-15C	USAF	33rd TFW	MIG-23	AIM-7
	F-15C	USAF	33rd TFW	MIG-23	AIM-7
	F-15C	USAF	33rd TFW	MIG-23	AIM-7
27 Jan	F-15C	USAF	4th TFW	MIG-23	AIM-9
	F-15C	USAF	4th TFW	MIG-23	AIM-9
	F-15C	USAF	4th TFW	MIG-23	AIM-7
	F-15C	USAF	4th TFW	Mirage F1	AIM-7
28 Jan	F-15C	USAF	33rd TFW	MIG-23	AIM-7
29 Jan	F-15C	USAF	32nd TFG	MIG-23	AIM-7
2 Feb	F-15C	USAF	36th TFW	IL-76	AIM-7
6 Feb	F-15C	USAF	4th TFW	MIG-21	AIM-9
	F-15C	USAF	4th TFW	MIG-21	AIM-9
	F-15C	USAF	4th TFW	Su-25	AIM-9
	F-15C	USAF	4th TFW	Su-25	AIM-9
	A-10A	USAF	926th TFG	Bo 105	GAU-8
7 Feb	F-14A	USN	VF-1	Mi-8	AIM-9
	F-15C	USAF	33rd TFW	Su-7/17	AIM-7
	F-15C	USAF	33rd TFW	Su-7/17	AIM-7
	F-15C	USAF	33rd TFW	Su-7/17	AIM-7
	F-15C	USAF	36th TFW	Helo	AIM-7
11 Feb	F-15C	USAF	36th TFW	Helo	AIM-7
15 Feb	A-10A	USAF	10th TFW	Mi-8	GAU-8
20 Feb	F-15C	USAF	36th TFW	Su-22	AIM-9
22 Mar	F-15C	USAF	36th TFW	Su-22	AIM-9
	F-15C	USAF	36th TFW	PC-9	Ground

NOTE: While the 4th TFW flew F-15Es, there were other units assigned to the 4th TFW that flew the F-15C, including elements of the 36th TFW.

By utilizing a "smart weapon," Allied pilots could guide a munition onto a target and avoid the collateral damage of destroying civilians and their dwellings. The use of smart munitions also cut down on the need for any additional attack missions, with one plane (for example the F-117 Stealth) capable of taking out a target like a bridge with a high probability of success. It would take ten regular bombs on five different aircraft to take out the same target. One of the stark contradictions between the Gulf War and the more total bombings — such as those that occurred in World War II in London and Berlin — was the absence of total destruction throughout entire sections of a city.

Unfortunately, sometimes smart munitions followed their guidance, but were guided to facilities that were not purely military. One such weapon landed on a suspect Iraqi communication bunker, which turned out to be a civilian bomb shelter. This incident led to the deaths of several hundred Iraqi civilians. On other occasions, smart munitions simply missed their targets and fell a few meters short or far of their desired targets.

The following list from the *Gulf War Air Power Survey* provides a good idea at the variety of munitions used by the United States during the Gulf War.

IRAQI CASUALTIES

One of the most asked questions of the Gulf War is "How many Iraqis were killed by Allied forces?" The answer, for many reasons, is a surprising "We don't know."

During the war, the media constantly pressured the military for figures on the Iraqi death toll. Military spokespeople, from General Schwarzkopf on down refused to provide any figures to the press as they did not want to engage in

TABLE 11.3

MUNITIONS EMPLOYED IN DESERT STORM

MUNITIONS	AIR FORCE	NAVY	MARINE CORPS	TOTAL
General Purpose Bombs				
MK-82 (500 lb)	59,884	10,941	6,828	77,653
MK-83 (1,000 lb)	10,125	8,893		19,018
MK-84 (20,00 lb)	10,467	971	751	12,189
MK-117 (B-52)	43,435			43,435
CBU-52 (fragmentation bomb)	17,831			17,831
CBU-87 (combined effects munition)	10,035			10,035
CBU-89/78 (Gator)	1,105	148	61	1,314
MK-20 (Rockeye)	5,345	6,814	15,828	27,987
Laser Guided Bombs				
GBU (Laser/Mk-82)	4,086	205	202	4,493
Air-to-Surface Missiles				
AGM-114 Hellfire (AH-64 and AH-1W)	2,876 (Army)	30	159	3,065
AGM-65 All Models	5,255	41		5,296

Priority one targets. This Iraqi command and control center just east of Kuwait City was destroyed in the air raids before the ground war began. *Source: Andy Lee Johnson*

a "body count." They were trying to avoid what happened with the Vietnam War when a weekly announcement of enemy killed became almost a game, with inaccurate information coming out for political reasons. Estimates made by members of the press often exceeded 100,000 Iraqi troops killed, although these figures were at best "guesstimates" by the media's private military consultants. During the war Iraq also released the figure of 1,591 civilian casualties, but this figure should be seen only as a base estimate at best, as Saddam Hussein has constantly reestimated this figure for political reasons, along with including additional casualties who have starved or died as a result of economic sanctions still in place against Iraq many years after the war had ceased.

Currently, the estimates of Iraqi casualties range between 3,000 to 8,000, with the only factual verifiable figure being the number of Iraqis buried by American troops (only 577). American sources do not seem too concerned with precisely determining this figure, allowing private estimates to go unchallenged. Depending upon the source, the number of Iraqis who have died as a result of sanctions varies between 10,000 to more than 500,000, with accurate figures simply being impossible to determine due to the political implications of both high and low estimates.

Although not as difficult to determine, but still subject to various interpretations, are the number of Iraqi vehicles destroyed. These figures have been estimated by military sources, based in large part by photographic proof and actual physical evidence.

One reported problem, however, was the fact that some Iraqi vehicles looked operational in reconnaissance photos, but on the interior were burned or gutted by Allied munitions. These total numbers are somewhat difficult to comprehend until they are compared with the extremely low losses of American equipment or the number of vehicles lost compared to the number actually deployed.

THE DOLLAR COST OF THE WAR

This question can never be properly answered. The reason behind this is that costs cannot be properly defined to anyone's satisfaction. For example, do you include the costs of the military facilities the United States built in Saudi Arabia in the 1980s and used in the Gulf War? Do you include the replacement costs of the aircraft lost? How about the food and pay for the troops? The list of questions like this is endless, and the answers difficult to agree upon.

In 1996, the figure generally thrown around was $61 billion, of which the United States paid $7.4 billion. Table 11.4 below gives a breakdown of the various coalition country's financial contributions — also known as burden-sharing. But it is important to remember that the U.S. continued presence in the region costs money as well. In fact, the United States spends almost $400 million a year to maintain air patrols in the no-fly areas of Iraq, and in October 1994, when Saddam was threatening Kuwait again, the United States spent $390 million to rush over reinforcements (although the Kuwaitis paid $226 million for that operation as well).

TABLE 11.4
FINANCIAL BURDENSHARING BY COUNTRY*

Country	Amount Paid
Saudi Arabia	$16.8 billion
Kuwait	$16.0 billion
United Arab Emirates	$4.1 billion
Japan	$10.0 billion
Germany	$6.5 billion
South Korea	$288 million
Others	$29 million

* Figures were compiled by the Department of Defense

SORTIES

During the daily press briefings conducted by the Allied forces, the one easily reportable figure to give the media was the number of sorties — a sortie is generally considered one mission conducted by one aircraft. American forces flew thousands of sorties a week in the KTO, and thousands more transporting equipment from the United States to Saudi Arabia.

Worthy of noting is the percentage of actual strategic attack sorties versus the number of total sorties as illustrated in Table 11.5 below. For example, a strike package of say eight planes required electronic jamming aircraft be sent

TABLE 11.5
STRATEGIC ATTACK SORTIES VERSUS TOTAL SORTIES

	Target Number of Strategic Sorties	Percentage of Strategic Missions to Overall Missions
Electrical power	215	1%
Naval	247	2%
National command	429	2%
Air defense	436	2%
Oil	518	3%
C3	601	3%
Railroads/bridges	712	4%
NBC	902	5%
Military support	2,756	15%
SCUDs/missiles	2,767	15%
Airfields	3,047	17%
Republican Guards	5,646	31%
Total		18,276

aloft, Wild Weasel air defense suppression planes be flying, tanker planes on stand-by for refueling, combat air patrols be overhead to protect aircraft from enemy air power, and search and rescue aircraft be on call for pilot recovery if necessary. In contrast to this, as pointed out considerably by the Air Force press office, was the Stealth Fighter, which flew in relatively unsupported through Iraqi air defense and air cover to strike its targets.

Approximately 16 percent of all sorties launched were strategic attack missions against the Iraqi infrastructure and war machine. Table 11.5 on the previous page, breaks down the attacks by target, but it is important to remember these numbers are illustrative of the entire war, whereas on any given day the majority of targets could have differed. It was not until some of the major Iraqi air defense systems and nuclear, biological, and chemical facilities were hit that the Allied war planners shifted their attention to the Republican Guard forces.

SOME FINAL THOUGHTS

Was this war a success? This question, despite the overwhelming military triumph in Kuwait is still asked and debated throughout the United States even today. To best answer it, you have to understand that war cannot be seen in isolation of its component parts. You can't look solely at the military battles. You can't examine only the domestic or international politics of the concerned parties. Nor can you focus merely on the fact that Saddam Hussein remains in office while George Bush does not. The Persian Gulf War has to be examined as a whole.

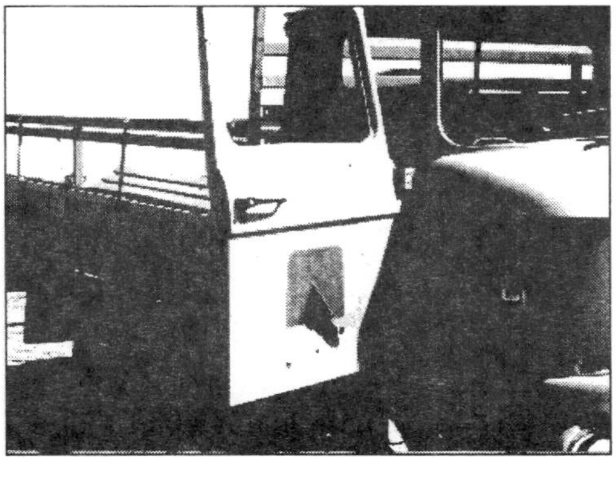

Republican Guard symbol. Once the Allied war planners knew that major Iraqi air defense and NBC facilities were destroyed, they began targeting the Iraqi Republican Guard forces. *Source: Andy Lee Johnson*

Our stated goal was the removal of Iraq from Kuwait — period. Destroying the Iraqi military was an understood consequence of this goal, and one most policymakers didn't mind accomplishing. However, following the Iraqi forces all the way back to their bases in Iraq, shooting them every step of the way, was not in the U.S. war plans. Nor was invading Baghdad to eliminate Hussein and his ruling party. We entered the war with fairly limited, publicly stated goals, from which we had some flexibility for accomplishing, but something that was not a carte blanche to do what we wanted in Iraq.

It is often spoken that the international military coalition would not stand for further operations to secure the capture of Saddam Hussein or even the continued destruction of Iraqi forces retreating northward after Kuwait had been liberated. Nor would the international diplomatic community sit idly if Allied forces pushed farther than their publicly stated goals. But it is also important to understand that American public opinion could have very easily shifted should U.S. policy had been altered.

While public opinion polls recorded unbelievably positive numbers for the president and his policies, these were the result of a quick and low casualty conflict that accomplished in days what most thought would take months and cost hundreds of American lives. As evidenced a few years later, when less than two dozen American special forces and Marines were killed in Somalia, the American public's tolerance for the loss of American lives is minimal when the policy does not have the public's full support. Pushing Iraq out of Kuwait was a goal reached through months of discussion, hearings on Capitol Hill, votes on use of force resolutions, and a general public debate. To simply go on attacking Iraq's forces when we had already destroyed so much of its offensive capabilities, or to put more American lives in jeopardy simply for the capture of Hussein may have been acceptable to many at first. But once the American death toll reached a certain point, the cries of "enough already" would have been so loud that the United States would have been forced to withdraw with its tail between its legs.

Leaving when it did provided the United States with a number of benefits. U.S. military personnel came home with relatively few casualties and a new found respect in the eyes of even the most vocal critic. A domestic political honeymoon for the president was now in place. Iraq's nuclear, chemical, and biological capabilities lay in tatters. Oil prices returned to their prewar levels. A great opportunity for Middle East peace talks existed where before there was little hope. And, the biggest threat to peace and stability in the Middle East was now licking his wounds in Baghdad for many years to come.

Chapter Twelve
The Aftereffects

A look beyond the victories and defeats of the Persian Gulf War will lead to an examination of the war's aftereffects. Similar to the aftershocks experienced following a major earthquake, the aftershocks of what occurred July 1990 through April 1991 will be felt well into the twenty-first century. This final chapter explores two of the war's most common and most controversial aftereffects — the Gulf War Syndrome and the environmental damage caused by the oil fires, oil spill, and other littering of the Arabian countryside.

GULF WAR SYNDROME

In the fog of war and the hectic nature of combat, a soldier with a cough or a headache was easily missed when casualties were counted. But as soon as troops began returning from the war, a whole series of ailments were becoming known to the veterans. Headaches, ulcers, dizziness, and other symptoms were widely reported. At first, these were dismissed as the result of climate, desert environment, and other easily explainable things. Many thought the problems would simply go away.

But the problems persisted. More and more soldiers, through a network of veterans groups and hospitals, began to relay their symptoms to one another, creating a database of information as to what was wrong with them. They brought this to the attention of the Pentagon, giving their affliction a name — the Persian Gulf War Syndrome.

Speculation centered around chemical or biological weapons release, or on the experimental medicine given to troops to counter these weapons. Hearings were held in Congress and researchers, both government and private, began a massive series of investigations. For years, the Pentagon stood behind the line that there was no "single" Gulf War syndrome, as the affliction varied from soldier to soldier, nor could any one cause be found that would have resulted in so various a number of symptoms.

However, as a result of heavy pressure from suffering veterans, the Pentagon later admitted that some chemical weapons were released during the destruction of a chemical facility and these weapons may have contaminated some coalition forces. (You can find more on this incident later in this chapter.) To better understand the controversy surrounding the Gulf War Syndrome, a study of the chemical weapons usage during Operation Desert Shield and Operation Desert Storm is necessary.

U.S. CHEMICAL WEAPONS

First of all, Iraq wasn't the one one with chemical weapons. The United States maintains a large arsenal of chemical weapons, although it has publicly stated its unwillingness to use these weapons of mass destruction in military conflicts. U.S. stockpiles are maintained in eight continental U.S. sites and on Johnston Atoll, a U.S. territory in the Pacific.

An illusion. When coalition forces found these unknown storage pods in this berm they had to call in intelligence units to search for the presence of chemical weapons. *Source: Andy Lee Johnson*

Unconfirmed reports continue to claim U.S. planners wanted to threaten (or did threaten) the Iraqis via secret diplomacy with a tactical nuclear attack if chemical weapons were employed. In *My American Journey*, written after the war, General Powell mentioned this plan, but said it was destroyed shortly after it was drafted. Whether this was just an example of the military looking at every contingency or part of an elaborate ruse may never be known.

IRAQ'S USE OF CHEMICAL WEAPONS

Iraq, on the other hand, has a history of using chemical weapons, even against its own people. During the Iran-Iraq War, chemical artillery shells were fired upon opposing forces on many occasions. Chemical weapons were also dropped on the Kurdish people in Iraq, who have long opposed the Iraqi government. Although chemical warfare manufacturing plants were targeted in the initial operations of Operation Desert Storm, Saddam Hussein stockpiled large quantities of chemical agents in a large number of storage facilities — which remained intact until after the war and are currently being destroyed by U.N. workers.

There are two known types of chemical weapons (mustard gas and nerve gas) that the Iraqis are believed to possess. Mustard gas, first used in WWI, has its name because of its noticeable smell. Today, the smell is gone but the devastating effect is still the same. Mustard gas is a blistering agent which, when in contact with exposed flesh, will cause huge and painful blisters. Should the gas be inhaled, the blistering effect is internal and oftentimes fatal. Nerve gas gets into the respiratory system and causes convulsions and respiratory failure. It is considered lethal in even the smallest doses when it comes in contact with the skin or is inhaled. The antidote kit requires an injection into the infected patient immediately, followed by more extensive medical care in a hospital.

Iraq had several different delivery systems for chemical weapons. The primary system was artillery shells, which have a lethal range of only a few hundred feet. Much more effective is air spraying — like a cropduster. But due to the Iraqi Air Force's inability to operate effectively during the Gulf War, this was not considered a great threat. On the other hand, SCUD missiles were believed to be capable of holding chemical warheads, but Saddam did not resort to chemical weapon use.

THE TERRORIZING EFFECT

Chemical weapons were not "used" in Operation Desert Storm, but their terrorizing effect was certainly felt. The first coalition troops through the lines attacked in full chemical protection gear. Further, on a number of occasions, the threat of chemical attack forced soldiers to suit up in the middle of operations. Intelligence gathered from Iraqi POWs indicated that the Iraqis were not comfortable using chemical weapons because much of their own defense against these gases was in poor condition. Subsequent searches in Kuwait after the war found no evidence of chemical weapons stores. According to the Department of Defense, more than 75 percent of the Iraqi's chemical weapons' capability was knocked out during the war.

THE KAMISIYAH INCIDENT

During 4 March through 15 March 1991, Army engineers conducted a controlled demolition of Iraqi ammunition bunkers near Kamisiyah, Iraq, to explode munitions that were captured by Allied forces. During this incident, several chemical alarms were activated and it is believed nerve

UNITS INVOLVED IN NOTIFICATION OF KAMISIYAH INCIDENT

Units associated with the 82nd Airborne Division

Headquarters, 82nd Airborne Division
Tactical Command Post, 1st Brigade, 82nd Airborne
Tactical Operations Center, 3rd Brigade, 82nd Airborne
1st Battalion, 504th Infantry
2nd Battalion, 504th Infantry
1st Battalion, 505th Infantry
2nd Battalion, 505th Infantry
3rd Battalion, 505th Infantry
4th Battalion, 325th Infantry
1st Battalion, 319th Field Artillery
3rd Battalion, 319th Field Artillery
1st Squadron, 17th Air Cavalry
3rd Battalion, 73rd Armor
313th Military Intelligence Battalion
307th Medical Battalion
307th Engineer Battalion
37th Engineer Battalion
450th Civil Affairs Battalion

Units associated with the 24th Infantry Division

Main Command Post, 24th Infantry Division
Headquarters, 197th Infantry Brigade
2nd Squadron, 4th Cavalry
24th Signal Battalion
724th Combat Support Battalion
1st Battalion, 5th Air Defense Artillery
Headquarters, 36th Engineer Group
3rd Engineer Battalion
5th Engineer Battalion
299th Engineer Battalion
362nd Engineer Company

agent that may have been stored in the facility with other munitions was released into the atmosphere. Alarms were sounding throughout the area surrounding Kamisiyah, and several tests were conducted of the air utilizing the M256 chemistry test — twelve of which indicated positive readings. But other tests, such as the M18A2, which is considered less likely to give false readings, indicated a negative presence of chemical weapons. After four hours, both tests indicated the area was clear and soldiers in the area de-masked.

Approximately 20,800 American soldiers were within a 30-mile radius of the explosion and may have been exposed to a sarin nerve agent. The Department of Defense and the Department of Veterans Affairs initiated a "notification" process to members of the several units to seek information about possible ailments from the explosion. This list is found on the previous page and below. Soldiers serving in these units are asked to call the Department of Defense Persian Gulf hotline at 800-472-6719 or the Department of Veterans Affairs Persian Gulf Registry at 800-749-8387.

Following the release of the units that may have been exposed in the Kamisiyah explosion, Congress undertook an inquiry into the Pentagon's handling of chemical weapons claims. Gripping testimony was offered by one serviceman whose friends he served with in the same unit have all died of puzzling ailments, and who himself suffers from significant medical problems following suspected chemical weapons exposure.

THE RESEARCH CONTINUES

In addition, recent studies by academic researchers have indicated that some of the anti-chemical weapons medication, when taken in combination with other anti-biological warfare medication, could have resulted in a dangerous toxin exposure to the servicemen and servicewomen. The Pentagon and the Veteran's Administration maintain large files on "Gulf War Syndrome," and numerous veteran's groups and congressmembers

UNITS INVOLVED IN NOTIFICATION OF KAMISIYAH INCIDENT (continued)

Units associated with the 101st Airborne Division (Air Assault)

Rear Command Post, 2nd Brigade, 101st Airborne Division
Headquarters, 101st Aviation Brigade
1st Battalion, 320th Field Artillery

Other Units

2nd Squadron, 3rd Armored Cavalry Regiment
Headquarters, 265th Engineer Group
Headquarters, 937th Engineer Group
12th Engineer Battalion
46th Engineer Battalion
264th Engineer Company
Tactical Command Post (TAC), XVIII Airborne Corps Artillery

Other Units (continued)

1st Battalion, 181st Field Artillery
1st Battalion, 623rd Field Artillery
Headquarters, 513th Military Intelligence Brigade
Headquarters, 12th Aviation Brigade
9th Chemical Company
36th Medical Detachment
5th Mobile Army Surgical Hospital
41st Medical Hospital
47th Combat Support Hospital
47th Field Hospital

continue to fight for a full accounting of the medical problems suffered by some Gulf War veterans.

In the fall of 1996 and spring of 1997, a presidential advisory committee on Gulf War veterans' illnesses issued a critical report of the Pentagon's handling of the Persian Gulf War Syndrome. It found that some in the military were slow to respond to the claims of veterans, oftentimes discounting them as simply stress related. Even the president's panel admitted that several of the symptoms, such as memory loss, diarrhea, fatigue, and insomnia could be blamed on symptoms unrelated to service in the Persian Gulf. However, the panel asked the Pentagon and the VA to continue their investigations into different causes of the sickness, including a possible chemical weapons link.

What had previously been placed on the back burner suddenly became a major concern for many inside Washington. Following this report, Congress undertook a series of hearings on the Gulf War Syndrome and the Pentagon's response. It is becoming clearer to many that the symptoms are not merely the results of incessant complaints, but actual ailments that need to be treated. At the Pentagon, the staff investigating Gulf War Syndrome was increased from 12 to 120 and a controversial chief investigator was replaced.

To date, 29,000 veterans have sought help from Department of Defense doctors concerning Gulf War Syndrome, and more than 68,000 have requested medical exams from the Veteran's Administration.

Interestingly, several other Allied servicemen and servicewomen, such as the British, have also reported similar symptoms. But French soldiers, who did not take the anti-chemical weapons pills nor use the insecticide DEET, remain the only ones who haven't reported any cases of Gulf War Syndrome. These pills — pyridostigmine bromide (PB) — and their combination with DEET are receiving greater interest as the investigations continue.

There still is no one, simple explanation behind Gulf War Syndrome, nor is there one easily prescribed cure. But a newfound investigative desire to solve this crisis, rather than just to push it away, seems to prevail amongst many in Washington. For a better understanding of how servicemen and servicewomen who may be suffering from Gulf War Syndrome can take advantage of the programs that exist, the VA fact sheet included at the end of this chapter highlights much of what is known to date.

ENVIRONMENTAL DAMAGE

Beyond the numbers of destroyed tanks and captured soldiers, the Gulf War took a toll on the Middle East environment — the likes of which have never been seen. The ecological warfare that took place — some of it intended and some of it the result of a modern military force — continues to affect the ecosystem of Kuwait, Iraq, and the Persian Gulf.

Perhaps the most visible damage came from Kuwaiti oil wells. Before retreating northward, Iraqi forces smashed open almost 800 oil wells and lit the spilling oil on fire. The first estimates called for one to five years to snuff out the fires that spewed black smoke over the Kuwaiti countryside. But a combination of American, Canadian, and other Allied firefighting teams were able to snuff out all the fires in six months. Even the famous Red Adair, who was memorialized in the John Wayne movie *Hell Fighters*, was called into action to help extinguish these fires. One unique firefighting company from Czechoslovakia utilized a surplus military fighter jet engine mounted on a tank's chassis to blow out the fires in one single effort, but this invention came late in the cleanup.

Those oil wells that did not go up in flames were left open to vent oil directly onto the sands of Kuwait. A giant oil pool of nearly 60 million barrels was spread onto the desert land, with nearly 49 square kilometers eventually being covered by oil. Reclamation efforts were successful in recycling about 21 million barrels of weathered crude oil. The

Firefighters in Kuwaiti oil fields. It was originally estimated that the fires would be contained over a period of several years, yet Allied firefighters managed to douse all of the fires in six months. *Source: Michael Lawson*

soil that was covered remains highly contaminated and has the potential to cause damage to the underground water supplies in the next few years.

At sea, oil was vented into the Persian Gulf, fouling the waters and threatening numerous sea birds and native fish species. About six to eight million barrels were released into the Persian Gulf. Balls of tar were found along the shores leading to a major clean-up effort estimated to cost Kuwait about $450 million dollars. Additional environmental dangers were the result of a modern military machine. Several stories have floated in the Middle Eastern press about the dangers of depleted uranium shells — the material of choice for many American munitions. The debate rages as to the lethal nature of these systems. Some say the shells are as harmless as any other piece of scrap metal. Others claim they are the functional equivalent of raw nuclear material littering the sands of Kuwait.

There have also been problems with unexploded ordnance that litters Kuwait and southern Iraq. Not only were nearly a million land mines spread throughout the region, but unexploded bombs and artillery shells lay buried under a shallow layer of sand, occasionally exploding when handled. Kuwait has spend some $800 million on ordnance removal, but many devices are still present and undiscovered.

Iraqi war materials also account for much of the environmental damage in the region. Rusting shells of Iraqi tanks and other vehicles have been left to rot in the desert sand, leaking oil and other fluids into the sand and, eventually, into the water supply. At sea, nearly 260 Kuwaiti and Iraqi vessels litter the bottom of the coastal regions, ranging in size from small pleasure craft to 100,000 ton oil tankers threatening the maritime environment.

International environmental conferences are continuously held to discuss solutions to many of the problems that continue to rage in the Middle East region. It will be years before some of the effects of the war can be accurately assessed. It may even take decades to determine and implement a solution to the environmental problems.

DEPARTMENT OF VETERANS AFFAIRS (VA) PROGRAMS FOR PERSIAN GULF VETERANS

The Department of Veterans Affairs (VA) offers Persian Gulf veterans physical examinations and special eligibility for follow-on care, and it operates a toll-free hotline at 800-749-8387 to inform these veterans of the program and their benefits. VA also is compensating veterans under unprecedented regulations addressing undiagnosed conditions. Special research centers and other investigations are searching for answers to aid seriously ill patients whose underlying disease is unexplained. Most Gulf veterans are diagnosed and treated; but for some, such symptoms as joint pain or fatigue have been chronic. Some respond to treatment of symptom even though their doctors have not yet identified an underlying illness or pathogenic agent.

UNEXPLAINED ILLNESS

The prevalence of unexplained illnesses among Persian Gulf veterans is uncertain. Data from special VA examinations show that 10,391 veterans had current symptoms and did not receive a diagnosis. This may be an overestimate or underestimate of the problem of "undiagnosed illnesses" as the diagnoses recorded may not explain all the symptoms. Further, VA does not have information on the chronology, severity or current existence of the symptoms. Answers about illness prevalence are expected through epidemiologic research involving representative samples of the Gulf veteran population.

PERSIAN GULF "SYNDROME" UNDEFINED

Several panels of government physicians and private-sector scientific experts have been unable to discern any new illness or unique symptom complex such as that popularly called "Persian Gulf Syndrome." "No single disease or syndrome is apparent, but rather multiple illnesses with overlapping symptoms and causes," wrote an outside panel led by professors from Harvard and John Hopkins University that convened for an April 1994 National Institute of Health (NIH) workshop. VA has neither confirmed nor ruled out the possibility of a singular Gulf syndrome.

RESEARCH AND RISK FACTORS

With variation in exposures and veterans' concerns ranging from depleted uranium in armaments to possible contamination from Iraqi chemical/biological agents, VA has

VA PROGRAMS FOR PERSIAN GULF VETERANS (continued)

initiated wide-ranging research projects evaluating illnesses as well as risk factors in the Gulf environment, spending $2.75 million in fiscal year 1995. The activation of three research centers conducting 14 protocols has enabled VA to broaden its activity from largely descriptive evaluations to greater emphasis on hypothesis-driven research.

STATISTICS

Some 945,000 servicemembers served in the Gulf from August 1990 through the end of 1994, nearly 697,000 of them serving in the first year. About 549,000 have become potentially eligible for VA care as veterans, having separated from the military or having become deactivated reservists or Guard members. More than 57,000 veterans have responded to VA's outreach encouraging any Gulf veteran to get a free physical exam under VA's Persian Gulf Program. Not all are ill. Twelve percent of the veterans who had the registry health exam had no health complaint (among the first 52,000 computerized records). Twenty-six percent of the same group rated their health as poor or very poor, while 73 percent reported their health as all right to very good (the remaining one percent did not have an opinion).

VA HEALTH PROGRAMS FOR GULF VETERANS

Special Health Examination

A free, complete physical examination with basic lab studies is offered to every Persian Gulf veteran, whether or not the veteran is ill. A centralized registry of participants, begun in August 1992, is maintained to enable VA to update veterans on research findings or new compensation policies through periodic newsletters. This clinical database also provides information about possible health trends and may suggest areas to be explored in future scientific research. The 57,000 Persian Gulf veterans who have taken advantage of the physical examination program become part of a larger Persian Gulf Registry. As defined by P.L.102-585, this includes 181,000 Gulf veterans (generally including those counted in the special examination program) who have been seen for routine VA hospital or clinic care, or who have filed compensation claims — or whose survivor registers a claim.

Persian Gulf Information Center

VA offers a toll-free information line at 800-PGW-VETS (800-749-8387) where operators are trained to help veterans with general questions about medical care and other benefits. It also provides recorded messages that enable callers to obtain information 24 hours a day. Information also is being disseminated 24 hours a day through a national computer bulletin board, VA ONLINE, at 800-US1-VETS (800-871- 8387). It also can be reached via the Internet at *telnet://vaonline.va.gov.*

Special Access to Follow-On Care

VA has designated a physician at every VA medical center to coordinate the special examination program and to receive updated educational materials and information as experience is gained nationally. Where an illness possibly related to exposure to an

VA PROGRAMS FOR PERSIAN GULF VETERANS (continued)

environmental hazard or toxic substance is detected during the examination, follow-up care is provided on a higher-eligibility basis than most non-service-connected care. As with the health examination registry, VA requested and received special statutory authority to bypass eligibility rules governing access to the VA health system.

Persian Gulf Referral Centers

If the veteran's illness defies diagnosis, the veteran may be referred to one of four Persian Gulf Referral Centers. Created in 1992, the first centers were located at VA medical centers in Washington, D.C.; Houston, Texas; and Los Angeles, California, with an additional center designated at Birmingham, Alabama, in June 1995. These centers provide assessment by specialists in such areas as pulmonary and infectious disease, immunology, neuropsychology, and additional expertise as indicated in such areas as toxicology or multiple chemical sensitivity. There have been approximately 296 veterans assessed at the centers; most ultimately are being diagnosed with known/definable conditions.

Standardized Exam Protocols

VA has expanded its special examination protocol as more experience has been gained about the health of Gulf veterans. The protocol elicits information about symptoms and exposures, calls the clinician's attention to diseases endemic to the Gulf region, and directs baseline laboratory studies including chest X-ray (if one has not been done recently), blood count, urinalysis, and a set of blood chemistry and enzyme analyses that detect the "biochemical fingerprints" of certain diseases. In addition to this core laboratory work for every veteran undergoing the Persian Gulf program exam, physicians order additional tests and specialty consults as they would normally in following a diagnostic trail — as symptoms dictate. If a diagnosis is not apparent, facilities follow the "comprehensive clinical evaluation protocol" originally developed for VA's referral centers and now used in VA and military medical centers nationwide.

The protocol suggests 22 additional baseline tests and additional specialty consultations, outlining dozens of further diagnostic procedures to be considered, depending on symptoms.

Risk Factors of Concern to Veterans

Veterans have reported a wide range of factors observed in the Gulf environment or speculative risks about which they have voiced concerns. Some are the subject of research investigations and none have been ruled out. There appears to be no unifying exposure that would account for all unexplained illnesses. Individual veterans' exposures and experiences range from ships to desert encampments, and differences in military occupational specialty frequently dictate the kinds of elements to which servicemembers are exposed. Veteran concerns include exposure to the rubble and dust from exploded shells made from depleted uranium (or handling of the shells); the possibility of a yet-unconfirmed Iraqi chemical-biological agent; and a nerve agent pre-treatment drug, pyridostigmine bromide.

VA PROGRAMS FOR PERSIAN GULF VETERANS (continued)

Many other risk factors also have been raised. In 1991, VA initially began to develop tracking mechanisms that matured into the Persian Gulf Registry as a direct consequence of early concerns about the environmental influence of oil wellfires and their smoke and particulate.

Interagency Coordination and White House Response

The federal response to the health consequences of Persian Gulf service is being led by the Persian Gulf Veterans Coordinating Board composed of the Department of Veterans Affairs and the Department of Defense and Health and Human Services. Working groups are collaborating in the areas of research, clinical issues and disability compensation. The board and its subgroups are a valuable vehicle for communication between top managers and scientists, including a staff office for the board that follows up on critical issues and promotes continuity in agency activities. President Clinton designated VA as the coordinating board's lead agency.

In March 1995, President Clinton announced formation of the Presidential Advisory Committee on Gulf War Veterans' Illnesses to review and make recommendations on: coordinating board activities; research, medical examination and treatment programs; federal outreach; and other issues ranging from risk factors to chemical exposure reports. It has been meeting since August 1995 and published its first report 15 February 1996.

MEDICAL RESEARCH

Environmental Hazards Research Centers

Through a vigorous scientific competition, VA developed major focal points for Gulf veteran health studies at three medical centers: Boston, Massachusetts; East Orange, New Jersey; and Portland, Oregon. With 14 protocols among them, the centers are conducting a variety of interdisciplinary projects, including some aimed at developing a case definition for an unexplained illness and clarification of risk factors. Some protocols involve areas of emerging scientific understanding, such as chronic fatigue syndrome or multiple chemical sensitivity, while others are evaluating or comparing factors in immunity, psychiatry, pulmonary response, neuroendocrinology and other body systems, some at the molecular level.

Health Survey and Mortality Study

VA's Environmental Epidemiology Service is surveying 15,000 randomly selected Gulf veterans and an equal size control group of veterans of the same time period (but who were not deployed) to compare symptoms in veterans and their family members, examining risk factors and providing physical examinations for a representative sample to help validate the self-reported health data.

That office also is engaged in a mortality study, analyzing death certificates to determine any patterns of difference in causes of deaths between deceased Gulf veterans and matched controls. Preliminary data have suggested the deployed veterans have a higher

VA PROGRAMS FOR PERSIAN GULF VETERANS (continued)

rate of post-war deaths due to accidents and traumatic injury as opposed to diseases or illness. Further analysis is continuing, with a report expected to be submitted for publication in a scientific journal later this year. (Independent of the study, VA has learned of 2,900 deaths among deployed veterans, which is lower than expected under general U.S. mortality rates.)

Exposure-Oriented Studies

Some current VA investigations are examining hypotheses of specific potential risks and comparing study subjects with controls who did not serve in the Gulf to determine differences in health patterns. A Baltimore project is following the health status of individuals who retained tiny embedded fragments of depleted uranium. A Birmingham, Alabama, pilot program offers an extensive battery of neurological tests aimed at detecting dysfunction that would be expected after exposure to certain chemical weapons.

Other Federal and Collaborative Studies

In its second annual report to Congress in March 1995, VA, on behalf of the Persian Gulf Veterans Coordinating Board participating agencies, detailed about 50 Persian Gulf research initiatives, reviews and clinical investigations, many involving VA. For example, VA investigators are collaborating with the Naval Medical Research Center in San Diego, California, in general epidemiological studies comparing Gulf veterans and control-group veterans (who served elsewhere) to detect differences in symptoms, hospitalizations, and birth outcomes in large cohorts of active duty servicemembers. A detailed research working plan is available online at *http://www.dtic.dla.mil/gulflink/varpt*.

Outside Reviews

With the Department of Defense (DOD), VA has contracted with the National Academy of Sciences (NAS) to review existing scientific and other information on the health consequences of Gulf operations. Congress has authorized VA and DOD to provide up to $500,000 annually to fund the review. In its first report issued in January 1995, a committee of the NAS Institute of Medicine called for systematic scientific research, including large epidemiological studies. Its recommendations urged greater coordination between federal agencies to prevent unnecessary duplication and assure high-priority studies are conducted.

Another nongovernment expert panel brought together at an NIH technology assessment workshop in April 1994 examined data and heard from both veterans and scientists, concluding that no single or multiple etiology or biological explanation for the reported symptoms could be identified and indicating it is impossible at this time to establish a single case definition for the health problems of Gulf veterans. A copy of this report is available through VA-ONLINE.

VA PROGRAMS FOR PERSIAN GULF VETERANS (continued)

VA Disability Compensation

On 3 February 1995, VA published a final regulation on compensation payments to chronically disabled Persian Gulf veterans with undiagnosed illnesses. The undiagnosed illnesses, which must have become manifest either during service in or within two years of leaving the Southwest Asia theater, may fall into 13 categories: fatigue; signs or symptoms involving skin; headache; muscle pain; joint pain; neurologic signs or symptoms; neuropsychological signs or symptoms; signs or symptoms involving the respiratory system (upper or lower); sleep disturbances; gastrointestinal signs or symptoms; cardiovascular signs or symptoms; abnormal weight loss; and menstrual disorders. While these categories represent the signs and symptoms frequently noted in VA's experience to date, other signs and symptoms also could qualify for compensation. A disability is considered chronic if it has existed for at least six months.

For claims considered under this special regulation, VA has a 29 percent approval rate among claims where the veteran has demonstrated symptoms within a required two-year period after leaving the Gulf. Among the remaining 71 percent, most are diagnosable conditions treated under conventional regulations, while some symptoms fail to meet the 6-month chronicity requirement or are found to be related to another known cause.

Outside of the new regulation, VA has long based monthly compensation for veterans on finding evidence a condition arose during or was aggravated by service. VA has approved 22,694 compensation claims of Gulf veterans for service injuries or illnesses of all kinds, including 1,033 claims in which the veteran alleged the cause was an environmental hazard, and within that group, 421 claims approved under the new undiagnosed illnesses regulation.

APPENDIXES

Appendix A
Army Units Deployed

Note to Readers: An asterisk in the second column indicates that this information was unavailable at the time of printing. For those readers who can supply additional information, please contact the author via email at *andrew@leyden.com*.

III Corps Artillery	Fort Sill, OK
VII Corps Artillery	Augsburg, Germany
VII Corps Aviation "Warriors" Brigade	*
VII Corps Division "Wagonmasters" Support Command	*
XVIII Airborne Corps Artillery	Fort Bragg, NC
1st Armored Division	Ansbach, Germany
1st Cavalry Division	Fort Hood, TX
1st Infantry Division (Mechanized)	Fort Riley, KS
2nd Corps Support Command	Stuttgart, Germany
Tiger Brigade, 2nd Armored Division (Forward)	Garlstedt, Germany
2nd Armored Cavalry Regiment	Nuremberg, Germany
3rd Armored Cavalry Regiment	Fort Bliss, TX
3rd Armored Division	Frankfurt, Germany
3rd Armored Division Combat Aviation Brigade	Frankfurt, Germany
3rd Infantry Division	Wurzburg,Germany
7th Medical Command	Heidelberg,Germany
11th Air Defense Artillery Brigade	Fort Bliss, TX
11th Armored Cavalry Regiment (4 Scout Platoons)	Fulda, Germany
42nd Field Artillery Brigade	Fort Polk, LA
72nd Field Artillery Brigade	Fort Sill, OK
75th Field Artillery Brigade	Fort Sill, OK
210th Field Artillery Brigade	Germany
212th Field Artillery Brigade	Fort Sill, OK
214th Field Artillery Brigade	Fort Sill, OK
31st Air Defense Artillery	Fort Hood, TX
3rd Field Artillery, 1st Battalion	Germany
92nd Field Artillery (MLRS)	Germany
5th Air Defense Artillery	Fort Hood, TX
43rd Air Defense Artillery	Fort Bliss, TX
11th Combat Aviation Brigade	Illesheim, Germany

12th Combat Aviation Brigade	Weisbaden, Germany
18th Aviation Brigade	Fort Bragg, NC
17th Air Cavalry	Fort Bragg, NC
13th Corps Support Command	Fort Hood, TX
24th Infantry Division (Mechanized)	Fort Stewart, GA
Division Artillery	
Aviation Brigade	
Division Engineer Brigade	
82nd Airborne Division	Fort Bragg, NC
101st Airborne Division (Air Assault)	Fort Campbell, KY
Artillery Brigade	
Aviation Brigade	
197th Infantry Brigade (Mechanized) (Separate)	Fort Benning, GA
HQ, 3rd U.S. Army	Fort McPherson, GA
HQ, VII Corps	Stuttgart, Germany
HQ, XVIII Airborne Corps	Fort Bragg, NC
44th Medical Brigade	Fort Bragg, NC
5th Special Forces Group	Fort Campbell, KY
3rd Special Forces Group (Abn)	Fort Bragg, NC
528th Special Operations Support Battalion	Fort Bragg, NC
112th Special Operations Signal Battalion	Fort Bragg, NC
A Company, 10th Special Forces Group	Fort Devens, MA
513th Military Intelligence Brigade	Fort Monmouth, NJ
15th Military Intelligence Battalion	*
11th Signal Brigade	Fort Huachuca, AZ
13th Signal Battalion	Fort Hood, TX
142nd Signal Battalion	Fort Hood, TX
1st Engineer Battalion	Fort Riley, KS
8th Engineer Battalion	Fort Hood, TX
7th Engineering Brigade	Fort Bragg, NC
20th Engineering Brigade	Fort Bragg, NC
14th Military Police Brigade	Germany
16th Military Police Brigade	Fort Bragg, NC
89th Military Police Brigade	Fort Hood, TX
3rd Personnel Group	Fort Hood, TX
5th Signal Corps	Germany
63rd Signal Battalion	Georgia
4th Psychological Operations Group	Fort Bragg, NC
6th Psychological Operations Group	Fort Bragg, NC
504th Military Intelligence Brigade	Fort Hood, TX
3rd Signal Corps	Fort Hood, TX
E Company, 304th Military Intelligence Battalion	*
207th Military Intelligence Brigade, VII Corps	Germany
94th Transportation Detachment	Fort Bragg, NC

502nd Forward Support Battalion	*
1022nd Air Ambulance Company	*

Detachment 1, 101 Military Intelligence Battalion, 1st Infantry Division

Goppingen, Germany

7th Signal Brigade

Mannheim, Germany

SPECIAL UNITS

Delta Force

USLOK – Security Assistance Team / U.S. Embassy

U.S. Special Operations Weather Teams (SOWTs)

SELECTED ARMY GUARD AND RESERVE UNITS ACTIVATED AS PART OF OPERATION DESERT SHIELD/STORM

Major Combat Units

1st Battalion, 108th Armor	Georgia
1st Battalion, 121st Infantry (Mechanized)	Georgia
1st Battalion, 141st Field Artillery	Louisiana
1st Battalion, 156th Armor	Louisiana
1st Battalion, 198th Armor	Mississippi
1st Battalion, 230th Field Artillery	Georgia
2nd Battalion, 121st Infantry (Mechanized)	Georgia
2nd Battalion, 156th Infantry (Mechanized)	Louisiana
2nd Battalion, 198th Armor	Mississippi
3rd Battalion, 141st Infantry (Mechanized)	Texas
3rd Battalion, 156th Infantry (Mechanized)	Louisiana
48th Infantry Brigade (Mechanized)	Georgia
1st Battalion, 142nd Field Artillery Brigade	Arkansas
2nd Battalion, 142nd Field Artillery Brigade	Arkansas
142nd Field Artillery Brigade	Arkansas
152nd Armored Battalion	Alabama
155th Armored Brigade	Mississippi
256th Infantry Brigade (Mechanized)	Louisiana
E Troop, 348th Armored Cavalry Regiment	Georgia

OTHER UNITS

Alabama

1241st Adjutant General Company	Guard
1207th Quartermaster Company	Guard
1207th U.S. Army Hospital	Reserve
314th Public Affairs Detachment	Reserve
322nd Military History Detachment	Reserve
318th Chemical Company	Reserve

Alabama (continued)

907th Chemical Detachment	Reserve
123rd Combat Support Company	Guard
715th Combat Support Company	Guard
1208th Quartermaster Company	Guard
1659th Transportation Detachment	Guard
490th Chemical Detachment	Reserve
851st Combat Support Group	Reserve
173rd Judge Advocate General Detachment	Reserve
81st Transportation Detachment	Reserve
287th Transportation Company	Reserve
1167th Transportation Detachment	Guard
731st Combat Support Battalion	Guard
226th Combat Support Company	Guard
778th Combat Support Company	Guard
638th Ordinance Company	Guard
1128th Transportation Company	Guard
377th Quartermaster Company (POL OPS)	Guard
781st Transportation Company	Reserve
1208th Quartermaster Company(Water Purification)	Guard
46th Engineer Battalion	Guard
226th Area Support Group	Guard

Arizona

348th Transportation Company	Reserve
2221st Quartermaster Company	Guard
2220th Transportation Company	Guard
222nd Transportation Company	Guard
2222nd Transportation Company	Guard
363rd EOD Detachment	Guard
416th Air Traffic Control	Guard
855th Military Police Company	Guard
259th Engineering Company	Guard
1404th Transportation Company	Guard
356th Signal Company	Guard
374th Medical Detachment	Reserve

Arkansas

299th Engineer Company	Reserve
296th Medical Company	Guard
374th Medical Company	Reserve
1122nd Transportation Detachment	Guard

California

419th Quartermaster Battalion	Reserve
316th Quartermaster Company	Reserve
2668th Transportation Company	Guard
224th Transportation Detachment	Guard
1113th Transportation Company	Guard

Colorado

1157th Transportation Detachment	Guard
1158th Transportation Detachment	Guard
193rd Military Police Battalion	Guard
220th Military Police Company	Guard
928th Medical Company	Guard
217th Medical Company	Guard
947th Medical Company	Guard

Connecticut

142nd Medical Company	Guard
344th Military Police Company	Reserve

District of Columbia

207th JAG Detachment	Reserve
547th Transportation Company	Guard
380th Combat Support Company	Guard
372nd Military Police Battalion	Guard

Florida

3220th U.S. Army Garrison	Reserve
337th Military Battalion	Reserve
160th Military Police Battalion	Reserve
351st Military Police Company	Reserve
810th Military Police Company	Reserve
351st Adjutant General Company	Reserve
320th Military Police Company	Reserve
146th Transportation Detachment	Reserve
322nd Quartermaster Detachment	Reserve
138th Aviation Company (EW)	Reserve
743rd Combat Support Company	Guard
325th Combat Support Company	Guard
873rd Quartermaster Detachment	Reserve
347th Medical Detachment	Reserve
653rd Signal Company	Guard
410th Quartermaster Detachment	Guard

Georgia

461st Adjutant General Company	Reserve
3299th Dental Detachment	Reserve
Operations Center Augmentation	Reserve
3297th Army Hospital	Reserve
433rd Chemical Detachment	Reserve
337th Military Battalion	Reserve
1015th Combat Support Company	Reserve
145th Medical Detachment	Reserve
190th Military Police Company	Guard
1148th Transportation Company	Guard
988th Combat Support Company	Reserve
Third U.S. Army	Reserve
165th Quartermaster Company	Guard
48th Armored Brigade	Guard
138th Medical Company	Guard
382nd Field Hospital	Reserve

Illinois

1138th Military Police Company	Guard
419th Transportation Detachment	Reserve
416th Engineer Command Detachment	Reserve
300th Adjutant General Detachment	Reserve
1544th Transportation Company	Guard
339th Transportation Detachment	Reserve
1244th Transportation Company	Guard
724th Transportation Company	Reserve
387th Quartermaster Battalion	Reserve
A-7/158 Aviation Regiment	Guard
108th Medical Battalion	Guard
882nd Military Police Company	Reserve
933rd Military Police Company	Guard
233rd Military Police Company	Guard

Indiana

838th Transportation Detachment	Guard
209th Combat Support Company	Reserve
1015 Adjutant General Unit	Guard
766th Transportation Detachment	Reserve
300th Combat Support Battalion	Reserve
1438th Transportation Detachment	Guard
21st Theater Area Army Command	Reserve
425th Adjutant General Company	Guard
425th Quartermaster Company	Reserve

Indiana (continued)

417th Quartermaster Company	Reserve
380th Quartermaster Company	Reserve
685th Transportation Company	Reserve
375th Medical Detachment	Guard
5030th Finance Support Company	Guard

Iowa

1133rd Transportation Company	Guard
4249th Military Police Detachment	Reserve
915th Transportation Company	Reserve

Kansas

170th Heavy Equipment Maintenance Company	Guard
13th Quartermaster Detachment	Reserve
129th Transportation Company	Reserve
842nd Quartermaster Company	Reserve
475th Engineer Detachment	Reserve
467th Engineer Detachment	Reserve
410th Evacuation Hospital	Reserve
793rd Military Police Battalion	*
144th Evacuation Hospital	Guard
1011th Quartermaster Company	Reserve

Kentucky

3346th Dental Detachment	Reserve
137th Transportation Detachment	Guard
217th Quartermaster Detachment	Guard
2123rd Transportation Detachment	Guard
623rd Field Artillery	Guard
438th Military Police Company	Guard
4th Training Support Brigade	Guard

Louisiana

312th Military Intelligence Battalion	Reserve
1086th Transportation Company	Guard
872nd Medical Detachment	Reserve
1190th Deployment Control	Reserve
1191st Transportation Terminal	Reserve
1192nd Transportation Terminal	Reserve
1090th Transportation Detachment	Guard
321st Logistics Center	Reserve
1083rd Transportation Company	Guard
1087th Transportation Company	Guard

Louisiana (continued)

57th Engineer Battalion	Guard
3673rd Comp. Service Company	Guard
256th Infantry Brigade	Guard

Maine

619th Transportation Company	Reserve
3620th Transportation Detachment	Guard
286th Supply and Service Battalion	Guard

Maryland

372nd Military Police Company	Reserve
352nd Civil Affairs Command	Reserve
417th Transportation Detachment	Reserve
1176th Transportation Terminal	Reserve
200th Military Police Company	Guard
290th Military Police Company	Guard
400th Military Police Battalion	Reserve
200th Transportation Detachment	Reserve
202nd Transportation Detachment	Reserve

Massachusetts

772nd Military Company	Guard
972nd Military Police Company	Guard
46th Judge Advocate General Detachment	Reserve
704th Transportation Detachment	Guard
324th Adjutant General	Reserve
1058th Transportation Company	Guard
181st Engineer Company	Guard
46th Combat Support Hospital	Reserve

Michigan

5064th U.S. Army Garrison	Guard
460th Combat Support Company	Guard
1009th Transportation Detachment	Guard
1461st Transportation Company	Guard
180th Transportation Company	Reserve
301st Military Police	Reserve
144th Military Police Company	Guard
210th Military Police Battalion	Guard
745th Ordnance Detachment	Guard
1776th Military Police Company	Guard

Minnesota

109th Combat Support Company	Guard
109th Light Equipment Maintenance Company	Guard
275th Military Police Company	Guard

Mississippi

1181st Transportation Terminal	Reserve
114th Military Police Company	Guard
365th Combat Support Detachment	Reserve
479th Ordnance Company	Reserve
193rd Transportation Battalion	Guard
162nd Military Police Company	Guard
112th Military Police Battalion	Guard
386th Transportation Company	Reserve
296th Transportation Company	Reserve
173rd Quartermaster Company	Reserve
786th Transportation Company	Guard
386th Personnel and Administrative Branch	Reserve

Missouri

624th Engineer Detachment	Reserve
858th Combat Support Detachment	Reserve
1138th Military Police Company	Guard
93rd Evacuation Hospital	Reserve
1267th Medical Company	Guard
35th Rear Area Operations Center	Guard
451st Medical Detachment	Reserve
376th Engineer Platoon	Reserve

Montana

370th Quartermaster Battalion	Reserve

Nebraska

1012th Combat Support Company	Reserve
172nd Transportation Company	Reserve
24th Medical Company (Air Ambulance)	Guard
Detachment 1, 1267th Medical Company (Air Ambulance)	Guard

New Hampshire

744th Transportation Company	Guard

New Jersey

253rd Transportation Company	Guard
328th Transportation Detachment	Guard
144th Supply Company	Guard

New Mexico

281st Transportation Company	Reserve
53rd Engineer Company	Reserve

New York

211th Military Intelligence Company	Reserve
1302nd Military Police Detachment	Reserve
10th Transportation Detachment	Guard
139th Transportation Detachment	Reserve
142nd Transportation Detachment	Reserve
423rd Medical Detachment	Reserve
318th Transportation Agency	Reserve
719th Transportation Company	Guard
623rd Transportation Company	Reserve
411th Engineer Brigade	Reserve
24th Military Intelligence Battalion	Reserve
159th Mobile Army Surgical Hospital	Reserve
639th Transportation	*
800th Military Police Brigade	Reserve

North Carolina

991st Transportation Company	Reserve
1450th Transportation Company	Guard
540th Quartermaster Detachment	Guard
121st Transportation Detachment	Guard
1454 Transportation Company	Guard
431st Quartermaster Detachment	Reserve
805th Military Police Company	Reserve
211th Military Police Company	Guard
398th Combat Support Company	Guard
385th Transportation Detachment	Reserve
315th Quartermaster Detachment	Reserve
210th Military Police Company	Guard
171st Combat Support Company	Reserve
337th Military Battalion	Reserve
382nd Public Affairs Detachment	Guard
3274th Army Hospital	Reserve
29th Transportation Detachment	Reserve
422 Civil Affairs Battalion	Reserve
28th Combat Support Hospital	Reserve

North Dakota

132nd Quartermaster Company	Guard
134th Quartermaster Detachment	Guard
131st Quartermaster Detachment	Guard
308th Engineer Detachment	Reserve

Ohio

2361st Mobile Signal Communications Center	Reserve
79th Quartermaster Detachment	Reserve
1001st Combat Support Company	Reserve
758th Combat Support Company	Reserve
828th Combat Support Company	Reserve
837th Combat Support Detachment	Reserve
870th Combat Support Detachment	Reserve
342nd Military Police Company	Reserve
316th Medical Detachment	Reserve
1052nd Transportation Company	Guard
350th Evacuation Hospital	Reserve
838th Military Police Company	Guard
1485th Transportation Company	Guard

Oklahoma

2120th Combat Support Company	Guard
158th Field Artillery (MLRS)	Guard
142nd Field Artillery Brigade	Guard
75th Field Artillery	Guard
745 Military Police Company	Guard
445th Military Police Company	Guard
245th Medical Company	Guard
120th Medical Battalion	Guard

Oregon

206th Transportation Detachment	Guard
2186th Light Equipment Maintenance Company	Guard

Pennsylvania

300th Field Hospital	Guard
316th Field Hospital	Reserve
121st Transportation Company	Guard
3623rd Maintenance Company	Guard
402nd Military Police	Guard
1185th Transportation Terminal	Reserve
442nd Combat Support Company	Reserve
635th Quartermaster Detachment	Reserve

Pennsylvania (continued)

298th Transportation Company	Reserve
228th Transportation Detachment	Guard
475th Quartermaster Detachment	Reserve
347th Quartermaster Company	Reserve
131st Transportation Company	Guard
14th Quartermaster Detachment	Reserve

Units formed, but never served due to SCUD attack at AJUN Compound include the 387th Transportation Company (PROVISIONAL) Fill from AD, USAR & NGR *and* 377th Transportation Company (PROVISIONAL). *The 387th had command and control of the AJUN Compound the night the SCUD hit. The units from Pennsylvania would not have been in the building twenty-four hours earlier or later.*

Puerto Rico

394th Quartermaster Battalion	Reserve
311th Quartermaster Company	Reserve
219th Quartermaster Detachment	Guard
276th Combat Support Company	Reserve
430th Combat Support Company	Reserve

Rhode Island

115th Military Police Company	Guard

South Carolina

265th Quartermaster Detachment	Guard
596th Transportation Detachment	Reserve
3271st Army Hospital	Reserve
3273rd Army Hospital	Reserve
413th Chemical Company	Reserve
187th Judge Advocate General Detachment	Reserve
132nd Military Police Company	Guard
747th Transportation Detachment	Guard
371st Chemical Company	Reserve
450th Ordinance Company	Reserve
941st Transportation Company	Reserve
120th Rear Area Operation Center	Reserve
251 Evacuation Hospital	Guard

South Dakota

57th Transportation Detachment	Guard
747th Transportation Detachment	Guard
452nd Ordnance Company	Reserve

Tennessee

130th Combat Support Center	Guard
176th Combat Support Detachment	Guard

Tennesse (continued)

3397th Army Garrison	Reserve
776th Combat Support Company	Guard
251st Combat Support Company	Guard
1175th Quartermaster Company	Guard
360th Quartermaster Detachment	Reserve
212th Engineer Company	Guard
382 Medical Detachment	Reserve
1032rd Transportation Company	Guard
181st Field Artillery Battalion	Guard
196th Field Artillery Brigade	Guard
984th Military Police Company	Guard
268th Military Police Company	Guard
269th Military Police Company	Guard
300th Mobile Army Surgical Hospital	Reserve
155th Engineer Company	Guard
775th Engineer Company Detachment	Guard
861st Quartermaster Company	*
1174 Transportation Company	Guard
912th Mobile Army Surgical Hospital	Reserve
332nd Medical Brigade	Reserve
807 Mobile Army Surgical Hospital	Reserve

Texas

4005th Army Hospital	Reserve
327th Chemical Company	Reserve
302nd Military Police Company	Reserve
601st Transportation Detachment	Reserve
541st Transportation Detachment	Reserve
1104th Transportation Detachment	Guard
340th Combat Support Company	Reserve
383rd Quartermaster Company	Reserve
149th Adjutant General Company	Guard
15th Quartermaster Detachment	Reserve
644th Transportation Company	Reserve
808th Engineer Company	*
273rd Medical Detachment	Reserve

Utah

120th Quartermaster Detachment	Guard
142nd Military Intelligence Battalion	Guard
144th Evacuation Hospital	Guard
403rd CSH, 322nd Medical Brigade	Guard
419th Transportation Unit	Reserve

Virginia

91st Transportation Detachment	Reserve
145th Transportation Detachment	Reserve
986th Medical Detachment	Guard
1033rd Transportation Company	Guard
1032nd Transportation Company	Guard
116 Military History Detachment	Guard
HHD, 1030 EN Battalion	Guard
183 Personal Service Company	Guard
229th Military Police Company	Guard
HHC, 176 EN Group	Guard

Washington

1444th Transportation Detachment	Guard
907th Engineer Platoon	Reserve
50th General Hospital	Reserve

West Virginia

328th Quartermaster Detachment	Reserve
313th Military Police Detachment	Reserve
646th Quartermaster Company	Reserve
388th Quartermaster Detachment	Reserve
351st Ordnance Company	Reserve
201st Field Artillery	Guard

Wisconsin

13th Evacuation Hospital	Guard
13th Combat Support Hospital	Guard
432nd Civil Affairs Group	Reserve
304th Transportation Detachment	Reserve
343rd Transportation Detachment	Reserve
826th Ordnance Company	Reserve
107th Combat Support Company	Guard
340th Transportation Detachment	Reserve
1122nd Transportation Detachment	Guard
890th Transportation Company	Reserve
1158th Transportation Company	Guard
395th Ordnance Company	Reserve
1157th Transportation Company	Guard

Wyoming

1022nd Medical Evacuation Company	Guard

Appendix B
Navy Units Deployed

Note to Readers: An asterisk in the second column indicates that this information was unavailable at the time of printing. For those readers who can supply additional information, please contact the author via email at *andrew@leyden.com.*

AIRCRAFT CARRIERS

CVN-62 Independence	*
CV-41 Midway	Yokosuku, Japan
CV-60 Saratoga	Mayport, FL
CV-61 Ranger	San Diego, CA
CV-66 America	Norfolk, VA
CV-67 John F. Kennedy	Norfolk, VA
CVN-71 Theodore Roosevelt	Norfolk, VA
CVN-69 Dwight D. Eisenhower	*

BATTLESHIPS

BB-63 Missouri	Long Beach, CA
BB-64 Wisconsin	Norfolk, VA

CRUISERS

CG-18 Worden	Pearl Harbor, HI
CG-20 Richmond K. Turner	Charleston, SC
CG-22 England	San Diego, CA
CG-30 Horne	*
CG-29 Jouett	*
CG-47 Ticonderoga	*
CG-31 Sterett	Subic Bay, Philippines
CG-34 Biddle	Norfolk, VA
CG-50 Valley Forge	San Diego, CA
CG-51 Thomas Gates	Norfolk, VA
CG-52 Bunker Hill	Yokosuku, Japan
CG-53 Mobile Bay	Mayport, FL
CG-54 Antietam	Long Beach, CA
CG-55 Leyte Gulf	Mayport, FL
CG-56 San Jacinto	Norfolk, VA
CG-58 Philippine Sea	Mayport, FL

CRUISERS (continued)

CG-59 Princeton	Long Beach, CA
CG-60 Normandy	Norfolk, VA
CGN-37 South Carolina	*
CGN-38 Virginia	Norfolk, VA
CGN-40 Mississippi	Norfolk, VA

DESTROYERS

DD-963 Spruance	*
DD-964 Paul F. Foster	Long Beach, CA
DD-966 Hewitt	Mayport, FL
DD-970 Caron	New Orleans, LA
DD-971 David A. Ray	Long Beach, CA
DD-972 Olendorf	Yokosuku, Japan
DD-975 O'Brien	San Diego, CA
DD-980 Moosbrugger	Charleston, SC
DD-986 Harry W. Hill	San Diego, CA
DD-991 Fife	Yokosuku, Japan
DD-993 Kidd	*
DD-984 Leftwich	*
DD-995 Scott	*
DD-983 John Rodgers	*
DDG-10 Sampson	Mayport, FL
DDG-39 MacDonough	Charleston, SC
DDG-46 Preble	Norfolk, VA
DDG-44 William V. Pratt	Charleston, SC
DDG-620 Goldsborough	*
DDG-19 Tattnall	*

FRIGATES

FFG-33 Jarrett	*
FFG-32 John Hall	*
FFG-8 McInerney	*
FFG-30 Reid	San Diego, CA
FFG-38 Curts	Yokosuku, Japan
FFG-40 Halyburton	Charleston, SC
FFG-46 Rentz	San Diego, CA
FFG-47 Nicholas	Charleston, SC
FFG-48 Vandergrift	Long Beach, CA
FFG-49 Robert G. Bradley	Charleston, SC
FFG-50 Taylor	Charleston, SC
FFG-53 Hawes	Charleston, SC
FFG-54 Ford	Long Beach, CA
FFG-58 Samuel B. Roberts	Newport, RI

FRIGATES (continued)

FF-1067 Francis Hammond	Long Beach, CA
FF-1068 Vreeland	Norfolk, VA
FF-1066 Shields	*
FF-1080 Paul	*
FF-1063 Reasoner	*
FF-1086 Brewton	*
FF-1082 Elmer Montgomery	Mayport, FL
FF-1088 Barbey	San Diego, CA
FF-1092 Thomas C. Hart	Norfolk, VA

SUBMARINES*

SSN-724 Louisville	San Diego, CA
SSN-750 Newport News	*
SSN-690 Philadelphia	*
SSN-720 Pittsburgh	*
SSN-721 Chicago	*

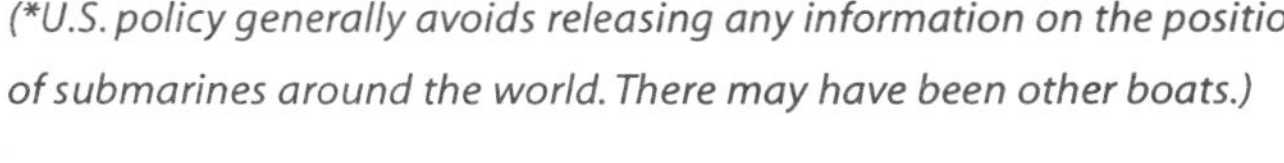
*(*U.S. policy generally avoids releasing any information on the position of submarines around the world. There may have been other boats.)*

HOSPITAL SHIPS

TAH-19 Mercy	Oakland, CA
TAH-20 Comfort	Baltimore, MD

AMPHIBIOUS ASSAULT SHIPS

LPH-2 Iwo Jima	Norfolk, VA
LPH-9 Guam	Norfolk, VA
LHA-4 Nassau	Norfolk, VA
LPH-12 Inchon	Norfolk, VA
LHA-1 Tarawa	San Diego, CA
LPH-10 Tripoli	San Diego, CA
LPH-11 New Orleans	San Diego, CA
LPH-3 Okinawa	San Diego, CA

LANDING SHIPS

LSD-41 Whidbey Island	Little Creek, VA
LSD-44 Gunston Hall	San Diego, CA
LSD-37 Portland	Norfolk, VA
LSD-38 Pensacola	Norfolk, VA
LST-1179 Newport	Little Creek, VA
LST-1193 Fairfax County	Little Creek, VA
LST-1188 Saginaw	Little Creek, VA
LST-1186 Cayuga	Long Beach, CA

LANDING SHIPS (continued)

LST-1184 Fredrick	*
LST-1192 Spartanburg County	Norfolk, VA
LST-1180 Manitowoc	Norfolk, VA
LST-1194 La Moure County	Norfolk, VA
LST-1183 Peoria	San Diego, CA
LST-1189 San Bernadino	Sasebo, Japan
LST-1195 Barbour County	San Diego, CA
LSD-36 Anchorage	Long Beach, CA
LSD-39 Mount Vernon	Long Beach, CA
LSD-40 Fort Fisher	San Diego, CA
LSD-41 Whidbey Island	*
LSD-43 Fort McHenry	Norfolk, VA
LSD-42 Germantown	San Diego, CA
LPD-1 Raleigh	Norfolk, VA
LPD-2 Vancouver	San Francisco, CA
LPD-5 Ogden	Long Beach, CA
LPD-8 Dubuque	Sasebo, Japan
LPD-9 Denver	San Diego, CA
LPD-10 Juneau	San Diego, CA
LPD-12 Shreveport	Norfolk, VA
LPD-13 Nashville	Norfolk, VA
LPD-14 Trenton	Norfolk, VA
LKA-114 Durham	San Diego, CA
LKA-115 Mobile	Long Beach, CA
LKA-116 Saint Louis	Sasebo, Japan
LST-1185 Schenectady	Long Beach, CA

FAST COMBAT SUPPORT SHIPS

AOE-1 Sacramento	Bremerton, WA
AOE-3 Seattle	Norfolk, VA
AOE-4 Detroit	Earle, NJ

COMMAND VESSELS

AGF-31 La Salle	Philadelphia, PA
LCC-19 Blue Ridge	Yokosuku, Japan

MINESWEEPERS

MSO-449 Impervious	Mayport, FL
MSO-490 Leader	Charleston, SC
MSO-509 Adroit	Norfolk, VA
MCM-1 Avenger	Charleston, SC

TENDERS

AD-41 Yellowstone	Norfolk, VA
AD-38 Puget Sound	Norfolk, VA
AD-42 Acadia	San Diego, CA
AD-18 Sierra	Charleston, SC
AS-41 McKee	San Diego, CA

REPAIR SHIPS

AR-8 Jason	San Diego, CA
AR-5 Vulcan	Norfolk, VA

RESERVE SHIP/TUG

ATS-2 Beaufort	Sasebo, Japan

OILERS

AOR-3 Kansas City	Oakland, CA
AOR-7 Kalamazoo	Norfolk, VA
AO-186 Platte	Norfolk, VA
AO-177 Cimarron	Oakland, CA

AMMUNITION SHIPS

AE-23 Nitro	Earle, NJ
AE-28 Santa Barbara	Charleston, SC
AE-33 Shasta	Concord, CA
AE-35 Kiska	Concord, CA
AE-25 Halekala	*
AE-29 Mount Hood	*
AE-21 Suribachi	Lenardo, NJ
AE-21 Flint	*

COMBAT SUPPLY SHIPS

AFS-1 Mars	San Francisco, CA
AFS-4 White Plains	Guam
AFS-7 San Jose	Guam
AFS-2 Sylvania	Norfolk, VA
AFS-3 Niagara Falls	Guam
AFS-6 San Diego	Norfolk, VA

OTHER UNITS

Navy Special Warfare Group One	*
Seal Team One (two platoons)	*
Seal Team Five (two platoons)	*
Swimmer Delivery Vehicle Team One (one platoon)	*
Special Boat Unit 12	*
Naval Special Warfare Development Group (high-speed boat detachment)	*

CARRIER AIR WINGS DEPLOYED

USS Eisenhower (CVN-69)
Carrier Air Group 7

Squadron	Aircraft
VF-142	F-14 Tomcat
VF-143	F-14 Tomcat
VFA-131	F/A-18 Hornet
VFA-136	F/A-18 Hornet
VA-34	A-6E and KA-6 Intruder
VAW-121	E-2C Hawkeye
VAQ-140	EA-6B Prowler
VS-31	S-3 Viking
HS-5	SH-3H Sea King

USS Independence (CVN-62)

Squadron	Aircraft
Carrier	Air Wing 14
VF-21	F-14 Tomcat
VF-154	F-14 Tomcat
VFA-25	F/A-18 Hornet
VFA-113	F/A-18 Hornet
VA-196	A-6E and KA-6 Intruder
VAW-113	E-2C Hawkeye
VAQ-139	EA-6B Prowler
VS-37	S-3 Viking
HS-8	SH-3H Sea King

CARRIER AIR WINGS
USS America (CV-66)
Carrier Air Wing 1

Squadron	Aircraft
VF-33	F-14A Tomcat
VF-102	F-14A Tomcat
VFA-82	F/A-18C Hornet
VFA-86	F/A-18C Hornet
VA-85	A-6E and KA-6D Intruder
VAW-123	E-2C Hawkeye
VAQ-137	EA-6B Prowler
VS-32	S-3 Viking
HS-11	SH-3H Sea King

USS Saratoga (CV-60)
Carrier Air Wing 17

Squadron	Aircraft
VF-74	F-14A+ Tomcat
VF-103	F-14A+ Tomcat
VFA-83	F/A-18 Hornet
VFA-81	F/A-18 Hornet
VA-35	A-6E and KA-6D Intruder
VAW-125	E-2C Hawkeye
VAQ-132	EA-6B Prowler
VS-30	S-3 Viking
HS-3	SH-3H Sea King

USS Ranger (CV-61)
Carrier Air Wing 2

Squadron	Aircraft
VF-1	F-14A Tomcat
VF-2	F-14A Tomcat
VFA-155	A-6E Intruder
VA-145	A-6E and KA-6 Intruder
VAW-116	E-2C Hawkeye
VAQ-131	EA-6B Prowler
VS-38	S-3A Viking
HS-14	SH-3H Sea King

USS Midway (CV-41)
Carrier Air Wing 5

Squadron	Aircraft
VFA-195	F/A-18 Hornet
VFA-151	F/A-18 Hornet
VFA-192	F/A-18 Hornet
VA-185	A-6E and KA-6D Intruder
VAW-115	E-2C Hawkeye
VAQ-136	EA-6B Prowler
HS-12	SH-3H Sea King

USS Roosevelt (CVN-71)
Carrier Air Wing 8

Squadron	Aircraft
VF-41	F-14A Tomcat
VF-84	F-14A Tomcat
VFA-15	F/A-18 Hornet
VFA-87	F/A-18 Hornet
VA-36	A-6E Intruder

USS ROOSEVELT (continued)

VA-65	A-6E Intruder
VAW-124	E-2C Hawkeye
VAQ-141	EA-6B Prowler
VS-24	S-3 Viking
HS-9	SH-3H Sea King

USS John Kennedy (CV-67)
Carrier Air Wing 3

Squadron	Aircraft
VF-14	F-14A Tomcat
VF-32	F-14A Tomcat
VA-46	A-7E Corsair II
VA-72	A-7E Corsair II
VA-75	A-6E and KA-6D Intruder
VAW-126	E-2C Hawkeye
VAQ-130	EA-6B Prowler
VS-22	S-3 Viking
HS-7	SH-3H Sea King

OTHER NAVY AIR WINGS DEPLOYED

HC-11	HC-1
HC-6	HC-8
HM-14	HSL-32
HSL-33	HSL-34
HSL-35	HSL-36
HSL-42	HSL-43
HSL-44	HSL-46
HSL-48	VP-11
VP-19	VP-23
VP-4	V-8
VP-40	VP-91
VPMAU	VPU-1
VPU-2	VQ-1
VQ-2	VR-24
VRC-30	VRC-50
VP-46	
VRC-50	
VR-56	
VR-47	
VR-59	
VR-55	

SELECTED NAVY RESERVE UNITS

Alabama

Naval Reserve Naval Hospital	Mobile

Alaska

WPNSTA Concord	Anchorage

Arizona

Naval Reserve Medical Unit	Phoenix
Naval Hospital San Diego	Phoenix
Marine Corps 29Palms Branch Hospital	Tucson

Arkansas

WPNSTA Concord	North Little Rock
WPNSTA Yorktown	Little Rock

California

Naval Reserve Medical IMA 12067A	San Francisco
Naval Reserve Medical IMA 12063A	Sacramento
Navy Reserve Naval Hospital San Diego	San Bernardino
Navy Reserve Naval Hospital Oakland	Stockton
Naval Reserve Medical Command San Francisco	Alameda
Navy Reserve Naval Hospital Lemoore	Pt. Mugu
Navy Reserve Naval Hospital Lemoore	Lemoore
Navy Reserve NAS Alameda Medical	Alameda
COMNAVIUWGRU ONE	San Diego
Mobile Inshore Undersea Warfare Unit	San Francisco
NR COMSCSEA	Pomona
NR COMSCPAC 120	Alameda
NR MSCO EAST PAC	Santa Barbara
NR COMSCPAC 220	Alameda
Navy Reserve Naval Hospital Camp Pendleton	Los Angeles
Naval Hospital Oakland Unit	Alameda
Naval Medical Clinic Port Hueneme	Encino
Naval Medical Command Northwest	Fresno
Naval Hospital Long Beach	Long Beach
Mobile Inshore Undersea Warfare	Long Beach
Naval Reserve NAS Moffett	Moffett Field
Naval Medical Command	Sacramento
Naval Hospital Oakland	San Jose
Naval Hospital San Diego Unit 519	San Diego
Naval Hospital San Diego Unit 449	San Diego
Medical Unit P-1942A	San Diego
Naval Hospital San Diego Unit 119	San Diego

California (continued)

Navy Reserve Naval Hospital San Diego	San Diego
Naval Reserve Medical Unit	Los Angeles
Medical Unit P-2067A	San Francisco
Naval Medical Command Northwest	San Francisco
Naval Reserve Medical P-1945A	Santa Ana
Naval Reserve Naval Hospital Camp Pendleton	Santa Ana
Naval Hospital Oakland	Vallejo
CBC PORT HUENEME	Santa Barbara
CBC PORT HUENEME DETACHMENT B	San Bruno
CTF-168-0794	San Diego
FIRSTPAC 1287	Alameda
FIRSTPAC 0894	San Diego
NTIC 0820	Alameda
IPAC 0319	San Diego
IPAC 0220	Alameda
WPNSTA Seal Beach 219	Los Angeles
WPNSTA Seal Beach 519	Pomona
WPNSTA Seal Beach HQ 119	Long Beach
WPNSTA Seal Beach Detachment 319	Encino
WPNSTA Concord	San Jose
WPNSTA Concord	Stockton
WPNSTA Concord	Fresno
WPNSTA Concord	Pacific Grove
CTF 168-0620	Alameda
Special Boat Unit 11	Vallejo
Special Boat Unit 13	San Francisco
Navy Special Warfare Group 1	Santa Barbara
Navy Special Warfare Unit 1	Vallejo
SEAL TEAMS 1/3/5	San Diego
Navy Special War Group 1	San Diego
NCSO Los Angeles	Los Angeles

Colorado

WPNSTA Seal Beach	Aurora
CNAVEUR 118	Aurora
VANOPINTCEN 0171	Aurora
CINCPACE/NSIU	Aurora
FIRSTPAC 1371	Aurora
IPAC 0171	Aurora

District of Columbia

Naval Hospital Bethesda Unit 2906	Washington
Medical Unit PO-655A	Washington

District of Columbia (continued)

Naval Reserve COMSC HQ Detachment 206	Washington
Naval Reserve NCSO Europe 206	Washington
NIC 0166	Washington
NIAC 0166	Washington
DEFATTACHE 0166	Washington
WPNSTA Yorktown Detachment B206	Washington
ABFC/AMCC	Washington
OPNAV 04 Detachment 0106	Washington
FOSIC Europe 0166	Washington
NAVOPINTCEN 0566	Washington
NAVOPINTCEN 0666	Washington
NICSEC 0166	Washington
DIA Current Intelligence 0166	Washington
CNO Plans 0166	Washington
CNO Analysis 0166	Washington
SECGRU 0706	Washington
NISRO 0166	Washington

Florida

Naval Reserve Navy Dental Clinic	Jacksonville
Navy Reserve Naval Hospital	Pensacola
Mobile Inshore Warfare Unit	Miami
Minesweeper Impervious	Jacksonville
CINCUSCENCOM108	Tampa
FIRSTEURLANT 0774	Jacksonville
CTF-168 0208	Jacksonville

Georgia

CINCEURINT 0167	Marietta
FIRSTEURLANT 0967	Marietta
Naval Reserve NSCO Mideast	Atlanta
Medical Individual Mobilization	Atlanta
Naval Reserve Naval Medical Clinic	Marietta

Hawaii

CINCPACFLT 120	Pearl Harbor
CINCPACFLT 1120	Pearl Harbor
IPAC 0468	Pearl Harbor
Naval Reserve CINCPACFLT	Honolulu
Naval Reserve ABFC	Honolulu

Illinois

Naval Reserve Naval Hospital Philadelphia	Forest Park

Illinois (continued)

Naval Reserve Medical Unit P-1326B	Great Lakes
Naval Control of Shipping Mideast	Forest Park
DEFINTERROG 372	Glenview
NCSO Korea/NZ 113	Forest Park
NCSO Chicago 413	Great Lakes
FIRSTEURLANT 1572	Glenview
NAVOPINTCEN 0872	Glenview

Indiana

Naval Reserve Naval Hospital Great Lakes	Indianapolis
Naval Reserve Naval Hospital Philadelphia	Terre Haute
WPNSTA Concord	South Bend
WPNSTA Concord	Terre Haute
WEPNSTA Yorktown Detachment B113	Gary

Louisiana

Naval Reserve Naval Hospital Pensacola	Alexandria
Naval Reserve Naval Hospital New Orleans	New Orleans
NCSO NOLA 110	New Orleans
COMFAIRMED HQ 1082	Belle Chase
FISTEURLANT 1182	Belle Chase

Maine

Naval Hospital Philadelphia 101	Augusta
Naval Reserve COMSCMED 201	Bangor

Maryland

WEPNSTA Yorktown Detachment A 206	Baltimore
Naval Hospital Bethesda Unit	Adelphi
Naval Hospital Bethesda Unit	Adelphi
Naval Reserve NCS COMSC/NCC/MARAD106	Adelphi
Uniformed Service University of Health Sciences	Adelphi
Medical Unit P-0605B	Baltimore
Medical Unit P-0605C	Baltimore
Naval Reserve NCSO Baltimore	Baltimore
Naval Medical Clinic Annapolis	Baltimore

Massachusetts

Naval Reserve Naval Medical NAS	South Weymouth
SECGRU CHICOPEE	Chicopee
NS Rota Det. 0391	South Weymouth
FIRSTEURLANT 0291	South Weymouth
FIRSTEURLANT 0191	South Weymouth

Michigan

Naval Hospital Patuxent River	Mount Clemens
SECGRU Detroit	Southfield
NAS Sigonella Detachment 0573	Mount Clemens
FIRSTEURLANT 1773	Mount Clemens
FIRSTEURLANT 1673	Mount Clemens

Minnesota

FIRSTPAC 0178	Minneapolis
FIRSTPAC 0278	Minneapolis
DIA H.Q. 0878	Minneapolis

Missouri

Mobile Inshore Undersea Warfare Unit 112	Bridgeton
WPNSTA Concord	Bridgeton
USTRANSCOM	Bridgeton
NIC 0218	Bridgeton

Nebraska

CNAVEUR 318	Omaha

Nevada

Naval Reserve Naval Hospital San Diego	Las Vegas
Naval Reserve NAS Fallon	Reno

New Hampshire

Mobile Inshore Undersea Warfare Unit	Portsmouth
AMCC Four/Six 101	Manchester

New Jersey

Naval Reserve Commander Military Sealift Command	Kearney

New York

Naval Reserve Naval Hospital Bethesda 802	Albany
Naval Reserve Naval Hospital Bethesda 1102	Poughskeepsie
COMFAIRMED NCSO 202	Mattydale
Naval Reserve Naval Hospital Bethesda 1402	Staten Island
Naval Hospital Bethesda	Brooklyn
Naval Hospital Bethesda	Mattydale
SECGRU AMITYVILLE	Amityville
NCSO Argentia	Bronx

North Carolina

Medical Unit P-0725A	Greensboro
Medical Unit P-0783A	Wilmington

North Carolina (continued)

Naval Hospital Camp Lejeune	Raleigh
Naval Hospital Cherry Point	Wilmington
NR Military Sealift Command Charleston	Raleigh
Naval Reserve Naval Hospital Camp Lejeune	Charlotte
Naval Reserve Naval Hospital Charleston	Asheville
Naval Hospital Camp Lejeune	Greensboro

Ohio

AMCC EIGHT/NINE 205	Dayton
Commander Middle East Force 105	Youngstown
FIRSTEURLANT 1081	Columbus
NTIC 0605	Columbus

Oklahoma

ABFC SSU 211	Oklahoma City

Oregon

Convoy Commander 122	Eugene
PHIB CB 1 DET 122	Eugene

Pennsylvania

Naval Reserve Medical IMA I0451A	Philadelphia
Naval Reserve Branch Medical CL 0193	Willow Grove
NISRO 0893	Willow Grove
FIRSTEURLANT 0693	Willow Grove
FIRSTEURLANT 0593	Willow Grove
NAVOPINTCEN 0102	Willow Grove
NAVOPINTCEN 0293	Willow Grove

Rhode Island

Naval Reserve Medical IMA 10143A	Providence

South Carolina

NAS Sigonella CHB 4 Detachment	Charleston
Naval Hospital Charleston	Charleston
AMCC Three/Ten 307	Greenville
Naval Hospital Charleston	Greenville

South Dakota

WPNSTA SEAL BEACH 716	Sioux Falls

Tennessee

Reserve NAS Chase Field MED 0179	Millington
CINCLANT/USCINCLANT 0209	Millington
FIRSTEURLANT 1379	Millington

Texas

Naval Reserve Naval Hospital Jacksonville	Austin
Naval Reserve Naval Hospital MEDUNIT	Austin
Naval Reserve Medical Unit P-0125B	Houston
MIUWU 108	Corpus Christi
NAS Kingsville MED 170	Dallas
Medical Unit P1046A	San Antonio
Naval Reserve Military Sealift Command	Orange
Naval Reserve Naval Hospital Corpus	Houston
NICHQ 0170	Dallas
COM 7th Fleet 111	Dallas
WPNSTA Seal Beach 411	El Paso
FIRSTPAC 0470	Dallas
FIRSTPAC 0370	Dallas
FIRSTPAC 1070	Dallas
DIAHQ	Dallas
NVOPINTCEN 0770	Dallas

Utah

Naval Reserve MED IMA 12065A	Salt Lake City
Naval Medical Command	Salt Lake City
Naval Hospital Oakland 920	Ogden
CBC Port Hueneme Detachment A	Salt Lake City

Vermont

Naval Reserve Naval Hospital	Burlington

Virginia

Naval Reserve Naval Station Norfolk BRCL 106	Norfolk
Naval Medical Services Unit P-0623A	Norfolk
Inshore Undersea Warfare Group Two	Norfolk
Minesweeper Androit	Norfolk
Naval Hospital Portsmouth	Roanoke
Naval Reserve NAB Little Creek	Norfolk
Naval Reserve Naval Hospital Portsmouth	Norfolk
Naval Reserve Naval Station Norfolk Clinic	Norfolk
Naval Reserve Medical Individual Mobilization	Portsmouth
Naval Reserve Hospital Quantico	Richmond
Naval Hospital Bethesda Unit 2806	Stauton
Naval Reserve Medical Unit P-0615A	Stauton
Naval Reserve Medical Unit P-0645A	Richmond
Special Boat Unit 24	Norfolk
NORVA NCSO 306	Norfolk
WEPNSTA Yorktown Detachment A 113	Stauton

Virginia (continued)

WEPNSTA Yorktown Detachment C 206	Stauton
FOSIF Rota 0186	Norfolk
CINCLANTFLT 0186	Norfolk
LANTJIC 0186	Norfolk
FIRSTEURLANT 0486	Norfolk

Washington

Medical Individual Mobilization	Seattle
Naval Reserve Naval Hospital	Oak Harbor
Naval Reserve MSCO PAC	Seattle
FISTPAC 1489	Oak Harbor
FISTPAC 1689	Oak Harbor
IPAC 0522	Oak Harbor
DIAHQ 0522	Oak Harbor

Wisconsin

Naval Control Shipping Office Mideast	Milwaukee
Naval Reserve Medical Unit P-1351A	*

West Virginia

Naval Reserve Medical Unit P-0650A	Charleston

Appendix C

Marine Corps Units Deployed

Note to Readers: An asterisk in the second column indicates that this information was unavailable at the time of printing. For those readers who can supply additional information, please contact the author via email at *andrew@leyden.com.*

I Marine Expeditionary Force (I MEF)	Camp Pendleton, CA
II Marine Expeditionary Force (II MEF)	Camp Lejeune, NC
III Marine Expeditionary Force (III MEF)	Okinawa
1st Marine Division	Camp Pendleton, CA
2nd Marine Division	Camp Lejeune, NC
1st Marine Expeditionary Brigade	Kaneohe, HI
5th Marine Expeditionary Brigade	Camp Pendleton, CA
4th Marine Expeditionary Brigade	Norfolk, VA
7th Marine Expeditionary Brigade	29Palms, CA
Maritime Prepositioned Ships MPS-1, MPS-2, MPS-3	Guam, Diego Garcia, and Norfolk, VA
Regimental Combat Team 7	29 Palms, CA
Brigade Service Support Group 7	Camp Pendleton, CA
Marine Aircraft Group 11	El Toro, CA
Marine Aircraft Group 13	Yuma, AZ
Marine Aircraft Group 16	Camp Pendleton, CA
Marine Aircraft Group 26	MCAS New River
Marine Air Control Group 38	El Toro, CA
Marine Wing Support Group 37	El Toro, CA

MARINE CORPS RESERVE UNITS DEPLOYED

4th Marine Division	*
4th Force Service Support Group	*
4th Marine Aircraft Wing	*

AVIATION UNITS

Marine Aircraft Group-41	*
Marine Aircraft Group-42	*
Marine Aircraft Group-46	*

AVIATION UNITS (continued)

Marine Aircraft Group-49	*
Marine Air Control Group-48	*
Marine Wing Support Group-47	*
HMA-775	*
HMA-773	*

GROUND UNITS

(These groups were composed of active duty servicemembers and Reservists from bases all over the world.)

1st Battalion, 14th Marines	*
2nd Battalion, 14th Marines	*
3rd Battalion, 14th Marines	*
2nd Battalion, 23rd Marines	*
3rd Battalion, 23rd Marines	*
1st Battalion, 24th Marines	*
2nd Battalion, 24th Marines	*
3rd Battalion, 24th Marines	*
1st Battalion, 25th Marines	*
2nd Battalion, 25th Marines	*
3rd Battalion, 25th Marines	*
3rd Civil Affairs Group	*
4th Civil Affairs Group	*
Combat Service Support Det-40	*
Combat Service Support Det-41	*
6th Engineer Support Battalion	*
4th Light Armored Vehicle Battalion	*
6th Motor Transport Battalion	*
4th Landing Support Battalion*	
8th Tank Battalion	*
4th Tank Battalion	*
4th Light Anti Air Defense Battalion	*
4th Assault Amphibian Battalion	*
4th Anti Aircraft Battalion	*
4th Combat Engineer Battalion	*
4th Reconnaissance Battalion	*
4th Maintenance Battalion	*
1st Military Police Company	*
6th Motor Transport Battalion	*
4th Medical Battalion	*
6th Engineer Support Battalion	*
6th Communication Battalion	*
4th Supply Battalion	*
8th Tank Battalion	*

Appendix D
Air Force Units Deployed

Note to Readers: An asterisk in the second column indicates that this information was unavailable at the time of printing. For those readers who can supply additional information, please contact the author via email at *andrew@leyden.com.*

FIGHTERS

1st Tactical Fighter Wing (F-15s)	Langley AFB, VA
4th Tactical Fighter Wing (F-15s)	Seymour-Johnson AFB, NC
10th Tactical Fighter Wing (A-10s)	RAF Alconbury, U.K.
17th Tactical Fighter Wing	*
20th Tactical Fighter Wing	RAF Heyford, U.K.
23rd Tactical Fighter Wing (A-10s)	England AFB, LA
33rd Tactical Fighter Wing (F-15s)	Eglin AFB, FL
35th Tactical Fighter Wing (F-4s)	George AFB, CA
36th Tactical Fighter Wing (F-15s)	Bitburg, Germany
37th Tactical Fighter Wing (F-117s)	Nevada
48th Tactical Fighter Wing (F-16s)	RAF Lakenheath, U.K.
50th Tactical Fighter Wing (F-16s)	Hahn AFB, Germany
52nd Tactical Fighter Wing (F-4s)	Sprangdahlem, Germany
345th Tactical Fighter Wing	*
347th Tactical Fighter Wing (F-16s)	Moody, GA
354th Tactical Fighter Wing (A-10s)	Myrtle Beach, SC
363rd Tactical Fighter Wing (F-16s)	Shaw AFB, SC
366th Tactical Fighter Wing (EF-111A)	Mountain Home AFB, ID
388th Tactical Fighter Wing (F-16s)	Hill AFB, UT
401st Tactical Fighter Wing (F-16s)	Torrejon AFB, Spain

BOMBERS

48th Tactical Fighter Wing (F-111s)	RAF Lakenheath, U.K.
306th Strategic Air Wing (F-111s)	Mildenhall, England
93rd Bombardment Wing (B-52s)	Castle AFB, CA
42nd Bombardment Wing (B-52s)	Loring AFB, ME
379th Bombardment Wing	Wurtsmith AFB, MI
2nd Bomb Wing (B-52G)	*
97th Bomb Wing (B-52Gs)	Eaker AFB, AK
416th Bomb Wing (B-52Gs)	Griffis AFB, NY

SUPPORT AND OTHER AIRCRAFT

411th JSTARS Sqadron (E-8A)	Melbourne, FL (in testing)
552nd Air Warning Wing (E-3 AWACs)	Tinker AFB, OK
26th Tactical Reconnaissance Wing (RF-4C)	Zweibrucken, Germany
41st Electronic Combat Squadron	Davis-Monthan AFB, AZ
42nd Electronic Combat Squadron (EC-130H)	Sembach, Germany
43rd Electronic Combat Squadron (EC-130H)	*
66th Electronic Wing (EF-111A)	Sembach, Germany
67th Tactical Recon Wing (RF-4s)	Bergstrom AFB, TX
507th Tactical Air Control Wing (OA-10)	Shaw AFB, SC
602nd Tactical Air Control Wing (OA-10)	Davis-Monthan AFB, AZ
366th Tactical Fighter Wing (EF-111)	Mountain Home AFB, ID
9th Strategic Reconnaissance Wing	Beale AFB, CA
17th Reconnaissance Wing	RAF Alconbury, UK
55th Strategic Reconnaissance Wing	Offut AFB, NE
314th Tactical Airlift Wing (C-130)	Little Rock AFB, AR
317th Tactical Airlift Wing (C-130)	Pope AFB, NC
374th Tactical Airlift Wing (C-130)	Yokota, Japan
435th Tactical Airlift Wing (C-130)	Rhein Main AFB, Germany
463rd Tactical Airlift Wing (C-130)	Dover AFB, DE
375th Tactical Airlift Wing (C-21s)	Scott AFB, IL
1st Special Operations Wing	Hurlbert Field, FL
39th Special Operations Wing	RAF Alconbury, UK
8th Special Operations Squadron (MC-130E)	Hulbert Field, FL
9th Special Operations Squadron (HC-130)	Eglin AFB, FL
16th Special Operations Squadron (HC-130N/P)	Eglin AFB, FL
20th Special Operations Squadron (MJ-53J)	Eglin AFB, FL
55th Special Operations Squadron (MH-60G)	Eglin AFB, FL
60th Military Airlift Wing	Travis AFB, CA
62nd Military Airlift Wing	McChord AFB, WA
63rd Military Airlift Wing	Norton AFB, CA
436th Military Airlift Wing	Dover AFB, DE
729 Tactical Air Control Squadron	*
1606th Security Police Sqadron	Kirtland AFB, NM
416th Air Traffic Control Platoon	*
437th Military Airlift Wing	Charleston AFB, SC
438th Military Airlift Wing	McGuire AFB, NJ
552nd Airborne Warning and Control Wing	Tinker AFB, OK
507th Tactical Air Control Wing	Shaw AFB, SC
602nd Tactical Air Control Wing	Davis-Monthan AFB, AZ
820th RED HORSE Civil Engineering Squadron	Nellis AFB, NV.
823rd RED HORSE Civil Engineering Squadron	Hurlburt Field, FL
27th Tactical Fighter Wing (support units)	Cannon AFB, NM

SUPPORT AIRCRAFT (continued)

7th Airborne Command Squadron (EC-130)	Kessler AFB
726 Tactical Control Squadron	Homestead
728th Tactical Control Squadron	Eglin AFB, FL
2nd Bomb Wing, tankers (KC-10A)	Barksdale
5th Bomb Wing, tankers (KC-135A)	Minot AFB
7th Bomb Wing, tankers (KC-135A)	Castle AFB, CA
9th Strategic Reconnaissance Wing, tankers	Beale AFB, CA
19th Air Refueling Wing	Robbins AFB, GA
22nd Air Refueling Wing	March AFB, CA
28th Bomb Wing, tankers (KC-135R)	Ellsworth AFB, ME
42nd Bomb Wing, tankers (KC-135R)	Loring AFB, ME
68th Air Refueling Wing (KC-10)	Seymour Johnson AFB, NC
92nd Bomb Wing (KC-135R)	Fairchild AFB, WA
93rd Bomb Wing, tankers (KC-135R)	Castle AFB, CA
96th Bomb Wing, tankers	Dyess AFB, TX
97th Bomb Wing, tankers (KC-135R)	Eaker AFB, AR
301 Air Refueling Wing	Malmstrom AFB, MT
305th Air Refueling Wing (KC-135R)	Grissom AFB, IN
319th Bomb Wing, tankers (KC-135R)	Grand Forks AFB, NE
340th Air Refueling Wing	Altus AFB
376 SW (KC-135R)	Kadena AB, Okinawa
379th Bomb Wing, tankers (KC-135A)	Wurtsmith AFB, MI
380th Bomb Wing, tankers (KC-135A)	Plattsburgh AFB, NY
383 Air Refueling Wing (KC0134R)	McConnell AFB, KS
416th Bomb Wing, tankers	Griffis AFB, NY

AIR FORCE GUARD AND RESERVE UNITS DEPLOYED

Alabama

187th Security Police Flight	Montgomery
117th Tactical Reconnaissance Wing	Birmingham
106th Air National Guard	*

Alaska

176th Security Police Flight	Anchorage
168th Air Refueling Group	Eielson AFB

Arizona

161st Civil Engineering Squadron	Phoenix
161st Air Refueling Group	Phoenix
162nd Civil Engineering Squadron	Tucson
162nd Air Refueling Group	Phoenix
939th Air Refueling Wing	Davis-Mothan AFB
944th Civil Engineering Squadron	Luke AFB

Arizona (continued)

944th Combat Support Squadron	Luke AFB
71st Special Operations Squadron	Davis-Monthan AFB, AZ

California

144th Civil Engineering Squadron	Fresno
301st Military Airlift Squadron (C-5s)	Travis AFB
312th Military Airlift Squadron (C-5s)	Travis AFB
708th Military Airlift Squadron (C-141s)	Travis AFB
445th Military Airlift Wing	Travis AFB
445th Civil Engineering Squadron	Mather AFB
42nd Aeromedical Staging Squadron	Norton AFB
336th AREFS	March AFB
940th Civil Engineering Squadron	Mather AFB
940th Air Refueling Group	Mather AFB
452nd Civil Engineering Squadron	March AFB
452nd Air Refueling Wing	March AFB
349th Civil Engineering Squadron	Travis AFB
452nd Security Police Fleet	March AFB
452nd USAF Clinic	March AFB
730th Military Airlift Squadron	Norton AFB
234th Combat Communications Squadron	Haywood
162nd Combat Communications Squadron	North Highland
149th Combat Communications Squadron	North Highland
445th Tactical Airlift Wing	March AFB

Colorado

140th Security Police Fleet	Denver

Connecticut

103rd Security Police Squadron	Bradley Air National Guard Base

Delaware

326th Military Airlift Squadron (C-5s)	Dover AFB
709th Military Airlift Squadron (C-5s)	Dover AFB
512th Military Airlift Wing	Dover AFB
512th Civil Engineering Squadron	Dover AFB
46th Aerial Port Squadron	Dover AFB
166th Tactical Airlift Group (C-130s)	Wilmington

Florida

290th Joint Chief of Staff Squadron	Tampa
125th Civil Engineering Squadron	Jacksonville
37th Aeromedical Evacuation Group	MacDill AFB

Florida (continued)

919th Security Police Squadron	Eglin AFB
919th Special Operations Group	Duke Field AFB

Georgia

224th Joint Chief of Staff Squadron	Brunswick
94th Airlift Wing	Dobbins AFB
64th Aeromedical Evacuation	Dobbins AFB

Idaho

124th Services Flight	Boise

Illinois

126th Air Refueling Wing	Chicago
932nd Civil Engineering Squadron	Scott AFB
182nd Tactical Air Support Group	Peoria
183rd Tactical Air Support Group	Springfield
108th Air Refueling Squadron	Chicago
126th Consolidated Aircraft Maintenance Squadron	Chicago

Indiana

122nd Security Police Fleet	Fort Wayne
181st Tac Clinic	Terre Haute
72nd Air Refueling Group	Grissom AFB
434th Air Refueling Wing	Grissom AFB

Iowa

132nd Civil Engineering Squadron	Des Moines
185th Civil Engineering Squadron	Sioux City

Kansas

190th Air Refueling Group	Topeka
184th Tactical Clinic	McConnell AFB

Louisiana

926th Tactical Fighter Group (A-10s)	New Orleans
706th Tactical Fighter Squadron	New Orleans

Maine

101st Air Refueling Wing	Bangor

Maryland

135th Civil Engineering Squadron	Baltimore
135th Mobile Aerial Port Fleet	Baltimore
756th Military Airlift Squadron (C-141s)	Andrews AFB
175th Security Police Flight	Baltimore

Massachusetts

102nd Civil Engineering Squadron	Otis
337th Military Airlift Squadron (C-5s)	Westover AFB
439th Security Police Squadron	Westover AFB
439th Combat Support Group	Westover AFB
439th MAW	Westover AFB

Michigan

127th Security Police Fleet	Selfridge
110th Civil Engineering Squadron	Battle Creek
191st Civil Engineering Squadron	Selfridge
927th Air Refueling Squadron	Selfridge

Minnesota

148th Civil Engineering Squadron	Duluth
109th Aeromed Evacuation Fleet	Minneapolis

Mississippi

183rd Military Airlift Squadron	Jackson
186th Security Police Fleet	Meridan
193rd Aeromedical Evac Fleet	Jackson

Missouri

131st Security Police Fleet	St. Louis
139th Tactical Airlift Group	St. Joseph
403rd Tactical Airlift Wing	Keesler

Montana

120th Civil Engineering Squadron	Great Falls
120th Tactical Clinic	Great Falls

Nebraska

922nd Civil Engineering Squadron	Offutt AFB

Nevada

152nd Tactical Recon Group (RF-4Cs)	Reno
192nd Tactical Fighter Squadron	Reno

New Hampshire

157th Air Refueling Group	Portsmouth

New Jersey

177th Civil Engineering	Atlantic City
170th Air Refueling Group	Bordentown
702nd Military Airlift Squadron	McGuire AFB

New Jersey (continued)

732nd Military Airlift Squadron (C-141s)	McGuire AFB
335th Military Airlift Squadron (C-141s)	McGuire AFB
514th Military Airlift Wing	McGuire AFB
35th Aerial Port Squadron	McGuire AFB

New Mexico

150th Security Police Fleet	Albuquerque

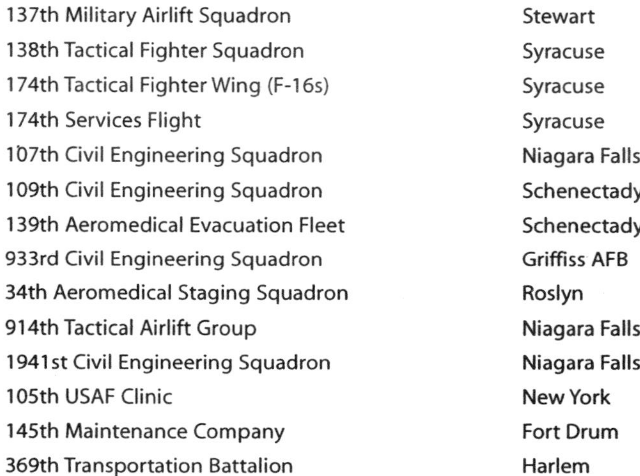

New York

137th Military Airlift Squadron	Stewart
138th Tactical Fighter Squadron	Syracuse
174th Tactical Fighter Wing (F-16s)	Syracuse
174th Services Flight	Syracuse
107th Civil Engineering Squadron	Niagara Falls
109th Civil Engineering Squadron	Schenectady
139th Aeromedical Evacuation Fleet	Schenectady
933rd Civil Engineering Squadron	Griffiss AFB
34th Aeromedical Staging Squadron	Roslyn
914th Tactical Airlift Group	Niagara Falls
1941st Civil Engineering Squadron	Niagara Falls
105th USAF Clinic	New York
145th Maintenance Company	Fort Drum
369th Transportation Battalion	Harlem

North Carolina

263rd Combat Command Squadron	Badin
156th Aeromedical Evacuation Fleet	Charlotte
916th Air Refueling Group	Seymour Johnson
916th Civil Engineering Squadron	Seymour Johnson
915th Civil Engineering Squadron	Pope
916th USAF Clinic	Seymour Johnson

North Dakota

119th Civil Engineering Squadron	Fargo

Ohio

121st Security Police Fleet	Columbus
907th Tactical Air Group	Rickenbacker AFB
178th Civil Engineering Squadron	Springfield
180th Civil Engineering Squadron	Toledo
160th Air Refueling Group	Columbus
76th Aerial Port Squadron	Youngstown

Oklahoma

137th Civil Engineering Squadron	Oklahoma City
137th Tactical Airlift Wing	Oklahoma City
138th Civil Engineering Squadron	Tulsa
137th Aeromedical Evacuation Fleet	Oklahoma City
72nd Aerial Port Squadron	Tinker AFB

Oregon

142nd Civil Engineering Squadron	Portland

Pennsylvania

112th Security Police Fleet	Pittsburgh
171st Air Refueling Wing	Pittsburgh
913th Medical Squadron	Willow Grove
92nd Aerial Port Squadron	Wyoming Valley
193 SOG (EC-130E)	Harrisburg
913th Tactical Air Group	Willow Grove

Puerto Rico

156th Security Police Fleet	Puerto Rico Int'l

Rhode Island

282nd Combat Command Squadron	Coventry

South Carolina

169th Tactical Fighter Group	Columbia
157th Tactical Fighter Squadron	*
240th Combat Command Squadron	Easton
169th Services Flight	Columbia
701st Military Airlift Squadron (C-141s)	Charleston
315th Military Airlift Wing	Charleston
38th Aerial Port Squadron	Charleston
315th Civil Engineering Squadron	Charleston

South Dakota

114th Security Police Fleet	Sioux Falls

Tennessee

164th Mobile Aerial Port Squadron	Memphis
164th Civil Engineering Squadron	Memphis
134th Air Refueling Group	Knoxville
18th Aeromedical Evacuation Fleet	Nashville

Texas

136th Mobile Aerial Port Squadron	Dallas
136th Tactical Airlift Wing	Dallas
149th Security Police Fleet	Kelly AFB
149th Tactical Clinic	Kelly AFB
147th Civil Engineering Squadron	Houston
301st Civil Engineering Squadron	Carswell AFB
68th Military Airlift Squadron	Kelly AFB
32nd Aeromedical Evacuation Group	Kelly AFB
24th Aeromedical Evacuation Squadron	*

Utah

151st Civil Engineering Squadron	Salt Lake City
151st Air Refueling Group	Salt Lake City
419th Civil Engineering Squadron	Hill AFB

Vermont

158th Civil Engineering Squadron	Burlington

Virginia

909th Civil Engineering Squadron	Langley AFB

Washington

141st Air Refueling Wing	Spokane
62nd Security Police Squadron	McChord AFB
97th Military Airlift Squadron (C-141s)	McChord AFB
446th Military Airlift Wing	McChord AFB
446th Civil Engineering Squadron	McChord AFB
36th Aerial Port Squadron	McChord AFB

Wisconsin

128th Air Refueling Group	Milwaukee

West Virginia

130th Tactical Airlift Group	Charleston
167th Aeromedical Evacuation Fleet	Martinsburg
167th Civil Engineering Squadron	Martinsburg

Wyoming

187th Aeromedical Evacuation Fleet	Cheyenne

Appendix E
Allied Units Deployed

ARGENTINA

Destroyer:	Admiral Brown
Corvette:	Spiro
100 ground troops	
Two (2) C-130s	
One (1) 707	

AUSTRALIA

Destroyer:	Brisbane
Frigates:	Sydney Adelaide Darwin
Support Ships:	Westralia Success
C-130 squadron	
Clearance Diving Team 3 (CDT3)	
Medical teams	

BANGLADESH

6,000 troops

BELGIUM

Minesweepers:	Iris Myosotis
Frigates:	Wandelaar Wielingen
Two (2) landing ships	

BRITAIN

(35,000 troops, 175 tanks, 8 warships)

1st Armoured Division

7th Armoured Brigade (The Desert Rats)

4th Armoured Brigade (Hell for Leather)

The Royal Scots Dragoon Guard

The Queen's Royal Irish Hussars

40th Field Regiment, Royal Artillery

BRITAIN (continued)

2nd Field Regiment, Royal Artillery
26th Field Regiment, Royal Artillery
39th Heavy Regiment, Royal Artillery
32nd Heavy Regiment, Royal Artillery
46th Air Defense Battery, Royal Artillery
10th Air Defense Battery, The Staffordshire Regiment
12th Air Defense Regiment, Royal Artillery
645th Squadron, Army Air Corps
4th Regiment, Army Air Corps
21st Engineer Regiment
23rd Engineer Regiment
23rd Engineer Regiment
32nd Armoured Engineer Regiment
1st Armoured Division Transport Regiment
4th Armoured Division Transport Regiment
1st Armoured Division Field Ambulance
5th Armoured Division Field Ambulance
3rd Ordnance Battalion, Royal Army Ordnance Corps
7th Armoured Workshop, Royal Electric and Mechanical Engineers
11th Armoured Workshop
205th General Hospital, Royal Army Medical Corps
24th Air Mobile Field Ambulance, Royal Army Medical Corps
22nd Field Hospital, Royal Army Medical Corps
32nd Field Hospital, Royal Army Medical Corps
33rd General Hospital, Royal Army Medical Corps
6th Armoured Workshop
207th Signals Squadron
204th Signals Squadron
The Life Guards
4th Royal Tank Regiment
1st Battalion, The Grenadier Guards
1st Battalion, The Devonshire and Dorset Regiment
1st Battalion, The Prince of Wales Own Regiment of Yorkshire
1st Battalion, Queen's Own Royal Highlanders
1st Battalion, The Royal Green Jackets
Three (3) squadrons (Tornado fighter/attack aircraft)
Three (3) squadrons (Nimrod aircraft for maritime patrol)
One (1) squadron (Jaguar attack aircraft)

Destroyers:	York Gloucester Cardiff Exeter

Frigates:	Jupiter Battleaxe Brilliant Brave Brecon Chatham London Brazen Broadsword
Support Ships:	Orangeleaf Olna Fort Grange Diligence Herald Sir Galahad Sir Percival Hecla Argus Dulverston Ledbury Sir Bedivere Sir Tristram Resource
Submarines:	Opposum Otus
Minesweepers:	Atherstone Cattistock Huntworth
Several other support vessels	

CANADA

Destroyers:	Terra Nova Athabaskan
Frigate:	Restigouce
Support Ship:	Protecteur
409 Tactical Fighter Squadron (CF-18s)	
Twelve (12) C-130 transport aircraft	
90th Canadian Headquarters Squadron	
Other support troops	

CZECHOSLOVAKIA

Medical team

Chemical decontamination unit

DENMARK

Frigate:	Olfert Fischer

EGYPT

(35,000 troops, 2 armor divisions, 400 M-60 tanks)

3rd Mechanized Infantry

3rd Armored Division

4th Armored Division

Twenty (20) aircraft

FRANCE

(17,000 troops, 7 warships, 120 helicopters, 350 tanks)

French Rapid Action Force

6th Light Armored Division

1st Spahis Cavalry Regiment

1st Foreign Armored Regiment

2nd French Foreign Legion Regiment

11th Marine Artigiment

5th Combat Helicopter Regiment

Carrier:	Clemenceau (transporting helicopters)
Cruiser:	Colbert
Destroyers:	La Motte-Piquet Montcalm Dupliex De Chayla Jeanne de Vienne
Frigates:	Commandante Ducuing Commandante Bodry Doudart De Lagree Protet
Hospital Ships:	Rance Foudre
Support Ships:	Var Rhin Berry

Several other auxiliary ships

Twenty-four (24) F3 Jaguar attack aircraft

Ten (10) Mirage 2000 fighters

Eight (8) F1 CR Mirage attack fighters

GERMANY

Five minesweepers:	Marburg Koblenz Wetzlar Loboe Vebehernn

GERMANY (continued)

Depot Ship:	Werro
Ammunition Ship:	Westerwold

GREECE

Frigates:	Elli
	Limnos

GULF STATES

17,000 troops composed of Kuwaiti refugees, troops from Bahrain, Qatar, Oman, and the United Arab Emirates,

200 tanks

15 aircraft

HONDURAS

200 troops

ITALY

Frigates:	Libeccio Orsa Zeffiro Lupo Saggitario
Corvettes:	Minerva Sfinge
Destroyer:	Audace
Assault Ship:	San Marco

Ten (10) Tornado aircraft from the 154th, 155th, and 156th groups

MOROCCO

1,500 troops

NETHERLANDS

Frigates:	Pieter Florisz Witte de With Jacob van Heemskerck Philips van Almonde
Support Ships:	Zuiderkruis Alkmaar Zierikzee

Army hospital unit

NEW ZEALAND

Two (2) C-130 transports, 40th Squadron

Medical team

NIGER

500 troops

NORWAY

Cutter:	Andenes
Other transport ships	

PAKISTAN

5,000 troops

POLAND

210 servicemen and servicewomen in KKMC	
Hospital Ship:	Wodnik

PORTUGAL

Logistics Ship:	Sao Miguel

SAUDI ARABIA

45,000 troops, 200 tanks, 250 aircraft

SENEGAL

500 troops

SPAIN

Frigates:	Diana
	Numancia
	Infanta Cristina
	Santa Maria
	Descubierta
	Cazadora
	Infanta Elena
	Victoria
	Vencedora
Transport aircraft	

SYRIA

20,000 troops in Saudi Arabia, 270 tanks

9th Armored Division

5,000 special forces paratroopers

More than 50,000 Troops in Syria

TURKEY

Two (2) frigates in the Gulf

100,000 troops in Turkey on the Iraqi border

ORDER OF BATTLE

Joint Forces Command – North

Syrian 45th Commando Brigade
- 122nd Special Forces Battalion
- 183rd Special Forces Battalion
- 824th Special Forces Battalion

Syrian 9th Armored Division
- 33rd Mechanized Brigade
- 43rd Mechanized Brigade
- 52nd Mechanized Brigade
- 89th Artillery Regiment
- 79th Anti-aircraft Brigade

Task Force Muthana
- Royal Saudi Land Forces 20th Mechanized Brigade
- Kuwaiti 35th Mechanized Brigade

Task Force Sa'ad
- Royal Saudi Land Forces 4th Armored Brigade
- Kuwaiti 15th Infantry Brigade

Reserves
- Kuwaiti "Haq" Brigade
- Kuwaiti "Khulud" Brigade
- Nigerian Infantry Battalion

Joint Forces Command – East

Royal Saudi Land Forces 10th Mechanized Brigade

UAE Mechanized Battalion

Northern Omani Brigade

Task Force Othman
- Royal Saudi Land Forces 8th Mechanized Brigade
- Kuwaiti "Al Fatah" Brigade
- Kuwaiti 2/15 Mechanized Battalion
- Bahraini Motorized Infantry Company

Task Force Abu Bakar
- Saudi Arabian National Guard 2nd National Guard Brigade

Task Force Tariq
- Royal Saudi Marine Battalion
- Moroccan 6th Mechanized Battalion
- Senegalese 1st Infantry Battalion

Reserves
- Qatari Mechanized Battalion Task Force
- 1st East Bengal Infantry Battalion
- Royal Saudi Land Forces 14th Field Artillery Battalion
- Royal Saudi Land Forces 18th Missile Battalion
- Royal Saudi Land Forces 6th Target Acquisition Battery

Egyptian II Corps

Egyptian 3rd Mechanized Division
- 23rd Armored Brigade
- 10th Mechanized Brigade
- 114th Mechanized Brigade
- 39th Artillery Brigade
- 126th Anti-aircraft Artillery Brigade

Egyptian 4th Armored Division
- 2nd Armored Brigade
- 3rd Armored Brigade
- 6th Mechanized Brigade
- 4th Artillery Brigade

Egyptian 1st Ranger Regiment

Joint Forces Command – Reserves

Saudi Attack Aviation Battalion

Royal Saudi Land Forces 15th MLRS Battalion

Royal Saudi Land Forces Anti-tank Company

Royal Saudi Land Forces 4th Airborne Battalion

Czech NBC Defense Company

1st Marine Expeditionary Force

1st Marine Division
- 1st Marine Regiment
- 3rd Marine Regiment
- 4th Marine Regiment
- 7th Marine Regiment
- 11th Marine (Artillery) Regiment

2nd Marine Division
- 6th Marine Regiment
- 8th Marine Regiment
- 10th Marine (Artillery) Regiment
- 1st "Tiger" Brigade/2nd Armored Division (U.S. Army)

2nd Marine Expeditionary Force

4th Marine Expeditionary Brigade

5th Marine Expeditionary Brigade

13th Marine Expeditionary Unit

U.S. VII Corps

1st Armored Division

1st Infantry Division (Mechanized)

1st "Cavalry" Division (Armored)

3rd Armored Division

2nd Armored Cavalry Regiment

- 1st British Armoured Division
    - 4th Armoured Brigade
        - 14/20 King's Hussars
        - 1st Royal Scots Infantry
        - 3rd Royal Fusiliers Infantry
        - 23rd Regiment, Royal Engineers
        - 46th Air Defense Battery (Javelin)
        - 2nd Field Regiment
    - 7th Armoured Brigade
        - Royal Scots Dragon Guards
        - Queen's Royal Irish Hussars
        - 1st Staffordshire Infantry
        - 39th Regiment, Royal Engineers
        - 664th Helicopter Squadron
        - 10th Air Defense Battery
        - 40th Field Regiment
    - 16/5 Queen's Royal Lancers Recon Battalion
    - 4th Army Air Regiment
    - 32nd Heavy Artillery Regiment
    - 29th Heavy Artillery Regiment
    - 12th Air Defense Regiment
    - 32nd Regiment, Royal Engineers
- 42nd Field Artillery Brigade
- 75th Field Artillery Brigade
- 142nd Field Artillery Brigade
- 210th Field Artillery Brigade
- 11th Aviation Brigade
- 7th Engineer Brigade
- 14th Military Police Brigade

U.S. XVIII Airborne Corps

- 24th Infantry Division (Mechanized)
- 101st Air Assault Division
- 82nd Airborne Division
- French 6th Light "Daguet" Armored Division (Reinforced)
    - Organic
        - 1st Foreign Legion Armored Regiment
        - 1st Regiment de Spahis
        - 2nd Foreign Legion Infantry Regiment
        - 21st Marine Infantry Regiment
        - 68th Marine Artillery Regiment
        - 6th Foreign Legion Engineer Regiment
    - 4th Airmobile Division
        - 5th Combat Helicopter Regiment

1st Transport Helicopter Regiment
1st Infantry Regiment (airmobile)
9th Marine Division
2nd Marine Infantry Regiment
Detachment, 3rd Marine Infantry Regiment
11th Marine Artillery Regiment
10th Armored Division
4th Dragoon Regiment
3rd Armored Cavalry Regiment
18th Airborne Field Artillery Brigade
75th Field Artillery Brigade
196th Field Artillery Brigade
212th Field Artillery Brigade
214th Field Artillery Brigade
20th Engineer Brigade
12th Aviation Brigade
18th Aviation Brigade
16th Military Police Brigade
89th Military Police Brigade
800th Military Police Brigade

Enemy Prisoner of War Guards

1st Coldstream Guards
Royal Highland Fusiliers
King's Own Scottish Borderers

ADDITIONAL BREAKDOWNS OF SPECIFIC U.S. UNITS

1st Armored Division

1st Brigade
4-66 Armored Battalion(+)
4-7 Mechanized Battalion(+)
1-7 Mechanized Battalion
2-41 Field Artillery Battalion
16th Engineer Battalion
2nd Brigade
2-70 Armored Battalion
1-35 Armored Battalion
4-70 Armored Battalion
6-6 Mechanized Battalion
2-1 Field Artillery Battalion
54th Engineer Battalion
3rd Brigade
1-37 Armored Battalion
3-35 Armored Battalion

7-6 Mechanized Battalion
3-1 Field Artillery Battalion
Task Force W Engineer Battalion

4th Brigade

1-1 Air Cavalry Squadron

2-1 Aviation Battalion

3-1 Aviation Battalion

A-94 Field Artillery Battalion

4-27 Field Artillery Battalion

19th Engineer Battalion

1-1 Cavalry Squadron

1st "Cavalry" Division (Armored)

1st Brigade
- 3-32 Armored Battalion
- 2-8 "Cavalry Battalion" (Armored)
- 2-5 "Cavalry Battalion" (Mechanized)

2nd Brigade
- 1-32 Armored Battalion
- 1-8 "Cavalry Battalion" (Armored)
- 1-5 "Cavalry Battalion" (Mechanized)
- 3-82 Field Artillery Battalion

3rd Brigade

4th Aviation Brigade
- 1-227 Aviation Battalion
- 1-3 Aviation Battalion
- 1-7 Air Cavalry Squadron
- A-21 Field Artillery Battalion (MRLS)
- A-92 Field Artillery Battalion (MRLS)

8th Engineer Battalion

1-82 Field Artillery (SP)

1-7 Cavalry Squadron

1st Infantry Division (Mechanized)

1st Brigade
- 1-34 Armored Battalion
- 2-34 Armored Battalion
- 5-16 Mechanized Battalion
- 1-5 Field Artillery Battalion
- 9th Engineer Battalion (Combat)
- 588 Engineer Battalion

2nd Brigade
- 3-37 Armored Battalion TF
- 4-37 Armored Battalion

2-16 Mechanized Battalion TF
4-5 Field Artillery Battalion
317 Engineer Battalion (Combat)
1st Engineer Battalion
3rd Brigade / 2nd Armored Division (Attached)
1-41 Mechanized Battalion
2-66 Armored Battalion
3-66 Armored Battalion
4-3 Field Artillery Battalion
176 Engineer Battalion
4th Brigade
1-1 Aviation Battalion
1-4 Air Cavalry Squadron
B-6 Field Artillery Battalion
1-4 Cavalry Squadron

2nd Armored Cavalry Regiment

1-2 Cavalry Squadron
2-2 Cavalry Squadron
3-2 Cavalry Squadron
4-2 Air Cavalry Squadron
210th Field Artillery Brigade
3-17 Field Artillery Battalion
4-27 Field Artillery Battalion(-)
6-41 Field Artillery Battalion
82nd Engineer

3rd Armored Division

1st Brigade
3-5 "Cavalry Battalion" (Mechanized)
5-5 "Cavalry Battalion" (Mechanized)
4-32 Armored Battalion
2-3 Field Artillery Battalion
2nd Brigade
4-8 Armored Battalion
3-8 Armored Battalion
4-18 Mechanized Battalion
2-82 Field Artillery Battalion
3rd Brigade
2-67 Armored Battalion
4-67 Armored Battalion
5-18 Mechanized Battalion
4-82 Field Artillery Battalion

4th Aviation Brigade
- 4-7 Air Cavalry Squadron
- 2-227 Aviation Battalion
- 1-27 Field Artillery Battalion
- A-40 Field Artillery Battalion

4-7 Cavalry Squadron
23rd Engineer Battalion

24th Infantry Division (Mechanized)

1st Brigade
- 2-7 Mechanized Brigade
- 3-7 Mechanized Brigade
- 4-64 Armored Brigade
- 1-41 Field Artillery Battalion

2nd Brigade
- 3-69 Armored Battalion(-)
- 3-15 Mechanized Battalion TF
- 1-64 Armored Battalion
- 3-41 Field Artillery Battalion

197th Infantry Brigade (Mechanized) (Attached)
- 1-18 Mechanized Battalion TF
- 2-18 Mechanized Battalion
- 2-69 Armored Battalion
- 4-41 Field Artillery Battalion

3rd Armored Cavalry Regiment
- 1-3 Cavalry Squadron
- 2-3 Cavalry Squadron
- 3-3 Cavalry Squadron
- 4-3 Air Cavalry Squadron
- 3-18 Field Artillery Battalion

Aviation Brigade
- 2-4 Air Cavalry Squadron
- 1-24 Aviation Battalion
- A-13 Field Artillery Battalion

212th Field Artillery Brigade
- 3-27 Field Artillery Battalion
- 2-18 Field Artillery Battalion

2-4 Cavalry Squadron
3rd Engineer Battalion

82nd Airborne Division

325th Parachute Regiment
504th Parachute Regiment
505th Parachute Regiment

101st Air Assault Division

2nd Brigade

- 3-502 Infantry Battalion
- 3-327 Infantry Battalion
- 1-502 Infantry Battalion
- 1-320 Field Artillery Battalion

327th Air Assault Regiment

502nd Air Assault Regiment

505th Air Assault Regiment

101st Aviation Brigade

- 1-101 Aviation Battalion
- 2-229 Aviation Battalion

Appendix F

Casualties and POWs

For the families of loved ones who died in the Gulf War, it doesn't really matter if their sons or daughters died in a SCUD attack or in a car crash — their losses can never be replaced. In the Persian Gulf War, more Allied servicemen died in non-combat related accidents than at the hands of the Iraqis. This includes the non-combat deaths that resulted from Operation Desert Shield.

During Operation Desert Shield, several major incidents led to significant numbers of American casualties. In the Port of Haifa Israel, a launch ferrying sailors from USS *Saratoga* sank, killing twenty-one. Early in the deployment, thirteen soldiers and airmen were killed when their C-5 Galaxy transport plane crashed in Ramstein, Germany. Ten crewmembers of USS *Iwo Jima* were killed in a major steam leak on 30 October 1990. In addition to these major catastrophes, several smaller accidents involving colliding aircraft and truck accidents took the lives of American servicemen.

The Pentagon released an official tally in 1991 of coalition casualties.

Coalition Casualties	Battle Deaths	Non-Battle Deaths	Wounded
U.S.	148	145*	467
Allies	99	unknown	434
Total	247	unknown	901

(*The list in this appendix includes 116 of the 145.)

Compiling an accurate list is a definite challenge because the "official" reason for a servicemember's death does not always conform with what his or her colleagues may say. Originally, few casualties were attributed to friendly fire, whereas later it was determined thirty-five Americans were killed by other Allied units. For more information on friendly fire incidents, see Chapter 8.

Sincerest apologies go out to the families and loved ones of any servicemember who was left off this list or misidentified. The author welcomes any necessary changes or additions to this list. Please contact him via email at *andrew@leyden.com.*

COALITION AIR LOSSES

Date	Service	Aircraft	Crew (KIA or killed, unless specified)
17 Jan	Navy	F/A-18	Lieutenant Commander Michael Scott Speicher
	Kuwaiti	A-4KU	
	French	Jaguar	
18 Jan	Navy	A-6E	Lieutenant Jeffrey Zaun (POW) Lieutenant Robert Wetzel (POW)
	Navy	A-6E	Lieutenant Charles Turner Lieutenant William T. Costen
	USAF	F-15E	Major Donnie R. Holland Major Thomas F. Koritz
	RAF	Tornado	
	RAF	Tornado	
	RAF	Tornado	
	RAF	Tornado	
	Marines	OV-10	Lieutenant Colonel Clifford M. Acree (POW) Chief Warrant Officer Guy L. Hunter (POW)
19 Jan	USAF	F-4G	Both crewmen recovered
20 Jan	USAF	F-15E	Colonel David W. Eberly (POW) Major Tomas E. Griffith (POW)
	USAF	F-16	Captain Harry M. Roberts (POW)
	USAF	F-16	Major Jeffrey S. Tice (POW)
	Army	UH-60	(non-combat) Staff Sergeant Garland V. Haily
	Navy	A-6E	Both crewmen safe Loss due to extensive damage Aircraft returned safely to carrier
	RAF	Tornado	
	RAF	Tornado	
21 Jan		Army	AH-64 (non-combat; both crewmen recovered)
	Navy	F-14	Lieutenant Lawrence R. Slade (POW) Lieutenant Devon Jones (rescued)
22 Jan	RAF	Tornado	
	Marine	AV-8B	(non-combat) Captain Manuel Rivera, Jr.
	Army	AH-1	(non-combat; crew recovered safely)
23 Jan	USAF	F-16	Pilot recovered safely
	Army	AH-64	(non-combat)
24 Jan	RAF	Tornado	
26 Jan	Navy	F/A-18	Pilot recovered safely

COALITION AIR LOSSES (continued)

Date	Service	Aircraft	Crew (KIA or killed, unless specified)
28 Jan	Marines	AV-8B	Captain Michael C. Berryman (POW)
	Army	AH-1	(non-combat)
29 Jan	Army	OH-58	(non-combat; no injuries)
31 Jan	USAF	AC-130	Lieutenant Tomas C. Bland, Jr. Staff Sergeant John P. Bleasinger Master Sergeant Paul G. Beuge Sergeant Berry M. Clark Captain Arthur Galvan Captain William D. Grimm Staff Sergeant Timothy R. Harrison Top Sergeant Robert K. Hodges Sergeant Damon V. Kanuhe Master Sergeant James B. May II Staff Sergeant John L. Oelschlager Staff Sergeant Mark J. Schmauss Captain Dixon L. Walters, Jr. Major Paul J. Weaver
2 Feb	Navy	A-6E	Lieutenant Commander Barry T. Cooke Lieutenant Patrick K. Conner
	USAF	A-10	Captain Richard D. Storr (POW)
	Marine	AH-1J	(Non-combat) Major Eugene McCarthy Captain Jonathan R. Edwards
3 Feb	USAF	B-52G	(Non-combat; three crewmen recovered safely) Captain Jeffry J. Olson First Lieutenant Jorge I. Artegga First Lieutenant Eric D. Hedeen
	Marines	UH-1	(Non-combat) Captain David R. Herr, Jr. Captain James K. Thorp Corporal Albert G. Haddad, Jr. Corporal Kurt A. Benz
5 Feb	Navy	F/A-18	Lieutenant Robert J. Dwyer
	Army	AH-1	(Non-combat; one minor injury)
6 Feb	Army	UH-1	(Non-combat) Chief Warrant Officer Richard R. Lee Four crewmen injured
7 Feb	Army	AH-1	(Non-combat; no injuries)
9 Feb	Marines	AV-8B	Captain Russell A. C. Sanborn (POW)
13 Feb	Saudi	F-5E	
	Saudi	F-15C	(non-combat)
14 Feb	Saudi	F-5E	

COALITION AIR LOSSES (continued)

Date	Service	Aircraft	Crew (KIA or killed, unless specified)
	RAF	Tornado	Flight Lieutenant Rupert Clark (POW) Flight Lieutenant Stephen Hicks
	USAF	EF-111	(Non-combat) Captain Paul R. Eichenlaub II Captain Douglas L. Bradt
15 Feb	Navy	A-6E	(Non-combat; both crewmen recovered safely)
	USAF	A-10	Captain Stephen R. Phillis
	USAF	A-10	First Lieutenant Robert J. Sweet (POW)
16 Feb	USAF	F-16	(non-combat; Captain Dale T. Cormier)
18 Feb	USAF	F-16	Pilot rescued
19 Feb	USAF	OA-10	Lieutenant Colonel Jeffrey D. Fox
21 Feb	Army	OH-58	Chief Warrant Officer Hal H. Reichle Specialist Michael D. Daniels
	USAF	F-16	(non-combat; pilot recovered safely)
	Navy	CH-46	(non-combat; Petty Officer James Crockford)
	Army	MH-60	(non-combat; Master Sergeant Eloy A. Rodriguez Captain Charles W. Cooper Sergeant Major Patrick R. Hurley Chief Warrant Officer Michael F. Anderson Master Sergeant Otto F. Clark Sergeant Christopher J. Chapman Sergeant Mario V. Valazquez
	Navy	SH-60	(non-combat)
23 Feb	Navy	CH-46	(non-combat)
	Marines	AV-8B	Captain James Wilbourn
25 Feb	Marines	AV-8B	Pilot rescued
	Army	AH-64	Pilots rescued
	Marine	OV-10	Major Joseph Small (POW) Captain David Spellacy
27 Feb	USAF	OA-10	First Lieutenant Patrick Olson
	USAF	F-16	Captain William Andrews (POW)
	Army	UH-60	Major (Dr.) Rhonda Cornum (POW) Specialist Troy Danlap (POW) Staff Sergeant Daniel Stamaris (POW) Chief Warrant Officer Robert Godfrey Staff Sergeant William Butts Chief Warrant Officer Phillip Garvey Sergeant Patbouvier E. Ortiz
	Marines	AV-8B	Captain Reginald Underwood
28 Feb	Army	UH-60	Sergeant Cheryl L. O'Brien Warrant Officer George Swartzendruber

COALITION AIR LOSSES (continued)

Date	Service	Aircraft	Crew (KIA or killed, unless specified)
			Sergeant First Class Gary Streeter Warrant Officer David Pleach Staff Sergeant Johnathan Kamm Sergeant Jason Carr First Lieutenant Donaldson P. Tiller Sergeant Lee Belas Warrant Officer John Morgan
	Army	UH-1	Staff Sergeant Michael R. Robson Warrant Officer Kerry Hein First Lieutenant Daniel Graybeal
1 Mar	Army	CH-47	(non-combat) Major Marie T. Rossi Chief Warrant Robert Hughes Staff Sergeant Mike Garrett Specialist William Brace
2 Mar	Army	UH-1	(non-combat; four crewman injured)
6 Mar	Marines	AH-1	(non-combat; two crewman injured)
8 Mar	Marines	(2) F-18	(non-combat collision; both pilots rescued)
13 Mar	USAF	F-16	(non-combat; pilot rescued)
	Army	UH-60	(non-combat)
19 Mar	Marines	AV-8B	(non-combat; pilot rescued)

CASUALTIES OF OPERATION DESERT SHIELD

Alabama

Major Barry Henderson, 40, of Tuscumbia. Killed on 8 October when his RF-4 crashed in Saudi Arabia. Survived by a wife and two children.

Major Stephen Schramm, 43, of Birmingham. Survived by a wife and two children.

Army Sergeant Arthur Jackson, 36, of Brent. Killed on 18 November when hit by a truck.

Marine Sergeant Larry Hogan, 33, of Birmingham. Killed on 7 January in a shooting.

Navy Petty Officer Timothy Jackson, 20, of Anniston. Died on 22 December in a boat accident near Haifa, Israel, while returning sailors to USS *Saratoga*.

Arizona

Marine Lance Corporal James Cunningham, 22 of Glendale. Killed on 8 November in an accidental shooting.

California

Air Force Staff Sergeant John Campisi, 30, of Covina.

Air Force Captain James Poulet, 34, of San Carlos. Died on 30 September in the crash of an F-15.

Air Force Major Peter S. Hook, 36, of Bishop. Died on 30 September in the crash of an F-15.

Corporal Timothy W. Romei, 22, of Alameda. Died on 8 October when his helicopter collided with another in the Arabian Sea.

Navy Petty Officer Andrew T. Cady, 25, of San Diego. Died on 19 December in helicopter accident off USS *Tripoli*.

Lieutenant James H. Love, 31, of El Cajon. Died on 19 December in helicopter accident off USS *Tripoli*.

Marine Warrant Officer Thomas Diffenbaugh, 34, of Bakersfield. Died in a vehicle collision. Survived by his wife and two children.

Colorado

Navy Petty Officer Michael L. Belliveau, 24, of Lakewood. Died on 22 December in a boat accident near Haifa, Israel, while returning sailors to USS *Saratoga*.

Florida

Air Force Staff Sergeant Marc Cleyman, 30, of Jacksonville Beach. Died on 28 August in the crash of a C-5 transport plane en route from Germany to the Persian Gulf.

Air Force Technical Sergeant Daniel G. Perez, 50. Died on 28 August in the crash of a C-5 transport plane en route from Germany to the Persian Gulf.

Army 2nd Lieutenant Shannon Kelley, 23, of Gulf Breeze. Killed in a shooting on 31 December.

Navy Petty Officer Delwin Delgado, 26, of Jacksonville. Died on 22 December in a boat accident near Haifa, Israel, while returning sailors to USS *Saratoga*.

Navy Boatswain's Mate Marvin Plummer, 27, of Ponte Vedra. Died on 22 December in a boat accident near Haifa, Israel, while returning sailors to USS *Saratoga*.

Navy Specialist Nathaniel H. Kemp, 18, of Greenwood. Died on 22 December in a boat accident near Haifa, Israel, while returning sailors to USS *Saratoga*.

Georgia

Navy Petty Officer Phillip L. Wilkinson, 35, of Savannah. Died on 22 December in a boat accident near Haifa, Israel, while returning sailors to USS *Saratoga*.

Georgia (continued)

Navy Airman Larry M. Clark, 21, of Decatur. Died on 22 December in a boat accident near Haifa, Israel, while returning sailors to USS *Saratoga*. Survived by his wife and daughter.

Navy Airman Apprentice Christopher B. Brown, 19, of Leslie. Died on 22 December in a boat accident near Haifa, Israel, while returning sailors to USS *Saratoga*.

Navy Clerk Timothy B. Seay, 22, of Thomaston. Died on 22 December in a boat accident near Haifa, Israel, while returning sailors to USS *Saratoga*.

Illinois

Marine Captain William Cronin, Jr., 29, of Elmhurst. Died on 8 October when his helicopter collided with another in the Arabian Sea.

Marine Captain William J. Hurley, 27, of Chicago. Died on 8 October when his helicopter collided with another in the Arabian Sea.

Marine Sergeant Kenneth T. Keller, 26, of Glenville. Died on 8 October when his helicopter collided with another in the Arabian Sea.

Marine Corporal Raymond Horwath, Jr., 26, of Waukegan. Died on 30 November of natural causes. Survived by his wife and son.

Navy Electrician's Mate Kevin J. Hills, 19, of Genoa. Killed on 23 December in a truck accident.

Indiana

Navy Apprentice Jeffrey Settimi, 25, of Fort Wayne. Died on 22 December in a boat accident near Haifa, Israel, while returning sailors to USS *Saratoga*.

Iowa

Army Specialist Steven Douglas Clark, 22, of Cedar Rapids. Died on 7 November in a truck accident.

Navy Fire Control Chief Jeffrey Shukers, 28, of Union. Died on 22 December in a boat accident near Haifa, Israel, while returning sailors to USS *Saratoga*.

Kentucky

Navy Airman Brent A. McCreight, 23, of Eminence. Died on 22 December in a boat accident near Haifa, Israel, while returning sailors to USS *Saratoga*.

Louisiana

Marine Lance Corporal Thomas R. Addams, 20, of Baton Rouge. Died on 8 October when his helicopter collided with another in the Arabian Sea.

Navy Radioman Roderick Stewart, 20, of Shreveport. Died on 22 December in a boat accident near Haifa, Israel, while returning sailors to USS *Saratoga*.

Massachusetts

Navy Petty Officer Daniel M. Jones, 19, of Wakefield. Electrocuted on 22 August aboard USS *Antietam*.

Marine Sergeant John R. Kilkus, 26, of Wakefield. Died on 8 October when his helicopter collided with another in the Arabian Sea. Survived by his wife and 5-month-old daughter.

Michigan

Navy Technician Tyrone Brooks, 19, of Detroit. Killed on 30 October in a boiler-room explosion on board USS *Iwo Jima*.

Mississippi

Army Sergeant James Wilcher, 25, of Crystal Springs. Died on 8 November of natural causes.

Missouri

Navy Petty Officer David Gililand, 21 of Rolla. Killed on 30 October in a boiler-room explosion on board USS *Iwo Jima*.

Missouri (continued)

Army Sergeant Dallas R. Cooper, 35, of Russellville. Died on 14 December in a helicopter crash near Houston, Texas. Survived by his wife and two children.

Navy Chief Warrant Officer Carol L. McKinery, 36, of Leslie. Died on 14 December in a helicopter crash near Houston, Texas.

Navy Airman Apprentice Alexander Jones, 19, of St. Louis. Died on 22 December in a boat accident near Haifa, Israel, while returning sailors to USS *Saratoga*.

Nebraska

Army 1st Lieutenant Peter J. Rose, 26, of Lincoln. Died on 14 December in a helicopter crash near Houston, Texas.

New Hampshire

Marine Captain Kevin R. Dolvin, 29, of Mineral City. Died on 8 October when his helicopter collided with another in the Arabian Sea. Survived by his wife and two children.

Air Force Captain Michael Chinburg, 26, of Durham. Died on 8 January in an F-16 crash. Survived by his wife.

New Jersey

Navy Lieutenant John Snyder, 25 of Milltown. Killed on 30 October in a boiler-room explosion on board USS *Iwo Jima*.

Army Specialist Jimmy Wesley, 22. Killed in a truck accident on 22 December.

New York

Navy Machinist's Mate Dale William Jock, 28, of Malone. Died on 11 September of a heart attack.

Navy Petty Officer Robert Volden, 38, of New York City. Killed on 30 October in a boiler-room explosion on board USS *Iwo Jima*. Survived by his wife, four children, and three grandchildren.

Army Private Scott Nolie Vigrass, 28, of Tonawanda. Killed in a truck accident on 9 December. Survived by his wife who was expecting in April 1991.

Navy Petty Officer Brian P. Weaver, 22, of Lockport. Killed on 23 December in a truck accident.

Marine Lance Corporal Anthony Stewart, 19, of Yonkers. Killed on 29 December in an accidental shooting.

Army Sergeant Tatiana Dees, 34, of Congers. Drowned on duty on 7 January.

Navy Petty Officer Anthony J. Fleming, 25, of Buffalo. Died on 22 December in a boat accident near Haifa, Israel, while returning sailors to USS *Saratoga*.

Navy AKAN Gilbert A. Fontaine, 22, of Spring Valley. Died on 22 December in a boat accident near Haifa, Israel, while returning sailors to USS *Saratoga*.

New Mexico

Navy Airman Randy Neel, 19, of Albuquerque. Died on 22 December in a boat accident near Haifa, Israel, while returning sailors to USS *Saratoga*.

North Carolina

Navy Petty Officer Fred Parker, Jr., 24, of Reidsville. Killed on 30 October in a boiler-room explosion aboard USS *Iwo Jima*.

Air Force Sergeant Melvin D. McDougle, 35, of Fayetteville. Killed on 23 December in a live-fire training exercise.

Army Sergeant Donald Danielson of Fort Bragg. Killed in an accident on 29 December.

Army Sergeant Tommy Blue, 33, of Spring Lake. Killed in a vehicle accident on 30 December.

North Carolina (continued)

Navy Petty Officer Jay Phillip Thomas, 25, of Chapel Hill. Killed in a vehicle accident on 30 December.

Ohio

Air Force Staff Sergeant Rande Hulec, 29, of Cleveland. Died on 28 August. Killed in the crash of a C-5 transport plane en route from Germany to the Persian Gulf.

Army Specialist Robert A. Noonan, 21, of Cincinnati. Died on 20 September in a car accident.

Air Force Captain Thomas R. Caldwell, 32, of Columbus.Died on 10 October in the crash of an F-111 fighter-bomber during training. Survived by a wife and a son.

Marine Corporal Dennis W. Betz, 22, of Alliance. Died on 9 December aboard USS Comfort of a brain hemorrhage. Survived by his wife and daughter.

Oregon

Navy Technician Matthew Schielder, 20, of Hubbard. Died on 22 December in a boat accident near Haifa, Israel, while returning sailors to USS *Saratoga.*

Pennsylvania

Marine Staff Sergeant Thomas J. Moran, 29, of Cornwells Heights. Died on 26 September of a gunshot wound.

Air Force Captain Fredrick A. Reid, 33, of Harrisburgh. Died on 10 October when his F-111 fighter-bomber crashed in a training mission. Survived by his wife.

Navy Petty Officer Daniel Lupatsky, 22 of Centralia. Killed on 30 October in a boiler-room explosion on board USS *Iwo Jima.* Survived by his wife.

Navy Technician Daniel McKinsey, 21, of Hanover. Killed on 30 October in a boiler-room explosion on board USS *Iwo Jima.* Survived by his wife who was expecting a child in March 1991.

Army Private First Class Jeffrey Speicher, 20, of Camp Hill. Killed in a truck accident on 4 January.

Army 1st Lieutenant Jeffrey Bnosky, 25 of Tamaqua. Killed on 13 January in a truck accident. Survived by his wife.

Navy Seaman Monray C. Carrington, 22, of North Braddock. Died on 22 December in a boat accident near Haifa, Israel, while returning sailors to USS *Saratoga.* Survived by his wife and son.

South Carolina

Marine Corps Sergeant Ernest Rivers, 26, of Anderson. Killed on 10 December aboard USS *Iwo Jima* of a suspected heart attack.

Tennessee

Navy Petty Officer James Smith, Jr., 22, of Somerville. Killed on 30 October in a boiler-room explosion aboard USS *Iwo Jima.* Survived by his 2-year-old daughter.

Army Lieutenant Colonel Joe Henry Hancock, Jr., 49, of Springfield. Killed on 5 December in an accidental shooting. Survived by a wife and two children.

Navy Airman Darrell K. Brown, 19, of Memphis. Died on 22 December in a boat accident near Haifa, Israel, while returning sailors to USS *Saratoga.*

Texas

Navy Lieutenant Daniel V. Hull, 31, of Chula Vista. Died on 19 December in a helicopter accident off USS *Tripoli.* Survived by his wife and one son.

Air Force Major Richard W. Chase, 43, of San Antonio. Died on 28 August in the crash of a C-5 transport plane en route from Germany to the Persian Gulf.

Air Force Master Sergeant Samuel Gardner, 35, of Idalou. Died on 28 August in the crash of a C-5 transport plane en route from Germany to the Persian Gulf.

Texas (continued)

Air Force Staff Sergeant Daniel Garza, 24, of San Antonio. Died on 28 August in the crash of a C-5 transport plane en route from Germany to the Persian Gulf.

Air Force Major John M. Gordon, 46, of Spring. Died on 28 August in the crash of a C-5 transport plane en route from Germany to the Persian Gulf.

Air Force Master Sergeant Rosendo Herrera, 45, of San Antonio. Died on 28 August in the crash of a C-5 transport plane en route from Germany to the Persian Gulf.

Air Force Technical Sergeant Lonty A. Knutson, 27, of San Antonio. Died on 28 August in the crash of a C-5 transport plane en route from Germany to the Persian Gulf.

Air Force Major Richard M. Price, 38, of San Antonio. Died on 28 August in the crash of a C-5 transport plane en route from Germany to the Persian Gulf.

Air Force Captain Bradley Schuldt, 27, of Arlington Heights. Died on 28 August in the crash of a C-5 transport plane en route from Germany to the Persian Gulf.

Air Force Staff Sergeant Edward E. Sheffield, 28, of San Antonio. Died on 28 August in the crash of a C-5 transport plane en route from Germany to the Persian Gulf.

Air Force Senior Master Sergeant Carpio Villarreal, Jr., of San Antonio. Died on 28 August in the crash of a C-5 transport plane en route from Germany to the Persian Gulf.

Army Specialist Gary Mahan, 23, of Waco. Killed on 3 January in a vehicle accident.

Rhode Island

Army 1st Lieutenant Tommie Bates, 27, of Coventry. Died on 14 September in a truck accident.

Virgin Islands

Navy Petty Officer Troy Josiah, 25, of St. Thomas. Died on 19 December in a helicopter accident off USS *Tripoli.*

Navy Fireman Wilton L. Huyghue, 20, of St. Thomas. Died on 22 December in a boat accident near Haifa, Israel, while returning sailors to USS *Saratoga.*

Virginia

Navy Technician Michael Manns, Jr., 23, of Bowling Green. Killed on 30 October in a boiler-room explosion on board USS *Iwo Jima.*

Army Private Hans Christian Richard Avery, 21, of Falls Church. Killed on 7 January in a truck accident.

Washington

Marine Lieutenant Michael Monroe, 27 of Auburn. Killed in a vehicle crash on 20 October.

Army Private First Class Dustin Craig LaMoureaux, 20, of Bremerton. Killed on 5 December in a truck accident.

West Virginia

Navy Petty Officer Mark Hutchinson, 27, of Elkins. Killed on 30 October in a boiler-room explosion on board USS *Iwo Jima.* Survived by his wife and two children.

Wisconsin

Army Private First Class Kevin Lee Calloway, 20, of Arpin. Killed on 24 November in a truck crash.

Air Force Airman 1st Class Rocky J. Nelson, 21, of New Auburn. Killed on 1 December in a vehicle accident. Survived by a wife and one daughter.

CASUALTIES OF OPERATION DESERT STORM Killed in Action (KIA)

Official reports put the number of KIA at 148, although some are lower, about 146. Listed below are 151, which included a some who were killed by land mines in the days immediately following the cessation of hostilities. As the circumstances surrounding the losses are investigated further, this list may be revised.

Alabama

Army Private First Class John W. Hutto, 19, of Andalusia. Died in a tank battle with Iraqi Republican Guard forces.

Army Chief Warrant Officer Robert Godfrey, 32, of Daleville. Died in a helicopter rescue mission on the last day of the ground war.

Marine Captain James N. Willbourn III, 28, of Huntsville. Died in a crash of his AV-8B Harrier near the Saudi border.

Alaska

Army Sergeant David Quentin Douthit, 24, of Soldotna. Died on 27 February.
Survived by his wife who, at the time of his death, was expecting their first child.

Arizona

Marine Lance Corporal Eliseo Felix, 19, of Avondale. Killed on 2 February by friendly fire while driving in a convoy of trucks.

Marine Corporal (posthumously made Sergeant) Aaron A. Pack, 22, of Phoenix. Died on 23 February from a friendly-fire incident from an A-6E.

Arkansas

Air Force Captain Paul R. Eichenlaub II, 29, of Bentonville. Killed on 14 February when his EF-111 crashed after a mission. Survived by his wife and two children.

Army Sergeant Scotty L. Whittenburg, 22, of Carlisle.

Army Specialist Steven G. Mason, 23, of Paragould. Killed in a SCUD missile attack on a U.S. barracks in Saudi Arabia on 25 February.

Army Sergeant Scott Lindsey, 27, of Springdale. Killed on 1 March when his vehicle hit a mine. Survived by his wife and three children.

Army Private First Class David Mark Wieczorek, 21, of Gentry. Died when he stepped on an unexploded bomb.

California

Marine Lance Corporal Thomas A. Jenkins, 20, of Mariposa. Killed on 30 January in fighting around the Saudi border town of Khafji.

Army Specialist Adrienne L. Mitchell, 20, of Moreno Valley. Killed on 25 February by a SCUD missile attack on U.S. barracks.

Army Sergeant Jimmy D. Haws, 28, of Traver. Killed on 20 February died when his vehicle was hit by Iraqi fire.

Army Sergeant Edwin B. Kutz, 26, of Sunnymeade. Suspected friendly fire.

Army Sergeant David R. Crumby, Jr., 26, of Long Beach. Killed by friendly fire from an M1-A1.

Army Private First Class David W. Kramer, 20, of Palm Desert. Killed by friendly fire from an M1-A1.

Army Sergeant Adrian L. Stokes, 20, of Riverside. Killed by Iraqi artillery.

Air Force Sergeant Damon V. Kanuha, 28, of San Diego. Died when the AC-130 Spectre Gunship in which he was flying in support of the Khafji attacks was shot down on 31 January.

Colorado

Army Sergeant Young Dillon, 27, of Aurora. Killed in a battle with the Iraqi Republican Guard Tawakalno Division. Survived by his wife who, at the time of his death, was expecting their second child.

Connecticut

Army Staff Sergeant William T. Butts, 30, of Waterford. Killed when his helicopter was shot down rescuing a downed pilot.

Army Specialist Cindy Beaudoin, 19, of Plainfield. Died when she stepped on a land mine trying to aid a soldier who was injured.

Delaware

Army Captain James R. McCoy, 29, of Wilmington. Survived by his wife and four children.

Florida

Navy Lieutenant Commander Michael Scott Speicher, 33, of Jacksonville. Died on 17 January when his F/A-18 was shot down on the opening day of the war. Shot down by a MIG-25PD in the only loss in an air-to-air combat. He was the father of two children.

Air Force Staff Sergeant John P. Blessinger, 33, of Fort Walton Beach. Died when the AC-130 Spectre Gunship in which he was flying in support of the Khafji attacks was shot down on 31 January.

Air Force Senior Master Sergeant Paul G. Buege, 43 of Mary Esther. Died when the AC-130 Spectre Gunship in which he was flying in support of the Khafji attacks was shot down on 31 January.

Air Force Sergeant Barry M. Clark, 26, of Hulburt Field. Listed as MIA when the AC-130 Spectre Gunship in which he was flying was shot down on 31 January. The gunship was believed to be involved in Special Forces operations.

Air Force Captain Arthur Galvan, 33, of Navarre. Died when the AC-130 Spectre Gunship in which he was flying in support of the Khafji attacks was shot down on 31 January.

Air Force Captain William D. Grimm, 28, of Hulburt Field. Died when the AC-130 Spectre Gunship in which he was flying in support of the Khafji attacks was shot down on 31 January.

Air Force Technical Sergeant Robert K. Hodges, 28, of Hulburt Field. Died when the AC-130 Spectre Gunship in which he was flying in support of the Khafji attacks was shot down on 31 January.

Air Force Master Sergeant James B. May II, 40, of Fort Walton Beach. Died when the AC-130 Spectre Gunship in which he was flying in support of the Khafji attacks was shot down on 31 January.

Air Force Staff Sergeant John L. Oelschlager, 28, of Niceville. Died when the AC-130 Spectre Gunship in which he was flying in support of the Khafji attacks was shot down on 31 January.

Air Force Staff Sergeant Mark J. Schmauss, 30, of Hulburt Field. Died when the AC-130 Spectre Gunship in which he was flying in support of the Khafji attacks was shot down on 31 January.

Air Force Captain Dixon L. Walters, Jr., 29, of Navarre. Died when the AC-130 Spectre Gunship in which he was flying in support of the Khafji attacks was shot down on 31 January.

Air Force Major Paul J. Weaver, 34, of Navarre. Died when the AC-130 Spectre Gunship in which he was flying in support of the Khafji attacks was shot down on 31 January.

Army Sergeant Dodge R. Powell, 28, of Hollywood.

Florida (continued)

Army Chief Warrant Officer Phillip Garvey, 39, of Pensacola. Died in the crash of a helicopter during a rescue mission on 28 February. Survived by his wife and two sons.

Army Staff Sergeant Michael Robson, 30, of Seminole. Died in the crash of a helicopter during a rescue mission on 28 February. Survived by his wife and four children.

Georgia

Army Specialist James Worthy, 22, of Albany. Killed on 23 February. Had just arrived in Saudi Arabia one week earlier. Killed by a SCUD missile attack on a U.S. barracks.

Marine Corporal Phillip J. Jones, 21, of Atlanta. Killed trying to clear a wet powder bag from a misfired M198 155 mm Howitzer. Unfortunately, while doing so, the Howitzer fired and he was struck in the head by the breach and killed. Survived by three children.

Army Private First Class Robert Wade, 31, of Savannah.

Guam

Army Specialist Roy Damian, Jr., 21, of Toto.

Hawaii

Marine Lance Corporal Frank C. Allen, 22, of Waianae. Killed on 30 January in fighting around the Saudi border town of Khafji.

Idaho

Army Sergeant Neis A. Moller, 23, of Aul. Died on 27 February. Survived by his wife.

Illinois

Marine Lance Corporal Christian J. Porter, 20, of Wood Dale. Killed in a tank battle with Republican Guard forces.

Air Force Captain Stephen Richard Phillis, 30, of Rock Island. Killed in action on 15 February.

Air Force Major Thomas F. Koritz, 37, of Rochelle. Listed as MIA on 18 January. Changed to KIA on 22 March. Shot down in an F-15 over Iraq.

Indiana

Army Captain Brian K. Simpson, 22, of Indianapolis. Killed in the SCUD missile attack on a U.S. Army barracks on 25 February. Survived by his wife.

Marine Lance Corporal Brian L. Lane, 20, of Bedford. Killed in the tank battle for the Kuwait City Airport.

Army Specialist James R. Miller, 20, of Decatur. Stepped on a land mine while taking supplies to the front on 1 March. Survived by his wife and a son, whom he never met, who was born on 21 February.

Iowa

Air Force Staff Sergeant Timothy R. Harrison, 31, of Maxwell.

Army Specialist Michael Mills, 23, of Panora. Killed on 25 February by a SCUD missile attack on a U.S. barracks. Survived by a wife and one son and by another child whose birth was expected in April 1991.

Army Specialist Ronald D. Rennison, 21, of Dubuque. Killed in a SCUD missile attack on a U.S. barracks on 25 February.

Kansas

Army Specialist Michael Daniels, 20, of Leavenworth. Killed on 21 February. Killed when his OH-58 helicopter was shot down. Survived by his wife.

Army Corporal Jeff Middleton, 26, of Oxford. Killed on 17 February when his Bradley fighting vehicle came under friendly fire from Allied aircraft. It was later discovered his unit was attacked by U.S. Apache helicopters. Survived by his wife of two years.

Army Private First Class Marty R. Davis, 19, of Salina. Killed by a hand grenade inside Kuwait.

Idaho (continued)

Army Sergeant First Class Gary Streeter, 40, of Manhattan. Died when his helicopter was shot down. Survived by his wife and two daughters.

Kentucky

Marine Captain Reginald Underwood, 33, of Lexington. His Harrier was shot down by a surface-to-air missile on the last day of the war. Survived by his wife and a daughter he had never met.

Louisiana

Air Force Lieutenant Colonel Donnie R. Holland, 42, of Bastrop. Listed as MIA on 18 January. Changed to KIA on 22 March. His F-15 was shot down over Iraq. He was the father of five children.

Army Corporal Rolando A. Delagneau, 30, of Gretna.

Maryland

Air Force 1st Lieutenant Thomas Clifford Bland, Jr., 26, of Gaithersburg. Died when the AC-130 Spectre Gunship in which he was flying in support of the Khafji attacks was shot down on 31 January.

Army Sergeant Ronald M. Randazzo, 24, of Glen Burnie. Killed on 20 February when his vehicle was attacked by Iraqi forces.

Massachusetts

Army Sergeant Russell G. Smith, Jr., 44, of Fall River. A 17-year veteran of the Army, he was killed by a land mine on the last day of the war in an Iraqi bunker. Survived by four daughters.

Michigan

Army Specialist Timothy Hill, 23, of Detroit.

Army Private First Class Aaron W. Howard, 20, of Battle Creek. Killed when clearing land mines in Iraq.

Army Specialist William E. Palmer, 23, of Hillsdale. Killed on 23 February near the Iraq/Kuwait border.

Army Corporal Stanley W. Bartusiak, 34, of Romulus. Killed on 25 February in a SCUD missile attack. Survived by his wife.

Army Sergeant Roger Brilinski, 24, of Ossineke. Killed on 27 February in a rescue attempt of a downed Air Force pilot.

Minnesota

Marine Lance Corporal Stephen E. Bentzlin, 23, of Wood Lake. Killed on 30 January in fighting around the Saudi border town of Khafji. Survived by his wife.

Army Specialist Glen D. Jones, 21, of Grand Rapids. Killed on 25 February by a SCUD missile attack on a U.S. barracks.

Navy Lieutenant Charles J. Turner, 29, of Richfield. Listed as MIA on 18 January. Changed to KIA on 17 March. Shot down in a Navy A-6 over Kuwait. Survived by a 6-month-old son.

Missouri

Army Specialist Steven P. Farnen, 22, of Salisbury. Killed on 25 February. Had a brother serving in the Gulf. Killed by a SCUD missile attack on U.S. barracks.

Army Specialist Phillip D. Mobley, 26, of Blue Springs. Killed when he stepped on a land mine.

Navy Lieutenant William T. Costen, 27, of St. Louis. Listed as MIA on 18 January. Changed to KIA on 17 March. Shot down in an A-6 Intruder.

New Hampshire

Army Warrant Officer David Plasch, 23, of Portsmouth.Killed in a rescue mission when his helicopter was shot down on the last day of the war. Survived by his wife.

New Jersey

Marine Sergeant Garett A. Mongrella, 25, of Belvidere. Killed on 30 January in fighting around the Saudi border town of Khafji. Survived by his wife and son.

New Jersey (continued)

Army Private Robert D. Talley, 18, of Newark. Killed on 17 February when his Bradley fighting vehicle came under friendly fire from Allied aircraft. It was later discovered his unit was attacked by U.S. Apache helicopters.

New York

Army Captain Mario Fajardo, 29, of Flushing. A graduate of the Citadel, he was killed in a minefield.

Marine Corporal Ismael Cotto, 27, of the Bronx. Killed on 30 January in fighting around the Saudi border town of Khafji. Believed to be killed by friendly fire from a TOW missile. Survived by his wife and daughter.

Army Staff Sergeant Patbouvier Ortiz, 27, of Queens. Killed in a helicopter crash while rescuing a downed pilot. Survived by his wife.

Army Master Sergeant Otto F. Clark, 35, of Corith. Killed on 25 February in helicopter crash. Survived by his wife and three children.

Army Specialist Thomas G. Stone, 20, of Falconer. Killed on 25 February by a SCUD missile attack on a U.S. barracks. Survived by his wife and 17-month-old daughter.

Marine Lance Corporal David T. Snyder, 21, of Kenmore. Killed on 30 January in fighting around the Saudi border town of Khafji.

Army Staff Sergeant David Ames, 30, of Herkimer. Killed in fighting on the Kuwait/Saudi border prior to the ground war. Survived by his wife and two children.

North Carolina

Army Specialist Kenneth J. Perry, 23, of Lake Waccamaw. Killed by a land mine.

Army Sergeant Michael A. Harris, Jr., 26, of Pollocksville. Killed clearing a mine field.

Air Force 1st Lieutenant Patrick B. Olson, 25, of Washington. Graduate of the U.S. Air Force Academy. Shot down on a reconnaissance mission over Kuwait.

Army Private First Class Jerry L. King, 20, of Winston-Salem. Died clearing a minefield on 28 February.

Ohio

Army Specialist Clarence A. Cash, 20, of Ashland. Died in a mortar attack on 27 February.

Army Specialist Anthony W. Kidd, 21, of Lima. Killed by friendly fire from an M1-A1.

Marine Lance Corporal James H. Lumpkins, 22, of New Richmond. Killed on 30 January in fighting around the Saudi border town of Khafji.

Navy Lieutenant Robert J. Dwyer, 32, of Worthington. Killed on 8 February when his F-18 was shot down on a bombing mission. Survived by his wife and daughter.

Army Chief Warrant Officer Hal H. Reichle, 27, of Cleveland. Died on 21 February when his OH-58 helicopter was shot down during a combat mission.

Army Staff Sergeant Johnathan Kamm, 25, of Mason. Killed on the last day of combat when his helicopter was downed.

Army Staff Sergeant Tony Applegate, 28, of Portsmouth. Killed by friendly fire. Survived by his wife and two children.

Marine Captain David Spellacy, 28, of Columbus.

Oklahoma

Army Warrant Officer George Swartzendruber, 25, of Adair. Died when his helicopter was shot down.

Oregon

Marine Lance Corporal Michael E. Linderman, Jr., 19, of Roseburg. Killed on 30 January in fighting around the Saudi border town of Khafji. Survived by his wife.

Army Private First Class Michael C. Dailey, 19, of Klamath Falls.Killed from wounds received from a mine. Survived by his wife.

Army Specialist Troy Wedgwood, 22, of The Dalles.

Pennsylvania

Army Specialist Steven Atherton, 25, of Dayton. Killed on 25 February by a SCUD missile attack on a U.S. barracks. Survived by his wife and one son.

Army Specialist John Boliver, 27, of Monongahela. Killed on 25 February by a SCUD missile attack on a U.S. barracks. Survived by his wife and two children.

Army Specialist Joseph P. Bongiomi III, 20, of Hickory. Killed on 25 February by a SCUD missile attack on a U.S. barracks.

Army Sergeant John Boxler, 44, of Johnstown. Killed on 25 February by a SCUD missile attack on U.S. barracks. A veteran of the Vietnam War, he was survived by his wife and two children.

Army Specialist Beverly Clark, 23, of Armagh. Killed on 25 February by a SCUD missile attack on U.S. barracks.

Army Major (Dr.) Mark Connelly of Lancaster. Killed trying to reach surrendering Iraqis when he stepped on a land mine. Survived by his wife and two children.

Army Sergeant Alan B. Craver, 32, of Penn Hills. Killed on 25 February in a SCUD missile attack.

Army Specialist Duane W. Hollen, Jr., 24, of Bellwood. Killed on 25 February in a SCUD missile attack.

Army Specialist Frank S. Keough, 22, of Rochester Mills. Killed on 25 February in a SCUD missile attack on U.S. barracks.

Army Specialist Anthony Madison, 27, of Monessen. Killed on 25 February by a SCUD missile attack on a U.S. barracks. Survived by his wife and two children.

Army Specialist Christine Mayes, 22, of Rochester Mills. Killed on 25 February by a SCUD missile attack on a U.S. barracks. Was engaged to be married just before leaving for the Gulf.

Army Private First Class Mark A. Miller, 20, of Cannelton. Killed when his truck was struck by enemy fire.

Army Specialist Stephen J. Siko, 24, of Latrobe. Killed on 25 February by a SCUD missile attack on a U.S. barracks. Father of a five-year-old son.

Army Specialist Richard V. Wolverton, 24. Killed on 25 February by a SCUD missile attack on U.S. barracks. Survived by his wife.

Army Specialist Frank J. Walls, 20, of Hawthorne. Killed on 25 February in a SCUD missile attack on a U.S. barracks.

Marine Lance Corporal James E. Waldron, 25, of Jennett. Killed in the battle for Kuwait International Airport. Survived by his wife and a son.

Tennessee

Army Specialist James D. Tatum, 22, of Athens. Killed on 25 February in SCUD missile attack.

Army Specialist Douglas L. Fielder, 22, of Nashville. Died in a small arms battle with Iraqi troops.

Army Private Roger E. Valentine, 19, of Memphis. Killed two days after the cease-fire.

Texas

Army Specialist Andy Alaniz, 20, of Corpus Christi. Killed when his tank was hit by a mine. Survived by his wife who, at the time of his death, was expecting their first child.

Army Specialist Tommy D. Butler, 22, of Amarillo.

Air Force Captain Douglas L. Bradt, 29, of Houston. Killed on 14 February when his EF-111 Raven crashed after a mission. Survived by his wife.

Army Specialist Melford Collins, 34, of Uhland. Killed by a land mine on the first day of the war. Survived by his wife and daughter.

Army Specialist Luis Delgado, 30, of Laredo. Killed clearing unexploded ordnance. Father of two children.

Marine Sergeant James D. Hawthorne, 24, of Stinnett. Killed clearing Iraqi equipment. Survived by his wife and daughter.

Marine Sergeant Candelario Montalvo, 25, of Eagle Pass. Killed clearing a land mine on 1 March. Survived by his wife and a daughter he never met.

Army Specialist James Murray, Jr., 20, of Conroe. Killed when his Bradley was hit by Iraqi fire. Survived by his wife and daughter he never met.

Army Staff Sergeant Christopher H. Stephens, 27, of Houston. Killed on 1 March. Survived by his wife and four children.

Marine Lance Corporal Daniel B. Walker, 20, of Whitehouse. Killed on 30 January in fighting around the Saudi border town of Khafji.

Army Private First Class Corey L. Winkle, 21, of Lubbock.

Army Staff Sergeant Harold P. Witzke III, 28, of Copperas Cove. Died on 26 February while storming an Iraqi bunker. Survived by his wife and two children.

Utah

Marine Lance Corporal Dion J. Stephenson, 22, of Bountiful. Killed on 30 January in fighting around the Saudi border town of Khafji. Survived by his brother and fellow Marine, Shaun, who was also serving in the Gulf.

Virginia

Army Sergeant Jason Carr, 24, of Halifax. Killed when his helicopter was downed.

Army Sergeant Kenneth B. Gentry, 32, of Ringgold. Killed by suspected friendly fire. Survived by his wife and two children.

Army 1st Lieutenant Terry L. Plunk, 25, of Vinton. Killed on 25 February while clearing mines in Kuwait. Graduate of the Virginia Military Institute.

Marine Lance Corporal Troy Lorrenzo Gregory, 21, of Richmond. Killed on 25 February from wounds caused by a land mine.

Army Corporal Jonathan M. Williams, 23, of Portsmouth. Killed on 25 February in a SCUD missile attack.

Army Private First Class Timothy Alan Shaw, 21, of Alexandria. Killed on 25 February in SCUD missile attack.

Army Major Thomas C.M. Zeugner, 36, of Petersburg. Killed trying to deactivate Iraqi land mines. Graduate of the Virginia Military Institute.

Navy Lieutenant Patrick K. Connor, 25, of Virginia Beach.

Navy Lieutenant Commander Barry T. Cooke, 35, of Virginia Beach.

Virginia (continued)

Army First Lieutenant Donaldson P. Tillar III, 25, of Miller School. Killed on the last day of fighting when his Blackhawk was shot down.

Washington

Army Private First Class Ardon B. Cooper, 23, of Seattle. Killed on 20 February when his vehicle was hit by Iraqi fire.

Army Sergeant Lee Belas, 22, of Port Orchard. Killed on last day of the war when his helicopter was shot down in Iraq.

Army Warrant Officer John Morgan, 28, of Bellevue. Killed when his Blackhawk was shot down over Iraq.

Wisconsin

Marine Private First Class Scott A. Schroeder, 20, of Wauwatosa. Killed on 30 January in fighting around the Saudi border town of Khafji.

Army Sergeant William A. Strehlow, 27, of Kenosha. Died deactivating an enemy bomb. Survived by his wife and three children.

Army Sergeant Brian P. Scott, 22, of Park Falls. Survived by his wife and a son he never met.

Army Sergeant Cheryl LaBeau-O'Brien, 24, of Racine. Survived by her husband who also served in the Gulf.

Army Private Michael L. Fitz, 18, of Horicon. Killed on the last day of fighting.

Wyoming

Army Specialist Manuel Davila, 22, of Gillette. Killed when his Bradley was hit by friendly fire. Survived by his wife and daughter.

BRITISH LOSSES

Conrad Cole, 17, from Rochdale, Lancs.

David Clifford, Royal Military Police.

Robert Consiglio, Special Air Services.

Paul Atkinson, 19, from Co Durham.

Richard Gillespie, 19, from Tynemouth.

Kevin Leech, 20, from Prudhoe, Northumberland.

Lee Thompson, 19, from Coventry.

Private John Lang, 19, from Munster, Germany.

Pte Neil Donald, 18, from Forres, Grampian.

Martin Ferguson, 21, from Fort William, Highland.

Sergeant Michael Dowling, 34, from Dorset.

Lance Corporal Francis Evans, 25, from Flint, Clwyd.

Corporal David Denbury, 26, from Ponthir, near Newport, Gwent.

Jason McFadden, 19, from Coventry.

Private Carl Moult, 22, from Burton-on-Trent.

Lance Corporal Terence Hill, 26, of the Royal Corps of Transport, from Middlesex.

Pte Shaun Taylor, 20, of the Staffordshire Regiment, from Stourbridge, West Midlands.

Pte Alistair Fogerty, 21, of the Royal Army Ordnance Corps, of Cheadle Hulme, Cheshire.

Pte Thomas Haggerty, 20, of the 1st Battalion Royal Scots, from Glasgow.

Gunner Paul Keegan, 20, of 32 Heavy Regiment, the Royal Artillery, of Kirkby, Merseyside.

Lance Corporal Stephen Crofts, 23, from Chippenham, Wilts.

Lance Corporal Robert Robbins, of the Royal Corps of Transport.

Major James Kinghan, 33, from Nottingham. Died in a road accident.

Royal Military Policeman Sergeant David Tite, 32, from Bulford, Wilts.

Sapper Richard Alan Royle, from Rochdale.

Lieutenant Colonel Alistair Wright, 49, of Kent.

Sergeant Donald Kinnear, 24.

Seaman Maurice Foy, 38.

Stephen Satchell, 18, from Rye, East Sussex.

"Legs" Lane, Special Air. Services

Vince Phillips, Special Air Services.

OTHER NON-COMBAT LOSSES OF OPERATION DESERT STORM

Air Force

Captain Jorge I. Arteaga
Captain. Dale Thomas Cormier
1st Lieutenant Eric D. Hedeen
Sergeant Leroy E. Hein, Jr.
Captain Jeffry J. Olson
Senior Airman Ramono L. Poole

Army

Chief Warrant Officer Michael F. Anderson
Staff Sergeant Russell F. Awalt
Specialist Charles L. Bowman, Jr.
Specialist William C. Brace
Private Cindy D.J. Bridges
Specialist James R. brown
Sergeant Paul Burt
Sergeant Christopher J. Chapman
Lars Chew (rank unknown)
Private Gerald A. Cohen
Captain Charles W. Cooper
Specialist Gary W. Crask
Specialist Mark Cronquist
Private Robert L. Daugherty
Chief Warrant Officer Patrick A. Donaldson
Private Dorothy Falls
Sergeant Ira L. Foreman
Specialist John Fowler
Staff Sergeant Mike A. Garrett
Major (Dr.) John H. Gillespie
Sergeant Mark J. Gologram
1st Lieutenant Daniel Graybeal
1st Lieutenant Thomas Haggerty
Staff Sergeant Garland V. Halley
Sergeant Tracy Hampton
Staff Sergeant Steven Hansen
Specialist Adrian Hart
Staff Sergeant Raymond Hatcher, Jr.
Specialist Wade Hector
Warrant Officer Kerry P. Hein
Specialist Luis A. Henry-Garay
Specialist Jame Heyden
Specialist David Heyman
Chief Warrant Officer Robert Hughes
Sergeant Major Patrick Hurley
Private First Class Kenneth J. Jackson
Specialist Jimmy W. James
Specialist Thomas R. Jarrell
Captain Joseph G. Kime, III
Private First Class Reuben G. Kirk, III
Chief Warrant Officer Richard R. Lee
Staff Sergeant Ralph E. Lewis
1st Lieutenant Joseph Maks
Warrant Officer1 George N. Malak
Warrant Officer1 Christopher Martin
Sergeant Kely Matthews
Sergeant Melvin McDougle
Chief Warrant Officer Carol McKinney
Specialist Bobby McKnight
Staff Sergeant Donald Morgan
Sergeant Jeffrey E. Mullin
1st Sergeant Joe Murphy
Specialist Donald Myers
Private First Class Shawnacee L. Noble
Specialist Robert Noonan
Private Anthony T. Patterson
Specialist Dale Paulson
Specialist Kelly Phillips
Private First Class Jeffrey D. Reel
Private First Class Todd C. Ritch
Sergeant Stephen R. Robinette
Master Sergeant Eloy A. Rodriguez, Jr.
Sergeant Jeffrey A. Rollins
Major Marie T. Rossi
Private First Class Scott A. Rush
Sergeant Leonard A. Russ
1st Sergeant Henry J. Sanders, Jr.
Specialist Manuel B. Sapien, Jr.
Sergeant Baldwin Satchell
Sergeant Michael S. Smith
Specialist John B. Stephens
Major Earl K. Stribling
Staff Sergeant Roy J. Sumerall
Specialist Peter L. Swano, Jr.
Specialist Steven R. Trautman
Sergeant Mario Vega Velazquez

Lieutenant Colonel (Dr.) Carlos A. Viquez
Private First Class Charles S. Walker
Specialist Thomas E. Walrath
Private First Class Patrick A. Wanke
Specialist Bobby M. Ware
Specialist Kevin E. Wright

Marines

Corporal Allen M. Auger
Corporal Kurt A. Benz
Lance Corporal Edward M. Codispodo
Staff Sergeant Michael R. Conner, Sr.
Corporal Ismael Cotto
Captain Jonathan R. Edwards
Lance Corporal Arthur O. Garza
Corporal Albert G. Haddad, Jr.
Captain David R. Herr, Jr.
Private First Class Adam T. Hoage
Corporal Victor T. Lake, Jr.
Major Eugene McCarthy
Private First Class Michael A. Noline
Lance Corporal Arthur D. Oliver
Lance Corporal Kip A. Poremba
Captain Manuel Rivera, Jr.
Lance Corporal Thomas J. Scholand
Staff Sergeant David A. Shaw
Corporal James H. Sylvia
Captain James K. Thorp
Chief Warrant Officer Bermard S. Winkley

Navy

Boiler Technician 2nd Class Alan H. Benningfield
Aviation Structural Mechanic-Structures 3rd Class James F. Crockford
Aerographers Mate 1st Class Shirley M. Cross
Lieutenant Mark D. Jackson
Chief Warrant Officer John M. Paddock
Lieutenant David A. Warne
Aviation Electricians Mate 2nd Class Brian P. Weaver

PRISONERS OF WAR IN OPERATION DESERT STORM

Alabama

Army Specialist David Lockett, 23, of Bessemer. Captured by the Iraqis on 30 January during the four Iraqi thrusts into Saudi Arabia. He was taken along with the first U.S. woman POW, Melissa Rathburn-Nealy. Carried as MIA throughout the war, he was released as a POW on 4 March.

California

Marine Corps Lieutenant Colonel Clifford M. Acree, 39, of Oceanside. Shot down in his OV-10 spotter plane. Released on 5 March.

Marine Corps Chief Warrant Officer Guy L. Hunter, 46, of Camp Pendleton. Shot down in an OV-10 Bronco. Released on 5 March.

Georgia

Air Force Captain Harry M. Roberts, 30, of Savannah. Released on 5 March.

Idaho

Army Sergeant Daniel Stamaris, 31, of Boise. Released as a POW on 5 March.

Illinois

Sergeant Troy Allen Dunlap, 20, of Massac. Released as a POW on 5 March.

Massachusetts

Air Force Lieutenant Colonel Jeffrey D. Fox, 39, of Fall River. Captured after his OV-10 was shot down in Kuwait. Released on 5 March.

Michigan

Army Specialist Melissa Rathburn-Nealy, 20, of Grand Rapids. Captured by the Iraqis on 30 January during the four Iraqi thrusts into Saudi Arabia. She was the first woman to be listed as missing in action and remained listed as MIA during the war. She was released on 4 March.

New Jersey

Navy Lieutenant Jeffrey N. Zaun, 28, of Cherry Point. Zaun was one of the POWs shown on Iraqi television with several injuries visible on his face. After his release on 4 March, Zaun said he injured himself to deter his Iraqi captors from showing his face on television. Zaun's copilot was Lieutenant Robert Wetzel, who was released on the same day.

New York

Air Force Captain William F. Andrews, 32, of Syracuse. Listed as MIA during the war, but was released as a POW on 5 March.

Major Rhonda L. Cornum, 36, of Freeville. Released as a POW on 5 March.

North Carolina

Air Force Colonel David W. Eberly, 43, of Goldsboro. Released on 5 March.

Air Force Major Thomas E. Griffith, 34, of Goldsboro. Released on 4 March.

Marine Captain Russell A.C. Sanborn, 27, of Havelock. Listed as MIA during the war, but was released as a POW on 5 March.

Ohio

Marine Captain Michael C. Berryman, 28, of Cleveland. Listed as MIA during the war, but was released as a POW on 5 March.

Pennsylvania

Air Force Major Jeffrey Scott Tice, 35, of Sellerville. Released on 5 March.

Air Force 1st Lieutenant Robert James Sweet, 24, of Philadelphia. Listed as MIA during the war, but was released as a POW on 5 March.

Virginia

Navy Lieutenant Lawrence Randolf Slade, 26, of Virginia Beach. Released on 4 March.

Navy Lieutenant Robert Wetzel, 30, of Virginia Beach. Listed as MIA on 18 January. Shot down in a Navy A-6. His copilot, Lieutenant Jeffrey Zaun, was captured by Iraqi soldiers and listed as a POW, but Wetzel's fate was unknown until the end of the war. Wetzel was listed as MIA throughout the conflict, but was released as a POW on 4 March.

Washington

Air Force Captain Richard D. Storr, 29, of Spokane. Listed as MIA during the war, but was released as a POW on 5 March.

Wisconsin

Marine Corps Major Joseph J. Small, 39, of Racine. Released as a POW on 5 March.

Glossary

A-10 (Warthog).

An anti-tank airplane designed to support troops on the ground.

AH.

An acronym for an attack helicopter. These two letters are followed by a number that indicates a model. The AH-1 is a Cobra; the AH-64 is an Apache. *See also* Cobra and Apache.

Air superiority.

A condition that exists when aircraft can operate in a theatre without serious threat from enemy forces. Although enemy forces still operate, they are not very successful in shooting down Allied aircraft.

Air supremacy.

A condition that exists when aircraft can operate with little or no threat from enemy forces. Enemy forces do not fight attacking aircraft with great effectiveness.

AK-47.

The standard machine gun in the Soviet Bloc and Iraqi arsenal. The more recent model is called the AK-74.

Amir.

Sometimes spelled emir, this man is the commander or leader in Arab-speaking countries.

Apache (AH-64).

The main attack helicopter in the U.S. Army, the Apache is used to defeat enemy armor and support ground troops.

Armored personnel carrier (APC).

A lightly armored vehicle used to transport troops into combat zones. *See also* BMP and BTR.

AV-8.

See Harrier.

AWACs.

An acronym for airborne warning and control system. Noticeable because of its large radar disk attached to its fuselage. The AWACs is capable of locating, identifying, and targeting enemy aircraft from long distances. Saudi Arabia purchased several AWACs in the early 1980s and the U.S. deployed a small unit in Operation Desert Storm.

B-52.

The U.S. strategic bomber for the last thirty years. It can deliver a devastating payload anywhere in the world.

Baghdad.

The capitol of Iraq.

Bandit.

A slang term used to describe enemy aircraft.

Blackhawk (UH-60).

The standard utility and transport helicopter in the U.S. military.

BMP.

A Soviet-built Iraqi armored personnel carrier.

Bogey.

A slang term used to describe an unidentified aircraft.

Bomb damage assessment.

A detailed process of examining photographs, interviewing pilots, and conducting intelligence to determine if bombing operations were successful in eliminating a threat. Bombs often hit their targets, but they do not always eliminate the threat.

Bradley fighting vehicle (M-2, M-3).

A U.S. armored personnel carrier currently being integrated into U.S. forces.

BTR.

A Soviet-built Iraqi armored personnel carrier. This designation is usually followed by a number that indicates which model it is.

C3.

A designation that identifies command, control, and communications priority targets in any attack.

Carpet bombing.

The massive bombing of a particular area, devastating all structures, personnel, and vehicles. Six B-52s can destroy a two-mile by one-half mile area.

CENTCOM.

One of eight joint commands in the U.S. military. CENTCOM had jurisdiction in the Middle East region. It was headed by General Norman Schwarzkopf during the Persian Gulf War.

CHAPPARAL.

A U.S. anti-aircraft missile system.

Close air support.

The use of aircraft to support troops on the ground with pinpoint bombing and strafing runs.

Cluster bomb.

An air-dropped bomb that releases hundreds of "bomblets" to destroy targets.

Cobra (AH-1).

An attack helicopter designed to support troops on the ground.

Combat Air Patrol (CAP).

A term that means aircraft on patrol over ships and airports to provide fighter cover to potential targets.

DEFCON.

An acronym used to imply defense condition. DEFCON1 means war.

E.

Standard designation for electronic warfare aircraft, most commonly used for radar jamming.

E-6 (Prowler).

A shipborne electronic warfare jet used to jam enemy communications and radar.

ECM.

Electronic countermeasures used to confuse and disrupt enemy communications and radars.

Exocet.

A French-made, Iraqi anti-ship missile. An Exocet destroyed USS *Stark* on 17 May 1987 and many oil tankers during the Persian Gulf War.

F-4 (Wild Weasel).

Air-defense suppression jet.

F-14 (Tomcat).

The primary air combat aircraft that was used aboard U.S. carriers in the Persian Gulf.

F-15 (Eagle).

An Air Force air combat aircraft. The F-15E is used for attack.

F-16 (Falcon).

An Air Force fighter and attack aircraft.

F-18 (Hornet).

The Navy and Marines fighter and attack aircraft.

F-111.

A medium-range, swept-wing bomber that operated out of Saudi Arabia and Turkey during the Persian Gulf War. Combat-proven in Vietnam and Libya, it is used for bombing operations that require a large quantity of explosives.

F-117 (Stealth).

This highly advanced fighter jet is used primarily for deep penetration attack missions.

FLIR.

An acronym for forward-looking, infra-red, which is a type of electronic vision used to detect targets at night.

Feet dry.

A slang term that describes aircraft crossing from sea to land.

Feet wet.

A slang term that describes aircraft crossing from land to sea.

Fox.

A pilot's codename for an aircraft missile.

Kuwaiti Theatre of Operations (KTO).

A military term that describes the overall location of U.S. forces in the Persian Gulf.

Kurds.

The minority in Iraq that is opposed to Saddam Hussein's rule. Thousands of Kurds were killed with chemical weapons in 1988.

HARM.

A U.S. missile system that hones in on enemy radar and destroys it.

Harrier.

A British-designed vertical takeoff and landing jet used by U.S. Marines.

HAWK.

A U.S. anti-aircraft missile. Its launcher holds three missiles.

HEAT.

A high-explosive, anti-tank shell used in the M-1 Abrams tank to destroy enemy armor. *See also* SABOT.

HIND.

A Soviet MI-24 attack helicopter. The variant is the HIND-D.

IFF.

An acronym for identification friend or foe. A computer system on board an American weapon that checks a target by reading its transponder code. If it is friendly, the weapon is not used. If it is an enemy, the weapon continues its mission.

Jihad.

An Arabic word meaning "holy war." Saddam called for a Jihad during the Persian Gulf War to whip up religious fervor against the Allied nations.

Joint Chiefs of Staff (JCS).

The chairman of the JCS is in charge of the different armed services and ensures that presidential orders are carried out. The chairman of the JCS during the Persian Gulf War was Colin Powell.

Landing craft, air-cushioned (LCAC).

A hovercraft vessel used to land Marines in shallow and mined waters.

Lock-on.

A term that indicates a radar has acquired an enemy target.

M-1.

A designation for a main U.S. battle tank.

M-3.

The scout version of the Bradley fighting vehicle.

M-16.

The standard machine gun used by U.S. forces.

M-60.

1) A medium-sized tank used by the Marine Corps.

2) A standard machine gun used by the infantry.

M-109.

A self-propelled artillery piece in both U.S. and Iraqi arsenals.

M-113.

The armored personnel carrier used by both the United States and Iraq.

Mecca.

The holiest of Islamic cities, Mecca is located in southern Saudi Arabia.

MI-24.

An Iraqi attack helicopter. *See also* HIND.

MIG.

A Soviet-made aircraft designed by Mikoyan and Gurevich, usually followed by a number that indicates which model it is.

Multiple Launch Rocket System (MLRS).

A U.S. rocket launcher used by artillery units.

Mossad.

The Israeli secret service. Any U.S. intelligence operation in the Middle East involves the Mossad.

Mustard gas.

WWI-era poison gas that causes skin irritation.
Compare sarin gas.

NBC.

An acronym for nuclear, biological, and chemical. Commonly used to describe target sets and defensive capabilities of Allied weapons and tanks.

Night vision goggles.

Goggles worn by troops that amplify available light thus enabling them to see clearly at night.

Organization of Petroleum Exporting Countries (OPEC).

A cartel designed to oversee oil production.

Patriot.

An anti-missile missile used to defend U.S. and Allied forces.

Reactive armor.

Explosive charges placed on tanks to deter armor-piercing shells. The explosion deflects the shell and prevents penetration of the armor.

Resolution 678.

The resolution passed by the United Nations that authorized the use of force against Iraq.

Riyadh.

The capitol of Saudi Arabia.

RPG.

The acronym for a rocket powered grenade. Small RPGs were used by the Iraqis against Allied armor with little effect due to the small size of the warhead.

SABOT.

The nickname for armor-piercing fin stabilized discarding sabot munitions used in the M-1 tanks as an armor-piercing round primarily used against enemy tanks.

SAM.

An acronym for a surface-to-air missile.

Sarin gas.

A nerve gas that affects the respiratory system and is considered lethal in even minute doses.

SCUD.

A Soviet-made surface-to-surface missile used by the Iraqis. *Compare* Patriot.

Security council.

A group of fifteen countries inside the U.N. that is responsible for maintaining peace around the world. The council consists of five permanent members and ten rotating members selected from the entire group of U.N. members. All resolutions against Iraq had to be authorized by the U.N. Security Council.

Sidewinder.

A heat-seeking anti-aircraft missile, used considerably by American forces.

Smart bomb.

A bomb capable of adjusting its flight to a more specific target.

Sortie.

A term used to describe one mission by one aircraft.

Sparrow.

A radar-guided anti-aircraft missile used primarily by American aircraft.

Squawk.

Military slang for the signal sent out by transponders on board an aircraft. "Squawk 334" is a command to send out the code 334 to all IFF weapons.

STINGER.

An acronym for a shoulder-launched anti-aircraft missile in the U.S. and Allied arsenals.

Strategic bombing.

Indicates the attacking of the infrastructure and industry of an enemy, along with military targets far behind the enemy lines.

SU.

The designation given to Soviet-made Sukhoi aircraft, usually followed by a number that indicates its model.

Tactical bombing.
A phrase that indicates the bombing of military targets that are threatening friendly forces.

Tomahawk.
A shipborne or airborne cruise missile that is guided to its target by computer and can deliver a conventional or nuclear warhead.

Tornado.
An English fighter/bomber used by British and Saudi air forces.

TOW.
An acronym for the tube-launched, optically-tracked, wire-guided anti-tank missile mounted on board HUMVEEs and Bradleys.

Tracer.
A shell coated in phosphorous to help guide a gunner to his target.

Transponder.
A device that emits a signal for identification purposes to IFF-equipped weapons.

UH-1 (Huey).
A Vietnam-era transport and utility helicopter still in service in the Gulf and is still in the fleet today.

UH-60 (Blackhawk).
The standard transport helicopter in use by U.S. forces.

Wild Weasel.
During the Gulf War this air-defense suppression jet, which was a Vietnam-era F-4 Phantom, was modified to destroy enemy radar and anti-aircraft weapons.

Bibliography

Atkinson, Rick. *Crusade: The Untold Story of the Persian Gulf War.* New York: Houghton, Mifflin, 1993.

Center for Defense Information. *Persian Gulf Handbook.* Washington, D.C.: Government Printing Office, 1991.

Chant, Christopher. *Air Forces of the World.* New York: Crescent Books, 1990.

Congressional Research Service. *Iraq-Kuwait: The United Nations Response.* Washington, D.C.: Library of Congress, 1991.

———. *Iraq-Kuwait Crisis: Major Issues for Congress.* Washington, D.C.: Library of Congress, 1991.

———. *Iraq-Kuwait Crisis: The International Response and Burdensharing Issues.* Washington, D.C.: Library of Congress, 1991.

———. *Iraq-Kuwait Crisis: U.S. Policy and Options.* Washington, D.C.: Library of Congress, 1991.

———. *Iraq's Invasion of Kuwait: A Review of Events.* Washington, D.C.: Library of Congress, 1991.

Coyne, James P. *Airpower in the Gulf.* Arlington: Air Force Association, 1992.

Department of Defense. *Conduct of the Persian Gulf War – Final Report to the Congress.* Washington, D.C.: Government Printing Office, 1992.

———. *Soviet Military Power 1987.* Washington, D.C.: Government Printing Office, 1987.

———. *Soviet Military Power 1988.* Washington, D.C.: Government Printing Office, 1988.

———. *Soviet Military Power 1989.* Washington, D.C.: Government Printing Office, 1989.

———. *Fact Sheet on Benefits for Reservists.* Washington, D.C.: Government Printing Office, 1991.

Dunnigan, James F. and Austin Bay. *From Shield to Storm.* New York: Morrow Books, 1992.

Friedman, Norman. *Desert Victory: The War For Kuwait.* Annapolis: Naval Institute Press, 1991.

Hutchinson, Kevin Don and John H. Admire. *Operation Desert Shield/Desert Storm: Chronology and Fact Book.* Texas: Greenwood Publishing Group, 1995.

Keaney, Thomas A. and Cohen A. Eliot. *Revolution in Warfare? Airpower in the Persian Gulf.* Annapolis: Naval Institute Press, 1995.

Kinzey, Bert. *The Fury of Desert Storm: The Air Campaign.* Blue Ridge Summit, PA: TAB Books, 1991.

Krause, Chaim. *A Guide to the Gulf Forces.* www.chaim.com/chaim/military/desert.html

Miller, David and Christopher F. Foss. *Modern Land Combat.* New York: Portland House, 1987.

Miller, Judith and Laurie Mylroie. *Hussein and the Crisis in the Gulf.* New York: Random House, 1991.

Pagonis, William G. *Moving Mountains: Lessons in Leadership and Logistics from the Gulf War.* Cambride, MA: Harvard Business School Press, 1992.

Paxton, John. *Statesman's Year Book, 1989–90.* New York: St. Martin's Press, 1990.

———. *Statesman's Year Book, 1990–91.* New York: St. Martin's Press, 1991.

Powell, Colin. *My American Journey.* New York: Random House, 1995.

Schwarzkopf, H. Norman. *Norman Schwarzkopf, the Autobiography: It Doesn't Take a Hero.* New York: Bantam Books, 1992.

Sharpe, Richard. *Jane's Fighting Ships 1989–90.* London: Jane's Publishing Company Limited, 1990.

Summers, Harry G. *Persian Gulf War Almanac.* New York: Facts on File, 1995.

U.S. Airforce. *Gulf War Air Power Survey*. Washington, D.C.: Government Printing Office, 1993.

U.S. Army. *Iraq – A Country Study.* Washington, D.C.: Government Printing Office, 1990.

———. *Saudi Arabia – A Country Study.* Washington, D.C.: Government Printing Office, 1990.

———. *Weapons Systems 1990.* Washington, D.C.: Government Printing Office, 1990.

U.S. Marine Corps. *Marine Corps Concepts and Issues 1990.* Washington, D.C.: Government Printing Office, 1990.

Winnefeld, James, David Niblack and David Johnson. *A League of Airmen: U.S. Air Power in the Gulf War.* Santa Monica, CA: Rand Project Air Force, 1994.

The Almanac of Seapower 1990. Arlington, Virginia: The Navy League of the United States, 1990.

Jane's Armour and Artillery 1989–90. London: Jane's Publishing Company Limited, 1990.

Jane's All the World's Aircraft 1989-90. London: Jane's Publishing Company Limited, 1990.

World Almanac 1990. New York: Pharos Books, 1990.

Order Directly

Call, Mail, or Fax Your Order to: PSI Research, 300 North Valley Drive, Grants Pass, OR 97526 USA
Phone USA & Canada: 800 228-2275 *Inquiries & International Calls:* +1 541 479-9464 *Fax :* 541 476-1479
Internet: http://www.psi-research.com Email: psi2@magick.net

TITLE	PRICE	QUANTITY	COST
GULF WAR DEBRIEFING BOOK An After Action Report			
ARMY MUSEUMS West of the Mississippi			
BYRON'S WAR I never will be young again...			
FROM HIROSHIMA WITH LOVE			

If your purchase is:	Shipping costs within the USA:
$0 - $25	$5.00
$25.01 - $50	$6.00
$50.01 - $100	$7.00
$100.01 - $175	$9.00
$175.01 - $250	$13.00
$250.01 - $500	$18.00
$500.01 +	4% of total merchandise

SUB-TOTAL $

SHIPPING (see chart below) $

TOTAL ORDER $

SOLD TO: *Please Give Street address*

NAME:

Street Address:

City/State/Zip:

Daytime Phone:

Email:

SHIP TO: *If different than above give street address*

NAME:

Street Address

City/State/Zip:

Daytime Phone

Hellgate PRESS

PAYMENT INFORMATION: *Rush service is available, call for details.*
International and Canadian Orders: Please call for quote on shipping.

☐ CHECK Enclosed payable to PSI Research ☐ Charge: ☐ VISA ☐ MASTERCARD ☐ AMEX ☐ DISCOVER

Card Number: Expires:

Signature: Name On Card:

CALL TOLL FREE TO ORDER 1-800-228-2275
PSI Research 300 North Valley Drive, Grants Pass, OR 97526 FAX 541-476-1479